Lecture Notes of the Institute for Computer Sciences, Social Informatics and Telecommunications Engineering   146

Shahid Mumtaz · Jonathan Rodriguez
Marcos Katz · Chonggang Wang
Alberto Nascimento (Eds.)

Wireless Internet

8th International Conference, WICON 2014
Lisbon, Portugal, November 13–14, 2014
Revised Selected Papers

 Springer

Editors

Shahid Mumtaz
University of Santiago
Aveiro
Portugal

Chonggang Wang
InterDigital Communications
King of Prussia, PA
USA

Jonathan Rodriguez
Institute of Telecommunication
Aveiro
Portugal

Alberto Nascimento
Departamento de Matemática e Engenharias
University of Madeira
Funchal
Portugal

Marcos Katz
Finland Technical
University of Oulu
Oulu
Finland

ISSN 1867-8211   ISSN 1867-822X (electronic)
Lecture Notes of the Institute for Computer Sciences, Social Informatics
and Telecommunications Engineering
ISBN 978-3-319-18801-0   ISBN 978-3-319-18802-7 (eBook)
DOI 10.1007/978-3-319-18802-7

Library of Congress Control Number: 2015938743

Springer Cham Heidelberg New York Dordrecht London

Printed on acid-free paper

Springer International Publishing AG Switzerland is part of Springer Science+Business Media
(www.springer.com)

Preface

We are living in exciting times, where the developments and achievements of information communication are not only shaking up some of the ways we are living and working, but they already became a key pillar of any competitive economy and inclusive society and we are just at the beginning of a revolution of the sector which will continue to change the way citizens, companies, governments, and public institutions operate and interact.

The 8th International Wireless Internet Conference - Symposium on Wireless and Vehicular Communication was held last year in the stimulating city of Lisbon. The committee had organized exciting programs for The 8th International Wireless Internet Conference with conference themes of "Wireless and Vehicular Communication." These themes cover the latest topics such as 5G mobile communications, Internet of Things (IoT), super Wi-Fi, and V2V/V2I. Moreover, on a technical note, following the gradual roll-out of the Third-generation Partnership Project's Long-Term Evolution (3GPP LTE) initiative, research is now well under way toward the definition of next-generation standards. The 3G High Speed Packet Access (HSPA) system also continues to evolve further toward increased-rate multi-carrier solutions using carrier aggregation, with the goal of maintaining the current momentum of increasing the achievable bitrate. In the past, each consecutive decade brought about a factor of ten bitrate improvement, as observed for the second-, third-, and fourth-generation wireless systems. Naturally, the associated three orders of magnitude throughput improvement were achieved at the cost of a substantially increased power consumption. In the light of the escalating energy prices, this motivated the design of "green radios," aiming for more power-efficient designs - all in all, an exciting era for our community.

The technical program consists of 12 tracks. The conference track chairs have selected 60 outstanding papers for the oral sessions. In addition to the oral sessions, we present one workshop and two keynote presentations. The creation of this impressive program would not have been possible without the voluntary support from an outstanding team of colleagues that we thank sincerely.

Special thanks go to the conference track chairs who have organized a very efficient and smooth review and session organization process, as well as the workshop. We also thank all the Technical Program Committee members and reviewers for their professional and timely review of technical contributions. Of course, making a successful technical conference would not have been possible without the participation from authors, to whom we express our gratitude for presenting and sharing their ideas and contributions with our community. We also thank the EAI Organizing Committee for their support. We express sincere appreciation to all of our colleagues for their concerted efforts, to all of the authors who submitted their valuable research contributions that will lead to very fruitful discussions, and to all of the participant's efforts to make this conference a success.

November 2014

Shahid Mumtaz
Jonathan Rodriguez
Marcos Katz
Chonggang Wang
Alberto Nascimento

Organization

String Committee

Imrich Chlamtac — Create-Net, Italy
Athanasios Vasilakos — Kuwait University, Kuwait
Xudong Wang — Shanghai Jiao Tong University, China
Hsiao-Hwa Chen — National Cheng Kung University, Taiwan

Organizing Committee

General Chair

Shahid Mumtaz — Instituto de Telecomunicações, Portugal

General Co-chairs

Jonathan Rodriguez — Instituto de Telecomunicações, Portugal
Stephen Wang — Toshiba Research Europe Limited, UK

Technical Program Committee Chair

Marcos Katz — University of Oulu, Finland

Technical Program Committee Co-chairs

Frank Fitzek — Aalborg University, Denmark
Lie-Liang Yang — University of Southampton, UK
Joaquim Bastos — Instituto de Telecomunicações, Portugal

Workshops Committee Chairs

Christos Verikoukis — Centre Tecnològic de Telecomunicacions de Catalunya, Spain
Du Yang — Instituto de Telecomunicações, Portugal

Publications Committee Chairs

Chonggang Wang — InterDigital Communications, USA
Alberto Nascimento — University of Madeira, Portugal

Contents

A Fast Handover Procedure
Based on Smart Association Decision for Mobile IEEE
802.15.4 Wireless Sensor Networks

Zayneb Trabelsi Ayoub[✉] and Sofiane Ouni

RAMSIS, CRISTAL Laboratory, Ecole Nationale des Sciences de l'Informatique,
Manouba, Tunisia
trabelsizayneb@yahoo.fr, Sofiane.ouni@insat.rnu.tn

Abstract. Recent technological progress in microelectronics has allowed a considerable development of Wireless Sensor Networks. These networks are deployed in several relevant applications such as healthcare and wildlife which require the support of sensor nodes mobility. However, this mobility is a real threat in breaking communications and packet loss accordingly. This paper proposes a fast handover procedure based on a smart association decision to handle mobility and to ensure continuous communication in IEEE 802.15.4 WSNs. In our proposed procedure, the mobile node can anticipate the coordinator change upon detecting the degradation of the link quality indicator. Then, it performs a fast re-association based on our smart criterion and it resumes the forwarding of stored packets. Simulations show that our fast handover procedure ensures better network performances than a similar approach.

Keywords: Mobility · Fast handover · Smart association · Wireless Sensor Networks · IEEE 802.15.4 · Energy · Reliability · Delay

1 Introduction

Wireless Sensor Network (WSN) consists of a set of small and low-power devices called sensor nodes which interact with the environment to sense physical phenomena. In fact, these sensor nodes collect environmental information and work together to transmit data to one or more collection points (called *sinks*) in an autonomous way.

The IEEE 802.15.4 standard [4] is a good candidate for WSNs application development since it allows the interconnection of wireless devices with low autonomy and not requiring a high bit rate. In such networks, the network topology is created by association procedure initiated by the PAN coordinator followed by other sensor nodes. Indeed, the PAN coordinator broadcasts beacon frames to allow the association of neighbor nodes. Similarly, the new associated nodes send beacon frames to allow the association of child nodes and so on, thus forming a tree topology. Recently, WSNs find their interests in various and innovative applications. However, some applications such as monitoring patients in hospitals and medical centers require the mobility of sensor nodes. This mobility can lead to the performance degradation. Given that,

© Institute for Computer Sciences, Social Informatics and Telecommunications Engineering 2015
S. Mumtaz et al. (Eds.): WICON 2014, LNICST 146, pp. 1–7, 2015.
DOI: 10.1007/978-3-319-18802-7_1

mobile nodes should be able to change their locations while ensuring continuous communication. Actually, the IEEE 802.15.4 standard lacks of effective procedure to handle mobility. In fact, if a mobile node moves away from the coverage area of its coordinator, it loses synchronization with this latter and becomes orphaned device. This orphaned device should try to find its current coordinator by performing the orphaned realignment procedure [4]. Otherwise, if it fails to reassociate to its current coordinator, the orphaned device should reset its MAC sub-layer and then perform a new association procedure to the network [4]. During the orphaned device realignment and/or re-association procedure, all received data packets will be discarded. This inaccessibility period cannot be tolerated especially in the case of critical and real-time applications. Several works investigated mobility management in WSNs. The authors of [7] show that the performance of IEEE 802.15.4/ZigBee networks degrades when the number of mobile nodes increases or when the node is moving fast. Thus, the association procedure is costly in terms of time and energy consumption because of the scan channels phase and CSMA/CA mechanism [7]. The authors of [2] propose an approach to handle mobility in IEEE 802.15.4/ZigBee networks with tree topology. This approach aims to anticipate the change of coordinators without losing connection based on a link quality threshold. Furthermore, the authors in [3] propose a handover mechanism for mobile healthcare WSNs based on detecting the need for changing the access point according to a link quality indicator comparison. In the same context, the authors in [5] propose a model introducing a new entity called 6LoWPAN proxy agent responsible to handle the mobility-related messages based on received signal strength indicator (RSSI) value of the link with the mobile node. We can notice that most of presented approaches are based on a frequent exchange of control messages. In WSNs, this frequent exchange is costly and energy consuming which can shorten the network lifetime. We can also note that none of them proposes a solution in order to reduce the packet loss during the handover procedure. So, in order to handle mobility, we propose a fast handover procedure to anticipate the coordinator change upon detecting a link quality degradation. Besides, our procedure is based on smart association decision without extra messages exchange to conserve energy and to reduce average delay.

The remainder of the paper is organized as follows. Section 2 describes our contribution, where we propose our fast handover procedure based on smart association decision. The performance evaluation is given in Sect. 3. Finally, Sect. 4 concludes the paper.

2   Proposed Fast Handover Procedure Based on Smart Association Decision

In the case of mobile WSNs, sensor nodes can often change their locations which can lead to synchronization loss and packet loss accordingly. In order to ensure a continuous communication in a mobile context, we propose a fast handover procedure. This procedure is triggered by a mobile node when it detects that the link quality with its current coordinator degraded under a predefined threshold. So, this mobile node should perform a fast re-association procedure in order to avoid breaking connection and the resulting packet loss. Actually, our proposed handover aims to conserve energy, to reduce end-to-end delay and to minimize packet loss. To do this, we focus on three major points:

- Anticipate the coordinator change based on link quality indicator values;
- Select the new suitable coordinator based on a smart association criterion allowing to optimize energy consumption and end-to-end delay;
- Inform child nodes so that they store all outgoing packets temporarily until the end of the handover procedure triggered by their parent coordinators.

We note that in our proposals, we take advantage from periodic beacons to exchange necessary information for fast handover and smart association decision, so that we avoid the exchange of extra messages. So, we extend the IEEE 802.15.4 standard [4] to get smart association relationships and to optimize the dynamic network topology according to nodes mobility.

2.1 Smart Association Decision

In order to optimize energy consumption and average communication delay, the mobile node should select the new coordinator based on a smart association criterion. Our proposed smart association criterion is the sum of the inverses of coordinators' remaining energy composing paths towards the sink (noted: *InvE*), investigated in our previous work [1]. This criterion allows to select the shortest path having the maximum remaining energy which can optimize energy consumption and latency [1].

2.2 Fast Handover Procedure

The fast handover mechanism is triggered when a mobile node moves away from the coverage area of its parent coordinator and detects that the link quality indicator degrades under the predefined threshold. Figure 1 describes the activity diagram of a mobile node during the fast handover procedure. In fact, it periodically receives beacons from its parent coordinator (Fig. 1, Activity 1). Upon receipt of each beacon, the node measures the LQI (*Link Quality Indicator*) with which it was received. Indeed, if the measured value of the LQI is below the predefined threshold (noted: *LQI_thresh*), the mobile node realizes that it should associate to another coordinator with better link quality. Therefore, it sends four *informing beacons* to its child nodes asking them to store all outgoing packets (Fig. 1, Activity 2). This ensures that packets will not be lost during the handover procedure. If the beacon was sent four times successfully, the mobile node must wait a random time to avoid simultaneous re-associations with its neighbors (Fig. 1, Activity 3). Then it disassociates from its old coordinator (Fig. 1, Activity 4). Then, it performs the re-association procedure. If it ever discovers several candidate coordinators in its coverage area, it associates to the one that meets our smart association criterion (Fig. 1, Activity 5). Then it updates its routing table in order to consider the new route resulting from the new parent-child relationship (Fig. 1, Activity 6). Finally, it sends four *re-informing beacons* to its child nodes asking them to transfer queued packets (Fig. 1, Activity 7).

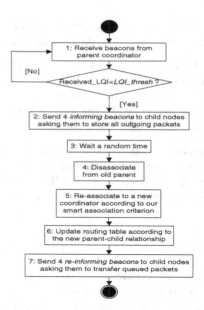

Fig. 1. Activity diagram of a mobile node during the fast handover procedure.

3   Performance Evaluation

In this section, we focus on performance analyses conducted from extensive simulations in order to investigate the efficiency of our fast handover procedure.

Our proposed procedure is validated by using NS-2. In fact, we modified its original version provided by Zheng and Lee in [9] in order to simulate our fast handover procedure based on smart association decision. In our simulation scenarios, we used a network composed of 49 nodes randomly deployed in the simulation area. We considered that all of sensors are mobile nodes except the sink (PAN coordinator) representing the root of the tree. We considered a CBR (*Constant Bit Rate*) traffic with a traffic rate varying from 1 pps to 6 pps. We set the transmitting and receiving power respectively to 31.32 mW and 35.28 mW (according to the study results of Chipcon CC2420 [6, 8]). In our scenarios, all of sensor nodes move randomly according to the Random Waypoint model with a random speed up to 2 m/s. This model is a widely used mobility model [10]. To investigate the efficiency of our fast handover procedure, we evaluate the packet delivery ratio, the communication average delay and the network throughput in our simulations. We compared our proposed procedure to a similar approach proposed by [2]. This approach [2] (that we denote *LQI_Approach*) aims to anticipate the coordinator change according to a link quality threshold.

Figure 2 shows the variation of packet delivery ratio by increasing the packet generation rate for our fast handover procedure compared to *LQI_Approach* proposed by [2]. We can notice (Fig. 2) that our fast handover procedure offers a relatively high ratio even by increasing the packet generation rate up to 4 pps, compared to *LQI_Approach* whose delivery ratio degrades under 30 %. This fact is due to storing all outgoing packets by child nodes during the coordinators handover process and resuming them upon their successful re-association.

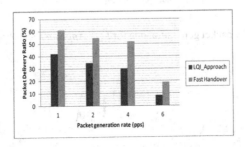

Fig. 2. Packet delivery ratio by packet generation rate for *LQI_Approach* and Proposed Fast Handover.

Figure 2 also shows that the network reached the congestion point with a packet generation rate of 6 pps, which explains the relatively low value of the packet delivery ratio under these conditions. Figure 3 shows the variation of the average delay by increasing the packet generation rate for our fast handover procedure compared to *LQI_Approach* proposed by [2]. We can see that our proposed procedure offers the lowest average delay. This result is obtained due to integrating our smart association criterion (*InvE*) that permits to select paths with reduced number of nodes which lead to reduce the average delay [1]. In addition, Fig. 3 shows that the average delay increases sharply with a generation rate of 6 pps because of collisions and resulting retransmissions. Figures 4a and b illustrate the variation of the network throughput over time for our fast handover and *LQI_Approach* respectively. We can notice that our proposed procedure provides a relatively high throughput compared to *LQI_Approach*, particularly by increasing the packet generation rate. Indeed, during the time interval [85 s, 165 s], our protocol allows to reach a steady throughput of 18000 b/s (Fig. 4a) whereas *LQI_Approach* can hardly provide 15000 b/s, with no mobility and a packet generation rate of 4 pps (Fig. 4b). Once the sensor nodes start moving (after the instant 165 s), our protocol keeps a quite high throughput (between 14000 b/s and 10000 b/s) according to Fig. 4a while throughput obtained by the *LQI_Approach* fluctuates frequently and can hardly reach 10000 b/s (Fig. 4b). However, by observing the Fig. 4a, we note some instantaneous throughput degradations that match the instants of coordinators' re-associations and storing outgoing packets by child nodes. Upon successful re-associations, all stored packets are forwarded and network throughput reaches a high level consequently.

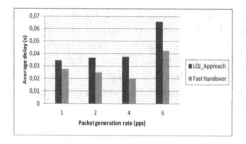

Fig. 3. Average Delay by packet generation rate for *LQI_Approach* and Proposed Fast Handover.

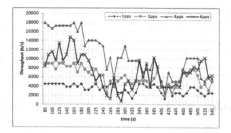
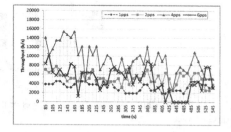

Fig. 4a. Network throughput by packet generation rate for Proposed Fast Handover.

Fig. 4b. Network throughput by packet generation rate for *LQI_Approach*.

4   Conclusion

In this paper, we have proposed a fast handover procedure based on a smart association decision for mobile IEEE 802.15.4 WSNs. In order to avoid the inaccessibility period caused by mobility and breaking communication, our fast handover procedure allows to anticipate the coordinator change upon detecting a link quality degradation. Besides, our procedure is based on a smart association decision in order to conserve energy and to reduce average delay. Furthermore, our proposed procedure permits to minimize packet loss by storing data packets during the handover process and forwarding them upon a successful handover. Simulations show that our fast handover procedure outperforms a similar approach in terms of packet delivery ratio, average delay and network throughput.

References

1. Ouni, S., Trabelsi Ayoub, Z.: Cooperative association/re-association approaches to optimize energy consumption for real-time IEEE 802.15.4/ZigBee wireless sensor networks. Wirel. Pers. Commun. **71**(4), 3157–3183 (2013)
2. Chaabane, C., Pegatoquet, A., Auguin, M., Ben Jemaa, M.: Energy optimization for mobile nodes in a cluster tree IEEE 802.15.4/ZigBee network. In: IEEE Computing, Communications and Applications Conference, Hong Kong, China, 11–13 January 2012

3. Caldeira, J.M.L.P., Rodrigues, J.J.P.C., Lorenz, P., Shu, L.: Intra-mobility handover enhancement in healthcare wireless sensor networks. In: 14th International Conference on E-Health Networking, Applications and Services, Beijing, China, 10–13 October 2012
4. IEEE-TG15.4: Part 15.4: Wireless Medium Access Control (MAC) and Physical Layer (PHY) specifications for low-rate Wireless Personal Area Networks (LR-WPANs), IEEE Standard for Information Technology 2011 (2011)
5. Zinonos, Z., Vassiliou, V.: Inter-mobility support in controlled 6LoWPAN networks. In: IEEE GLOBECOM Workshops, Miami, FL, 6–10 December 2010, pp. 1718–1723 (2010)
6. Gao, B., He, C.: An individual beacon order adaptation algorithm for IEEE 802.15.4 networks. In: Proceedings of IEEE ICCS, November 2008
7. Sun, T., Liang, N., Chen, L., Chen, P., Gerla, M.: Evaluating mobility support in ZigBee networks. In: EUC 2007, Taipei (Taiwan), 17–20 December 2007
8. Bougard, B., Catthoor, F., Daly, D.C., Chandrakasan, A., Dehaene, W.: Energy efficiency of the IEEE 802.15.4 standard in dense wireless microsensor networks: modeling and improvement perspectives. In: Proceedings of the Conference on Design, Automation, and Test in Europe Conference and Exhibition (DATE 2005), pp. 196–201, March 2005
9. Zheng, J., Lee, M.: NS2 Simulator for IEEE 802.15.4 (2004). http://ees2cy.engr.ccny. cuny.edu/zheng/pub/
10. Camp, T., Boleng, J., Davies, V.: A survey of mobility models for ad hoc network research. Wirel. Commun. Mob. Comput. 2(5), 483–502 (2002)

Building Efficient Multi-level Wireless Sensor Networks with Clustering

Hnin Yu Shwe$^{(\boxtimes)}$ and Peter Han Joo Chong

School of Electrical and Electronic Engineering,
Nanyang Technological University, Singapore, Singapore
{hninyushwe, EHJChong}@ntu.edu.sg

Abstract. Wireless sensor networks will be responsible for the majority of the growth in smart building systems over the next decade. In resource constrained wireless sensor networks, it is very important to design the protocols with energy efficiency to prolong the lifetime of the sensor networks. Node clustering and data aggregation become popular since cluster-based sensor network can enhance the whole network throughput by aggregating the collected sensory information in each cluster. In such a network, the cluster head nodes play an important role in forwarding data originated from other common nodes to the sink. As a consequence, the cluster head nodes will have the problem of quick energy depletion upon multiple packets forwarding in high data load sensor networks. In this paper, we proposed a simple cluster-based linear network coding protocol in which random linear network coding is applied at cluster head nodes in order to minimize the number of forward packets to the sink. Simulation results are provided to show the efficacy of the proposed method in terms of the throughput and end-to-end delay.

Keywords: Wireless sensor network · Building · Clustering

1 Introduction

Availability of low-cost sensing and processing modules as well as recently developed efficient wireless communication protocols for building automation applications provide the basic enabling tools for the application domain of smart buildings. Smart building systems are becoming more and more vital due to the improvement they provide to the quality of life. One of the key components of a smart building system is a wireless sensor network (WSN), which provides the necessary information to the smart building system, allowing it to control and monitor the physical environment.

A WSN is formed by a large number of sensor nodes to monitor the objects of interest or environmental conditions such as sound, temperature, light intensity, humidity, pressure, motion and so on through wireless communications [1]. As the technology of WSNs matures, the scope of their applications has become more extensive, e.g., environmental monitoring, home automation, intelligent office, energy saving, intelligent transportation, health care, and security monitoring [2]. A major limitation of untethered nodes is finite battery capacity and memory and thus power efficient configuration of WSN has become a major design goal to improve the

© Institute for Computer Sciences, Social Informatics and Telecommunications Engineering 2015
S. Mumtaz et al. (Eds.): WICON 2014, LNICST 146, pp. 8–13, 2015.
DOI: 10.1007/978-3-319-18802-7_2

performance of the network. Due to the limited resources of sensor nodes, it is very important to design a routing protocol with energy efficiency to extend the lifetime of the WSN. Several solution techniques have been proposed to maximize the lifetime of battery-powered sensor nodes. Among the various techniques, it is well-known that cluster architecture enables better resource allocation and helps to improve power control.

In the clustered environment, the data gathered by the sensors are communicated to the base station (BS) through a hierarchy of cluster-head (CH) nodes [3]. With clustering in WSN, the randomly distributed sensor nodes are formed as many clusters and each sensor node has to transmit the collected data to its CH. After deployment, the CH is responsible for collecting data from its cluster member sensors, and those collected sensor data are aggregated and then forwarded to the BS via the sink. Thus, the CH plays an important role in aggregating and forwarding data sensed by other common nodes and as a consequence CH consumes more energy than the other member sensors. In addition, another limitation of the sensor node is the buffer size and it is also very important to efficiently utilize the limited buffer of the sensors. In this paper, we propose architecture of cluster-based WSN with the use of linear network coding at CH nodes to optimize the throughput and delay of high data load sensor networks.

The remaining of this paper is organized as follows. We first discuss the related works in Sect. 2. We then briefly present our proposed network architecture in Sect. 3. Simulation results and discussions are presented in Sect. 4. Finally, we conclude our paper and present our future work in Sect. 5.

2 Related Works

WSNs are event-based systems based on the collaboration of several micro-sensor nodes [4]. The high density of sensor nodes is vital for sensing, intrusion detection, and tracking applications. When an event is detected in the network, the aggregated collaborative report of the detecting nodes is delivered to the sink. Clustering mechanisms enable the sensor nodes to collect and aggregate data at nodes called CHs in each cluster. However, due to the high data load nature of monitoring sensor networks, the cluster head nodes will suffer from the problem of packet overwhelming over the time [5].

Since the packet transmission is the most power consuming action for sensor nodes and the network coding technique reduces the number of packet transmissions, network coding becomes useful to reduce the energy consumption in WSN. Network coding technique [6] allows cluster head node to produce the linear combination of the received packets from its cluster member nodes before sending the data to the sink. The operations are computed in the finite field and thus the result of the operation is also of the same length. The original packets can be recovered at the sink by solving the set of linear equations just after receiving the required number of linearly independent packets [7, 8].

The AODV Routing Protocol [9] uses an on-demand approach for finding routes, that is, a route is established only when it is required by a source node for transmitting data packets. AODV is suitable for dynamic wireless networks where nodes can enter and leave the network at will. To find a route to a particular destination node, the source node broadcasts a RREQ to its immediate neighbors. If one of these neighbors has a route to the destination, then it replies back with a RREP. Otherwise the neighbors in turn rebroadcast the request. This continues until the RREQ hits the final destination or a node with a route to the destination. At that point a chain of RREP messages is sent back and the original source node finally has a route to the destination.

3 Proposed Method

In this section, we will illustrate the network model of our study. We consider a simple cluster-based monitoring WSN where hundreds of sensor nodes generate the readings on every unit time and those sensory data are sent to the sink via CH. The network architecture of our proposed cluster-based linear network coding for WSN is illustrated in Fig. 1(a). As it can be seen in the figure, we logically consider the network as 2-level network. In level-1, the whole network is broken into set of clusters and member nodes send data to associated CH. In level-2, data communication is carrying out only among CHs in order to forward data to BS.

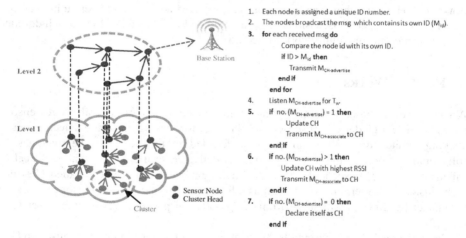

Fig. 1. (a) Architecture of proposed protocol (b) Algorithm for cluster forming.

Our proposed system can be mainly classified into two phases: (1) Cluster forming phase and (2) Data collection phase.

(1) Cluster Forming Phase: After all nodes are deployed, clusters are formed according to the algorithm shown in Fig. 1(b). In our algorithm, CH nodes are chosen based on the highest node ID (HID) and the received signal strength (RSSI). We assume that each sensor node has its own ID. In the beginning of the clustering phase, the nodes broadcast the message which contains its own ID. Due to the broadcast nature of the sensor networks, all the nodes in its communication range will receive that message. For each received message, the node will compare the embedded ID with its own ID.

If a node found that its own ID is greater than the entire received ID, it will broadcast the cluster head advertisement message ($M_{CH\_advertise}$). Entire nodes in the network will listen to the cluster head advertisement for the unit time T_w. After time T_w, if a node receives only one cluster head advertisement message, it means $no.(M_{CH\_advertise}) = 1$, it joins in that cluster and sends cluster head associate message ($M_{CH\_associate}$) back to that CH node then it updates its associate cluster head node. For the nodes who received more than one cluster head advertisement message, it means $no.(M_{CH\_advertise}) > 1$, sensor node decides which cluster to join based on the received signals strength. After choosing the cluster head, it sends cluster head associate message ($M_{CH\_associate}$) back to that CH node then it updates its associate cluster head node. For the nodes who did not receive any cluster head advertisement message in T_w, it means $no.(M_{CH\_advertise}) = 0$, it advertises itself as cluster head and form an isolated cluster. After joining cluster, sensor nodes send their data only to the associated CH node. In our cluster forming phase, we ensure that every node in the same cluster is in one-hop distance.

(2) Data Collection Phase: In the data collection phase, each node in the cluster sends its own packet to the associated CH. Only CH node performs network coding upon the packets in its own cluster. In here, we adopt the simple random liner network coding where CH node encodes N-packets in its buffer as one encoded packet and broadcasts the encoded packets only. The use of network coding has several benefits: reduce the transmission energy and enhance the network throughput.

Upon receiving n originated packets ($M^1, M^2, ..., M^n$) from its member nodes, the sequence of coefficients ($g_1, g_2, ..., g_n$) are chosen uniformly at random over the finite field f_2s. Then the associated CH node generates the encoded packet P by this equation:

$$P = \sum\nolimits_{i=0}^{n} g_i M^i$$

Intermediate CH node acts as a relay in order to help the packets successfully arrive to the sink. Upon receiving the n-linearly independent encoded packets, the original packets can be decoded by the linear equation at the sink.

4   Simulation Results

4.1   Simulation Setting

We perform computer simulation using NS-2, a standard tool in sensor network simulation. The detail parameter setting for the simulations is shown in Table 1. In our simulation, we assume sensor nodes are stationary after deployment. All nodes in the network are homogeneous and energy constrained. The location of the sink node fix and far from the sensor network and the data sensed by the sensors can be reached to the sink node via CH nodes. We use CBR (constant bit rate) as traffic source and numbers of sources are 20, 40, 60, 80 and 100 separately.

Table 1. Simulation parameters

Parameters description	Values
Simulation area (m)	100 × 100
Network size (nodes)	100
Data packet size	512 Bytes
Transmission range (Sensors)	15 m
Transmission range (CH)	30 m
Simulation time (s)	500

4.2   Simulation Results

In order to evaluate the performance of our proposed protocol, we computed the packet delivery ratio and end-to-end delay with a period of 500 s under the proposed protocol and compared our proposed scheme with the standard routing protocol, AODV [9].

In Fig. 2, the first row shows the simulation results of packet delivery rate on different number of source nodes. This measurement was done assuming each sensor node in the network has fixed buffer size of 10. As we can see from the figures, the packet delivery ratio of our proposed method is higher than AODV in various number of source nodes. Although the performance is not very significant in low packet rate (1 Pkt/s), we can see the significant results in packet rate of 5 Pkt/s and 10 Pkt/s.

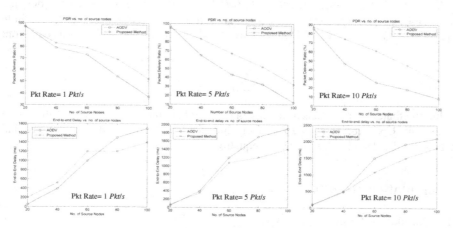

Fig. 2. Simulation results for PDR and end-to-end delay with various no. of source nodes.

We then plot the end-to-end delay as a function of the number of source nodes. We compare the average delay between our proposed protocol and AODV during the simulation time. With low packet rate which is 1 Pkt/s, our proposed protocol has more delay than AODV for the number of sources less than 60. This is because the CH node keeps the data packet until it receives enough packets to encode. However, when load becomes heavy which is greater than 60 sources, the performance of our proposed protocol becomes better.

In last two figures, even though the performance of our proposed protocol and AODV is not much different for sources less than 40, it is obvious to see that our proposed protocol outperform AODV for the heavy load which is sources greater than 60. From the results, we conclude that our proposed protocol is able to optimize the packet delivery ratio and end-to-end delay for the heavy load sensor networks.

5 Conclusion and Future Work

In this paper, a cluster-based network coding architecture for WSN was introduced and discussed. The basis of our protocol is using linear network coding only at the CH nodes in order to increase the throughput of the whole sensor network. Since only CH nodes perform data encoding and take responsibility to send the data to the sink node, it causes energy saving of member sensor nodes. Simulation results show that our proposed scheme outperform AODV in terms of PDR and end-to-end delay. In the future, we will research on the energy consumption and lifetime of the network.

Acknowledgement. This research is funded by the Republic of Singapore's National Research Foundation through a grant to the Berkeley Education Alliance for Research in Singapore (BEARS) for the Singapore-Berkeley Building Efficiency and Sustainability in the Tropics (SinBerBEST) Program. BEARS has been established by the University of California, Berkeley as a center for intellectual excellence in research and education in Singapore.

References

1. Karl, H., Willig, A.: Telecommunication Networks Group: A Short Survey of Wireless Sensor Networks, October 2003
2. Kuorilehto, M., Hannikainen, M., Hamalainen, T.D.: A survey of application distribution in wireless sensor networks. EURASIP Trans. Wirel. Commun. Netw. 5(5), 774–788 (2005)
3. Haenggi, M.: Opportunities and challenges in wireless sensor networks. In: Handbook of Sensor Networks: Compact Wireless and Wired Sensing Systems, pp. 1.1–1.14. CRC Press, Florida (2004)
4. Akyildiz, F., et al.: Wireless sensor networks: a survey. Comput. Netw. 38, 393–422 (2002)
5. Shan-Shan, L., Pei-Dong, Z., Xiang-Ke, L., Wei-Fang, C., Shao-Liang, P.: Energy efficient multipath routing using network coding in wireless sensor networks. In: Kunz, T., Ravi, S.S. (eds.) ADHOC-NOW 2006. LNCS, vol. 4104, pp. 114–127. Springer, Heidelberg (2006)
6. Ahlswede, R., Cai, N., Li, S.Y.R., Yeung, R.W.: Network information flow. IEEE Trans. Inf. Theor. 46, 1204–1216 (2000)
7. Fragouli, C., Wismwer, J., Le Boudec, J.Y.: A network coding approach to energy efficient broadcasting: from theory to practice. In: Proceedings of ACM MobiSys 2006 (2006)
8. Katti, S., Rahul, H., Hu, W., Katabi, D., Medard, M., Crowcroft, J.: Xors in the air: practical wireless network coding. In: Proceedings of ACM SIGCOMM 2006, September 2006
9. Perkins, C.E., Royer, E.M.: Ad-hoc on-demand distance vector routing. In: Proceedings of the Second IEEE Workshop on Mobile Computing Systems and Applications, pp. 90–100, February 1999

Delay Accounting Optimization Procedure to Enhance End-to-End Delay Estimation in WSNs

Pedro Pinto[1]([✉]), António Pinto[2], and Manuel Ricardo[3]

[1] ESTG, Instituto Politécnico de Viana do Castelo and INESC TEC,
Viana do Castelo and Porto, Portugal
pedropinto@estg.ipvc.pt
[2] CIICESI, ESTGF, Politécnico do Porto and INESC TEC, Porto, Portugal
apinto@inescporto.pt
[3] INESC TEC, Faculdade de Engenharia, Universidade do Porto, Porto, Portugal
mricardo@inescporto.pt

Abstract. Real-time monitoring applications may generate delay sensitive traffic that is expected to be delivered within a firm delay boundary in order to be useful. In this context, a previous work proposed an End-to-End Delay (EED) estimation mechanism for Wireless Sensor Networks (WSNs) to preview potential useless packets, and to early discard them in order to save processing and energy resources. Such estimation mechanism accounts delays using timers that make use of an Exponentially Weighted Moving Average (EWMA) function where the smoothing factor is a constant defined prior to the WSN deployment. Later experiments showed that, in order to enhance the estimation results, such smoothing factor should be defined as a function of the network load.

The current work proposes an optimization of the previous estimation mechanism that works by evaluating the network load and by adapting the smoothing factor of the EWMA function accordingly. Results show that this optimization leads to a more accurate EED estimation for different network loads.

Keywords: End-to-End Delay · Delay Estimation · EWMA · Smoothing factor

1 Introduction

Real-time applications may generate packet flows requiring specific service levels from the network. Applications that use delay sensitive flows can assume that such flows are only useful if received within a strict delay limit and useless otherwise. The deployment of these applications on top of Wireless Sensor Networks (WSNs) with scarce energy and processing resources, requires additional efforts in order to preview and avoid the transmission of potential useless data packets. Our previous work [1] presents an End-to-End Delay Estimation Mechanism (EEDEM) for delay sensitive applications deployed on a WSN that tries to accurately classify the usefulness of data packets in real-time. EEDEM estimates the

© Institute for Computer Sciences, Social Informatics and Telecommunications Engineering 2015
S. Mumtaz et al. (Eds.): WICON 2014, LNICST 146, pp. 14–19, 2015.
DOI: 10.1007/978-3-319-18802-7_3

End-to-End Delay (EED) based on the internal delays experienced by previously sent packets, and delay information from other nodes through the use of Routing Protocol for Low-power and Lossy Networks (RPL). All internal delays are accounted using an Exponentially Weighted Moving Average (EWMA) function, which defines the weight of the last value in relation to the history value, using a constant smoothing factor (β) defined *a priori*. In order to enhance the EED estimation, the β factor should be defined as a function of the network load.

This paper presents a Delay Accounting Optimization Procedure (DAOP) which dynamically applies, at each node, the best β as function of the network load. Thus, DAOP enables the lowest estimation error for multiple network loads.

The structure of this paper is as follows. Section 2 presents the related work. Section 3 details the preliminary experiments conducted. Section 4 describes the current proposal. Section 5 shows the results obtained. Section 6 concludes paper.

2   Related Work

EEDEM [1] assumes that a set of generator/forwarder nodes generate and forward data to a sink node, and that the sink node is the ultimate destination of all data. Each node accounts for the time elapsed while the packet is processed within the stack of the generator node, the time elapsed while in the MAC layer queuing, and the time elapsed in packet transmissions. Delay accounting is accomplished by using timers that register delays between labels inserted into parts of the code where the data passes through, ranging from the application in the generator node to the application in the sink node (see Fig. 1).

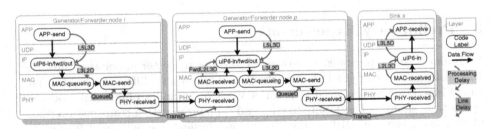

Fig. 1. EEDEM overview

The internal delays used are: 1) Generation Internal Delay (GenIntDelay) registered when packets are generated; 2) Forward Internal Delay (FwdIntDelay) registered when packets are being forwarded; 3) Receiving Internal Delay (RecIntDelay) registered when packets reach the destination. The *GenIntDelay* obtained at a node i with a parent p is calculated as follows:

$$GenIntDelay_{ip} = L5L3D_i + L3L2D_i + QueueD_i + TransD_{ip} \qquad (1)$$

The *FwdIntDelay* obtained at a node p with a parent s is calculated as follows:

$$FwdIntDelay_{ps} = FwdL2L3D_p + L3L2D_p + QueueD_p + TransD_{ps} \qquad (2)$$

The *RecIntDelay* obtained at the sink s node is calculated as follows:

$$RecIntDelay_s = L2L3D_s + L3L5D_s \qquad (3)$$

where *LxLyD* is the delay between layer x and layer y, *QueueD* is the MAC queuing delay, and *TransD* is the transmission delay.

Each node calculates the delay of all the path up to the sink node by using a feedback mechanism that announces back the cumulative delays to other nodes using RPL [2] with delay-based metrics (RPLMetrics). Each node provides a real-time EED estimation up to the sink, per generated packet, by combining the internal delays with the *RPLMetrics*. In [3] a set of RPL modifications was proposed to improve EEDEM work. Regarding the internal delay, each component (*GenIntDelay*, *FwdIntDelay* and *RecIntDelay*) is obtained by using EWMA. The last delay and the all delay history values, for a packet n, are calculated using a β as follows:

$$Delay^n = \beta.Delay^{last} + (1 - \beta).Delay^{n-1} \qquad (4)$$

Our previous EEDEM work estimates delays using a constant value for the β, defined *a priori*. Better estimation results are achieved when using different β values, adapted depending on the network load. Other research efforts use or adapt EWMA for estimation purposes. In [4] authors present an adaptive forecast method based on EWMA. In [5] authors propose the use of routing metrics that are obtained using EWMA.

3   Preliminary Experiments

Preliminary experiments were performed in order to better understand how the EED estimation error (EED_Error) changes in relation to different β values. The Cooja simulator [6] was used to setup a WSN of 16 nodes plus a sink node, all nodes were simulated as Tmote Sky [7] and configured with a transmission range of 30 m using the Unit Disk Graph Medium as physical channel model. The nodes ran the Contiki OS 2.5 and were deployed in a grid topology within an area of $100\,\mathrm{m}^2$. The application layer used UDP and it generated packets of 100 Bytes in a constant rate here defined as Inter-packet Generation Intervals (IGI). Simulations were configured to stop whenever the sink node received 100 packets from each node, and were repeated 10 times using random seeds. The simulator was configured to output the instant of time when a packet was generated and when a packet reached the destination application. For each generated packet, the estimated EED (estEED) was collected and later compared with the real EED (realEED). Finally, when the simulation ended, the EED_Error for N samples was obtained using the difference between estEED and realEED calculated using the Symmetric Mean Absolute Percentage Error (SMAPE) according to Eq. 5, expressed in a value between 0 % and 200 %. SMAPE compares the difference between estEED and realEED with the mean of these two values, thus treating over and under estimations equally, avoiding distortion on the average value.

$$EED\_Error_{(SMAPE)}(\%) = \frac{1}{N} \sum_{n=1}^{N} \frac{|estEED_n - realEED_n|}{(estEED_n + realEED_n)/2} \qquad (5)$$

The results obtained for the EED_Error and its confidence interval are shown in Fig. 2. Different β values were used for IGIs of 1, 2.5, 5, and 10 s. The results show that for high network loads (lower IGIs) a high β provided the lowest EED_Error, while for low network loads (IGI above 2.5 s) a lower β should be used. Whenever a node is experiencing a high network load, the EED values will vary with a higher amplitude, thus, in order to enhance EED estimation, the last EED sample must have a higher weight than the EED history. In short, a high β value should be used in high network loads.

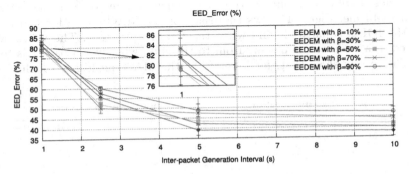

Fig. 2. EED_Error using β varying from 10 % to 90 %

4   Delay Accounting Optimization Procedure

The preliminary experiments demonstrated that, in order to minimize the EED_Error, each node must be aware of its network load. Our proposal Delay Accounting Optimization Procedure (DAOP) infers the network load by monitoring the real-time usage of the MAC queue and then, based on the size of the queue, selects the best β value and applies it in all internal timers. Figure 3 shows how the DAOP is integrated within the EEDEM. The DAOP assumes 4 intervals within the MAC-queueing block: i1, i2, i3, and i4. In interval i1 (from 0 up to 2 packets in the MAC queue) the DAOP assumes a low network load, in interval i2 (3 or 4 packets) and i3 (5 or 6 packets) the DAOP assumes a medium network load, and in interval i4 (from 7 up to the queue limit, i.e. 8 packets) it assumes a high network load. When a node sends a packet the queue usage is monitored and for intervals i1, i2, i3, or i4, a β value of 10 %, 30 %, 50 % or 70 % is applied, respectively, in all internal timers (β of 90 % was not used since it introduces higher EED_Error using DAOP). Since β values are calculated when packets are sent, the computational cost of DAOP will grow linearly with the sent packets, i.e., the procedure complexity is $O(n)$.

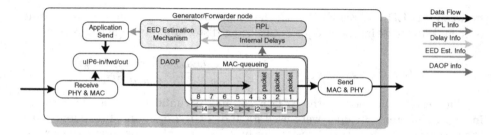

Fig. 3. DAOP integration in EEDEM

5 Results

The proposed solution monitors the MAC queue usage to infer the network load in real-time. Figure 4 shows the usage of the MAC queue for two cases: when the IGI is equal to 1, and when the IGI is equal to 5. The values were obtained in a node one hop away from to the sink, whenever a packet is to be sent. The results show that, for lower IGIs, the MAC queue has roughly 6 or

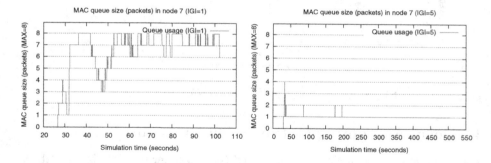

Fig. 4. MAC queue usage. Left: IGI=1 Right: IGI=5

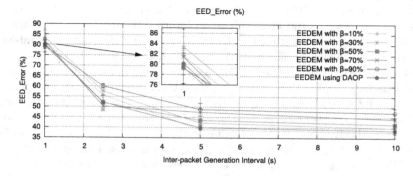

Fig. 5. EED_Error for EEDEM using different β and using DAOP

more packets, on average, and for an IGI equal to 5, the MAC queue has roughly 1 packet during all the simulated time.

Figure 5 compares the EED_Error obtained using the proposed solution with those obtained with constant β values of 10 %, 30 %, 50 %, 70 % and 90 %, for different IGI values. The results show that, by monitoring the MAC queue usage, the proposed DAOP dynamically infers network load and applies a β value that matches the best ones for each IGI in the preliminary experiments. Thus, DAOP presents the lowest EED_Error for all the different network loads.

6 Conclusions

Our previous proposal to estimate EED accounts for internal delays and uses RPL to feedback delays to the remaining nodes. The internal delays are accounted using an EWMA function, where the smoothing factor β is constant and defined *a priori*. Experimentation showed that the best EED estimation error results are obtained by varying the β value as a function of the network load.

This paper proposes a delay accounting procedure that dynamically adapts the β value inferring the network load by actively monitoring the node's MAC queue size. The results obtained show that the current solution provides a more accurate EED estimation for different network loads than our previous solution.

References

1. Pinto, P., Pinto, A., Ricardo, M.: End-to-end delay estimation using RPL metrics in WSN. In: IFIP Wireless Days (WD), pp. 1–6 (2013)
2. Winter, E.T., Thubert, E.P., Brandt, A., Hui, J., Kelsey, R., Levis, P., Struik, R., Vasseur, E.J.P., Alexander, R.: RPL: IPv6 Routing Protocol for Low-Power and Lossy Networks. RFC 6550, March 2012
3. Pinto, P., Pinto, A., Ricardo, M.: RPL modifications to improve the end-to-end delay estimation in WSN, In: Proceedings of the 11th International Symposium on Wireless Communication Systems (ISWCS), Barcelona, Spain, August 2014
4. Nembharda, H.B., Kaoa, M.S.: Adaptive forecast-based monitoring for dynamic systems. Technometrics **45**(3), 208–219 (2003)
5. Li, H., Cheng, Y., Zhou, C., Zhuang, W.: Routing metrics for minimizing end-to-end delay in multiradio multichannel wireless networks. IEEE Trans. Parallel Distrib. Syst. **24**(11), 2293–2303 (2013)
6. Osterlind, F., Dunkels, A., Eriksson, J., Finne, N., Voigt, T.: Cross-level sensor network simulation with COOJA. In: Proceedings of 31st IEEE Conference on Local Computer Networks, pp. 641–648 (2006)
7. Tmote Sky Project. http://www.snm.ethz.ch/Projects/TmoteSky
8. Contiki OS. http://www.contiki-os.org

Effects of Cooperation on Wireless Ad Hoc Network Performance

Maurizio D'Arienzo[1]([✉]) and Simon Pietro Romano[2]

[1] Dipartimento di Scienze Politiche, Seconda Università di Napoli,
Caserta, Italy
maudarie@unina.it
[2] DIETI, Università di Napoli Federico II, Naples, Italy

Abstract. Unfairness in wireless ad hoc networks is often due to the
different ways the single nodes decide to participate in relay operations.
We propose to introduce a dedicated ad hoc routing protocol based on
results of game theory to force the cooperation of less operative nodes and
mitigate the effort of overwhelmed ones. Simulations on an experimental
testbed show a better distribution of the energy consumption and an
increased fairness in the average delivery ratio achieved by nodes, as well
as a prolonged network lifetime.

Keywords: Game theory in wireless networks · Cooperation · Energy
efficiency

1 Introduction

Ad hoc networks are composed of several wireless nodes with limited power
resources usually provided by accumulators. In these networks each node is an
end system and a router at the same time. The limited energy is then not only
used to deliver one's own packets to the destinations but also to serve other nodes
as message relayer [1,2]. Current routing protocols do not implement any mechanism to verify if other nodes are participating in relay operations, so certain
nodes have the chance not to cooperate.

This situation can affect the final performance achieved by single nodes
as well as that of the entire network. For instance, the presence of malicious
nodes in the network can have a negative impact on the final delivery ratio
achieved by well behaving nodes compared to that achieved by uncooperative
ones. At the opposite, too much cooperation can lead to an unfair energy consumption because certain nodes, usually the inner nodes of a topology, are more
involved than others in relay operations and this causes a greater drain of their
energy compared to that spent by border nodes.

In the presence of a behavior detection system, well behaving nodes can deal
with uncooperative ones, for instance by refusing to relay packets coming from
them. In this way, the malicious nodes experience a delivery ratio reduction and
are in fact rather pushed towards a more cooperative attitude. We also aim

S. Mumtaz et al. (Eds.): WICON 2014, LNICST 146, pp. 20–25, 2015.
DOI: 10.1007/978-3-319-18802-7_4

at minimizing the residual energy variance, that means to improve the fairness among nodes and avoid an irregular shut down of single nodes. To this purpose, overloaded nodes can periodically switch to a defection state to preserve their own energy, hence inducing a better energy balance among the nodes.

Rather than introducing new energy aware features into the routing protocols, we rely on a decentralized algorithm to track down the behavior of network nodes in order to quickly find alternative paths. We demonstrate that the proposed approach allows for a better balance of energy among the nodes. The algorithm takes inspiration from the results of game theory and enhances an existing ad hoc routing protocol.

2   Related Work

Most of the proposals to mitigate the unfair consumption of energy rely on energy aware routing mechanisms [3]. Similarly to our proposal, [4] proposes to control the energy consumption in each discovered route, and then monitor their state in the following manteinance process. Rather than considering an adaptation at MAC or network layer, the work in [5] formulates the fair energy distribution problem with the same objective functions as our proposal: minimizing the residual energy variance at the same time maximizing the minimum residual node energy.

To address the fair energy consumption issue, in [6] a fair cooperative protocol (FAP) is proposed to improve the overall performance of the whole network. Each node calculates a *power reward* to evaluate the power contributed to and by the others. The work done in [7] still relies on cooperation among nodes. However, it makes the assumption that only a subset of nodes belonging to the same group can be interested in a mutual cooperation instead of a full cooperation involving all nodes.

3   Game Theory Applied to Track Nodes Behaviour

Although game theory is a branch of applied mathematics, it witnessed a great success thanks to the application of its results to a wide selection of fields, including social sciences, biology, engineering and economics, as welll as the study of ad hoc networks [8]. Games can be classified according to various properties. Here we are mainly interested in the difference between *cooperative* and *non-cooperative* games as well as the difference between *strategic games* (played once) and *extensive games* (played many times). A well known non-cooperative game is the *prisoner's dilemma*. In its basic form the prisoner's dilemma is played only once and has been applied to many real life situations of conflict, even comprising thorny issues of state diplomacy. A different version of the prisoner's dilemma is played repeatedly rather than just once and is known as iterated prisoner's dilemma (IPD), which turned out to be a cooperative game under certain circumstances [9]. One of the main result of IPD game is that it stimulates cooperation. We base our algorithm to mitigate the node selfishness on the results of this version of the game.

In an ad hoc network, the number of nodes and links can change during time, so we consider the number of nodes $N(t)$ as a function of time t. We also define a dynamic array $C(t)$ of $N(t)$ elements for each node of the network. The generic element $c_i(t)$ of $C(t)$ assumes the values (UNKNOWN, COOPERATE, DEFECT) meaning that the behavior of node i at time t is respectively unknown, cooperative or non cooperative. At time $t = 0$ all the values are set to UNKNOWN, since at the beginning each node is not aware of the behavior of the other nodes.

Suppose the generic node s of the network needs to send some traffic to the destination d. The first task is to discover an available path, if it exists, to reach the destination. To this purpose, we consider a source based routing protocol capable of discovering a list $A(t)_{(s,d)i}$ $\forall i : 0 < i < P$ of P multiple paths. All the nodes in the list $A(t)_{(s,d)i}$ are considered under observation and marked as probably defecting in the array $C(t)$ unless a positive feedback is received before a timeout expires. The sender s starts sending his traffic along all the discovered paths. If the destination node generates D acknowledgement messages containing the list of all the nodes $L_{(s,d)i}$ $0 < i < D$ traversed, as it happens in some source based routing protocols, the sender s is informed about the behavior of intermediate nodes. For each acknowledgement message received, the sender s can make a final update of the array $C(t)$ by setting the matching elements between the list $L_{(s,d)i}$ and list $A(t)_{(s,d)i}$ as *cooperative*. The mismatches are instead set to *defective* Notice that the last update overwrites the previous stored values and represents the most recent information concerning the behavior of a node.

At the same time, intermediate nodes (those not generating or receiving traffic but still involved in a path) can keep trace of other nodes' behaviors. As soon as a packet to be forwarded (and containing the complete routing list) is received, all the nodes on the path *preceding* the current node are marked as cooperative. Similarly, when an acknowledgement packet is received, all the nodes on the path *following* the current node are marked as cooperative. Missing acknowledgements cause instead a defective mark in the list. Given this algorithm, each node is aware of the behavior of other nodes and can react in the most appropriate way.

The algorithm has been implemented in an existing source based routing protocol for ad hoc networks, the AH-CPN (Ad Hoc Cognitive Packet Network) [10]. AH-CPN is designed to support QoS (Quality of Service) and make an intense use of acknowledgement messages independently from the transport protocol in use. We first modified this protocol to support the search of multiple paths, and then included the new algorithm for the identification of non cooperative nodes [11]. Implementation details are omitted due to limited space.

4   Testbed and Experiments

We tested the proposed routing protocol on a simulated testbed in the ns-2 simulator under different working conditions. The testbed is composed of 25 nodes arranged in a 5×5 grid topology labeled from 0 to 24. At the end of each of the experiments run on the testbed, we measure the delivery ratio dr_i, the average residual energy of all the nodes μ, their variance ν, as well as the energy e_i spent by node i to successfully deliver one single byte to the destination, which is computed as: $e_i = \frac{Ec_i}{(s_i + rl_i)} * \frac{s_i}{r_i}$, being Ec_i the energy consumed by node i, s_i the total number of bytes sent to the destination, rl_i the number of bytes relayed from node i, and r_i the bytes correctly received at destination. e_i has a dimension of $[Joule/bytes]$.

In the first series of experiments we consider the presence of malicious nodes, which clearly have a negative impact on the final performance of cooperative nodes. In the 25 nodes testbed, nodes $1, 3, 6, 8, 12, 16, 18, 21, 23$ decide to either cooperate or defect for the entire duration of the experiment. The remaining nodes are instead always cooperative. We consider six cases: (i) all nodes cooperate; (ii) node 12 does not cooperate; (iii) nodes $6, 12, 18$ do not cooperate; (iv) nodes $6, 8, 12, 16, 18$ defect; (v) nodes $1, 3, 6, 8, 12, 16, 18$ defect; (vi) all nodes $1, 3, 6, 8, 12, 16, 18, 21, 23$ do not cooperate. A total number of 10 CBR (Constant Bit Rate) UDP traffic sessions are generated between each pair of nodes $(0, 24)$, $(24, 0)$, $(4, 20)$, $(20, 4)$, $(6, 9)$, $(8, 5)$, $(13, 10)$, $(11, 14)$, $(16, 19)$, and $(18, 15)$. Each experiment lasts $720\,s$.

By looking at the first histogram in Fig. 1(a), we can observe how the presence of malicious nodes affects the final performance. Also, in lack of a tracing algorithm, the delivery ratio of defective nodes (marked as def) outperforms that achieved by the cooperative ones ($coop$), whatever the number of defective nodes is. At the opposite, the introduction of the tracing algorithm always favors cooperative nodes ($coop_T$), whose delivery ratio is constantly kept higher than that of defective ones (def_T).

We then evaluate the energy e_i spent to successfully deliver a single byte to the destination in the second row of histograms in Fig. 1(b). Again, the behavior tracking algorithm $mPath$-T is able to reverse the values achieved with the plain version of the AH-CPN protocol. While in the basic protocol version the value e_i of cooperative nodes increases at a pace which closely mirrors the increase in the number of defecting nodes, when the tracing algorithm is enabled such a value is kept low as the number of defecting nodes increases. Also, the energy e_i of defecting nodes shows a raising exponential slope. To balance the unfair energy consumption among the nodes we propose to deliberately push overwhelmed nodes in defection mode for short time intervals. During this second series of experiments the percentage of cooperation of the inner nodes $6, 7, 8 - 11, 12, 13 - 16, 17, 18$ changes over time. In the first experiment, all nodes cooperate. In the second experiment nodes, inner nodes cooperate for a total time of 75 % out of the total experiment duration. In the third and last experiment, the defection intervals are extended, so the percentage time interval of cooperation is of about 60 % with respect to the overall duration of the experiment. This time, defective nodes do not send traffic during the above mentioned intervals since their action aims at preserving the energy rather than cheating the other nodes.

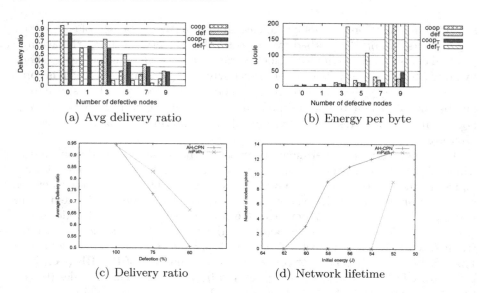

(a) Avg delivery ratio

(b) Energy per byte

(c) Delivery ratio

(d) Network lifetime

Fig. 1. Experimental results

The average residual energy and their variance is significantly reduced when the defection interval of inner nodes increases. The introduction of the proposed tracking algorithm do not show significant improvement with respect to the basic protocol. Notice however that if we look at the comparison of delivery ratio achieved by the two versions of the protocol in Fig. 1(c) (labeled as *basic* (AH-CPN), and *mPath-T* the version with the proposed tracking algorithm), the behavior tracking algorithm clearly outperforms the counterpart when the percentage of cooperation of inner nodes goes down.

We arranged a further experiment to analyze network nodes lifetime. To this purpose we make the testbed start from a situation of low energy and we count the number of nodes that shut down before the natural end of the experiment. As witnessed by the comparative results presented in Fig. 1(d), the introduction of the behavior tracking system again helps reduce the number of node shutdowns as long as the initial energy level is higher than 54 *Joule*. Notice also how the slope of basic protocol is linear, while that of the tracing algorithm looks like an impulse, which again indicates a fairer distribution of residual energy among nodes and then a longer lifetime for the whole network.

5   Conclusions

Current ad hoc routing protocols do not take into account the amount of work done to relay other nodes' traffic, which impacts the residual energy available for a node's own transmissions. This inevitably brings to a situation of unfair energy consumption for certain nodes in favor of other, less involved, ones. In this paper we propose to introduce some modifications in ad hoc routing protocols to support the identification of nodes' behaviors. Behavioral information gives the busiest nodes a chance to temporarily stop serving the others, while the routing protocol helps discover alternative paths allowing to keep both the residual energy and the overall network performance at fair levels. The improved distribution of energy consumption also prevents the irregular shut down of overloaded nodes, thus increasing the overall network lifetime. Among some possible enhancements we envision the introduction of a self-regulated system to switch the status of each node according to the received behavioral information.

References

1. Anastasi, G., Conti, M., Di Francesco, M., Passarella, A.: Energy conservation in wireless sensor networks: a survey. Ad Hoc Netw. **7**(3), 537–568 (2009). ISSN 1570–8705
2. Feng, D., Jiang, C., Lim, G., Cimini Jr., L.J., Feng, G., Li, G.Y.: A survey of energy-efficient wireless communications. IEEE Commun. Surv. Tutorials **15**(1), 167–178 (2013)
3. Mehta, S., Tamanna, Kumar, M.: A comparative study of power aware routing protocols of Ad Hoc network. In: IJCA Proceedings on National Workshop-Cum-Conference on 2011 RTMC (15), pp. 3–7. Foundation of CS, New York, May 2012
4. Asha, T.S., Muniraj, N.J.R.: Energy efficient topology control approach for mobile ad hoc network. Int. J. Comput. Sci. Issues (IJCSI) **10**(4), 289 (2013)
5. Singh, N.K., Simha, R., Narahari, B.: Energy balance in wireless networks using connection segmentation and range control. IEEE Wirel. Commun. Network. **3**, 1871–1876 (2003)
6. Dai, L., Chen, W., Cimini, L.J., Letaief, K.B.: Fairness improves throughput in energy-constrained cooperative ad-hoc networks. IEEE Trans. Wirel. Commun. **8**(7), 3679–3691 (2009)
7. Guha, R.K., Gunter, C.A., Sarkar, S.: Fair coalitions for power-aware routing in wireless networks. IEEE Trans. Mob. Comput. **6**(2), 206–220 (2007)
8. Srinivasan, V., Nuggehalli, P., Chiasserini, C.F., Rao, R.R.: Cooperation in wireless ad hoc networks. In: INFOCOM 2003. vol. 2, pp. 808–817, April 2003
9. Axelrod, R., Dion, D.: The further evolution of cooperation. Science **242**(4884), 1385–1390 (1988)
10. Gelenbe, E., Lent, R.: Power-aware ad hoc cognitive packet networks. Ad Hoc Netw. **2**(3), 205–216 (2004). ISSN: 1570–8705
11. D'Arienzo, M., Oliviero, F., Romano, S.P.: Can cooperation improve energy efficiency in ad hoc wireless networks? Comput. Commun. **35**(14), 1707–1714 (2012). ISSN: 0140–3664

Revisiting IEEE 802.11 Backoff Process Modeling Through Information Entropy Estimation

Faisal Iradat[(✉)] and Sayeed Ghani

Faculty of Computer Science,
Insitute of Business Administration, Karachi, Pakistan
{firadat,sghani}@iba.edu.pk

Abstract. In this paper, we propose a more accurate model, than many existing models, to evaluate the throughput performance of the IEEE 802.11 distributed coordination function. The proposed model is based on a novel approach to modeling the backoff process where the average backoff window size is measured through information entropy estimation. Our approach provides a better description of the backoff process as compared to some of the models available in the literature. The behavior of the proposed model is validated via simulations and compared against that of some known models across a wide range of settings.

Keywords: IEEE 802.11 · DCF · Throughput performance · Information entropy

1 Introduction

In recent years, the world has witnessed tremendous growth and popularity of the IEEE 802.11-based wireless local area networks (WLANs). Capable of delivering "all-time-on" seamless wireless connectivity to local area networks, these systems have been massively deployed in business, residential, and public areas.

The IEEE 802.11 standard [1] is an adaptation of the Ethernet protocol for wireless networks. It inherits many advantages of the Ethernet protocol in terms of design, simplicity, and higher performance. In the original IEEE 802.11 standard [2], two medium access control (MAC) mechanisms were defined: distributed coordination function (DCF) and point coordination function (PCF). The DCF mechanism is the fundamental MAC procedure of the IEEE 802.11 standard. In the DCF, WLAN stations (STAs) contend for the channel access by using carrier sense multiple access with collision avoidance (CSMA/CA). THE CSMA/CA protocol uses slotted binary exponential backoff (BEB) algorithm [3]. Whenever a backoff process is initially invoked, each STA randomly and uniformly chooses a backoff from the range $[0, CW]$, where CW is equal to CW_{min}, where the default value of CW_{min} is 31. After each unsuccessful transmission attempt, the value of the CW doubles until the maximum backoff window size CW_{max}, is reached. If there are a maximum of m backoff stages than $CW_{max} = 2^m CW$. CW will reset to CW_{min} after a successful transmission or remain at CW_{max} until it is reset to CW_{min}. The retry limit defines when the frame is dropped after

© Institute for Computer Sciences, Social Informatics and Telecommunications Engineering 2015
S. Mumtaz et al. (Eds.): WICON 2014, LNICST 146, pp. 26–38, 2015.
DOI: 10.1007/978-3-319-18802-7_5

which CW resets to CW_{min}. On the other hand, the PCF method provides polling-based contention free access to the channel. Although the PCF was originally designed to support real time services, it has never been widely implemented due to more complex quality of service (QoS) management. In the IEEE 802.11 standard, the PCF mechanism is thus optional. As such, the standard does not enforce vendors to provide support for the PCF mechanism in their devices.

The DCF scheme is therefore the fundamental channel access mechanism. Consequently, it has received significant research attention. Several analytical models have been proposed in the literature to evaluate its performance. At the heart of these studies is the classical decoupling assumption [3, 4] for saturated load conditions. Fundamentally, this assumption means decoupling interactions between saturated sources. That is the re-transmission processes at the sources are mutually exclusive and can be analyzed independently. Through this property, a fixed-point formulation can be reached and thus allowing one to relate per station transmission attempt rate with constant and independent collision probability of a packet. Different approaches in the literature have been followed to reach this fixed-point formulation. Bianchi [4] used a bi-dimensional Markov chain technique for modeling the backoff process. Tay and Chua [5] used an average value analysis. Alternatively, a p-persistent CSMA/CA model was used by Cali, Conti, and Gregori in [6]. The model initially proposed by Bianchi [4] for saturated load conditions and later extended by Tickoo and Sikdar in [7] to analyze the DCF performance under unsaturated load conditions are most commonly cited. This is due to their simple design and relatively high accuracy.

However, according to some recent studies [8–11], several details of the DCF protocol were not modeled properly in the earlier works [4, 7, 12–15]. Details that were addressed later include the concept of freezing counters [16, 17], backoff decrement probabilities [16], and frame error probability considerations under error-prone channel conditions [18]. Although these shortcomings were addressed, the improved models have lower accuracy as compared to the results of the original approach in [4]. These inaccuracies were subsequently indicated in [18, 19]. Later, an enhanced model was also proposed in [10] to provide a possible solution.

It transpires from the above discussion that despite the fact that the necessary details of the DCF protocol were considered, modeling accuracy was not improved. Apparently, the focus of existing studies in literature [4, 7] has been limited to modeling the backoff process under the assumption that the probabilities assigned to the different outcomes of CW are equal under arbitrary load conditions. Due to complete lack of knowledge on outcomes and in accordance with the principle of indifference [20], such an assumption may be valid. However, as discussed later in this paper, there are situations where definite knowledge about the outcomes of the backoff process exists and thus the principle of indifference may not be applicable. Thus, in a case when an outcome is definitely known, measuring the outcome has no intrinsic value. Rather, the situations which represent incomplete information are of interest. These conditions need to be analyzed to accurately estimate the probability for accuracy.

In an attempt to address the these issues and provide a possible solution, in this paper we describe situations in saturated and unsaturated load conditions which are predictable. Then by measuring the disorder through information entropy for other situations, which represent a great deal of information, we provide an augmentation to the model proposed by Tickoo in [7]. In this paper the analysis has been limited to studying the throughput performance under saturation. In [14], we have shown that by revisiting the assumptions in [4, 7] a more accurate model for unsaturated load condition can be developed. With our general approach, we have taken both saturated and unsaturated load conditions into consideration while proposing a new modeling approach. The results obtained within this framework have been validated through extensive simulations using ns-2 [21] and compared to the results from the existing models in [4, 7].

The rest of the paper is organized as follows. In Sect. 2, the analytical framework is presented. In Sect. 3, the analytical results are verified through simulations and compared with the related work. Finally, in Sect. 4, we give the concluding remarks.

2 Analytical Framework

To model the MAC layer with respect to packet delays or throughput performance, it is essential to describe the exponential backoff procedure of the IEEE 802.11 MAC. The IEEE 802.11 DCF is based on CSMA/CA access method for frame transmission and random backoff mechanism to resolve collisions. Each STA that has a frame to transmit first senses the channel for possible activity. If the channel is idle for a period of distributed inter-frame space (DIFS), the STA starts decrementing its backoff counter. The STA whose backoff counter has had decremented to zero begins transmission while all other STAs freeze their backoff counters and defer communication. The backoff counter decrement is reactivated whenever the channel is sensed idle. The events that follow a successful frame transmission are of great importance when modeling the IEEE 802.11 DCF. After the successful frame transmission, the transmission queue at each STA might be empty or full depending on the current offered load conditions. In saturated load conditions, the transmission queue at each STA always has backlogged frames. With multiple STAs contending for the channel access, the frames are more susceptible to collisions as the chances are higher that two or more STAs will pick up the same backoff counter. To avoid such conditions, after each unsuccessful transmission attempt the contention window doubles CW until the maximum backoff window size CW_{max} is reached. This way, the probability of selecting exactly the same backoff value by two or more STAs reduces further with successive collisions. Thus, collisions are resolved. However, the downside of this process is that now STAs on average have to suffer longer waiting times before a transmission attempt. Hence, there is a tradeoff between waiting longer and colliding more.

Modeling the backoff process for saturated load conditions is comparatively easier than modeling the unsaturated load scenarios, as queueing dynamics can be ruled out. Since the queue is always assumed to be non-empty, every frame collides with a constant and independent probability p (decoupling assumption), regardless of the number of (re)transmissions suffered. In [4], it was shown that once p is assumed constant, a bidirectional discrete time Markov chain [22] can be developed to represent user behavior. By deriving balance equations [23], a simple closed form solution can also be obtained. Readers are referred to [3] for an in-depth study on the justification and the use of decoupling assumption to analyze the performance of random multi-access algorithms.

In saturated load conditions, if collision probability p is assumed to be a constant value, then the probability that the contention window CW a frame experiences at the end of i unsuccessful attempts can be expressed as:

$$P_{CW=2^{i-1}CW_{min}} = p^{i-1}(1-p)$$
$$P_{CW=CW_{max}} = p^m \tag{1}$$

where $1 \leq i \leq m$. Similarly, the probability of a backoff counter event $P_{BC=j}$ is given by

$$P_{BC=j} = \begin{cases} \frac{(1-p)}{CW_{min}}, & 1 \leq j \leq CW_{min} \\ \sum_{i=0}^{m-1} \frac{p^i(1-p)}{2^i CW_{min}} + \frac{p^m}{CW_{max}}, & 2^{i-1}CW_{min} \leq j \leq 2^{i-1}CW_{min} \\ \frac{p^m}{CW_{max}} & j \leq CW_{max} \end{cases} \tag{2}$$

With no limit on the number of retransmissions suffered, in arbitrary load conditions the average backoff window seen by the frames when the STA experiences a collision rate of p is given by

$$\overline{CW} = (1-p) + \frac{1-p-p(2p)^m}{1-2p}.E[CW_{min}] + 2^{m+1}.\frac{CW_{min}}{2} \tag{3}$$

Where $E[CW_{min}] = CW_{min}/2$ is the uniformly distributed contention window. Under extremely low load conditions, the average backoff window size is exactly $1 - p$. Whereas in extremely heavy load conditions, the average backoff window size is $2^{m+1}.(CW_{min}/2)$; the maximum contention window.

In arbitrary load conditions, every frame starts out with a minimum window of size of CW_{min}, since there is always a frame in the transmission queue, the average backoff window $E[CW_{min}]$ is invoked for every transmission attempt. Upon a successful transmission, the frame starts out with an average backoff window of $CW_{min}/2$ and the probability $1 - p$. If the frame is successfully transmitted in the second attempt, it is transmitted with $p(1 - p)$ probability with a window size of $2 \times CW_{min}/2$. Similarly, other cases can be worked out and the Eq. (3) can be driven. The average backoff window analysis presented above relates the collision probability to the average window size.

2.1 Analysis of the Backoff Process Through Measures of Information Entropy

In order to demonstrate our proposed amendment, we draw the reader's attention to the backoff process and try to explain its behavior in terms of measure of disorder associated with assigning probabilities to different outcomes of CW_{min} under variable offered load conditions.

The network can be analyzed under two different conditions: saturated load and unsaturated load. As per the standard, regardless of the current offered load situation, the backoff process should be invoked even for the first attempt of transmitting a packet. Therefore, after a successful transmission, the corresponding STA must choose a value from the uniformly distributed range $[0, CW_{min}]$ and then wait for the respective interval before transmitting. The STA transmits when the backoff counter decrements to zero. Now if a collision occurs the backoff interval is doubled and a value from the larger range is randomly picked up to avoid subsequent collision. Thus, it seems from the ongoing discussion that regardless of the offered load conditions on the network, every packet has to undergo a backoff process before being transmitted. Under such rules and in accordance to the principle of indifference [20], it would be appropriate to assign a probability of $1/CW_{min}$ to each outcome of CW_{min}. This rule for assigning probabilities is only applicable to situations where there is complete lack of knowledge on the outcome of CW_{min}. However, if some definite knowledge about the backoff process exists, there is no reason to include these in measurements. Rather, only the outcomes which represent a good deal of information need to be measured for obtaining higher accuracy.

Working on these lines, we identify two situations where the outcomes are almost always predictable. In unsaturated load conditions, after each successful transmission, the transmitting STA initiates a "post-backoff" procedure. In a post-backoff state, the backoff timer continues to decrement even when the queue is empty [24]. If a packet from higher layers arrives at the station and finds the queue empty, with the latest post-backoff has already finished and the medium is idle, the frame may be transmitted immediately [25]. Under such circumstances, the STA does not have to wait for any backoff time. On the other hand, if the offered load on the network is extremely high, each packet will always have to suffer longer waiting times due to backoff process. These scenarios are highly predictable and represent no information. Hence, there is no need to include them in measurements.

By eliminating the highly predictable cases, which would yield virtually no additional information on the outcome, we can then focus on the situations that represent a great deal of information. As such, by measuring the disorder in the information, the precision of measurements can be improved. In information theory, the entropy of a system is a measure of its degree of disorganization [26]. Shannon quantified the expected value of the information content using a logarithmic measure [27]. In this paper, we refer to the disorder in information as to information entropy. Therefore, the conditions where packets may experience an on /off backoff process represent significant information, i.e. macroscopic[1] description of the situation. However, to specify the microstate[2] given the macroscopic description, additional information is needed. To measure the disorder in the information given the macrostate, we use the following measure of information entropy [28]:

---

[1] In statistical mechanics, the macrostate refers to the macroscopic properties of the system.

[2] A specific microscopic configuration given for a given macrostate.

$$I(E[CW_{\min}]) = log_{10}\left(\frac{CW_{\min}}{2}\right) \tag{4}$$

Equation (4) gives us a measure of disorder in the information in base 10 Hartleys [29]. We believe that information entropy would provide a better estimate than the equal probability assumption.

Therefore, substituting $I(E[CW_{\min}])$ in Eq. (3), the average backoff window can be computed more accurately and expressed as follows:

$$\overline{CW} = I(1-p)|_{=0} + \frac{1-p-p(2p)^m}{1-2p}.I(E[CW_{\min}]) + I(2^{m+1}.\frac{CW_{\min}}{2})\Big|_{=0} \tag{5}$$

To compute the average throughput performance under saturated load condition, the remaining equations are provided below. A summary of notations is given in Table 1 below:

Table 1. Summary of notations

Notations	Descriptions
T^S and T^C	Denote successful transmission (T) and collision (C) outcomes when computing the transmission time of a frame
STA	WLAN station
N	Number of transmitting stations/nodes
PKT	Packet
K	Transmitting station buffer size of a STA in PKTs
δ	Propagation delay – IEEE 802.11 PHY layer parameter (IEEE 802.11-1999 2003)
CW_{min}	Minimum contention window – IEEE 802.11 MAC layer parameter (IEEE 802.11-1999 2003)
m	Maximum number of contention stages (also backoff stages)
σ	Slot time (secs) – IEEE 802.11 MAC layer parameter (IEEE 802.11-1999 2003)
$\bar{\sigma}$	Average time between successive backoff counter decrements in the units of time (secs)
p	Packet collision probability
$Pr(TS)$	Probability that a station successfully transmits, (TS) in a slot time σ
λ	Arrival rate (number of packets arriving at each STA) in units of (packets/sec)
$Pr(X)$	Probability of an event 'X' e.g. X could be Idle Slot, Successful Slot, Collision Slot, transmission and etc.

From the law of total probability, the transmission probability $Pr(TS)$ is the pair wise union of the transmission probability given that the station finds the queue empty QE, and when the queue is non empty QNE

$$Pr(TS) = Pr(TS|QE)Pr(QE) + Pr(TS|QNE)Pr(QNE) \tag{6}$$

In saturated load conditions, the possibility of having an empty queue is typically very low. Therefore, the probability of transmitting a packet under saturated load conditions while the queue is empty is highly unlikely. Whereas if the queue is not empty which is highly probable under saturated conditions, the STA will transmit with a probability of $\rho/\overline{CW}$

$$Pr(TS) = Pr(TS|QE)\,Pr(QE) + Pr(TS|QNE)\,Pr(QNE)$$

$$Pr(TS) = 0.(1-\rho) + 1.\left(\frac{\rho}{\overline{CW}}\right) = \left(\frac{\rho}{\overline{CW}}\right) \tag{7}$$

$$Pr(TS) = \frac{1-2p}{1-p-p(2p)^m} \cdot \frac{\rho}{\overline{CW}}$$

Once the transmission scenarios have been modeled, the collisions can also be expressed in terms of $Pr(TS)$. If there are N stations in the network, then a collision will occur when any one or more of the remaining N–1 stations also transmits in the same slot. Therefore, the collision probability p can be expressed as follows:

$$p = 1 - (1 - Pr(TS))^{N-1} \tag{8}$$

Combining the Eqs. (7) and (8), p can be expressed as

$$p = 1 - \left(1 - \frac{1-2p}{1-p-p(2p)^m} \cdot \frac{\rho}{\overline{CW}}\right)^{N-1}$$

The total normalized offered load on the network, ρ, can be computed when the average service rate, $\bar{\mu}$, is known. A station transmits a frame successfully in a slot σ, when the remaining N–1 stations do not transmit in the same slot.

As such, on a discrete time scale, once the steady state has been achieved, $\bar{\mu}$ can be expressed as:

$$\bar{\mu} = \frac{Pr(TS)(1 - Pr(TS))^{N-1}}{\bar{\sigma}} \tag{9}$$

Since ρ is the total normalized offered load on the network, the packet arrival rate per station, λ, can be computed as follows:

$$\lambda = \frac{\rho.(T^{PKT})}{N} \tag{10}$$

where $T^{PKT} = \frac{8*Packet\ Size}{Data\ Rate}$.

In IEEE 802.11, the time is slotted in basic constant time units, σ, which are needed to detect the transmission of a frame from any other station. A slot can be in one of the three possible states: idle, successful transmission, or collision. Since these states are independent and mutually exclusive, the average time between the successive counter decrements, $\bar{\sigma}$, can be given as:

$$\bar{\sigma} = [\Pr(Idle\ Slot) + \Pr(Successful\ Slot) + \Pr(Collision\ Slot)] \tag{11}$$

Where

$$\Pr(Idle\ Slot) = (1 - \Pr(TS))^{N-1} \tag{12}$$

$$\Pr(Successful\ Slot) = (N-1).\Pr(TS).(1 - \Pr(TS))^{N-1}.(T^S + \sigma) \tag{13}$$

$$\Pr(Collision\ Slot) = p - [(N-1).\Pr(TS).(1 - \Pr(TS))^{N-1}.(T^C + \sigma)] \tag{14}$$

The successful and collision transmission times of a single frame transmission are given in Eqs. (15) and (16) below:

$$T^S = T^{RTS} + SIFS + \delta + T^{CTS} + SIFS + \delta + T^{(H+PL)} + SIFS + \delta + T^{ACK} + DIFS + \delta \tag{15}$$

$$T^C = T^{RTS} + DIFS + \delta \tag{16}$$

Finally, p can be obtained by substituting the remaining parameters given above in Eq. (11). The expression for computing the average saturation throughput given by [3] has been reformulated as follows:

$$
\begin{aligned}
\gamma &= X/Y \\
X &= \Pr(Successful\ Slot).\Pr(Transmission).T^{PKT} \\
Y &= ((1 - \Pr(Transmission)).\sigma) + (\Pr(Transmission).\Pr(Successful\ Slot).T^S) \\
&\quad + (\Pr(Transmission).(1 - \Pr(Successful\ Slot).T^C)
\end{aligned} \tag{17}
$$

$$\Pr(Transmission) = (1 - (1 - \Pr(TS))^N) \tag{18}$$

3 Model Verification

To verify the outcomes of the proposed model in comparison with the results from existing models [4, 7], extensive simulations were carried out in ns-2 [21]. The values for the default parameters are given in Table 2, which have been set in accordance with [4, 7, 12, 14, 30] and IEEE 802.11b [2]. The legacy technology is addressed here for the sake of fairness when comparing with the known models:

The model assumes:

1. For channel reservations, all the STAs exchange RTS and CTS frames.
2. Ideal channel conditions.
3. Packets are only lost due to collisions

Table 2. Default values of parameters used in [4, 7, 12, 14, 30] and also in this paper

Parameter	Value	Unit
T^{RTS}	$= \left(\dfrac{(RTSPKT\ Size\ *\ 8)}{Data\ Rate} + \dfrac{PHY\ Header}{Basic\ Rate} \right)$ $= \dfrac{(20*8)}{Data\ Rate} + \dfrac{(24*8)}{Basic\ Rate}$	μsecs
$T^{CTS/ACK}$	$= \left(\dfrac{(CTS/ACKPKT\ Size\ *\ 8)}{Data\ Rate} + \dfrac{PHY\ Header}{Basic\ Rate} \right)$ $= \dfrac{(14*8)}{Data\ Rate} + \dfrac{(24*8)}{Basic\ Rate}$	μsecs
T^{PKT}	$= \left(\dfrac{(PKT\ Size\ *\ 8) + MAC\ Header}{Data\ Rate} + \dfrac{PHY\ Header}{Basic\ Rate} \right)$ $= \dfrac{(PKT\ Size\ *\ 8) + (28*8)}{Data\ Rate} + \dfrac{(24*8)}{Basic\ Rate}$	(μsecs)
IEEE 802.11b Data Rates	11	(Mbps)
IEEE 802.11b Basic Rate	1	(Mbps)
DIFS	50	(μsecs)
SIFS	10	(μsecs)
δ	2	(μsecs)
σ	20	(μsecs)
m	5	
CW_{min}	31	
K	50	(packets)
R	5	

4. Collision probability experienced by each STA is constant and independent under saturated load conditions
5. All the STAs are within the sensing range of each other.
6. No mobility is assumed.
7. Each STA is modeled as a finite M/M/1/K queue with Poisson arrivals, exponential service time, and the queue length of size K packets.

The typical network layout is shown in Fig. 1 below. Each simulation is conducted for 200 s with 3 repetitions. All simulation results have been obtained with 95 % confidence level.

The saturation conditions are assumed. Figures 2 and 3 plot the throughput versus packet sizes of contending stations exchanging packets at the data rate of 11 Mbps. The simulation results are compared with three different analytical models: Tickoo's model in [7], Bianchi's model in [4], and the proposed model. From the figures, with the use of minimum measure of information, we can see that the results of the proposed model are more accurate as compared to the results of models proposed by Tickoo and Bianchi and are closer to simulation results.

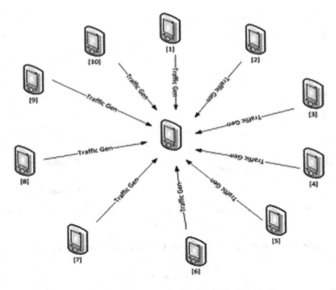

Fig. 1. Network scenario for 11 WLAN stations

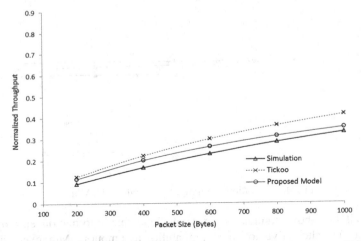

Fig. 2. Normalized (maximum) throughput versus packet size (data rate = 11 Mbps)

In Fig. 4, the saturation throughput versus the number of contending stations exchanging packets is plotted for the data rate of 11 Mbps. The results of the proposed model approach closer to the simulation curve as the number of stations keeps increasing. However, one thing is quite interesting to observe. The deviations can be observed at very low number of stations and high number of stations. We suspect that this may be due to longer waiting times where fewer packets are transmitted and thus the throughput drops.

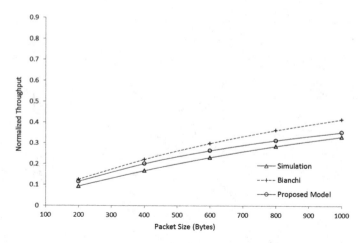

Fig. 3. Normalized (maximum) throughput versus packet size (data rate = 11 Mbps)

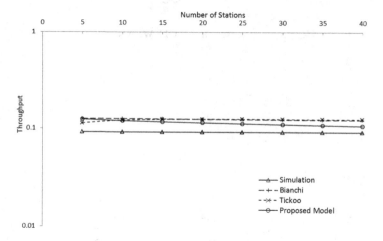

Fig. 4. Saturation throughput (data rate = 11 Mbps)

Given all the above figures, we can conclude that information entropy might provide a better alternative to equal probability assumption. Moreover, since the measure always gives a lower bound, we suspect that the proposed model may also provide accurate results for unsaturated load scenarios. However, a detailed investigation will further justify the applicability of the proposed approach.

4   Conclusion

The analytical modeling of the IEEE 802.11 DCF mechanism is a fairly established research area. Several models in the literature have been proposed for modeling the backoff process under saturated load conditions. However, how closely a model follows the actual backoff process of the IEEE 802.11 DCF mechanism still remains an open issue.

In this paper, we indicate that by assigning equal probability to the outcomes of CW_{min} when a station randomly requests for backoff value may result in inaccuracies. In past and existing models, this assumption is generally made on the basis of complete lack of knowledge. In such situations, with accordance to the principle of indifference, each outcome is assigned equal probability. In this paper, we have shown that there are situations when a definite knowledge about the backoff process exists. Hence, there is no reason to include these in measurements. Rather, only the outcomes which represent a great deal of information need to be considered for obtaining higher accuracy. By measuring the disorder in the information through information entropy estimates, we provide a better approximation for estimating the average window size. The results in this paper are validated through simulations. They are found to be more accurate in comparison with some of the widely-used existing models.

References

1. IEEE 802.11-2012: IEEE Standard for Information technology–Telecommunications and information exchange between systems Local and metropolitan area networks–Specific requirements Part 11: Wireless LAN Medium Access Control (MAC) and Physical Layer (PHY) Specifications. IEEE, 802.11-2012 (2012)
2. IEEE 802.11-1999: IEEE Standard for Information Technology- Telecommunications and Information Exchange Between Systems- Local and Metropolitan Area Networks- Specific Requirements- Part 11: Wireless LAN Medium Access Control (MAC) and Physical Layer (PHY) Specifications. ANSI IEEE Std 80211 1999 Ed. R2003, pp. 1–513 (2003)
3. Bordenave, C., McDonald, D., Proutière, A.: Random multi-access algorithms - a mean field analysis. In: Proceedings of ACCCC 2005, Monticello, IL, USA (2005)
4. Bianchi, G.: Performance analysis of the IEEE 802.11 distributed coordination function. IEEE J. Sel. Areas. Commun. 18(3), 535–547 (2000)
5. Tay, Y.C., Chua, K.C.: A capacity analysis for the IEEE 802.11 MAC protocol. Wirel. Netw. 7(2), 159–171 (2001)
6. Cali, F., Conti, M., Gregori, E.: Dynamic tuning of the IEEE 802.11 protocol to achieve a theoretical throughput limit. IEEE ACM Trans. Netw. 8(6), 785–799 (2000)
7. Tickoo, O., Sikdar, B.: Modeling queueing and channel access delay in unsaturated IEEE 802.11 random access MAC based wireless networks. IEEE ACM Trans. Netw. 16(4), 878–891 (2008)
8. Sharma, G., Ganesh, A., Key, P.: Performance analysis of contention based medium access control protocols. IEEE Trans. Inf. Theory 55(3), 1665–1682 (2009)
9. Cho, J., Le Boudec, J.Y., Jiang, Y.: On the validity of the fixed point equation and decoupling assumption for analyzing the 802.11 MAC protocol. SIGMETRICS Perform. Eval. Rev. 38(2), 36–38 (2010)
10. Tinnirello, I., Bianchi, G., Xiao, Y.: Refinements on IEEE 802.11 distributed coordination function modeling approaches. IEEE Trans. Veh. Technol. 59(3), 1055–1067 (2010)
11. Dai, L., Sun, X.: A unified analysis of IEEE 802.11 DCF networks: stability, throughput and delay. IEEE Trans. Mob. Comput. 99, 1 (2012)
12. Duffy, K., Malone, D., Leith, D.J.: Modeling the 802.11 distributed coordination function in non-saturated conditions. IEEE Commun. Lett. 9(8), 715–717 (2005)

13. Pham, P.P., Perreau, S., Jayasuriya, A.: Performance analysis of the IEEE 802.11 DCF. In: Proceedings of APCC 2005, Perth, Australia, pp. 764-768 (2005)
14. Iradat, F., Andreev, S., Ghani, S., Nabi, S.I., Arain, W.: Revisiting assumptions in backoff process modeling and queueing analysis of wireless local area networks (WLANs). Comput. J. **57**(6), 924–938 (2014)
15. Iradat, F., Andreev, S., Ghani, S.: Load based approach for backoff process modeling and queueing analysis of IEEE 802.11 based wireless LANs. In: Proceedings of NZCSRSC 2012. University of Otago, Otago (2012)
16. Ziouva, E., Antonakopoulos, T.: CSMA/CA performance under high traffic conditions: throughput and delay analysis. Comput. Commun. **25**(3), 313–321 (2002)
17. Foh, C.H., Tantra, J.W.: Comments on IEEE 802.11 saturation throughput analysis with freezing of backoff counters. IEEE Commun. Lett. **9**(2), 130–132 (2005)
18. Chatzimisios, P., Boucouvalas, A.C., Vitsas, V.: IEEE 802.11 wireless LANs: performance analysis and protocol refinement. EURASIP J. Wirel. Commun. **2005**(1), 67–78 (2005)
19. Felemban, E., Ekici, E.: Single hop IEEE 802.11 DCF analysis revisited: accurate modeling of channel access delay and throughput for saturated and unsaturated traffic cases. IEEE Trans. Wirel. Commun. **10**(10), 3256–3266 (2011)
20. Keynes, J.M.: A treatise on probability. Ann. Intern. Med. **128**(4), 288 (1998)
21. The Network Simulator - ns-2. http://www.isi.edu/nsnam/ns/
22. Kleinrock, L.: Queueing Systems, vol. 1. Wiley-Interscience, New York (1975)
23. Schwartz, M.: Telecommunication Networks: Protocols, Modeling and Analysis. Addison-Wesley Longman Publishing Co., Inc., Boston (1986)
24. Wang, X., Min, G., Guan, L.: Performance modelling of IEEE 802.11 DCF using equilibrium point analysis. Int. J. Wirel. Mob. Comput. **3**(3), 201–209 (2009)
25. Rathod, P., Dabeer, O., Karandikar, A., Sahoo, A.: Characterizing the exit process of a non-saturated IEEE 802.11 wireless network. In: Proceedings of MobiHoc, New Orleans, Louisiana, USA, pp. 249–258 (2009)
26. Wiener, N.: The Human Use of Human Beings: Cybernetics and Society. Doubleday, New York (1954)
27. Shannon, C.E.: A mathematical theory of communication. ATT Tech. J. **27**(1), 379–423 (1948)
28. Ramage, M., Chapman, D.: Perspectives on Information. Routledge, New York (2011)
29. Hartley, R.: Transmission of Information. ATT Tech. J. **7**(3), 535–563 (1928)
30. Zhao, Q., Tsang, D.H.K., Sakurai, T.: Modeling nonsaturated IEEE 80211 DCF networks utilizing an arbitrary buffer size. IEEE Trans. Mob. Comput. **10**(9), 1248–1263 (2011)

Transmission Window Optimization for Caching-Based Transport Protocols in Wireless Sensor Networks

Nestor Michael C. Tiglao[1](✉) and António M. Grilo[2]

[1] Ubiquitous Computing Laboratory EEE Institute,
University of the Philippines Diliman, 1101 Quezon City, Philippines
nestor@eee.upd.edu.ph
[2] INESC-ID/INOV/IST Rua Alves Redol, N° 9, 1000-029 Lisboa, Portugal
antonio.grilo@inov.pt

Abstract. Traditional transport protocols have been designed to perform end-to-end transmission and retransmission. In terms of choosing the optimal transmission window, previous works suggest a value based on the bandwidth-delay product (BDP). For wireless networks, the BDP value is related to the round-trip hop length. However, there exists a new class of transport protocols that use intermediate caching which can drastically improve the performance even in the presence of high packet error rates. In this paper, we show that using a window size related to the BDP could lead to sub-optimal performance for caching-based protocols. Furthermore, we present a heuristic for choosing the optimal transmission window such that the optimal value is related to the average cache size in the intermediate nodes.

Keywords: Wireless sensor networks · DTSN · Transmission window · Intermediate caching · Optimization

1 Introduction

Previous studies have shown that the transmission capacity of wireless ad hoc networks is related to the network size. Specifically, in [1] it was shown that the ideal capacity of a long chain of nodes is 1/4 of the raw channel capacity of the radio. In another work [2], the authors have shown that an upper bound on the bandwidth-delay product (BDP-UB) exists and is a function of the number of hops in the path. Furthermore, their study indicates that applying this BDP value to TCP's congestion window limit effectively improves the performance of TCP.

Datagram Transport Protocol for Ad Hoc Networks (DTPA), a reliable protocol designed for ad hoc networks, uses a fixed transmission window based on the bandwidth delay product for wireless networks (BDP-UB). However, such choice could lead to sub-optimal performance when applied to a caching-based protocols since intermediate caching improves packet delivery in the presence of packet loss compared with non-caching protocols [3].

© Institute for Computer Sciences, Social Informatics and Telecommunications Engineering 2015
S. Mumtaz et al. (Eds.): WICON 2014, LNICST 146, pp. 39–46, 2015.
DOI: 10.1007/978-3-319-18802-7_6

Reliable transport protocols require packets transmitted from the source to be acknowledged by the destination. Unacknowledged packets are deemed lost and are retransmitted by the source. The source may transmit multiple packets into the network before expecting any acknowledgment depending on its transmission window size. This value also corresponds to the maximum number of in-flight packets. The window size can be set dynamically (e.g., TCP [7]) or set to a fixed value (e.g., DTPA [5]). The window size must be optimized properly because it directly affects the end-to-end throughput, such that setting it too high can lead to congestion while setting it too low can result in low throughput.

With TCP, the transmission window is controlled by the congestion control algorithm (i.e., AIMD). End-to-end performance depends not upon the transfer rate itself, but rather upon the product of the transfer rate and the round-trip delay. This bandwidth-delay product (BDP) measures the amount of data that would fill the network pipe. This BDP also dictates the buffer space required at sender and receiver to obtain maximum throughput on the TCP connection over the path.

The traditional TCP has a maximum transmission window of 64 K bytes. For wired networks, this value works well in medium-sized pipes. For long fat pipes, the BDP exceeds this value and the 64 KB limit in the TCP header needs to be increased. However, for small-sized pipes where the BDP is well below 64 KB, such as in wireless networks, the BDP normally comprises a few packets only.

Distributed Transport for Sensor Networks (DTSN) [6] belongs to a class of transport protocols that leverage intermediate caching. DTSN supports both full and differentiated reliability and employs selective repeat ARQ using ACK and NACK semantics. When the DTSN receiver detects a lost packet, it creates a NACK packet indicating missing packet numbers in the current DTSN window. As the NACK traverses the network, the intermediate nodes will examine the NACK to see if there are any copy of missing packets in their cache. If copy is found, that packet is sent to the DTSN receiver and the NACK packet is modified (removing that packet number) and forwarded on towards the DTSN sender. In this way, end-to-end retransmission is reduced.

Paper contributions: This paper makes the following contributions: (1) We show that using a transmission window value based on the bandwidth-delay product leads to sub-optimal performance of caching-based transport protocols and (2) we develop a heuristic for choosing the optimal value for DTSN. To the best of our knowledge, this work is the first to consider the problem of choosing the optimal transmission window for caching-based protocols such as DTSN.

The rest of the paper is structured as follows. Section 2 presents the related work. Section 3 explains the simulation environment and protocol parameters used in this work. Section 4 presents our results. Finally, Sect. 5 concludes the paper.

2   Related Work

The work of [2] has established that the upper bound on the BDP for 802.11-based MANETs cannot exceed kN, where N is the round-trip hop length and

$1/8 < k < 1/4$ is the reduction factor due to transmission interference at the MAC layer. A larger k would suggest that the interference is smaller and that the chain network can accommodate for in-flight packets. In the said work, the authors obtained the value of k empirically to be equal to 1/5. DTPA [5] proposes a fixed optimal transmission window size equal to BDP-UB + 3. In our study, we have established that using a BDP-based value leads to sub-optimal performance and that the optimal transmission window size is equal to the cache size allocated to the flow. While this is most evident in high packet error rates, this is also true even in lower packet error rates where packet collisions can occur. Table 1 summarizes the protocols we considered in this thesis. For the 9-hop linear chain topology we considered, the value of the transmission window were set to 3 for DTPA-BDP and 6 for DTPA.

Table 1. Approaches to optimal transmission window.

Approach	Protocol used	Caching	Strategy
Chen, et al. [4]	TCP	N	Set congestion window limit to BDP-UB where BDP-UB=1/5 * round-trip hop length
Li, et al. [5]	DTPA	N	Set fixed window size to BDP-UB+3
Our Work	DTSN	Y	Set fixed window size to the cache size assigned to the flow

3   Simulation Environment

We implemented the DTSN protocol in ns-2 [8] and conducted extensive simulations. We consider a linear network topology consisting of 10 nodes with a single source (node 0) and destination (node 9). All the intermediate nodes have the same cache size. The source sends 500 packets of 500 bytes each in a realible stream-type transfer similar to TCP. We consider a network scenario considering uniform Frame Error Rate (FER) and we vary the FER from 0 to 0.70. The MAC retry limit is set to 3 (default value) unless specified otherwise. The DTSN EAR interval is set to 200 msec which is equal to the default minimum RTO setting in ns-2.

In order to conduct a comparison and analysis of the effect of our mechanisms on protocol performance, we fix the FER and network topology for each case. For each experiment, we conducted 20 simulation runs and obtained the 95 % confidence intervals. Table 2 provides a summary of the simulation parameters.

4   Results

We performed a comparative analysis of the following protocols to determine the effect of the transmission window:

Table 2. Simulation parameters

Parameter	Value
Network topology	Linear chain
Packet size	500 bytes
DTSN ACK window size	20 packets
DTSN cache size	20 packets
DTSN EAR interval	1 sec
Routing protocol	Static
MAC protocol	802.11 b
MAC retry limit (default)	3
PHY bandwidth	50 Kbps
PHY error model	Binary Symmetric Channel

- DTPA – The DTPA protocol as described in [5].
- DTPA-BDP – The DTPA protocol with the transmission window set to the value of the wireless bandwidth-delay product (BDP) [2].
- DTSN$^+$ – The DTSN protocol with the enhanced NACK repair and adaptive MAC retry limit mechanisms [9].
- TCP$^-$ – The TCP protocol without the RTO exponential backoff.

The goodput performance results (Fig. 1) show that the transmission window has a significant impact on the overall performance. Note that DTPA and DTPA-BDP only differs in the size of the transmission window (6 and 2, respectively). Both of these protocols use a fixed window size while TCP uses a dynamic window. However, all them perform end-to-end loss recovery. On the other hand, DTSN leverages on intermediate caching.

Furthermore, we studied the effect of the transmission window on DTSN by varying the acknowledgment window (AW) size. In order to simplify our network

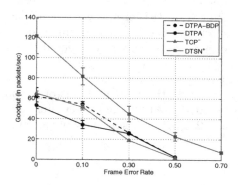

Fig. 1. Goodput performance comparison

configuration, we assume that all intermediate nodes have the same cache size (CS) and we vary the AW. We obtained both goodput and transmission cost as performance metrics. The transmission cost is the average number of link-wise packet transmissions including control and MAC layer packets and computed as follows:

$$\text{tx\_cost} = \frac{N_{data} + N_{ack} + N_{nack} + N_{mack}}{pktno} \tag{1}$$

where N_{data} is the total number of data packets transmitted, N_{ack} is the total number of transport-layer ACKs, N_{nack} is the total number of transport-layer NACKs, N_{mack} is the total number of MAC-layer ACKs, and $pktno$ is the total number of packets that need to be delivered end-to-end.

Figure 2 compares the goodput for CS=10 and CS=20. For CS=10, the optimal (i.e., maximum) goodput is achieved at AW_{opt}=[10,20] while for CS=20 optimal goodput is achieved at AW_{opt}=[20,30] as shown in Figs. 2(a) and (b), respectively.

In terms of energy efficiency, we see that the transmission cost is minimized in the same corresponding range of AWs as shown in Figs. 3(a) and (b). It can be seen that each figure shows a minimum value that corresponds to the optimal value of the transmission window.

Figure 3 shows that for high framer error rates (i.e., FER $\geq$ 0.5), the transmission cost at AW=5 is higher than at AW=1. This can be explained by the fact that at such high error rates, the cache hits are so low resulting in fewer RNACKs. Another factor is that with only one in-flight packet, contention is greatly reduced.

To quantify the optimality of the transmission window size, we calculate the overall gain of the goodput and transmission cost at a given AW relative to the worst case value (i.e., minimum goodput or maximum cost, respectively) using the following equations:

$$Gain_{Goodput} = \frac{Goodput_{AW} - min(Goodput)}{min(Goodput)} \tag{2}$$

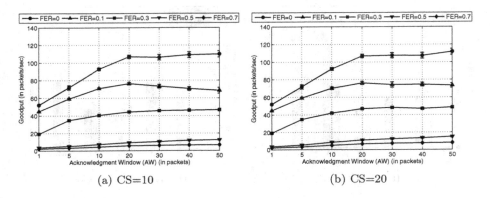

(a) CS=10   (b) CS=20

Fig. 2. Goodput, as a function of AW

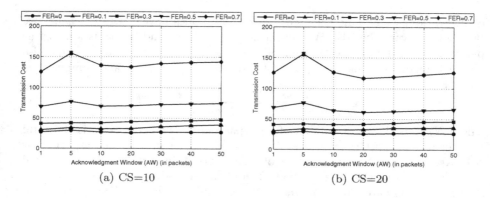

(a) CS=10   (b) CS=20

Fig. 3. Transmission cost, as a function of AW

where $Gain_{Goodput}$ = goodput gain,
        $Goodput_{AW}$ = goodput at a specific AW,
        $min(Goodput)$ = overall minimum goodput.

$$Gain_{Cost} = \frac{max(Cost) - Cost_{AW}}{Cost_{AW}} \tag{3}$$

where $Gain_{Cost}$ = transmission cost gain,
        $Cost_{AW}$ = transmission cost at a specific AW,
        $max(Cost)$ = overall maximum transmission cost.

Figure 4 shows the gain for CS=10. The goodput gain for AW=10 is lower than for AW=20 but the transmission cost gain of the former is higher than the latter. This can be explained by the fact the energy efficiency is achieved when the intermediate caching mechanism is maximized (i.e., maximum cache hits).

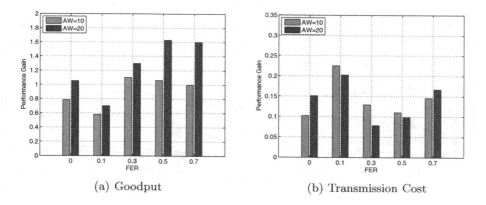

(a) Goodput   (b) Transmission Cost

Fig. 4. Performance gain histograms, CS=10.

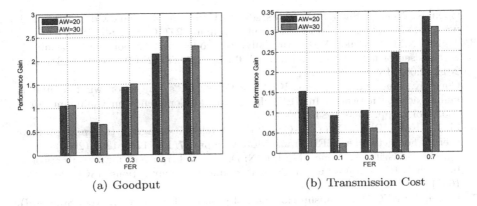

Fig. 5. Performance gain histograms, CS=20.

This occurs when the transmission window is equal to the cache size. However, in terms of goodput, a higher number of in-flight packets will tend to increase goodput since more packets can be delivered within the same period. This same pattern is observed for CS=20 as displayed in Fig. 5.

In our study, we assume uniform allocation for cache size on all nodes in the path. We have seen that for a given cache size (CS), the optimal energy efficiency (minimum transmission cost) is obtained when the transmission window (AW) when $AW = CS$ while the optimal goodput (maximum goodput) is obtained when $AW = CS + 10$. Thus, in general, the optimal transmission window is in the range $AW_{opt} = [CS, CS + 10]$.

5 Conclusion and Future Work

Recent works have highlighted the tremendous benefit of caching-based transport protocols in improving network performance in the presence of high packet error rates such as in Wireless Sensor Network. These necessitates a study in the optimal transmission window for these new class of protocols. Basing it on wireless bandwidth-delay product values leads to sub-optimal performance. In this paper, we have determined a heuristic in choosing the optimal transmission window for DTSN which is a function of the cache size in the intermediate nodes. Our future work shall include testing this heuristic on more complex and dynamic network scenarios as well implementing a suitable congestion control mechanism.

References

1. Li, J., Blake, C., De Couto, D.S., Lee, H.I., Morris, R.: Capacity of Ad hoc wireless networks. In: Proceedings of the 7th Annual International Conference on Mobile Computing and Networking, MobiCom 2001, pp. 61–69. ACM, New York (2001)

2. Chen, K., Xue, Y., Shah, S.H., Nahrstedt, K.: Understanding bandwidth-delay product in mobile ad hoc networks. Comput. Commun. **27**(10), 923–934 (2004)
3. Tiglao, N.M.C., Grilo, A.M.: An analytical model for transport layer caching in wireless sensor networks. Perform. Eval. **69**(5), 227–245 (2012). doi:10.1016/j.peva.2011.12.002. ISSN 0166–5316
4. Chen, K., Xue, Y., Nahrstedt, K.: On setting TCP's congestion window limit in mobile ad hoc networks. In: IEEE International Conference on Communications 2003, vol. 2, pp. 1080–1084 (2003)
5. Li, X., Kong, P.-Y., Chua, K.-C.: DTPA: A reliable datagram transport protocol over ad hoc networks. IEEE Trans. Mob. Comput. **7**(10), 1285–1294 (2008)
6. Marchi, B., Grilo, A., Nunes, M.: DTSN: Distributed transport for sensor networks. In: 12th IEEE Symposium on Computers and Communications. ISCC 2007, pp. 165–172 (2007)
7. Postel, J.,: RFC 793. Transmission control protocol. RFC 793 (Internet Standard), 1981. Updated by RFCs 1122, 3168, 6093, 6528, IETF. http://www.ietf.org/rfc/rfc793.txt
8. McCanne, S., Floyd, S.: The network simulator, 2012. http://www.isi.edu/nsnam/ns/
9. Tiglao, N.M.C., Grilo, A.M.: Caching based transport optimization for wireless multimedia sensor networks. IJARAS **5**(1), 30–48 (2014). Web. 15 Aug. 2014

Improved p-norm Energy Detector in AWGN Channel for Spectrum Sensing in Cognitive Radio

Vaibhav Kumar$^{(\boxtimes)}$, Monika Jain, Ranjan Gangopadhyay, and Soumitra Debnath

Department of ECE, The LNMIIT, Jaipur, India
vaibhav@lnmiit.ac.in

Abstract. The classical energy detection (CED) system is a well-known technique for spectrum sensing in cognitive radio application. Generalized p-norm detector for spectrum sensing has been shown to provide improved performance over CED under certain conditions. Further, improved algorithm exists which works better than the classical energy detection algorithm. The present paper highlights the combined benefit of the p-norm detector and an improved algorithm for spectrum sensing in achieving a higher performance gain.

Keywords: p-norm detector · Improved algorithm · Energy detection · Spectrum sensing · Cognitive radio

1 Introduction

In cognitive radio, spectrum sensing is the key technology that enables the secondary users (SUs) to access the licensed frequency bands without affecting the quality-of-service (QoS) of the primary users (PUs). Various spectrum sensing techniques have been suggested in the past [1], among which the classical energy detector (CED) is the simplest and well accepted technique for its low implementation cost and less complexity. However, the performance of the energy detector is limited by high susceptibility of the detection threshold to noise uncertainty and interference level. An improved energy detector (IED) has been proposed [2] which outperforms the CED with almost same algorithmic complexity and applicability without the need for a-priori information about the PU's signal format.

Another interesting improvement strategy for energy detection based on p-norm detector was first proposed by Chen [3], where the conventional energy detector is modified by replacing the squaring operation of the signal amplitude by arbitrary positive power p. The application of p-norm detector in fading channel and for diversity reception has been very well investigated recently [4]. In the present work, we have evaluated the performance benefit of spectrum sensing in AWGN channel by considering both the p-norm detector and the IED algorithm combinedly for efficient spectrum sensing.

© Institute for Computer Sciences, Social Informatics and Telecommunications Engineering 2015
S. Mumtaz et al. (Eds.): WICON 2014, LNICST 146, pp. 47–52, 2015.
DOI: 10.1007/978-3-319-18802-7_7

2   Spectrum Sensing

The spectrum sensing may be modeled as a binary hypothesis testing problem as:

$$
\begin{aligned}
H_0 : & \quad y[n] = w[n] \\
H_1 : & \quad y[n] = s[n] + w[n]
\end{aligned}
\tag{1}
$$

where, $y[n]$ is the signal sample detected by the SU, $s[n]$ is the signal transmitted by the PU, and $w[n]$ is the zero-mean additive white Gaussian noise (AWGN) with variance σ_w^2.

The hypotheses H_0 and H_1 correspond to the binary space, representing the absence and the presence of the PU respectively. In order to analyze the performance of the sensing scheme, the probability of false alarm, P_{fa}, and the probability of detection, P_d, need to be evaluated. The parameters are defined as follows:

$$
\begin{aligned}
P_{fa} &= P\left(H_1|H_0\right) \\
P_d &= P\left(H_1|H_1\right)
\end{aligned}
\tag{2}
$$

where, $P(\cdot|\cdot)$ denotes the conditional probability. The expression for these probabilities are obtained in the next section.

2.1   Classical Energy Detector (CED)

In CED, the decision variable $T_i(y_i)$ at the ith sensing event can be represented as:

$$
T_i(y_i) = \frac{1}{N} \sum_{n=1}^{N} \left| \frac{y_i(n)}{\sigma_w} \right|^2
\tag{3}
$$

where, N is the number of samples per sensing event. The decision rule can be modelled as:

$$
\begin{aligned}
H_0 : & \quad T_i(y_i) < \lambda \\
H_1 : & \quad T_i(y_i) \geq \lambda
\end{aligned}
\tag{4}
$$

where, λ is the decision threshold. For the number of samples $N \gg 1$, the decision variable can be well approximated as a Gaussian distribution [2], i.e.,

$$
T_i(y_i) = \begin{cases} \mathcal{N}\left(1, \frac{2}{N}\right) & : H_0 \\ \mathcal{N}\left((1+\gamma), \frac{2}{N}(1+\gamma)^2\right) & : H_1 \end{cases}
\tag{5}
$$

where, $\gamma = \frac{\sigma_s^2}{\sigma_w^2}$ is the signal-to-noise ratio (SNR) of the received signal, σ_s^2 is the signal power. For the AWGN channel, P_{fa}^{CED} and P_d^{CED} can be expressed as [2]:

$$
P_{fa}^{CED} = Q\left(\frac{\lambda - 1}{\sqrt{2/N}} \right)
\tag{6}
$$

$$P_d^{CED} = Q\left(\frac{\lambda - (1+\gamma)}{\sqrt{(2/N)(1+\gamma)^2}}\right) \tag{7}$$

where, $Q(x) = \int_x^\infty e^{-t^2} dt$, is the Gaussian tail probability function. From (6), the expression for λ can easily be obtained as:

$$\lambda = \sqrt{2/N}Q^{-1}\left(P_{fa}^{CED}\right) + 1 \tag{8}$$

2.2   Improved Energy Detector (IED)

In IED, the decision for the presence of the primary user is done based on the average of last L test statistics T_i^{avg} at the ith interval T_i, which is defined as:

$$T_i^{avg}(T_i) = \frac{1}{L}\sum_{l=1}^{L} T_{i-L+l}(y_{i-L+l}) \tag{9}$$

Out of the last L sensing events, $M \in [0, L]$ is the total number of events in which the primary signal was actually present. In IED algorithm, two additional checks are aimed to improve the detection probability as well as the probability of false alarm [2]. Since $T_i^{avg}(T_i)$ is the average of independent and identically distributed Gaussian random variables, it is also normally distributed:

$$T_i^{avg}(T_i) \sim \mathcal{N}(\mu_{avg}, \sigma_{avg}^2) \tag{10}$$

where, μ_{avg} and σ_{avg}^2 are obtained as:

$$\begin{aligned}
\mu_{avg} &= \frac{M}{L}(1+\gamma) + \frac{L-M}{L} \\
\sigma_{avg}^2 &= \frac{M}{L^2}\left(\frac{2}{N}(1+\gamma)^2\right) + \frac{L-M}{L^2}\left(\frac{2}{N}\right)
\end{aligned} \tag{11}$$

Based on the above assumptions, P_{fa}^{IED} and P_d^{IED} can be easily derived as [2]:

$$\begin{aligned}
P_{fa}^{IED} &= P_{fa}^{CED} + P_{fa}^{CED}(1 - P_{fa}^{CED})Q\left(\frac{\lambda - \mu_{avg}}{\sigma_{avg}}\right) \\
P_d^{IED} &= P_d^{CED} + P_d^{CED}(1 - P_d^{CED})Q\left(\frac{\lambda - \mu_{avg}}{\sigma_{avg}}\right)
\end{aligned} \tag{12}$$

2.3 p-norm Detector

The decision variable for the p-norm detector $(p > 0)$ is obtained by modifying (3) as:

$$T_i^p(y_i) = \frac{1}{N}\sum_{n=1}^{N}\left|\frac{y_i(n)}{\sigma_w}\right|^p \tag{13}$$

It may be noted that $p = 2$ in (13) leads to the CED case. The decision statistics may be well approximated by Gaussian distribution for $N \gg 1$ as follows [3]:

$$T_i^p(y_i) = \begin{cases} \mathcal{N}\left(\mu_{0,p}, \sigma_{0,p}^2\right) & : H_0 \\ \mathcal{N}\left(\mu_{1,p}, \sigma_{1,p}^2\right) & : H_1 \end{cases} \tag{14}$$

where,

$$\mu_{0,p} = \frac{2^{p/2}}{\sqrt{\pi}}\Gamma\left(\frac{p+1}{2}\right), \qquad \sigma_{0,p}^2 = \frac{2^p \Gamma\left(\frac{2p+1}{2}\right)}{N\sqrt{\pi}} - \frac{2^p}{N\pi}\left\{\Gamma\left(\frac{p+1}{2}\right)\right\}^2$$

$$\mu_{1,p} = \frac{2^{p/2}}{\sqrt{\pi}}\Gamma\left(\frac{p+1}{2}\right)\gamma_p^{p/2}, \quad \sigma_{1,p}^2 = \left[\frac{2^p \Gamma\left(\frac{2p+1}{2}\right)}{N\sqrt{\pi}} - \frac{2^p}{N\pi}\left\{\Gamma\left(\frac{p+1}{2}\right)\right\}^2\right]\gamma_p^p \tag{15}$$

where, $\gamma_p = 1 + \gamma$ and $\Gamma(\cdot)$ is the Gamma function. The probability of false alarm, P_{fa}^p and the probability of detection, P_d^p in the case of p-norm detector may be readily obtained as:

$$P_{fa}^p = Q\left(\frac{\lambda_p - \mu_{0,p}}{\sigma_{0,p}}\right), \ P_d^p = Q\left(\frac{\lambda_p - \mu_{1,p}}{\sigma_{1,p}}\right) \tag{16}$$

where, λ_p is the threshold for the p-norm detector to ensure a target P_{fa}^p.

2.4   Improved p-norm Energy Detector

By replacing the squaring operation of the signal amplitude in IED by an arbitrary positive power p, $T_i^{avg}(T_i^p)$ may be well approximated by a Gaussian distribution as:

$$T_i^{avg}(T_i^p) = \mathcal{N}\left(\mu_{avg,p}, \sigma_{avg,p}^2\right) \tag{17}$$

where, $\mu_{avg,p}$ and $\sigma_{avg,p}^2$ are the mean and the variance of $T_i^{avg}(T_i^p)$ defined as follows [2]:

$$\mu_{avg,p} = \frac{M}{L}\mu_{1,p} + \frac{L-M}{L}\mu_{0,p}$$

$$\sigma_{avg,p}^2 = \frac{M}{L^2}\sigma_{1,p}^2 + \frac{L-M}{L^2}\sigma_{0,p}^2 \tag{18}$$

Hence, according to the above assumptions, the probability of false alarm, $P_{fa}^{IED,p}$, and the probability of detection, $P_d^{IED,p}$, may be expressed as:

$$P_{fa}^{IED,p} = P_{fa}^p + P_{fa}^p\left(1 - P_{fa}^p\right)Q\left(\frac{\lambda_{IED,p} - \mu_{avg,p}}{\sigma_{avg,p}}\right)$$

$$P_d^{IED,p} = P_d^p + P_d^p\left(1 - P_d^p\right)Q\left(\frac{\lambda_{IED,p} - \mu_{avg,p}}{\sigma_{avg,p}}\right) \tag{19}$$

where $\lambda_{IED,p}$ is the threshold for the improved p-norm energy detector.

3   Results and Discussion

In this section, the results for the combined benefit of the improved energy detector algorithm as well as the p-norm detector are highlighted for spectrum sensing in AWGN channel. For a given target false alarm probability, the threshold value of λ is chosen; and for a given SNR γ, the optimal value of p is determined which yields the highest value of the probability of detection. In Fig. 1, the comparison of the receiver operating characteristics (ROCs) for CED ($p = 2$), IED ($p = 2$), CED with optimal p, and IED with optimal p has been depicted. It is clearly evident that the IED with optimal p outperforms all other schemes considered here for a low probability of false alarm. In Fig. 2, the variation of the probability of detection against SNR at a fixed target false alarm probability of 0.01

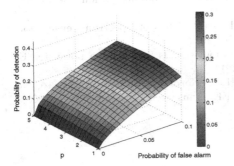

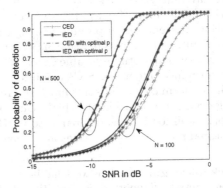

Fig. 1. Comparison of receiver operating characteristic for CED and IED with $p = 2$ and optimal p for $N = 100$ and $\gamma = -10$ dB.

Fig. 2. Probability of detection versus SNR for CED and IED with $p = 2$ and optimal p for $N = 100$ and 500, $\gamma = -10$ dB, $P_{fa,target} = 0.01$.

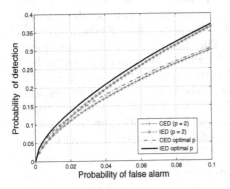

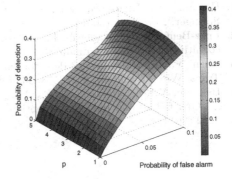

Fig. 3. Surface plot for probability of detection using CED in AWGN channel with $N = 100$ and $\gamma = -10$ dB.

Fig. 4. Surface plot for probability of detection using IED in AWGN channel with $N = 100$ and $\gamma = -10$ dB.

has been shown with the number of samples per sensing event, $N = 100$ and $N = 500$ as a parameter. It is interesting to note that the performance of both IED and CED remains optimal at $p = 2$, for a large value of N as well as for high value of SNR, as observed in [3].

To provide practical design guideline for a spectrum sensing system with p-norm detector with either CED/IED algorithms, Fig. 3 and Fig. 4 provide the surface plots for the probability of detection with variation of p and the probability of false alarm for CED and IED schemes respectively, each obtained for $N = 100$ and $\gamma = -10$ dB.

4   Conclusion

We have analyzed the sensing performance of an improved energy detector algorithm with the optimal p-norm value. The performance gain depends upon the various system design parameters, e.g., SNR, the probability of false alarm and the number of samples per sensing event, N. The theoretical results confirm that there exists an optimal p value other than 2, for which the detector gives the best performance under low SNR condition and with low probability of false alarm. The performance gain is not much significant, if the number of samples per sensing event, N is considerably high. But for the low value of N, a p-norm detector works well for IED as compared to CED. By combining both, the IED and the optimal p-norm detector, one can achieve a considerable performance gain.

Acknowledgments. The work has been carried out under the project, "Mobile Broadband Service Support over Cognitive Radio Networks," sponsored by Information Technology Research Academy (ITRA), Department of Electronics and Information Technology (DeitY), Govt. of India.

References

1. Hossain, E., Bhargava, V.K.: Cognitive Wireless Communication Networks. Springer, New York (2007)
2. Lpez-Bentez, M., Casadevall, F.: Improved energy detection spectrum sensing for cognitive radio. IET Commun. **6**(8), 785–796 (2012)
3. Chen, Y.: Improved energy detector for random signals in Gaussian noise. IEEE Trans. Wirel. Commun. **9**(2), 558–563 (2010)
4. Banjade, V.R.S., Tellambura, C., Jiang, H.: Performance of p-norm detector in AWGN, fading and diversity reception. IEEE Trans. Veh. Technol. **63**(7), 3209–3222 (2014)

Middleware Solution for HealthCare IoT Applications

José Cecílio[✉] and Pedro Furtado

University of Coimbra, Coimbra, Portugal
{jcecilio,pnf}@dei.uc.pt

Abstract. Advances in Internet of Things (IoT) technologies present enormous potential for the intensified healthcare support of senior or disabled citizens. Everyday objects will have the capability of directly interacting with each other and with humans. In this context we propose NCeH – a middleware solution that hides heterogeneity and offers a single common configuration and processing component for all nodes of IoT applications developed on top of it. The middleware is intended for the caring of people with special needs, such as video-vigilance, monitoring and so on, with multi-function, and is currently applied as a prototype in collaboration with cerebral palsy, blind and seniors caring institutions.

Keywords: Internet of things · Senior or disabled citizens · Middleware · Heterogeneity · Interoperability

1 Introduction

The Internet of Things (IoT) is one of the recent technological and social trends that will have a significant impact in the delivery of healthcare. IoT represents a vision in which Internet extends to the real world, everything is interconnected and has a digital entity. The impact of IoT will not be the same in all sectors, healthcare being the one to play a leadership role. IoT will enable the patient to stay longer and safer at home, since smart devices can alarm the hospital in case of critical conditions. Furthermore, due to constant monitoring, the patient can be relieved from the hassle of routine checks, replacing costly travel and reducing patient stress. Using implantable wireless devices to store health records could save a patient's life in emergency situations.

Currently, the services and technologies for accessing real world information are typically closed, leading to vertically integrated solutions for niches of applications. This approach leads to inefficient and expensive service infrastructures that lack interoperability. In this context we propose a middleware solution based on a single node component and a remote configuration/code loading component. The proposed solution ensures that all nodes will have at least a uniform configuration interface, important remote management and processing capabilities without any further programming or gluing together.

The proposed approach advances the current state-of-the-art, by providing a model whereby a single but powerful component is deployed in any node, regardless of its underlying differences, and the system is able to remotely manage and process data in a flexible way.

© Institute for Computer Sciences, Social Informatics and Telecommunications Engineering 2015
S. Mumtaz et al. (Eds.): WICON 2014, LNICST 146, pp. 53–59, 2015.
DOI: 10.1007/978-3-319-18802-7_8

In the literature, there are some middleware solutions for IoT and sensor networks. Most of the middleware are built on top of specific Operating Systems (mainly tinyOS) and almost all of them assumed it as a requirement and were not designed for abstracting away heterogeneous contexts. TinyDB [1], Agilla [2], Impala [3] are examples of middleware approaches designed to operate within sensor networks. On the other hand, Borealis [4], GSN [5] and IrisNet [6] are examples of middleware approaches that do not operate within sensor networks. Our approach can be deployed in any device, including embedded devices of any type.

For more information on sensor networks middleware, internet–of–things, and the relation between IoT and WSN, please consult [12].

Our work focuses on providing a device-independent middleware for operating with any IoT nodes, targeted at healthcare applications.

2   IoT HealthCare Application Scenarios and Requirements

IoT technologies and architectures could potentially impact a number of healthcare applications, such as medical treatment, pre- and post-hospital patient monitoring [7], people rescue [8–10], and early disease warning systems [11].

The healthcare application scenario is a very special scenario, since nodes store the data until some instant in time. All sensors are connected to one node, which is an embedded device. The node is placed on the body (human or animal body). Store and processing capabilities are the most important aspect in this scenario, because the node must collect and process data until a decision support system requests it. For instance, if a patient goes to the hospital and uses body sensors to monitor the heartbeat during a day [8], the node must be able to store the data it collects during a day and unload the data only when the patient returns to the hospital. Another application scenario [9] referring node processing and actuation is when a diabetic patient is monitored for insulin injection.

Several middleware requirements can be extracted from the previous scenarios. We consider data acquisition and processing, system configuration as functional requirements, while heterogeneity, interoperability and adaptability are considered as nonfunctional requirements.

Data Acquisition and Processing: Data have to be acquired and stored, processed (e.g., format adaptation, filtering), transferred, further processed or merged and delivered to users.

Heterogeneity: The middleware should be modular and based on drivers and interfaces, which allow it to run over different hardware and software platforms.

Interoperability: All nodes have to be provided with standard interfaces to access the data (different nodes have to be abstracted and accessed in the same way using a common API).

Flexibility: The middleware must be flexible and adaptive. Each application context (e.g. measurements of blood pressure, glycemic levels) will demand a slightly different mix of operations, sample rates and response times.

System Configuration and Adaptability: It should be necessary to deploy the system, configure it and it should be up and running. In other scenarios, it may be necessary to program part of the applications, using a common dialect and calling standard API functions.

To end this section, we describe a simple example scenario. A glucometer sends readings to a smartphone using a Zigbee communication. The smartphone uses GSM to exchange data and commands with a server. Each of these devices has exactly the same node component software, although developed for different platforms. Additionally, it was not necessary to code, since data sensing, storage and sending is configurable in the middleware.

3 Architectural Design

In this section we propose the IoT architecture. It provides remote access for configuration and processing capabilities to any device. The proposed architecture builds an intermediate computing layer which will serve as an abstraction hiding different hardware implementations.

Figure 1 shows the proposed architecture. It defines a node component (NCeH) that must be included in all node devices, including computers and data servers.

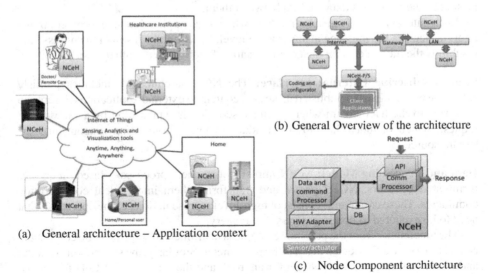

(a)   General architecture – Application context

(b) General Overview of the architecture

(c) Node Component architecture

Fig. 1. NCeH architecture.

The architecture works on top of a network communication infrastructure that is used to exchange data messages between nodes, send configuration commands to nodes and send acknowledgements from them.

The NCeH (represented in Fig. 1 c) runs at application level and has a set of modules that provide: **communication capabilities (Comm processor and API)**, whereby the node will be able to exchange messages with any other node in the system; **data and command processing capabilities (Data and Command Processor)**, whereby the node will be able to configure itself based on remote commands, look and compute on data it collects from either sensors or other nodes, to take decisions and to route data; **acquisition/actuation capabilities (HW Adapter)**, whereby sensor nodes will be able to periodically acquire sensing values or issue actuation commands.

The NCeH was designed to provide mechanisms to handle node referencing, heterogeneity and platform and communication protocol independency.

Platform and Communication Protocol Independency: In order for NCeH to run over different hardware and communication protocols, it needs drivers to manage files, handle different communication protocols and sensors, as well as drivers to handle timer events and memory requirements. When developing NCeH for a not-yet-supported operating system, the programmer needs to develop a set of drivers that offer a common architecture defined API, translating the corresponding calls to operating system calls.

Node Referencing and Heterogeneity: In order to handle communication protocol heterogeneity, NCeH defines a gateway component. This provides support for communication with non-IP embedded devices. Each gateway implements two communication protocols and translates data packets between them.

Each gateway has a Translator module, which is an application level protocol translator. It receives the message at application level, looks up the destination address, and resubmits the message using the communication function on the other side.

Publish/Subscribe External Interface: The NCeH architecture includes publish/subscribe mechanisms to publish data stream content to external applications. Users can subscribe to the data stream where each subscription is represented by a "subscribe" request, which includes the subscriber address, port, a connection timeout, and the stream source.

Data and Processing Model: NCeH implements a query processor. Based on queries formulated by users, NCeH parses and transforms them into logical configuration commands. These commands consist of high-level representations of the operations that need to be executed to obtain answers to the query.

The glucometer from the previous example is instrumented with the node component NCeH binaries for the device that has the glucometer. Similarly, the smartphone running android is instrumented with NCeH for android, and the server runs NCeH for Linux. The user sends configuration commands (read glucose every second; send to smartphone; store for 1 day; send to sever). Each of the keywords - glucose, smartphone, server - are defined using a simple mechanism (we do not explain further for lack of space).

4 Experimental Evaluation

As NCeH can be deployed for embedded devices or more powerful nodes, such as computers, in this section we will evaluate the NCeH when implemented in computer, Raspberry PI, TelosB and Arduino platforms.

We have developed NCeH for the devices listed above. Next, we configured the devices remotely using the remote configurator with an application that samples temperature sensors periodically, stores them and sends the data to a central server. This was a straightforward Java application that called the APIs of the middleware for interacting with the resources. In the rest of the experimental section, we focus on the issues related to development and porting of the middleware.

4.1 Development and Porting Between Platforms

The middleware must be developed once only for each type of platform/operating system. We have developed the middleware for the above listed platforms. Our experience from the development was that the first implementation that was done (the TelosB/Contiki one) required us to design all the structures and mechanisms of the middleware. However, the resulting code was used as a template for th remaining developments. This way, porting to other devices was quite easy. In agreement with the definition of NCeH, all functionalities were isolated from the operating system and hardware by using drivers. Additionally, some of the devices, such as the computer and Raspberry PI are less constrained, therefore we could make use of more memory and other resources.

From these implementations and porting we concluded that the reference architecture of NceH is quite helpful, since it specifies which modules to implement and how should work. Porting to new platforms is also simple.

4.2 Memory and Performance

In this sub-section we will detail the amount of memory needed to implement NCeH in chosen platforms. Figure 2 shows the amount of memory needed by each component of NCeH in the different platforms. From Fig. 2 we can conclude that NCeH implementation was significantly small to fit all devices that were tested. Implementations for either computer or Raspberry nodes need less than 60 KB (without operating systems). These consume more space than implementations for other platforms because they are java-based, but both computers and Raspberry PI resources do not pose any constraints on such code sizes. The Arduino implementation is smaller than the other ones, because it is written in C++ and it is not loaded with a full Operating System.

Another important issue for some embedded devices with constrained resources is the quantity of RAM memory needed to run each implementation. Figure 2 also shows the amount of memory needed by each component and in total for each platform.

From Fig. 2 we conclude that the Contiki-C version is the implementation that needs less RAM. However, this is not accounting for the RAM used by the Contiki Operating System. In general, the amount of RAM needed is small and fits nicely into each platform.

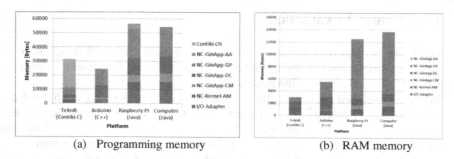

(a) Programming memory   (b) RAM memory

Fig. 2. Memory consumption.

5 Conclusions

In this paper we proposed an IoT architecture for healthcare applications. It offers easy and uniform configuration and operation for embedded devices and nodes such as computers or data servers. The model advances the state-of-the-art since it views the whole system as a distributed system and any computing device as a node, regardless of hardware or operating system. We have described main mechanisms and details of the architecture. Then we develop the architecture to show that the system is ease to implement and port for different classes of devices.

Acknowledgments.   This work was supported by the iCIS project (CENTRO-07-ST24-FEDER-002003).

References

1. Madden, S.R., Franklin, M.J., Hellerstein, J.M., Hong, W.: TinyDB: an acquisitional query processing system for sensor networks. ACM Trans. Database Syst. **30**(1), 122–173 (2005)
2. Fok, C.L., Roman, G.C., Lu, C.: Rapid development and flexible deployment of adaptive wireless sensor network applications. In: 25th IEEE International Conference on Distributed Computing Systems, ICDCS 2005, pp. 653–662 (2005)
3. Liu, T., Martonosi, M.: Impala: a middleware system for managing autonomic, parallel sensor systems. System **38**(10), 107–118 (2003)
4. Abadi, D.J., Ahmad, Y., Balazinska, M., Hwang, J., Lindner, W., Maskey, A.S., Rasin, A., Ryvkina, E., Tatbul, N., Xing, Y., Zdonik, S.: The design of the borealis stream processing engine. In: Time, pp. 277–289 (2005)
5. Aberer, K., Hauswirth, M., Salehi, A.: The global sensor networks middleware for efficient and flexible deployment and interconnection of sensor networks. In: Network, no. 5005 (2006)
6. Gibbons, P.B., Karp, B., Nath, S., Seshan, S.: IrisNet: an architecture for a worldwide sensor web. IEEE Pervasive Comput. **2**(4), 22–33 (2003)
7. Lo, B.P.L., Thiemjarus, S., King, R., Yang, G.-Z.: Body sensor network – a wireless sensor platform for pervasive healthcare monitoring. Architectural Des. **13**(2–3), 77–80 (2005)

8. Blount, M., Batra, V.M., Capella, A.N., Ebling, M.R., Jerome, W.F., Martin, S.M., Nidd, M., Niemi, M.R., Wright, S.P.: Remote health-care monitoring using personal care connect. IBM Syst. J. **46**(1), 95–113 (2007)
9. Zhou, F., Yang, H., Álamo, J.M.R., Wong, J.S., Chang, C.K.: Mobile personal health care system for patients with diabetes. In: Lee, Y., Bien, Z., Mokhtari, M., Kim, J.T., Park, M., Kim, J., Lee, H., Khalil, I. (eds.) ICOST 2010. LNCS, vol. 6159, pp. 94–101. Springer, Heidelberg (2010)
10. Lopes, I.M., Silva, B.M., Rodrigues, J.J.P.C., Lloret, J., Proenca, M.L.: A mobile health monitoring solution for weight control. In: 2011 International Conference on Wireless Communications and Signal Processing, WCSP, pp. 1–5 (2011)
11. Gao, T., Greenspan, D., Welsh, M., Juang, R., Alm, A.: Vital signs monitoring and patient tracking over a wireless network. In: Proceedings of the International Conference of IEEE Engineering in Medicine and Biology Society, vol. 1, pp. 102–105, September 2005
12. Cecílio, J., Furtado, P.: Wireless Sensors in Heterogeneous Networked Systems: Configuration and Operation Middleware. Springer, Switzerland, pp. 1–143 (2014)

A Survey on Short-Term Electricity Price Prediction Models for Smart Grid Applications

John S. Vardakas$^{(\boxtimes)}$ and Ioannis Zenginis

Iquadrat, Barcelona, Spain
jvardakas@iquadrat.com

Abstract. In this paper we present a survey of recent trends on short-term electricity-price prediction models. We classify the proposed price prediction methods based on the forecasting horizon into short- medium-and long-term approaches. We provide the key features of the medium-and long- solutions, while we emphasize on short-term prediction models, by providing their classification into statistical, computational intelligent and hybrid methods. We also highlight the key characteristics of the available prediction methods, while the strengths and weaknesses of these solutions are also discussed and analyzed. These important aspects should be considered by researchers that target on the derivation of more efficient and accurate electricity-price prediction models, especially for smart grid applications.

Keywords: Electricity pricing · Prediction method · Price forecasting · Computational intelligence · Smart grid

1 Introduction

The emergence of the smart grid has expanded the capabilities of the power grid's generation, transmission and distribution systems, in order to provide better control of energy supply and demand. This intelligent power grid is based on the continuous observation of power generation and consumption patterns, which enables the efficient management of the energy sources, while it also enhances the effectiveness of the electricity pricing strategies [1]. In this new environment, the transition from flat pricing into a variable electricity pricing procedure is inevitable and has triggered the design of pricing strategies with the aim of matching supply with demand [2].

The design of an efficient electricity pricing scheme is a crucial component of the future power grid. It is therefore necessary to develop methods and mechanisms that can provide the means for the application of a pricing procedure that not only motivates consumers to participate into Demand Side Management (DSM) programs, but also maximizes the social welfare [3]. To this end, electricity price prediction methods are resourceful tools that can be used by power utilities in order to enhance their decision making mechanisms. By predicting the electricity prices, utilities are able to strengthen their investments,

© Institute for Computer Sciences, Social Informatics and Telecommunications Engineering 2015
S. Mumtaz et al. (Eds.): WICON 2014, LNICST 146, pp. 60–69, 2015.
DOI: 10.1007/978-3-319-18802-7_9

to prevent the passing of unpredictable costs to the consumers and to provide competitive and attractive contracts to the consumers [4].

In general, electricity-price prediction methods can be classified according to the forecasting horizon into long-, medium- and short-price forecasting. Long- and medium-price forecasting methods consider prediction times from weeks up to even years and are mainly used for risk management, analysis of profitability of investments and long-term planning. As reported in [5], medium- and long-term predictions are usually performed by simulations, game theoretic approaches, production cost models or fundamental methods. On the other hand, a variety of methods have been used for short-term price forecasts, mainly due to their importance on the design of the future smart grid. The research efforts on short-term forecasting until 2006 have been extensively surveyed in [5]. To this end, in this paper we present the key characteristics of recent research efforts on electricity-price prediction models with a forecasting horizon of up to a few days. These methods are classified into statistical, computational intelligence and hybrid methods. We present the key characteristics of these prediction methods, while we highlight the strengths and weaknesses of each method, mainly in terms of prediction accuracy.

The rest of the paper is organized as follows. Section 2 provides the main features of the methodology that is used in electricity price prediction. Section 3 presents the three main categories of price prediction models, where recent research efforts are presented and analyzed. Finally, we conclude in Sect. 4.

2   Electricity Price Prediction Methodology

The main target of an electricity price prediction model is to provide the important inputs to the decision making mechanism of a utility company or a large commercial/industrial consumer. Both power utilities and large consumers can benefit from an accurate prediction of the volatile wholesale prices, in order to adjust their bidding strategies or their electricity production/consumption, so that any risks are reduced, while their profit is maximized. However, a number of challenges and constraints may affect the accuracy of the predicted electricity price, since electricity market does not allow for continuous trading, due to its "day-ahead market" nature. Furthermore, forecasting models should consider that in most cases electricity prices are determined for the next day by taking into account the same information, in order to match supply with demand.

It should be noted that although a large number of forecasting methods target the determination of electricity prices for the following day, there are a number of models that consider different forecasting horizons. In general, based on the forecasting horizon, models may provide predictions for short, medium or long periods. Short-term price forecasting models provide predictions from a few minutes up to a few days; a typical example is the day-ahead market. Medium-term models consider time periods from a few days up to a few months and are used for risk-management cases. Finally, long-term forecasting models refer to periods up to a few years and are mainly used for analyzing the investment profitability on new power plants and/or new fuel sources.

The accuracy of each electricity-price prediction model is determined by considering various accuracy metrics. The most widely-used accuracy metric refers to the *absolute error* AE_t for a time horizon t, which is equal to:

$$AE_t = |P_t^{real} - P_t^{pred}| \tag{1}$$

where P_t^{real} and P_t^{pred} are the actual and predicted prices, respectively. However, absolute errors may not provide efficient information when different datasets are considered. Other accuracy metrics that are considered to mitigate this problem include the *absolute percentage error*, which is the normalized absolute error by the real data, and the *Mean Absolute Percentage Error* (MAPE), which is the mean of a number of N of APE_t. The latter accuracy metric has been widely used, although it may provide misleading results when prices are close to zero [6]. Furthermore, the *Mean Absolute Scaled Error* (MASE) is defined as [7]:

$$MASE_{T,n} = \frac{1}{N} \sum_{n=1}^{N} \frac{\left|P_t^{real} - P_t^{pred}\right|}{\frac{1}{N-c} \sum_{n=c+1}^{N} \left|P_t^{real} - P_{t-c}^{pred}\right|} \tag{2}$$

where c is the cycle length. Another normalization metric is the *Daily (or Weekly)-weighted Mean Absolute Error* (DMAE, WMAE), which is defined as:

$$DMAE_{N=24}, WMAE_{N=168} = \frac{1}{N} \sum_{n=1}^{N} \frac{\left|P_t^{real} - P_t^{pred}\right|}{\frac{1}{N} \sum_{n=1}^{N} P_n^{real}} \tag{3}$$

Finally, the *Root Mean Square Error* (RMSE) is defined as the square root of the mean square differences between real and predicted electricity prices [8]:

$$RMSE_{N=24\,or\,168} = \sqrt{\frac{1}{N} \sum_{n=1}^{N} \left(P_t^{real} - P_t^{pred}\right)^2} \tag{4}$$

3 Classification of Price Prediction Methods

Various methods have been proposed for short-term electricity pricing forecasting. These methods can be classified into three general categories, according to their complexity, to statistical (or time-series) methods, computational intelligence methods and hybrid methods. The following subsection present the main characteristics and the research efforts on these three general prediction methods. The methods that are presented in the following sections are summarized in Fig. 1.

3.1 Statistical Methods

Statistical electricity-price prediction models target on the derivation of the price forecast based on a number of equations that include all the features of the

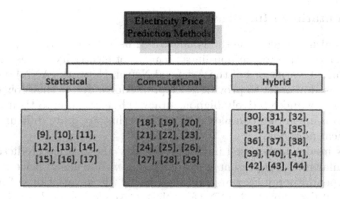

Fig. 1. Classification of electricity price prediction models.

problem. Therefore, the main challenge is the incorporation of all the problem's features into a linear model; this task significantly increases the complexity of the solution method. Statistical methods (or time series methods) include regression methods, such as Auto-Regressive Integrated Moving Average (ARIMA), Moving Average (MA), Autoregressive Moving Average (ARMA), ARMA with exogenous variables (ARMAX) models and Kalman filtering. It should be noted that these methods are also used for medium- and long-term forecasts and their main disadvantage is the fact that they are mainly based on linear equations, while in general, electricity price is a non-linear function of its input features. Furthermore, the MAPE of the following proposed methods of has been reported to be from 4 % to 22 %.

The ARMA method has been used in [9] for the day-ahead prediction of electricity prices. This model was combined with Generalized AutoRegressive Conditional Heteroskedacity (GARCH). The latter method has also been used in [10] to model and forecast hourly ahead electricity prices. On the other hand, ARIMA has been applied in [11] for day-ahead prediction, by using 10 years of observations, while some extensions of ARIMA based on EGARCH and GIGARCH models have been proposed in [12,13], respectively, in order to provide more accurate predictions. However, most of the ARIMA models cannot capture the characteristics of high volatility. Furthermore, ARMAX, has been used in [14] for providing day-ahead price predictions for the UK Power Exchange, together with Linear Regression (LR), Time-Varying parameter Regression (TVR) and Markov regime Switching model (MS) methods. ARMAX has also been used in [15] for hourly electricity pricing predictions for five MISO pricing hubs (Cinergy, First Energy, Illinois, Michigan, and Minnesota). Finally, the authors in [16,17] use the Kalman filtering method for day-ahead and seasonal price predictions, respectively. In the former case, real data taken from the Italian energy market have been used, while the resulted predictions were very close to those obtained with the empirical approaches.

3.2   Computational Intelligence Methods

Computational intelligence methods have been used for electricity price predictions in order to capture the non-linear feature of electricity prices more accurately. In general, variations of the Artificial Neural Network (ANN) model have been widely used in order to provide price predictions, due to their low computational complexity and relatively high accuracy, while also due to their capability of learning non-linear and complex relationships that are quite difficult to model with statistical methods.

An ANN model is proposed in [18] for the day-ahead price prediction, while in [19] a similar model is presented for delivering m-day ahead price predictions for the European Energy Exchange market. In [20] three variations of ANN have been deployed: Feed Forward ANN (FFANN), Cascade Forward ANN (CFANN) and Generalized Regression ANN (GRANN) for day ahead price forecasting. These methods were applied on Spanish market during 2002 and New York electricity market during 2010, providing high accuracy price predictions. Another variation of the ANN is the Recursive Neural Network (RNN) technique, which has been used in [21,22] for providing efficient and accurate day-ahead electricity price predictions for the PJN electricity market. The PNN model is based on the Similar Days (SD) method, which adopts the information of days similar to that of the forecast day. Furthermore, the discrete cosine transforms (DCTs) based Neural Network approach (DCT-NN) is used in [23] for providing electricity price predictions for the electricity markets of Spain and New York. The neural network that is proposed in [24] to forecast the market-clearing prices for day-ahead energy markets has a three-layer back propagation network structure. The results of this method indicate its high efficiency for predicting pricing in days with normal prices, but also the inability to provide accurate predictions for days with price spikes.

Another computational intelligence method is the Support Vector Machine (SVM). This method has been used in [25] for providing both short- and long-term predictions. For the short-term case, the proposed method has been tested on the experimental stage of 3 different electricity markets: the Spanish market, the New York market and the New England market. Furthermore, in [26] a SVM approach is used in order to forecast next day hourly electricity prices, which is based on a two-stage hybrid network. In the first stage a self organized map is used for clustering the input data into a number of clusters, while the SVM is applied to each cluster and an overall price is derived. A multiple SVM method is proposed in [27], where data classification and the price prediction modules are designed to first pre-process the input data into corresponding price zones, and then forecast the electricity price. Based on the presented results, this multiple SVM approach shows higher accuracy compared to a single SVM method.

An interesting study on the performance of statistical methods and ANN methods has been presented in [28]. The authors have compared these methods based on the forecasting horizon, the input and output variables, and the data points used for the evaluation. The result of this study is that although ANN methods are better in many cases in terms of accuracy, a general conclusion on the superiority of one method or another could not be deduced. Another comparison between models of these two categories has been conducted in [29]. More specifically, the authors in [29] perform day-ahead predictions for the Spanish energy market by using ANN and ARIMA methods. Their results indicate the superiority of ANN in terms of lower MAPE values. Another interesting conclusion of their work is that the predicting results for working days are more accurate than the predicting results for weekends or holidays.

3.3 Hybrid Prediction Models

Hybrid prediction models target on providing more accurate electricity-price predictions by combining either statistical or computational prediction methods. The main objective for the combination of different prediction methods is the derivation of electricity price predictions through the utilization of the unique features of each method for capturing the different data sets. To this end, various combinations of statistical and computational prediction methods appear in the literature. A well investigated combination refers to prediction models based on the ARIMA and neural networks. This combination is used in [30] for providing day-ahead price predictions for the Australian electricity market. However, the results showed that the combined ARIMA-ANN method is significantly more accurate than the ARIMA method but slightly more accurate than the ANN method. A similar combination is presented in [31], where the ARIMA is used together with the Radial Basis Function Neural Network (RBFN) approach, for the prediction of electricity prices of the Spanish electricity market. In addition, ARIMA together with Empirical Mode Decomposition (EMD) method, First Definite Season Index method is used in [32] to provide half-hourly prices; EMD is used to detach high volatilities, the First Definite Season Index method to detach periodicity, and the ARIMA model to predict the electricity prices. A variation of ARIMA, the Auto-Regressive Fractionally Integrated Moving Average (ARFIMA) model is combined with a neural network model in [33]. This model is examined by using data from the Nordpool electricity market and its accuracy found to be better compared to either the ARFIMA or the ANN results.

The ARIMA method has been combined not only with ANN models, but also with other solutions. In [34], the authors present a price prediction model based on the combination of ARIMA, GARCH and wavelet transform. The latter method is used in order to decompose the historical data, which are then reconstructed into a single approximation series and a number of detailed series. Then, ARIMA and GARCH are used for the extraction of the price forecast by composing the forecasts of each subseries. The performance of this combined method is evaluated by considering data from the Spanish market, and compared to results from various neural network approaches; the comparison of the price-prediction results showed the superiority of the proposed solution over the other ANN-based approaches, in terms of MAPE and error variance. Similarly, in [35] the authors combine ARIMA and a wavelet transform to provide price predictions. However, in this approach the least squares support vector machine (LSSVM) optimized by Particle Swarm Optimization (PSO) is also applied together with ARIMA, in order to predict electricity prices. The proposed method has been compared with various other prediction solutions (ARIMA, LSSVM, PSO LSSVM, ARIMA + LSSVM and ARIMA + PSO LSSVM) in terms of MAPE and found to be highly accurate with a significantly lower MAPE than that of all other methods.

ANN methods have been combined with various techniques, other than the ARIMA method. In [36] a recurrent neural network model is combined with time scales of the Fitz-Hugh Nagumo (FHN) method. The former model is used for regulating the related parameters, while the FHN method is used to accurately predict the electricity prices. On the other hand, the Enhanced Probability Neural Network (EPNN) is a combination of the probability neural network method and the Orthogonal Experimental Design (OED) and has been used in [37] to provide electricity price predictions. The use of the OED method improves the traditional probability neural network method by smoothing the related parameters and reducing the accuracy errors. Furthermore, in [38] ANN is combined with evolutionary algorithms. A Discrete Wavelet Transform (DWT) is used to decompose the data, ANN and evolutionary algorithms are used as forecasters. The authors compared their method with the method in [22] and showed the higher accuracy of their method over the RNN technique of [22].

A two stage electricity price prediction method is proposed in [39], where in the first stage a feature selection technique is applied, while in the second stage a cascaded neural network is used, and features of the two stages are selected for the 24 forecasters prediction engine. The performance of this combined method is evaluated by using data from the Spanish and Australia's electricity markets. Another two-stage prediction methodology is proposed in [40], where in the first stage a composite neural network is used, while in the second stage a few auxiliary predictors have been applied. This two-stage feature selection technique has also two filtering stages in order to remove non-relevant and redundant inputs, respectively, while its performance is evaluated by using data from Spain, PJM and California's electricity markets. In the same way, the authors in [41] propose a combined method of the Self-Organizing Map neural network (SOM) and SVM models in order to provide 24 hourly predicted prices. In this work the parameters of the SVM have been automatically selected by the PSO algorithm; this procedure is used in order to avoid the tester's arbitrary parameters decisions.

Apart from ANN- or ARIMA-based solutions and their combinations, other hybrid models appear in the literature for providing electricity price predictions. In [42], the proposed approach is based on particle swarm optimization and adaptive-network based fuzzy inference system, in order to perform electricity price predictions with forecasting horizon of one week. The authors compare their approach with ARIMA, mixed-model, ANN, wavelet-ARIMA, WNN, FNN, HIS, AWNN, NNWT, and CNEA techniques and showed that their model provides lower MAPE and error variance results, compared to the aforementioned approaches. On the other hand, the authors in [43] present a price prediction model that considers both a preprocessor and a Hybrid Neuro-Evolutionary System (HNES). The input features of the HNES are selected by the preprocessor based on the Maximum Relevance Minimum Redundancy (MRMR) principal. The HNES, which comprises of three neural networks and an evolutionary algorithm, is used to perform the price predictions. The authors also perform comparisons of the results from their proposed method and corresponding results from ARIMA, Wavelet-ARIMA, and FNN; this comparison showed that MAPE and error variance results of the proposed hybrid solution are significantly lower than of the other solutions. Finally, in [44] the authors use the combination of wavelet transform, Chaotic Least Squares Support Vector Machine (CLSSVM) and Exponential Generalized Autoregressive Conditional Heteroskedastic (EGARCH) models, for conducting day-ahead price predictions. As in the previous cases, the results of this approach were derived by using data from the Spanish electricity market, while they were compared with results from other approaches, showing the superiority of the model of [44], in terms of MAPE and error variance.

4 Conclusion

In this paper we presented the background and key characteristics of electricity-price prediction models. We provided an overview of the proposed forecasting methods by considering the general classification of statistical, computational intelligence and hybrid methods. We highlighted various factors of the prediction models, such as the forecasting horizon, the accuracy and the error evaluation procedure. This survey will provide the means to develop more accurate prediction models, by identifying the weaknesses of the current research efforts, and develop models that can be applied to a wider range of electricity markets.

Acknowledgment. This work has been funded by the E2SG project, an ENIAC Joint Undertaking under grant agreement No. 296131.

References

1. Fang, X., Misra, S., Xue, G., Yang, D.: Smart grid-The new and improved power grid: a survey. IEEE Commun. Surv. Tutor. **14**(4), 944–980 (2012)
2. Warrington, J., Mariethoz, S., Jones, C.N., Morari, M.: Predictive power dispatch through negotiated locational pricing. In: Proceedings of IEEE PES ISGT Europe (2010)
3. Dong, Q., Yu, L., Song, W. Z., Tong, L., Tang, S.: Distributed demand and response algorithm for optimizing social-welfare in smart grid. In: Proceedings of 26th IEEE IPDPS, pp. 1228–1239 (2012)
4. Bunn, D.W. (ed.): Modelling Prices in Competitive Electricity Markets. Wiley, New York (2004)
5. Weron, R.: Modeling and Forecasting Electricity Loads and Prices. Wiley, Chichester (2006)
6. Hyndman, R., Koehler, A.B.: Another look at measures of forecast accuracy. Int. J. Forecast. **22**, 679–688 (2006)

7. Garcia-Ascanio, C., Mate, C.: Electric power demand forecasting using interval time series: a comparison between VAR and iMLP. Energy Policy **38**(2), 715–725 (2010)

8. Cuaresma, J.C., Hlouskova, J., Kossmeier, S., Obersteiner, M.: Forecasting electricity spot-prices using linear univariate time-series models. Appl. Energy **77**(1), 87–106 (2004)

9. Swider, D., Weber, C.: Extended ARMA models for estimating price developments on day-ahead electricity markets. Electr. Power Syst. Res. **77**, 583–593 (2007)

10. Liu, H., Shi, J.: Applying ARMA-GARCH approaches to forecasting short-term electricity prices. Energy Econ. **37**, 152–166 (2013)

11. Jakasa, T., Androcec, I., Sprcic, P.: Electricity price forecasting- ARIMA model approach. In: Proceedings of 8th International Conference on the European Energy Market, pp. 222–225 (2011)

12. Nicholas, B., James, E.: Short term forecasting of electricity prices for MISO hubs: evidence from ARIMA-EGARCH models. Energy Econ. **30**(6), 3186–3197 (2008)

13. Abdou, K., Dominique, G., Bertrand, V.: Forecasting electricity spot market prices with a k-factor GIGARCH process. Appl. Energy **86**(4), 505–510 (2009)

14. Bordignon, S., Bunn, D.W., Lisi, F., Nan, F.: Combining day-ahead forecasts for British electricity prices. Energy Econ. **35**, 88–103 (2013)

15. Hickey, E., Loomis, D.G., Mohammadi, H.: Forecasting hourly electricity prices using ARMAX-GARCH models: an application to MISO hubs. Energy Econ. **34**, 307–315 (2012)

16. Crisostomi, E., Tucci, M., Raugi, M.: Methods for energy price prediction in the Smart Grid. In proceedings of IEEE ISGT Europe (2012)

17. Sherman, P.J., Jonsson, T., Madsen, H.: A Kalman filter based DSP method for prediction of seasonal financial time series with application to energy spot price prediction. In: proceedings of IEEE SSP, pp. 33–36 (2011)

18. Neupane, B., Perera, K., Aung, Z., Woon, W.: Artificial neural network-based electricity price forecasting for smart grid deployment. In: proceedings IEEE ICCSII (2012)

19. Pao, H.-T.: A neural network approach to m-daily-ahead electricity price prediction. In: Wang, J., Yi, Z., Żurada, J.M., Lu, B.-L., Yin, H. (eds.) ISNN 2006. LNCS, vol. 3972, pp. 1284–1289. Springer, Heidelberg (2006)

20. Anbazhagan, S., Kumarappan, N.: A neural network approach to day-ahead deregulated electricity market prices classification. Electr. Power Syst. Res. **86**, 140–150 (2012)

21. Mandal, P., Srivastava, A.K., Senjyu, T., Negnevitsky, M.: A new recursive neural network algorithm to forecast electricity price for PJM day-ahead market. Int. J. Energy Res. **34**(6), 507–522 (2010)

22. Mandal, P., Senjyu, T., Urasaki, N., Funabashi, T., Srivastava, A.K.: A novel approach to forecast electricity price for PJM using neural network and similar days method. IEEE Trans. Power Syst. **22**(4), 2058–2065 (2007)

23. Anbazhagan, S., Kumarappan, N.: Day-ahead deregulated electricity market price classification using neural network input featured by DCT. Int. J. Electr. Power Energy Syst. **37**(1), 103–109 (2012)

24. Singhal, D., Swarup, K.S.: Electricity price forecasting using artificial neural networks. J. Electr. Power Energy Syst. **33**(3), 550–555 (2011)

25. Gao, C., Bompard, E., Napoli, R., Cheng, H.: Price forecast in the competitive electricity market by support vector machine. Physica A: Stat. Mech. Appl. **382**(1), 98–113 (2007)

26. Fan, S., Mao, C., Chen, L.: Next-day electricity-price forecasting using a hybrid network. Proc. Inst. Eng. Tech. Gener. Transm. Distrib. **1**, 176–182 (2007)
27. Yan, X., Chowdhury, N.A.: Mid-term electricity market clearing price forecasting: a multiple SVM approach. Int. J. Electr. Power Energy Syst. **58**, 206–214 (2014)
28. Aggarwal, S.K., Saini, L.M., Kumar, A.: Electricity price forecasting in deregulated markets: a review and evaluation. Int. J. Electr. Power Energy Syst. **31**(1), 13–22 (2009)
29. Pino, R., Parreno, J., Gomez, A., Priore, P.: Forecasting next-day price of electricity in the Spanish energy market using artificial neural networks. Eng. Appl. Artif. Intell. **21**(1), 53–62 (2008)
30. Areekul, P., Senjyu, T., Toyama, H., Yona, A.: Notice of violation of IEEE publication principles a hybrid ARIMA and neural network model for short-term price forecasting in deregulated market. IEEE Trans. Power Syst. **25**(1), 524–530 (2010)
31. Shafie-khah, M., Moghaddam, M.P., Sheikh-El-Eslami, M.K.: Price forecasting of day-ahead electricity markets using a hybrid forecast method. Energy Convers. Manag. **52**, 2165–2169 (2011)
32. Dong, Y., Wang, J., Jiang, H., Wu, J.: Short-term electricity price forecast based on the improved hybrid model. Energy Convers. Manag. **52**(8), 2987–2995 (2011)
33. Chaabane, N.: A hybrid ARFIMA and neural network model for electricity price prediction. J. Electr. Power Energy Syst. **55**, 187–194 (2014)
34. Tan, Z., Zhang, J., Wang, J., Xu, J.: Day-ahead electricity price forecasting using wavelet transform combined with ARIMA and GARCH models. Appl. Energy **87**(11), 3606–3610 (2010)
35. Zhang, J., Tan, Z., Yang, S.: Day-ahead electricity price forecasting by a new hybrid method. Comput. Ind. Eng. **63**(3), 695–701 (2012)
36. Sharma, V., Srinivasan, D.: A hybrid intelligent model based on recurrent neural networks and excitable dynamics for price prediction in deregulated electricity market. Eng. Appl. Artif. Intell. **26**(5), 1562–1574 (2013)
37. Lin, W.M., Gow, H.J., Tsai, M.T.: Electricity price forecasting using enhanced probability neural network. Energy Convers. Manag. **51**(10), 2707–2714 (2010)
38. Amjady, N., Keynia, F.: Day ahead price forecasting of electricity markets by a mixed data model and hybrid forecast method. Int. J. Electr. Power Energy Syst. **30**(9), 533–546 (2008)
39. Amjady, N., Keynia, F.: Day-ahead price forecasting of electricity markets by a new feature selection algorithm and cascaded neural network technique. Energy Convers. Manag. **50**(12), 2976–2982 (2009)
40. Keynia, F.: A new feature selection algorithm and composite neural network for electricity price forecasting. Eng. Appl. Artif. Intell. **25**(8), 1687–1697 (2012)
41. Niu, D., Liu, D., Wu, D.D.: A soft computing system for day-ahead electricity price forecasting. Appl. Soft Comput. **10**(3), 868–875 (2010)
42. Pousinho, H.M.I., Mendes, V.M.F., Catalao, J.P.S.: Short-term electricity prices forecasting in a competitive market by a hybrid PSO-ANFIS approach. J. Electr. Power Energy Syst. **39**(1), 29–35 (2012)
43. Amjady, N., Keynia, F.: Application of a new hybrid neuro-evolutionary system for day-ahead price forecasting of electricity markets. Appl. Soft Comput. **10**(3), 784–792 (2010)
44. Zhang, J., Tan, Z.: Day-ahead electricity price forecasting using WT, CLSSVM and EGARCH model. Int. J. Electr. Power Energy Syst. **45**(1), 362–368 (2013)

Analysis of RF-based Indoor Localization with Multiple Channels and Signal Strengths

José M. Claver[1](✉), Santiago Ezpeleta[1], José V. Martí[2], and Juan J. Pérez-Solano[1]

[1] Department of Computer Science, University of Valencia, Avd. Universitat, 46100 Burjassot, Spain
{jclaver,sezpelet,jjperez}@uv.es
[2] Computer Science and Engineering Department, Jaume I University, Avd. Sos Baynat, 12071 Castellón, Spain
vmarti@uji.es

Abstract. In this paper, the influence and improvement of the localization accuracy achieved using a fingerprint database with information coming from different channels and radio signal strength levels is evaluated. This study uses IEEE 802.15.4 networks with different power levels and carrier frequency channels in the 2.4 GHz band. Experimental results show that selecting part of this information with a cleverer data processing can provide similar or better localization accuracy than using the whole database.

Keywords: Indoor location · Fingerprinting · IEEE 802.15.4

1 Introduction

The location information promises attractive services on future applications where determining the location of a target in a given environment triggers a set of actions related to it. For outdoor environments, Global Positioning System (GPS), complemented with the use of Cell-ID for cell phones, provides a precise location system for applications of mobile devices around the world. Neither of these technologies can be used in the case of indoor environments (there is not a GPS for indoors). In this case, radio frequency (RF) technologies as Wi–Fi and cellular signals, and RF signals from Wireless Sensor Networks (WSN) like ZigBee can be used for location and tracking purposes.

In outdoor applications, several analytic location systems can be used to calculate the distance between every beacon and the transmitter using the original signal strength and the propagation coefficient in the medium. However, in indoor environments the behavior of the RSSI (Received Signal Strength Indicator) can be harshly altered by the interactions with other electromagnetic waves and the obstacles around. To improve the analytic methods accuracy, fingerprinting techniques are used [2,8]. These methods start measuring the signal strengths in the

© Institute for Computer Sciences, Social Informatics and Telecommunications Engineering 2015
S. Mumtaz et al. (Eds.): WICON 2014, LNICST 146, pp. 70–75, 2015.
DOI: 10.1007/978-3-319-18802-7_10

chosen indoor area to create a database that will be used in the location phase to estimate the transmitter's real position. The main drawback of these methods is the time and effort needed to build the database. Additionally, the computing processes involved in the location need a large amount of memory and computational resources to carry out the location in real time.

This paper analyzes the information provided by network beacons using different channels and power levels, and how it can be taken into account to improve the location method. In the next section, some existing RF location and tracking techniques proposed until now for indoor applications are described. Section 3 describes the base RF location methodology using multiple channels and signal strengths. Experimental results showing the advantages of our approach are presented in Sect. 4. Finally, concluding remarks are given in Sect. 5.

2   Related Work

Many RF-based strategies have been proposed in the last decade for indoor location and tracking combining radio signal strength (RSS) and fingerprinting. This methodology is based on a first stage of training or preliminary exploration, in which the signal strength from all the beacons or base stations deployed in the localization scenario is obtained for a set of reference points. In the location stage, a metric to compare the signal strength of the test points with the collected information is applied. Around this idea, improvements to increase the location accuracy based on probabilistic techniques, pattern recognition, spatial filters, different number of beacons, etc. have been introduced.

One of the first approaches using RF signals was RADAR [3], which uses available WLAN based on Wi-Fi, and MoteTrack [4], which uses WSN based on IEEE 802.15.4. Some algorithms estimate the spatial position exploring the received signal strength information [1] improving the results presented in [3]. Statistical estimation methodologies for increasing the location accuracy have also been proposed [6].

The use of only one channel in RF-based location has been the norm in previous works. However, a very large number of carriers (500 channels) have been used in [7] for indoor location based on cellular telephony, where classification data has been carried out using Support Vector Machine techniques. This technique involves long training and higher computational complexity over previous methods, but good quality location results have been obtained. A recent proposal [5] uses the flexibility of current WSN with reconfigurable channels and RSS values to increase the amount of information available per location point in the fingerprint. Thus, by adding more information of channels and signal strengths more accurate locations may be achieved.

3   RF-based Localization Analysis

The location method presented in [5] relies on the flexibility of current WSN devices to configure the frequency channel and the signal strength involved in a packet transmission. Using several transmissions at different frequency channels and signal strengths, the total amount of information that is available during the location estimation is increased. The method consists of two phases: Training and Location estimation.

In the training stage, a mobile node is placed at a set of reference points with coordinates (i, j) forming a grid that covers the location scenario. The mobile node takes RSSI samples exchanging packets with every network beacon (b) at different signal strengths (p) and frequency channels (c). Thereby, at every reference point a vector of $p \times c \times b$ components is conformed and stored in a centralized database. It should be noticed that each component contains two RSSI values taken at the two different elements involved in the packets exchange. One RSSI value is taken at the beacon, after the first packet transmission from the mobile sensor, and a second RSSI sample is acquired at the mobile sensor, when the beacon replies in the opposite direction. In order to avoid sampling errors, 5 five consecutive packets exchanges are performed providing a group of 10 RSSI values (5 RSSI values in each direction) that can be averaged later on.

In the location estimation stage, a variation of the K-Nearest Neighbor (KNN) method [5] is applied. This algorithm (named Proposal Method or PM) has better average location accuracy, 2.09 m (meters), for the scenario described in the next section, in comparison with other alternative methods, such as: (a) Location Engine (system integrated in the CC2431 from Texas Instruments), 8.72 m, (b) the standard KNN algorithm, 2.59 m, and (c) a neural network based algorithm [5] implemented using a multilayer feed-forward network, 3 m.

The use of more channels increases the amount of information provided at each reference point. It is supposed that this increase allows more accurate locations, but some information may be redundant or it could even add more noise and degrade the location precision. The spacing of frequency channels used in WSN is small and there should be no significant differences between them. However, some channels can be affected by interferences from other RF waves present in the medium. As a consequence, the RSSI value can be altered and some channels can introduce an undesirable noise in the location process.

On the other hand, several studies show that the location accuracy for points that are too distant or too close to a beacon depends on the signal strength. Weak signals have problems for distant points due to packet losses, although they provide more information for nearby points. In contrast, strong signals are little discriminant for close points, but they are very useful for distant points. Thus, the combination of different signal strengths can provide more information and increase the accuracy. However, this behavior may vary for different scenarios.

4   Experimental Results

In this section, experimental results using the case study shown in Fig. 1 are presented. The experimental setup includes a Zigbee subsystem implemented using Texas Instruments CC2431 circuits.

The beacons are placed at positions B1, B2, B3, and B4 (see Fig. 1) and the mobile sensor is moved and placed sequentially at each position in the set of

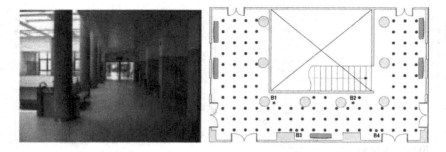

Fig. 1. Photograph and map of the testing scenario.

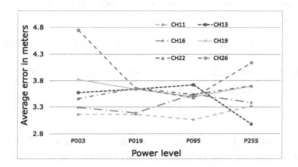

Fig. 2. Location accuracy for every channel and each one of the power levels.

122 reference points (with a distance of one meter between them) marked in Fig. 1. During the training stage, six channels: CH11, CH13, CH16, CH19, CH22, CH26 (frequencies (MHz): 2405, 2415, 2430, 2445, 2460, and 2480, respectively), and four power levels: P3, P19, P95, P255 (gains (dBm): -25.2, -5.7, -0.4, and 0.6, respectively) were chosen. So, at each reference point the mobile sensor exchanges packets with the 4 beacons, using 6 different channels and 4 power levels. Thus, the system takes 192 RSSI samples at each reference point, since it saves the two RSSI values received at both sides (the mobile sensor and the beacon). All the information is saved in a database that contains 111,360 RSSI values.

Next, a study about the location accuracy for different channels and RSSI strengths is presented. Results are obtained using the algorithm from [5]. These results point out which channels and strengths provide better information. The location error at every testing point of the grid in Fig. 1 is calculated comparing the location result with the real testing point position. Figure 2 shows the average error when the location algorithm uses a combination of only one channel and one power level. As it can be noticed, lower channels (e.g., 11 and 16) present a lower average error that is quasi constant independently of the power level. It can be also drawn that power level P3 provides a more stable behavior.

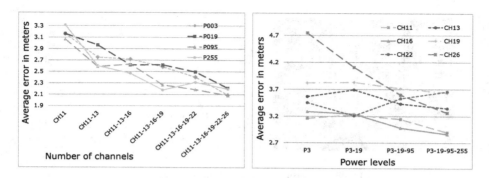

Fig. 3. Location accuracy for: (left) one power and a different number of channels; (right) one channel and an increasing number of power levels.

Table 1. Average localization accuracy for different algorithms.

PM(11)	PM(11,13)	PM(11,13,16)	PM(all)	NM(11,13,16)
3.16	2.75	2.71	2.09	2.05

Figure 3 (left) shows the average error for each power level and different combinations of channels. Notice that, as the number of channels increases, the error decreases. This is because of the number of points in the database to compare is higher and this aggregation decreases the average error. Figure 3 (right) depicts the average error for individual channels when more power levels are combined. Now, the average error usually decreases as the number of power levels is increased, but this effect is less significant than in the case of adding channels.

Thus, it can be concluded that it is not necessary to include all the channels and power levels for improving the location accuracy. Table 1 shows the average error for the algorithm PM considering only power level P3 with three different combinations of channels: (a) CH11, b) CH11-CH13, and (c) CH11-CH13-CH16. These values are compared to PM with all the database, PM(all), and a new variation of the PM algorithm, named NM (New PM), with only channels CH11-CH13-CH16 and the power level P3.

The NM algorithm starts with the 8 candidates that the PM algorithm provides for channels CH11-CH13-CH16. Then, NM applies the following conditions:

- if the first two candidates for CH11 are inside a radium ($r_p \leq 2d$) and the difference with the first candidates of CH13 and CH16 are inside a distance radium ($r_g \leq 2r_p$), the average between the two first candidates is taken.
- if the first three candidates for CH11 are inside a radium ($r_m \leq 1.5r_p$), the average among the three first candidates is taken.
- otherwise, the average of the eight candidates from the three channels is taken. If the average provides a location outside the fingerprint area, the most frequent coordinate among the candidates is taken.

5   Concluding Remarks

In this paper we conclude that, although the use of more channels increases location accuracy, a previous analysis and a clever selection of them can provide a similar location accuracy but with less computational requirements. The use of more power levels has a minor effect in the location accuracy. Additionally, lower levels of signal strength provide more significant information, but this effect may vary for different scenarios. Finally, a selected subset of all the available channels can provide the same or better location accuracy using an improved location algorithm, but this is a subject that requires further studies.

References

1. Alippi, C., Mottarella, A., Vanini, G.: A RF map-based localization algorithm for indoor environments. In: IEEE International Symposium on Circuits and Systems, ISCAS 2005, vol. 1, pp. 652–655 (2005)
2. Azizyan, M., Constandache, I., Choudhury, R.R.: Surroundsense: mobile phone localization via ambience fingerprinting. In: Proceedings of the 15th Annual International Conference on Mobile Computing and Networking, MobiCom 2009, pp. 261–272. ACM, New York (2009)
3. Bahl, P., Padmanabhan, V.N.: Radar: an in-building RF-based user location and tracking system. In: Proceedings INFOCOM 2000, Nineteenth Annual Joint Conference of the IEEE Computer and Communications Societies, vol. 2, pages 775–784. IEEE (2000)
4. Lorincz, K., Welsh, M.: MoteTrack: a robust, decentralized approach to RF-based location tracking. In: Strang, T., Linnhoff-Popien, C. (eds.) LoCA 2005. LNCS, vol. 3479, pp. 63–82. Springer, Heidelberg (2005)
5. Marti, J.V., Sales, J., Marin, R., Jimenez-Ruiz, E.: Localization of mobile sensors and actuators for intervention in low-visibility conditions: the zigbee fingerprinting approach. Int. J. Distrib. Sens. Netw. 1–10, 2012 (2012)
6. Milioris, D., Tzagkarakis, G., Papakonstantinou, A., Papadopouli, M., Tsakalides, P.: Low-dimensional signal-strength fingerprint-based positioning in wireless LANs. Ad Hoc Netw. Spec. Issue: Model. Anal. Simul. Wirel. Mob. Syst. **12**, 100–114 (2014)
7. Oussar, Y., Ahriz, I., Denby, B., Dreyfus, G.: Indoor localization based on cellular telephony RSSI fingerprints containing very large numbers of carriers. EURASip J. Wirel. Commun. Network. **2011**(1), 81 (2011)
8. Yao, Q., Wang, F.-Y., Gao, H., Wang, K., Zhao. H.: Location estimation in zigbee network based on fingerprinting. In: IEEE International Conference on Vehicular Electronics and Safety, 2007, ICVES. pp 1–6 (2007)

Can We Apply Clustering in Fast Moving Objects?

Victor Sucasas[1,2]([✉]), Ayman Radwan[1], Hugo Marques[1], Jonathan Rodriguez[1], Seiamak Vahid[2], and Rahim Tafazolli[2]

[1] Instituto de Telecomunicações, Aveiro, Portugal
vsucasas@av.it.pt
[2] Institute for Communication Systems, University of Surrey, Guildford, UK

Abstract. Clustering has been recently suggested in VANETs to support privacy preserving systems and to provide LTE scalability. First, cluster formation has been suggested to share traffic using short range communication links, aggregate this traffic in one vehicle, and to relay this aggregated traffic hiding the transmitters identities. Second, teaming up vehicles into groups to aggregate traffic can also reduce the number of LTE uplink connections. In this framework, mobility-aware clustering techniques are fundamental to increase the lifetime of mobile clusters. In this paper we provide an insight on what is the achievable cluster lifetime when applying mobility-aware clustering to fast moving objects, and the penalties in terms of control overhead and convergence time. We provide simulation results in ns2 and compare these results with analytical results.

1 Introduction

Clustering is considered the core of ad hoc networks technology, and it has been highly researched in the past two decades. Emergency and military applications were the first scenarios that fostered research on this topic. Clustering is oriented to cover the lack of network infrastructure by supporting on demand node coordination. Nodes form virtual groups that cooperate to achieve contention free intra-cluster communications and scalable routing protocols for inter-cluster communications. This approach however has not driven more research efforts lately in these scenarios, that have moved to other alternatives such as heterogeneous infrastructure-based networks [1]. Recently clustering has been suggested for a different kind of scenarios and for different purposes. Vehicular networks VANETs is one of these cases, where clustering is applied apart of the network infrastructure to provide scalability [2] or to support privacy preserving services [3]. Vehicles form virtual groups in order to share traffic through Dedicated Short Range Communication (DSRC) 802.11p links and to relay this traffic to base stations through LTE links. This approach reduces the number of LTE uplink connections and hides the 802.11p communications from network eavesdroppers.

In this framework, mobility-aware clustering techniques play an important role. These algorithms use mobility information to form virtual groups in order to

© Institute for Computer Sciences, Social Informatics and Telecommunications Engineering 2015
S. Mumtaz et al. (Eds.): WICON 2014, LNICST 146, pp. 76–84, 2015.
DOI: 10.1007/978-3-319-18802-7_11

maximize the time of contact between nodes. However, cluster lifetime (average time of availability of these virtual groups) can be severely affected by nodes mobility. Moreover, clustering requires a periodic control message exchange. Hence, solutions for VANETs that involve clustering must consider the overhead required and the achieved clustering lifetime. In this paper we undertake simulations in ns2 to investigate what is the achieved clustering stability and the required overhead. We implement a well-known mobility-aware algorithm and compare the results with an analytical model we proposed in [4]. The results show that cluster lifetime is severely affected by nodes speed. Moreover, at high speeds the periodicity of the control message exchange must be increased to maintain a connected topology. When the periodicity of control information is not sufficient, some nodes (the most unstable) are excluded from clusters. This fact has a negative and positive effect, first some nodes are out of clusters, hence they cannot communicate through 802.11p links with cluster-members, but the remaining nodes form clusters that are more stable (higher cluster lifetime). We explore this trade-off, and find that the efficiency in terms of achieved cluster-lifetime per transmitted overhead can be highly increased when some nodes are excluded from the topology.

The rest of the paper is structured as follows: Sect. 2 describes the system model; Sect. 3 provides the analytical model; Sect. 4 describes the simulation framework; Sect. 5 describes simulation results; Sect. 6 provides the energy efficiency evaluation; Sect. 7 evaluates clustering convergence time; and finally Sect. 8 concludes this paper.

2   System Model

The scenario considered is a vehicular network where vehicles team up in clusters. Short range communication between members of the same cluster is achieved through 802.11p whereas LTE is used to connect clusterheads to the network infrastructure. Figure 1 depicts the system model.

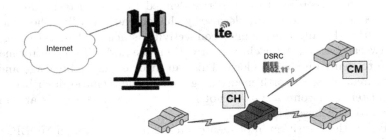

Fig. 1. System model of a hierarchical mobile network. CH refers to clusterhead and CM to cluster-member.

Clusters are formed with a mobility-aware clustering algorithm. The majority of clustering algorithms follow the same strategy for cluster formation and maintenance. Nodes transmit the same packet (which receives the name of *Hello message*) periodically including mobility information. Upon reception of control messages from neighboring nodes, nodes evaluate the neighborhood according the clustering algorithm predefined rules (which vary depending on the algorithm selected) to select clusterheads, leaders of the virtual group, and join clusters. After the completion of the clustering topology the nodes keep broadcasting hello messages for maintenance purposes. Maintenance is event-driven in most of the algorithms, affecting only the clusters where the event happens. Hence, for cluster formation and maintenance, nodes repeat continuously the same actions depicted in Fig. 2.

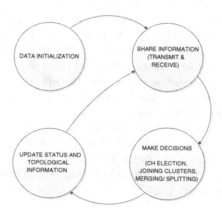

Fig. 2. Behavior of a node when performing clustering related operations with one control message per broadcast period.

Although the actions performed by the nodes are always the same, the decisions taken by nodes are different depending on the clustering phase. As depicted in Fig. 3: Nodes first select the most stable nodes as clusterheads (nodes to lead the groups according to the metric defined by the clustering algorithm); Then nodes join the most suitable nearby clusterhead according their mobility characteristics; Finally cluster inter-connectivity is achieved by selecting gateways between clusters; After cluster formation, the nodes keep control message exchange to maintain the topology. This can involve cluster breakage and new cluster formation. It is worth mentioning that in the scenario described in this paper, cluster inter-connectivity is not required since clusterheads are directly connected to LTE base stations.

MOBIC is the algorithm implemented in ns2 for our study. In MOBIC nodes obtain the mobility of the neighboring nodes by evaluating the variability of the signal strength in two consecutive Hello messages. This evaluation, called relative mobility (RM) is then used to compute the so called Mobility Prediction (MP). Nodes with the lowest mobility prediction are selected as clusterheads. Equation (1) defines the RM_i of a node i w.r.t. a neighbor j and the MP_i of i where $\{j_1, \ldots, j_n\}$ is the set of neighbors of node i. This algorithm has been

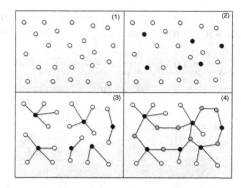

Fig. 3. The three-step division of the cluster formation process: election of cluster-heads (picture 2); cluster-members join clusters (picture 3); establishment of inter-connectivity (picture 4).

criticized due to its inaccuracy in scenarios with strong fading and multipath effects, since it affects the mobility metrics. In our simulation framework however, we do not simulate fading or multipath since we are only interested in the achievable cluster lifetime in comparison with the periodicity of control message exchange and the speed of the nodes.

$$RM_{i,j} = 10\log_{10}(\frac{RSS_{new}}{RSS_{old}})$$
$$MP_i = var_0(RM_{i,j_1}, \ldots, RM_{i,j_n}) \tag{1}$$

3 Analytical Model for Cluster Lifetime

In order to compare the simulation results with analytical results we adopt the model proposed in [5]. This model uses an adaptation of the Gambler's Ruin problem with windfalls and catastrophes described in [6], Fig. 4. This Markov chain models a cluster that has an initial number of members, N_m, and gets and loses members till reaching the zero members state. The zero members state represents cluster breakage. The duration of this game, the cluster lifetime, depends on the probability of gaining or losing members (p and q respectively) that for this simplified model is $p = q = 0.5$, since λ and μ are equivalent ([5] proposes different probabilities p and q since the model considers cluster merging events). The parameters λ and μ depend on the time of contact between nodes $E[t_c]$. And this time of contact depends on the relative velocity between nodes v_r. The pdf of v_r only depends on the mobility model and the average velocity of nodes, v, and for the random direction model is well known [7], Eq. 4. The analytical model for random direction is well known and accurate, thus in our simulation scenario we consider random mobility although we are targeting vehicular networks. It is worth mentioning that for a clustering algorithm, vehicular mobility models only differ from random mobility in that relative mobility between nodes is lower for the same nodes speed. Hence, with random mobility we are covering the same scenario than with vehicular mobility for a higher speed range.

$$p = \frac{\lambda}{\lambda + \mu} \; ; \; q = \frac{\mu}{\lambda + \mu}; \mu = \lambda = N_m / E[t_c] \qquad (2)$$

$$E[t_c] = \frac{4r}{\pi E[v_r]} \qquad (3)$$

where the probability density function of v_r is:

$$v_r = 2v \sin(\frac{\alpha}{2})$$

$$f_{v_r}(v_r) = \frac{2}{\sqrt{4v^2 - v_r^2}} \frac{1}{\pi} \quad \text{where } v_r \in [0, 2v] \qquad (4)$$

The average cluster lifetime, $E[CL]$, has a closed form expression, Eq. 5. The first parameter $1/(\lambda + \mu)$ models the average time per transient state in the Markov Chain while the rest of the expression evaluates the average number of transient states before reaching the state of zero members. In this equation $H = 3N_m$ is the maximum cluster-members considered and $k = N_m$ is the average number of members per cluster. Both values were obtained through simulations.

$$E[CL] = (\frac{1}{(\lambda + \mu)}) \cdot \left[\frac{2\sqrt{pq}}{H} (\sum_{u=1}^{H} \frac{\sin(\frac{u\pi}{H}) \sin(\frac{u\pi k}{H})}{(1 - 2\sqrt{pq} \cos(\frac{u\pi}{H}))^2} \right.$$
$$\left. + \frac{2\sqrt{pq}}{H} (\sum_{u=1}^{H} \frac{\sin(\frac{u\pi(H-1)}{H}) \sin(\frac{u\pi k}{H})}{(1 - 2\sqrt{pq} \cos(\frac{u\pi}{H}))^2} \right] \qquad (5)$$

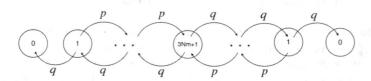

Fig. 4. Adaptation of the Markov model for Gambler's Ruin. Every transient state represents the number of members in the cluster.

4   Simulation Framework

The simulation parameters are summarized in Table 1. The clustering algorithm was implemented in ns-2 and the scenarios were generated with bonnmotion-2.0 [8].

We provide results for a fixed broadcast period, 2 s, that is always the same for all speeds. Then we repeat the same simulations for a variable broadcast period, decreasing the period according to the increase in the speed. Table 2 shows the broadcast periods (in seconds) used for each speed configuration.

Table 1. Simulation parameters

Simulation framework	ns-2.34
Number of nodes	100
Mobility model	Random Direction $500 \times 500\,\text{m}$
Wireless interface	802.11
Speed	1,2,4,8,12,16,24,32 and $40\,\text{m/s}$
Transmission range	50, $100\,\text{m}$
Simulation time	$2000\,\text{s}$
Broadcast interval	Variable
Propagation model	Free Space

Table 2. Broadcast period

Speed (m/s)	1	2	4	8	12	16	24	32	40
Fixed BP (s)	2	2	2	2	2	2	2	2	2
Variable BP (s)	2.5	1.9	0.9	0.45	0.3	0.24	0.15	0.09	0.07

5 Simulation Results

We first obtain the simulation results for cluster lifetime for both fixed and variable broadcast period that are presented in Figs. 5 and 6 respectively. We compare this results with analytical results to validate our simulations. It is worth noting that only the variable broadcast period achieves the analytical results. Cluster lifetime for fixed broadcast period has a higher cluster lifetime since the unstable nodes are excluded from clusters.

This effect can be appreciated in Fig. 7, that shows the percentage of nodes inside clusters for variable and fixed broadcast periods obtained through simulations. It can be appreciated that only a variable broadcast period can maintain the topology highly connected. Figure 8 also shows this effect, it represents the average number of clusters and members per cluster in the topology.

It can be concluded that a highly connected network can only be achieved with a high frequent control message exchange. With a low frequent message exchange (2 s) the hierarchical network cannot cover all nodes, but the clusters formed are more stable.

6 Clustering Efficiency

In this section we provide the efficiency of both strategies, reducing the broadcast period with the increase in the speed of nodes or maintaining a high broadcast period. We evaluated efficiency in terms of the achieved cluster lifetime and energy consumed by control overhead, $EE = Clifetime\ (sec)/Overhead\ (\mu J)$. The energy model is taken from [9]. We weight the EE with the percentage of

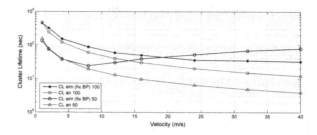

Fig. 5. Ananlytical and simulation results for cluster lifetime with a fixed broadcast period.

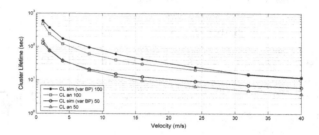

Fig. 6. Ananlytical and simulation results for cluster lifetime with a variable broadcast period.

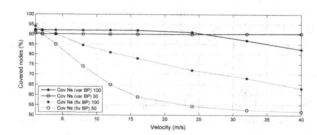

Fig. 7. Simulations results for the percentage of nodes inside the clustering topology.

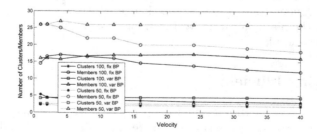

Fig. 8. Simulations results for the average number of cluster and members per cluster for fixed and variable broadcast periods.

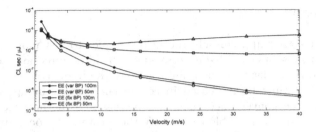

Fig. 9. Simulations results for the clustering efficiency (Cluster lifetime/energy in overhead) for fixed and variable broadcast periods.

nodes covered by the hierarchical topology, $EE' = (\%coverednodes)EE$. Figure 9 shows this efficiency for both strategies. It is appreciable that a fixed broadcast period is amply more efficient. The only advantage of a variable period is a more connected topology, since more nodes belong to clusters. This result suggest that it can be profitable to leave some nodes uncovered and connected directly with LTE links to the base station, the clustered nodes can still form stable groups and use 802.11p to reduce uplink connections.

7   Convergence

As described in previous sections, the advantage of reducing the broadcast period is a more connected topology. There is more energy consumption and less cluster lifetime, but the network can be highly connected. This connectivity however is achieved after a long period of cluster formation. We measured the time required to get 80 % of nodes covered by the clustering topology starting from a flat network, shown in Fig. 10. It can be appreciate that when the nodes speed increases this time is considerable, reaching the order of minutes.

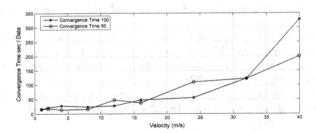

Fig. 10. Simulations results for the convergence time from a flat network to a 80 % of nodes included in clusters. Measured for a variable broadcast period for 100 m and 50 m transmission range.

8 Conclusion

We can conclude that applying clustering techniques to fast moving vehicles is possible, but it presents a trade-off between overhead required and connectivity. To cover all nodes under the clustering topology the frequency of control information exchange must be increased in concordance with the speed of nodes. In such a case the convergence time also increases with the speed of nodes. On the other hand it is possible to simplify the clustering process by excluding the most unstable nodes. This can be achieved by keeping a low frequency control message exchange, the outcome is a less connected clustering topology with a higher cluster lifetime. In such a scenario the unconnected nodes can establish directly LTE links while the clusterized nodes can share and aggregate data over 802.11p links. The strategy of leaving unstable nodes unconnected can be valid to reduce the number of LTE uplink connections. For privacy preserving systems however, all nodes should be covered by clusters, hence it requires a higher frequency of control information exchange.

References

1. Chiti, F., Fantacci, R., Maccari, L., Marabissi, D., Tarchi, D.: A broadband wireless communications system for emergency management. IEEE Wirel. Commun. **15**(3), 8–14 (2008)
2. Remy, G., Senouci, S.M., Jan, F., Gourhant, Y.: LTE4V2X—Collection, dissemination and multi-hop forwarding. In: 2012 IEEE International Conference on Communications (ICC), pp. 120–125, June 2012
3. Sampigethaya, K., Li, M., Huang, L., Poovendran, R.: Amoeba: robust location privacy scheme for vanet. IEEE J. Sel. Areas Commun. **25**(8), 1569–1589 (2007)
4. Sucasas, V., Radwan, A., Marques, H., Rodriguez, J., Vahid, S., Tafazolli, R.: On the efficiency of merging procedures in hierarchical mobile cooperative networks. In: 2014 IEEE International Conference on Communications (ICC), pp. 30–35, June 2014
5. Sucasas, V., Radwan, A., Marques, H., Rodriguez, J., Vahid, S., Tafazolli, R.: On the efficiency of merging procedures in hierarchical mobile cooperative networks. In: IEEE ICC 2014 (2014)
6. Hunter, B., Krinik, A.C., Nguyen, C., Switkes, J.M., Von Bremen, H.F.: Gambler's Ruin with catastrophes and windfalls. J. Stat. Theory Pract. **2**, 199–219 (2008)
7. Namuduri, K., Pendse, R.: Analytical estimation of path duration in mobile ad hoc networks. IEEE Sens. J. **12**(6), 1828–1835 (2012)
8. Aschenbruck, N., Ernst, R., Martini, P.: Evaluation of wireless multi-hop networks in tactical scenarios using bonnmotion. In: 2010 European Wireless Conference (EW), pp. 810–816, April 2010
9. Heinzelman, W.B., Chandrakasan, A.P., Balakrishnan, H.: An application-specific protocol architecture for wireless microsensor networks. IEEE Trans. Wireless Commun. **1**(4), 660–670 (2002)

Product Network Codes for Reliable Communications in Diamond Networks

Riccardo Bassoli[1,2]($\boxtimes$), Vahid N. Talooki[1], Hugo Marques[1,2],
Jonathan Rodriguez[1], and Rahim Tafazolli[2]

[1] Instituto de Telecomunicações, Aveiro, Portugal
{bassoli,vahid,hugo.marques,jonathan}@av.it.pt
[2] Centre for Communication Systems Research, Surrey, UK
r.tafazolli@surrey.ac.uk

Abstract. In wireless networks, mobile users connect either with other devices or with base stations. They can experience high errors caused by losses, low levels of signals or disconnections. Due to these aspects, it is important to find ways to make the communication reliable. Product network codes represent a way to improve error-correction capability. The main idea is to use a powerful error correction code in time with random linear network coding in space domain. This paper analyses the error-correcting capabilities of product network codes composed by either Luby transform (LT) codes or Reed-Solomon (RS) codes, and RLNC. The kind of errors are burst errors. The results quantify how product network codes improve reliability in case of high burst error probability.

Keywords: Random linear network coding · Reed-Solomon codes · LT codes · Burst errors

1 Introduction

In current mobile networks, wireless connections can experience high errors. These errors can be caused by losses, low levels of signals or disconnections: these events generate errors in a burst. Burst errors are significantly responsible for low quality of the communications and high energy consumption because of retransmissions. Due to these aspects, it is important to find efficient ways to reduce the impact of these errors on the communication.

During last years, network coding [1] represented a novel way to achieve higher capacity and higher error correction. In 2011, product network codes were proposed by [2]. The main idea is to encode source messages by adding redundant symbols with a systematic error-correcting code with powerful error-detection capability. The systematic code is applied to protect the link layer transmissions.

The research leading to these results has received funding from the European Community's Seventh Framework Programme (FP7/2007–2013) under grant agreement 264759 (GREENET).

© Institute for Computer Sciences, Social Informatics and Telecommunications Engineering 2015
S. Mumtaz et al. (Eds.): WICON 2014, LNICST 146, pp. 85–90, 2015.
DOI: 10.1007/978-3-319-18802-7_12

Firthermore, the encoded information is also given to random linear network coding (RLNC) encoder which is used to protect the whole multicast (network layer transmission).

This work analyses the error-correcting capabilities of product network codes composed by either Luby transform (LT) codes or Reed-Solomon (RS) codes, and RLNC. In this paper we proposed a different approach: the encoding and decoding operations of the link-layer codes are only performed at source and destination. The intermediate nodes can only re-code the messages with RLNC. The kind of errors considered are burst errors: in particular, the source faces very high error probability. This allows the evaluation of the codes in very unreliable scenarios as well.

The paper is organized as follow. Section 2 briefly presents product network codes. Section 3 provides some preliminaries to clarify the achieved results, desc- ribes the model used in the rest of the work and how the system is implemented for the simulations. Finally, Sect. 4 shows the simulation results of the product network coding schemes.

2 Product Network Codes

Product codes are codes that use NEC in the space domain, and the classical error correction code in the time domain. In this paper we implement a method slightly different from the one used by the unpublished work mentioned in [2].

Here, the source message is protected by encoding it with an error-correcting code and then is mapped into source packets. Next, the packets are given to RLNC encoder and then linearly combined. These product codes can guaran- tee higher error-correcting capabilities than only a 'classical' erasure code or a random linear network code in case of burst erasures.

The product codes investigated in this work are the ones constituted by either LT or RS codes in time domain, and RLNC in space domain. The encoder and decoder of both error-correcting code and RLNC are placed end-to-end, respectively at source and destination. The intermediate nodes are only able to re-code packets by using RLNC. The time-domain code has a rate $R = k/n$. After time-domain encoding, RLNC encoder linearly combines the packets constituted by the n encoded symbols. The sink receives the messages and decodes them first with Gaussian elimination and then with BP decoding.

3 System Model

Figure 1 represents the diamond scenario studied in this work. The outgoing links of the source are very unreliable and their packets are subject to high burst errors. The intermediate nodes (Node 1 and 2) re-code the messages received via RLNC. The investigated product network codes are constituted by either RS codes or LT codes and RLNC.

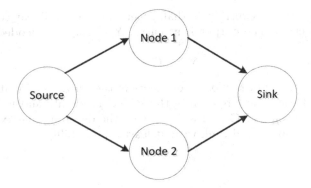

Fig. 1. Diamond scenario, in which a source communicates with a sink via two inter-mediate nodes. The source transmits encoded packets on both outgoing links: these links are the ones that experience burst errors.

RS codes [3] are non-binary erasure codes with symbols belonging to a Galois field $GF(q)$, with $q = 2^m$. RS codes are very powerful codes for burst error correction. The complexity of RS codes increases with the redundancy: so it is important to pay attention to the trade-off between error-correcting capability and complexity of operations. Because of that, the most interesting RS codes are the ones with high code rates and with small m.

LT codes [4] are a practical implementation of fountain codes. The encoder can generate a variable quantity of encoded symbols according to the needs. The encoder receives a stream of L source bits which are partitioned into $k = L/m$ input symbols over $GF(q)$. The encoder creates symbols according to the so called Robust Soliton distribution. In particular, this probability distribution is the sum between the distribution

$$\tau(i) = \begin{cases} S/ik \text{ for } i = 1, \ldots, k/S - 1 \\ S\log(S/\delta)/k \text{ for } i = k/s \\ 0 \text{ for } i = k/S + 1, \ldots, k \end{cases} \tag{1}$$

and the ideal Soliton distribution

$$\rho(1) = 1/k$$
$$\rho(i) = 1/i \ (i - 1) \text{ for } i = 2, \ldots, k. \tag{2}$$

Hence, after normalising, it results to be

$$\beta = \sum_{i=1}^{k} \rho(i) + \tau(i)$$
$$\mu(i) = (\rho(i) + \tau(i))/\beta \text{ for } i = 1, \ldots, k. \tag{3}$$

The parameter δ represents the upper bound on the failure probability at the decoder, given a set of n encoded symbols. Next, the variable S is defined as $c\sqrt{k}\log(k/\delta)$, where $c > 0$ is a constant. The decoder that is used in this paper is a belief propagation (BP) decoder.

Next, RLNC is a network code that generates random linear combinations of the input packets. The output is a matrix $\mathbf{Y}$ of n_{RLNC} encoded rows. The structure of $\mathbf{Y}$ is

$$\mathbf{Y} = \begin{bmatrix} \mathbf{C} & \tilde{\mathbf{Y}} \end{bmatrix} \tag{4}$$

where $\mathbf{C}$ is the matrix of random coefficients of the linear combinations and $\tilde{\mathbf{Y}}$ is the matrix of the codewords. Since the RLNC randomly and independently chooses the coefficients of $\mathbf{C}$ over a finite field, the decoding matrix is random. This matrix may not be full rank with at least a probability

$$P_e \propto \frac{1}{q}. \tag{5}$$

The burst erasure probability is defined as b_e. Each outgoing link of the source has its b_e that is grater than or equal to 0.1.

4   Analysis and Simulation Results

The first simulated scenario uses a product code of LT codes and RLNC. The source has blocks of information of 1.5 kb. The LT encoder has $\delta = 0.02$. It maps binary data in a finite field with $m_{LT} = 8$. Next, it encodes the k source symbols in $GF(q)$ into n_{LT} symbols according to rate $R = k/n_{LT}$. The packets which contain these n_{LT} symbols are passed to RLNC encoder that linearly combines them.

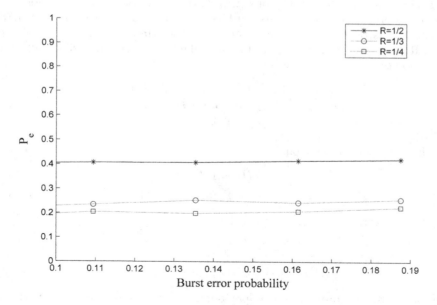

Fig. 2. Decoding error probability for product network codes in diamond scenario. The codes are constituted by LT codes and RLNC. The burst error probability b_e of the horizontal axis is the one of each one of the outgoing links.

The coefficients of the linear combinations and the coded packets are sent on both outgoing links with fixed burst erasure probabilities. The intermediate nodes re-encode the ingoing packets and transmit their linear combinations on the outgoing links. Finally, the sink collects k linearly independent encoded packets from the two ingoing links and decodes them first with Gaussian elimination and then with BP decoder. Figure 2 depicts the results of the simulations: in particular, the simulations consider high burst error probabilities (> 0.1). The errors are only at the outgoing links of the source.

The second scenario uses RS codes and RLNC. The size of source information is as above. The size of RS finite field is $m_{RS} = 8$. After RS encoding operations, RLNC encodes the packets and sends them on the outgoing links.

By comparing Figs. 2 and 3 it is possible to see the behaviour of the two schemes. The performances of the codes are evaluated in terms of error decoding probability (P_e). Product codes that use RS codes have higher error-correcting capabilities than the ones that use LT codes. On the other hand, the complexity of LT codes is lower than the one of RS codes. Furthermore, the performance of product network codes is not very influenced by the increase of burst error probability in both cases.

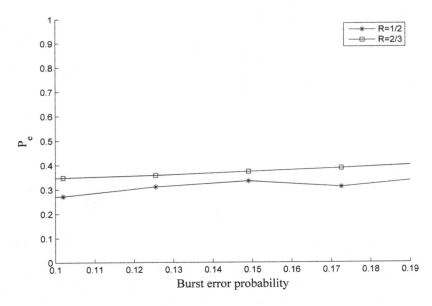

Fig. 3. Decoding error probability for product network codes in diamond scenario. This codes are constituted by RS codes and RLNC. The burst error probability b_e of the horizontal axis is the one of each one of the outgoing links.

5   Conclusion

This paper quantified the good performance of product network codes in presence of high burst error probability. The error decoding probability of product codes is slightly influenced by the increase of errors. Next, it was presented that the use of RS codes allows to achieve lower P_e with higher coding rates (i.e. lower redundancy). However, if low complexity is required instead of very high reliability, the use of product codes that combine LT codes and RLNC is suggested.

References

1. Ahlswede, R., Cai, N., Li, S.-Y.R., Yeung, R.: Network information flow. IEEE Inf. Theo. **46**(4), 1204–1216 (2000)
2. Zhang, Z.: Linear network error correction codes in packet networks. IEEE Trans. Inf. Theo. **54**(1), 209–218 (2008)
3. Lin, S., Costello Jr., D.J.: Error Control Coding: Fundamentals and Applications. Prentice-Hall, Englewood Cliffs (1983)
4. Luby, M.: LT codes, In: Proceedings the 43rd Annual IEEE Symposium on Foundations of Computer Science 2002, pp. 271–280 (2002)

Analysis of the Impact of Denial of Service Attacks on Centralized Control in Smart Cities

Evariste Logota$^{(\boxtimes)}$, Georgios Mantas, Jonathan Rodriguez, and Hugo Marques

Instituto de Telecomunicações, Aveiro, Portugal
{logota,gimantas,jonathan,hugo.marques}@av.it.pt

Abstract. The increasing threat of Denial of Service (DoS) attacks targeting Smart City systems impose unprecedented challenges in terms of service availability, especially against centralized control platforms due to their single point of failure issue. The European ARTEMIS co-funded project ACCUS (Adaptive Cooperative Control in Urban (sub) Systems) is focused on a centralized Integration and Coordination Platform (ICP) for urban subsystems to enable real-time collaborative applications across them and optimize their combined performance in Smart Cities. Hence, any outage of the ACCUS ICP, due to DoS attacks, can severely affect not only the interconnected subsystems but also the citizens. Consequently, it is of utmost importance for ACCUS ICP to be protected with the appropriate defense mechanisms against these attacks. Towards this direction, the measurement of the performance degradation of the attacked ICP server can be used for the selection of the most appropriate defense mechanisms. However, the suitable metrics are required to be defined. Therefore, this paper models and analyzes the impact of DoS attacks on the queue management temporal performance of the ACCUS ICP server in terms of system delay by using queueing theory.

Keywords: Smart city security · Denial of service attacks · Security modeling · Queueing theory

1 Introduction

Denial of Service (DoS) attacks are one of the oldest and most serious threats on the Internet. The main objective of DoS attacks is to prevent legitimate access to services of a target machine by overwhelming its resources (e.g., CPU, memory, network bandwidth). Essentially, DoS attacks are a type of attacks against availability of the targeted machine, which is an important security property for modern Internet-based systems. There are two main categories of DoS attacks: network layer DoS attacks and application layer DoS attacks [1, 2]. Network layer DoS attacks are carried out at the network layer and they attempt to overwhelm the network resources of the targeted victim with bandwidth-consuming assaults such as TCP SYN, ICMP or UDP flooding attacks. On the other hand, application layer DoS attacks are more sophisticated attacks that exploit specific characteristics and vulnerabilities of application layer protocols (e.g., HTTP, DNS, VoIP or SMTP) and applications running on the victim system in order to deplete its resources [1].

© Institute for Computer Sciences, Social Informatics and Telecommunications Engineering 2015
S. Mumtaz et al. (Eds.): WICON 2014, LNICST 146, pp. 91–96, 2015.
DOI: 10.1007/978-3-319-18802-7_13

Specifically in the case of Smart Cities, the effect of both categories of DoS attacks on any platform providing centralized control in these environments can be catastrophic since any unavailability of the platform (single point of failure) would plunge the cities into chaos. For example, the ongoing European research project ACCUS (Adaptive Cooperative Control in Urban (sub) Systems) [3] aims to provide a centralized Integration and Coordination Platform (ICP) for urban systems to leverage real-time collaborative applications across them. Furthermore, ACCUS is defining an adaptive and cooperative control architecture and the corresponding algorithms for urban subsystems in order to optimize their combined performance in Smart Cities. Thus, it becomes clear that DoS attacks on the ACCUS ICP server can jeopardize the safety and well-being of the ACCUS citizens. Additionally, there are huge incentives for cyber-criminals to launch DoS attacks against Smart Cities, like ACCUS City, ranging from financial gain to cyberwarfare.

Taking into consideration all the above mentioned, it is of utmost importance for ACCUS ICP to be protected with the appropriate defense mechanisms against these types of attacks in order to provide reliable and secure services to citizens. Towards this direction, the study and analysis of the impact of DoS attacks on the performance of the ICP server can play a critical role. Due to the fact that the impact of DoS attacks on the victim's performance is a key characteristic of them, the measurement of the performance degradation of the ACCUS ICP server imposed by these attacks can be used by the ACCUS ICP city planners to evaluate existing defense mechanisms. Then, it will enable them to select the most appropriate ones. However, the appropriate metrics are required to be defined firstly. Therefore, in this paper, as an initial step towards the definition of the appropriate metrics, we model and analyze the impact of DoS attacks on the queue management temporal performance within the ACCUS ICP server in terms of system delay by using queueing theory.

The rest of this paper is organized as follows. Section 2 demonstrates a scenario of ACCUS ICP server under a DoS attack. In Sect. 3, the model for analyzing the impact of DoS attacks on the ACCUS ICP server is presented. In Sect. 4 the performance evaluation takes place in order to assess the impact of DoS attacks on the ACCUS ICP server. Finally, Sect. 5 concludes the paper.

2   DoS Attack Threat Against ACCUS Smart City

The ACCUS ICP targets at interconnecting many communicating entities geographically distributed over a heterogeneous communication network and handling different types of data derived from many different sources. These entities include urban subsystems (e.g., traffic and energy subsystems) and end-users' devices (e.g., smartphones) supporting appropriate applications in the ACCUS Smart City, as in Fig. 1. As everything is interconnected through the ICP, any damage of it, due to DoS attacks, can severely affect not only the subsystems but also the end-users.

Especially, the level of their severity can grow dramatically as attackers take advantage of the botnet technology. A botnet is a network of compromised machines (e.g., legitimate PCs, laptops), commonly referred to as bots, which are under the control of an attacker through central Command & Control (C&C) servers.

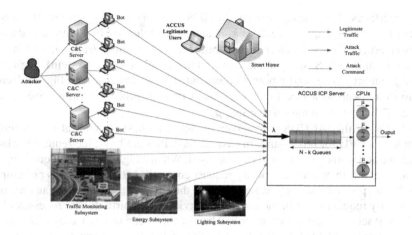

Fig. 1. ACCUS ICP server under DDoS attack.

Hence, the attacker is able to access and manage the botnet remotely via the central C&C servers. A depiction of a typical botnet architecture is included in Fig. 1. Botnets usually consist of several thousand bots and enable the attacker to launch Distributed Denial of Service (DDoS) attacks causing serious performance degradation on the victim's side (e.g., web server). DDoS attacks are a variation of the typical DoS attacks, where a single attacking host targets a single victim. Particularly, in contrast to DoS attacks, DDoS attacks deploy multiple attacking entities (e.g., bots), often located in disparate locations, in order to achieve their goal. The multiple attacking entities and the fact that they can be located in different locations are two factors that make the detection and mitigation of these attacks more challenging. Besides, it is worthwhile to mention that the legitimate user of a bot has no knowledge that his/her machine has been compromised and is taking part in a DDoS attack [4, 5]. It turns out that the ACCUS ICP server's protection is of paramount importance to guarantee reliability and security for ACCUS users.

Due to the fact that the impact of DoS attacks on the victim's performance is a key characteristic of them, it can be used as a feature for evaluation and accurate selection of existing defense mechanisms by the ACCUS ICP city planners. In this sense, the following section provides our analysis of the impact of this threat on the ACCUS ICP server.

3   A Model for Analyzing DoS Attack Impact on ACCUS ICP

The main objective of this section is to provide a model for analyzing the impact of DoS attacks on the queue management temporal performance of the ACCUS ICP server in terms of the system response time. To facilitate the understanding of the description of this work, we use queueing theory and emulate the ACCUS ICP server depicted in Fig. 1. For simplicity, we assume that the ACCUS ICP server is made up of k Central Processing Units (CPUs), a corresponding queue of size Q, and the Input/

Output interfaces. This means that the ACCUS ICP server can accommodate a total number of $N = Q + k$ queries, where k, N and Q are integers. In addition, λ_i denotes a Poisson process-based request arrival rate for an incoming traffic i, which may originate from ACCUS subsystems (e.g., traffic monitoring subsystem), legitimate users (e.g. Smart Home) and a botnet commanded by an attacker (see Fig. 1). Hence, the sum of λ_i, denoted λ (see Fig. 1), is also a Poisson process. Besides, we assume that each CPU has the same service rate μ.

Basically, in this ACCUS ICP server model, a request arriving at the system is submitted to a CPU for processing. In case all the CPUs are busy, the request is placed in the queue and waits for its turn to be processed. When a higher priority request arrives in the ICP server, then a lower priority request currently getting service is pre-empted and the higher priority request gets service from the CPU. In the same way, an incoming lower priority request waits in the queue for service. Such birth-death processes of the ACCUS ICP server's operations described herein above can be studied by using the M/M/k/N queueing model [6]. Hence, let P_n be the probability that exactly n requests are in the ACCUS ICP server. Thus, as described in [7], we express the steady-state distribution of requests into the ICP server as:

$$
P_n = \left\{
\begin{array}{ll}
\dfrac{\lambda^n}{n! \times \mu^n} \times P_0 & , \quad for \ \ 0 \leq n \leq k \\[2mm]
\dfrac{\lambda^n}{k^{n-k} \times \mu^n \times k!} \times P_0 & , \quad for \ \ k < n \leq N
\end{array}
\right\}.
\tag{1}
$$

To obtain the mean response time denoted $E[D]$, we first deduce the mean queue length denoted $E[Q]$ by using the Eq. (1) and the work in [7] as follows:

$$
E[Q] = \sum_{n=k+1}^{N} (n-k) \times P_n = \sum_{n=k+1}^{N} (n-k) \times \frac{\lambda^n}{k^{n-k} \times \mu^n \times k!} \times P_0 = \frac{P_0 A^k \rho}{k!} \sum_{i=1}^{N-k} i\rho^{i-1}.
\tag{2}
$$

where, $A = \frac{\lambda}{\mu}$ and $\rho = \frac{A}{k}$.

In addition, let's simplify the Eq. (2) further by considering the two cases of $\rho = 1$ and $\rho \neq 1$ as follows:

$$
\sum_{i=1}^{N-k} i\rho^{i-1} = \left\{
\begin{array}{ll}
1 + 2 + \ldots + N - k = \dfrac{(1+N-k)(N-k)}{2} & , \quad for \ \rho = 1 \\[3mm]
\dfrac{d}{d\rho}\left(\displaystyle\sum_{i=0}^{N-k} \rho^i\right) = \dfrac{d}{d\rho}\left(\dfrac{1-\rho^{N-k+1}}{1-\rho}\right) & , \quad for \ \rho \neq 1
\end{array}
\right.
\tag{3}
$$

From the Eqs. (2) and (3), we have:

$$
E[Q] = \left\{
\begin{array}{ll}
\dfrac{P_0 A^k \rho(1+N-k)(N-k)}{2k!} & , \quad for \ \rho = 1 \\[3mm]
\dfrac{P_0 A^k \rho[1-\rho^{N-k+1}-(1-\rho)(N-k+1)\rho^{N-k}]}{k!(1-\rho)^2} & , \quad for \ \rho \neq 1
\end{array}
\right.
\tag{4}
$$

By applying the Eq. (4) to Little's formula, we obtain the mean response time $E[D]$ imposed by the ICP server on incoming requests as:

$$E[D] = \frac{E[Q]}{\lambda} = \begin{cases} \frac{P_0 A^k \rho (1+N-k)(N-k)}{2\lambda k!} & , \ for \ \rho = 1 \\ \frac{P_0 A^k \rho [1-\rho^{N-k+1}-(1-\rho)(N-k+1)\rho^{N-k}]}{\lambda k!(1-\rho)^2} & , \ for \ \rho \neq 1 \end{cases} \tag{5}$$

4   Performance Evaluation

In order to assess the impact of DoS attacks on the ACCUS ICP server we implemented the ICP model described earlier in this work (M/M/k/N model) in Matlab by configuring each CPU service rate $\mu = 30$ requests/(time unit) and the ICP server's queue size $Q = 400$ requests. We simulated a DoS attack scenario (i.e., Distributed DoS attack) by increasing the overall request arrival rate, λ, from light traffic load perspective until the ICP is completely overloaded. The overloading occurs when $\lambda = \mu * k$. In addition, we run the simulation for different number of CPUs (for $k = 2$, 3 and 4) so as to evaluate how increasing the processing capacity of the ICP server could alleviate the impact of DDoS attacks on the ACCUS service delivery performance. In this way, we are able to study the degradation of the ACCUS queue management temporal performance under DoS attacks.

Thus, Fig. 2(a) shows that the mean response time increases with the increase of the request arrival rate, as we expected. Also, one can observe in Fig. 2(a) that, the response time improves with the increase of the number of CPUs in the ACCUS ICP. However, Fig. 2(b) warns that the queue utilization increases rapidly and reaches full utilization of 100 %, regardless of the number of CPUs running in the ACCUS ICP server. This effectively demonstrates the negative impact that DoS attacks can impose on the ICP server even if one can keep increasing its capacity in an attempt to improve its performance.

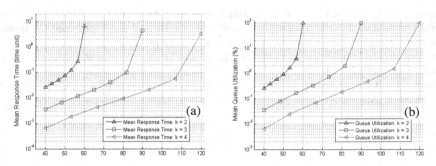

Fig. 2. Mean response time (a) and mean queue utilization (b).

5 Conclusion and Future Work

In this paper, we have focused our attention on the measurement of the performance degradation of the ACCUS ICP server imposed by DoS attacks, since it can be used by the ACCUS ICP city planners to evaluate existing defense mechanisms and select the most appropriate ones. Therefore, we modeled and analyzed the impact of DoS attacks on the queue management temporal performance of the ACCUS ICP server in terms of system delay by using queueing theory. As a result of this work, the mean response time and the mean queue utilization can be used as metrics for measuring the negative impact that DoS attacks can impose on the ACCUS ICP server's performance.

As future work, we plan to evaluate further, through a series of experiments, the mean response time and the mean queue utilization as metrics for accurate measurement of the performance degradation of the ACCUS ICP server due to DoS attacks. We also plan to use these metrics as parameters for the evaluation of existing defense mechanisms against DoS attacks.

Acknowledgments. The research leading to these results has received funding from the ARTEMIS Joint Undertaking Project ACCUS (ACCUS–ARTEMIS-005-2012/GA number 333020).

References

1. McGregory, S.: Preparing for the next DDoS attack. Netw. Secur. **5**, 5–6 (2013)
2. Zargar, S.T., Joshi, J., Tipper, D.: A survey of defense mechanisms against distributed denial of service (DDoS) flooding attacks. IEEE Commun. Surv. Tutorials. **15**(4), 2046–2069 (2013)
3. ACCUS (Adaptive Cooperative Control in Urban (sub) Systems). http://projectaccus.eu
4. Freiling, F.C., Holz, T., Wicherski, G.: Botnet tracking: exploring a root-cause methodology to prevent distributed denial-of-service attacks. In: di de Capitani di Vimercati, S., Syverson, P.F., Gollmann, D. (eds.) ESORICS 2005. LNCS, vol. 3679, pp. 319–335. Springer, Heidelberg (2005)
5. Specht, S.M., Lee, R.B.: Distributed denial of service: taxonomies of attacks, tools and countermeasures. In: 17th International Conference on Parallel and Distributed Computing Systems, San Francisco, California, USA, pp. 543–550 (2004)
6. Zukerman, M.: Introduction to Queueing Theory and Stochastic Teletraffic Models (2014). http://arxiv.org/pdf/1307.2968.pdf
7. Sztrik, J.: Basic Queueing Theory (2012). http://irh.inf.unideb.hu/~jsztrik/education/16/SOR_Main_Angol.pdf

Quadratic Programming for Demand-Side Management in the Smart Grid

Firooz B. Saghezchi[1]([⊠]), Fatemeh B. Saghezchi[2], Alberto Nascimento[3], and Jonathan Rodriguez[1]

[1] Instituto de Telecomunicações, Aveiro, Portugal
{firooz,jonathan}@av.it.pt
[2] Departamento de Economia, Gestão e Engenharia Industrial,
Universidade de Aveiro, Aveiro, Portugal
fatemeh@ua.pt
[3] Departamento de Matemtica e Engenharias,
Universidade da Madeira, Funchal, Portugal
ajn@uma.pt

Abstract. Demand-Side Management (DSM) is an effective means to optimize resource utilization in the electricity grid. It makes the electricity consumption pattern of users more even, reducing the Peak-to-Average demand Ratio (PAR) in the power system. The utility company can monitor and shape the hourly electricity consumption of the users by adopting an appropriate pricing strategy and advertising it online exploiting the underlying Smart Grid infrastructure. On the other hand, the users can monitor the hourly price of electricity in the market and based on the price variation, they can schedule their appliances to minimize their electricity payment, without compromising their daily need. In this paper, we consider a DSM problem where the company adopts a quadratic pricing strategy to encourage the users to have a flat consumption pattern. We formulate the problem incorporating Quadratic Programming (QP). The simulation results show that the QP approach reduces the PAR drastically.

Keywords: Smart grid · Demand-Side Management · Par shaving · Pricing strategy · Quadratic programming · Appliance scheduling

1 Introduction

Improving the social welfare, Demand-Side Management (DSM) can benefit both the utility company and the users [1–9]. Reducing the Peak-to-Average demand Ratio (PAR) helps the company (i) to shut down the inefficient power plants used only during peak hours and (ii) to avoid overdesigned thick transmission lines that operate in full capacity only few hours in a day, or even few days in a year. On the other hand, a price-aware user may shift its price elastic demand such as washing machine and Plug-in Hybrid Electric Vehicle (PHEV) from peak hours, when electricity is expensive, to off-peak hours, when it becomes more affordable.

© Institute for Computer Sciences, Social Informatics and Telecommunications Engineering 2015
S. Mumtaz et al. (Eds.): WICON 2014, LNICST 146, pp. 97–104, 2015.
DOI: 10.1007/978-3-319-18802-7_14

Adopting an effective pricing strategy by the company and an efficient scheduling strategy by a user are the main challenges for a successful DSM program. Inclining Block Pricing (IBP) has traditionally been practiced for many years to make electricity affordable for low-income people while charging higher rates for users who consume more to fulfill their non-basic needs such as air conditioning. Several other pricing strategies also exist for DSM, including Critical-Peak Pricing (CPP), Time-of-Use Pricing (TUP), Real-Time Pricing (RTP), and Day-Ahead Pricing (DAP) [2]. For example, in DAP strategy, the utility company sets the price of energy for the next 24 hours and advertises it to the users. However, in RTP strategy, the company does not determine the price in advance, rather it sets the price instantaneously based on the instantaneous demand.

A taxonomy for different DSM techniques is provided in [3], and [4] classifies DSM techniques to price-based and incentive-based techniques, highlighting the benefits and costs of a DSM program in a deregulated market. Li et al. [5] address pricing strategies that can align individual optimality to social optimality, so even if the users act selfishly and optimize their own utility, they automatically optimize the social welfare too. In [6], the authors address real-time pricing strategy and model users' preferences as a utility function, providing distributed algorithms for the company and the users to maximize the social welfare. A Vickery-Clarke-Grove (VCG) mechanism, which aims at maximizing the aggregate utility of all users while minimizing the total cost of power generation, is proposed in [7]. In [2], the authors propose an optimal scheduling technique which attempts to achieve a trade-off between minimizing the electricity expenditure of the user and minimizing the waiting time for operation of each appliance in presence of a RTP combined with IBP. In [8], the authors present a distributed game-theoretic algorithm for DSM when the users have full mesh network connectivity, elaborating efficient energy cost models and formulating optimization problems for minimizing either the PAR or energy cost. Finally, [9] addresses game-theoretic approach for distributed demand response optimization and formulates a Mixed Integer Linear Programming (MILP) problem for optimally scheduling users' appliances when the company adheres to the DAP strategy.

In this paper, we consider a DSM problem including a utility company serving several residential users. The company adopts a quadratic price function to charge the users. Every user has two sets of appliances (shiftable and non-shiftable) and uses Quadratic Programming (QP) to schedule its shiftable appliances to minimize its daily energy expense. However, it simultaneously minimizes the PAR due to the convexity of the price function. The constraints include power consumption rates of appliances and the user's preferences for their operating intervals. Last but not least, we assume that the power consumption of each shiftable appliance can be controlled between 0 and its power consumption rate.

The rest of this paper is organized as follows. Section 2 describes the system model. Section 3 formulates the QP scheduling problem. Section 4 depicts the simulation setup, and Sect. 5 provides the simulation results. Finally, Sect. 6 concludes the paper.

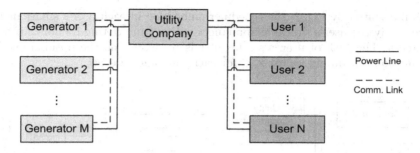

Fig. 1. Considered Demand-Side Management (DSM) scenario

2   System Model

We assume a DSM problem consisting of a utility company and multiple residential users, illustrated by Fig. 1.

To formulate the problem, let $\mathcal{N} = \{1, ..., N\}$ denote the set of users. For each user $n \in \mathcal{N}$, let l_n^h denote the load at hour $h \in \mathcal{H} = \{1, ..., H\}$, where $H = 24$. The daily load for user n is denoted by $l_n = [l_n^1, ..., l_n^H]$. The aggregate load of all users at hour $h \in H$ can be calculated as follows.

$$L_h = \sum_{n \in \mathcal{N}} l_n^h \tag{1}$$

The daily peak and average load levels are calculated as

$$L_{peak} = \max_{h \in \mathcal{H}} L_h \tag{2}$$

and

$$L_{avg} = \frac{1}{H} \sum_{h \in \mathcal{H}} L_h, \tag{3}$$

respectively. Therefore, the PAR is calculated as

$$PAR = \frac{L_{peak}}{L_{avg}} = \frac{H \max_{h \in \mathcal{H}} L_h}{\sum_{h \in \mathcal{H}} L_h}. \tag{4}$$

For each user $n \in \mathcal{N}$, let $\mathcal{A}_n$ denote the set of household appliances such as refrigerator. For each appliance $a \in \mathcal{A}_n$, we define an energy consumption scheduling vector

$$\mathbf{x}_{n,a} = [x_{n,a}^1, ..., x_{n,a}^H] \tag{5}$$

where scalar $x_{n,a}^h$ denotes the corresponding one-hour energy consumption that is scheduled for appliance $a \in \mathcal{A}_n$ by user $n \in \mathcal{N}$ at hour $h \in \mathcal{H}$. The total load of user $n \in \mathcal{N}$ at hour $h \in \mathcal{H}$ is obtained as

$$l_n^h = \sum_{a \in \mathcal{A}_n} x_{n,a}^h, \ h \in \mathcal{H}. \tag{6}$$

As illustrated by Fig. 2, the scheduler embedded in each user's smart meter controls only the user's shiftable appliances without interfering its non-shiftable appliances. The task of user n's scheduler is to determine the optimal energy consumption scheduling vector $\mathbf{x}_{n,a}$ for each appliance $a \in \mathcal{A}_n$.

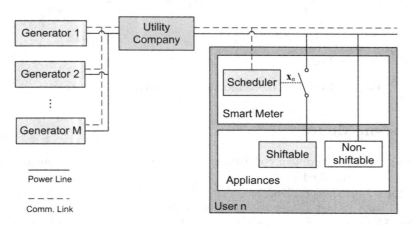

Fig. 2. Scheduler embedded in each user's Smart Meter to schedule its shiftable appliances

Now, we identify the feasible set of the energy consumption scheduling vector based on a user's demand and its preferences. For each user $n \in \mathcal{N}$ and each appliance $a \in \mathcal{A}_n$, we denote the predetermined total daily energy consumption as $E_{n,a}$. Note that the scheduler does not aim to change the amount of energy consumption, but instead to systematically manage and shift it, e.g., in order to reduce the PAR or minimize the energy cost. The user needs to determine the beginning $\alpha_{n,a} \in \mathcal{H}$ and the end $\beta_{n,a} \in \mathcal{H}$ of a time interval that appliance a can be scheduled. Clearly, $\alpha_{n,a} \leq \beta_{n,a}$. For example, a user may select $\alpha_{n,a} = $ 6:00 PM and $\beta_{n,a} = $ 8:00 AM for its PHEV to have it ready before going to work. This imposes certain constraint on scheduling vector $\mathbf{x}_{n,a}$. Furthermore, we denote that

$$\sum_{h=\alpha_{n,a}}^{\beta_{n,a}} x_{n,a}^h = E_{n,a} \tag{7}$$

and

$$x_{n,a}^h = 0, \ \forall h \in \mathcal{H} \backslash \mathcal{H}_{n,a} \tag{8}$$

where $\mathcal{H}_{n,a} = \{\alpha_{n,a}, ..., \beta_{n,a}\}$. For each appliance, the time interval provided by the user needs to be larger than or equal to the time interval needed to finish the task. The daily load of the system is equal to the total energy consumed by all appliances over the 24 hours. That is, we always have the following relationship.

$$\sum_{h\in\mathcal{H}} L_h = \sum_{n\in\mathcal{N}} \sum_{a\in\mathcal{A}_n} E_{n,a}. \tag{9}$$

In general, some appliances may not be shiftable and may have strict energy consumption scheduling constraints. For example, a refrigerator may have to be on all the time. In that case, $\alpha_{n,a} = 1$ and $\beta_{n,a} = 24$.

We define the minimum standby power level $\gamma_{n,a}^{min}$ and the maximum power level $\gamma_{n,a}^{max}$ for each appliance $a \in \mathcal{A}_n$ and for each user $n \in \mathcal{N}$. We assume that

$$\gamma_{a,n}^{min} \leq x_{n,a}^h \leq \gamma_{n,a}^{max}, \; \forall h \in \mathcal{H}_{n,a}. \tag{10}$$

We introduce vector $\mathbf{x}_n$ for each user $n \in \mathcal{N}$, which is formed by summing up energy consumption scheduling vectors $\mathbf{x}_{n,a}$ for all appliances $a \in \mathcal{A}_n$. In this regard, we can define a feasible set for energy consumption scheduling vector for user $n \in \mathcal{N}$ as follows.

$$\mathcal{X}_n = \{\mathbf{x}_n | \sum_{h=\alpha_{n,a}}^{\beta_{n,a}} x_{n,a}^h = E_{n,a}, \; x_{n,a}^h = 0 \; \forall h \in \mathcal{H}\backslash\mathcal{H}_{n,a},$$
$$\gamma_{n,a}^{min} \leq x_{n,a}^h \leq \gamma_{n,a}^{max} \; \forall h \in \mathcal{H}_{n,a}\}. \tag{11}$$

An energy consumption scheduling vector calculated by user n's smart meter is valid if and only if $\mathbf{x}_n \in \mathcal{X}_n$.

3   Quadratic Programming Problem

We assume that the company uses a quadratic price function as follows to calculate the cost of electricity at hour $h \in \mathcal{H}$

$$p(h) = \alpha L_h^2, \tag{12}$$

where $\alpha \in \mathbb{R}$ is a real constant and L_h is the aggregate load at hour $h \in \mathcal{H}$.

Hence, to minimize the energy cost, every user independently composes and solves the following QP optimization problem to schedules its own appliances.

$$\min_{\mathbf{x}_n \in \mathcal{X}_n} \sum_{h=1}^{h=24} \left(\sum_{a \in \mathcal{A}_n} x_{n,a}^h \right)^2 \tag{13}$$

Recall $\mathcal{X}_n$ is the feasible set for $\mathbf{x}_n$, defined by (11). Obviously, the objective function is the sum of squares of hourly energy consumption of all appliances of user n, including both shiftable and non-shiftable ones. Note that although there is no freedom for scheduling non-shiftable appliances, they are included in the optimization problem since their consumption affects the price.

4   Simulation Setup

We assume a scenario where a utility company serves 10 residential users. Each user has a mixture of shiftable and non-shiftable appliances. Tables 1 and 2

Table 1. Non-shiftable appliances

Appliance	Power (W)	Start	End
Light	200	19:00	24:00
Refrigerator	30	00:00	24:00
Stove	1200	12:00	13:00
		18:00	19:00
TV	200	11:00	24:00
Kettle	2000	08:30	08:35
		16:00	16:05
		20:00	20:05

Table 2. Shiftable appliances

Appliance	Power (W)	Start	Deadline	Duration (h)
PHEV	1100	19:00	08:00	9
Space Heater	1200	01:00	24:00	2
Ventilation	250	01:00	24:00	1
Washing Machine	200	10:00	20:00	2
Tumble Dryer	2100	12:00	22:00	2

present respectively the list of assumed non-shiftable and shiftable appliances along with their power consumption and the users' preferences, including start and end times as well as durations and deadlines for shiftable appliances. Each table has two parts, separated by a double horizontal line. The upper part includes 3 basic appliances that every user has, while the lower part includes 2 more optional appliances that every user may have. For each user, we generate a random integer between 0 and 2 to determine the number of optional non-shiftable appliances. Then, we generate another similar random integer to determine the number of shiftable appliances.

We use *quadprog* function of MATLAB to solve the QP problem formulated in the previous section. We assume that the SM can control the power consumption of every shiftable appliance between 0 and the power consumption rate. For example, the power consumption of the PHEV can be controlled between 0 and 1100 W. For the purpose of comparison, we conduct two experiments. In the first experiment, we do not utilize the QP scheduler and simply schedule the shiftable appliances at the most convenient time for the user (i.e., the start time). However, in the second experiment, we activate the QP scheduler to schedule the shiftable appliances at the best time possible that meets the deadlines.

5   Simulation Results

Figure 3 shows the hourly aggregate demand for 24 hours without and with QP scheduling. As seen from the figure, the QP scheduler successfully shaves the

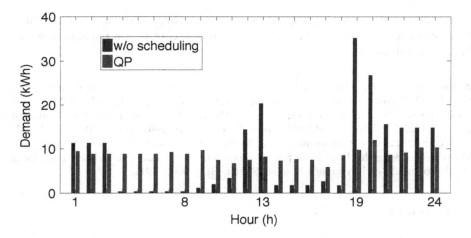

Fig. 3. Aggregate demand with and without QP scheduling

PAR, and results in a quite even demand pattern. The proposed QP approach reduces the PAR from 4.08 to 1.38, reducing the PAR by almost three times. Recall that the case "without scheduling" means that the shiftable appliances are scheduled at the user's most convenient time which is their start time as listed in Table 2.

In conclusion, QP is an efficient approach, for it alleviates the shortcomings of DAP strategy and the MILP approach proposed in [9]. The crucial weakness of DAP strategy is that when demand is highly elastic (i.e., the portion of shiftable demand is high), increasing the price during the peak-hours while decreasing it during off-peak hours simply shifts the peak-demand to other hours without reducing the PAR considerably. However, the QP approach not only shaves the existing peak-demand, but also avoids creating a new peak-demand in other hours.

6   Conclusion

We addressed DSM problem in the Smart Grid. We assumed multiple residential users connected to a utility company through a two-way digital communication infrastructure. The company adopted a quadratic price model to encourage users to reduce their PAR. Responding to this strategy, the users employed QP to schedule their appliances to minimize their electricity bills while meeting their daily need and preferences for the operating intervals of the appliances. We simulated a scenario with 10 users where each user had a set of shiftable and non-shiftable appliances. Specifically, each user had 3–5 shiftable appliances and another 3–5 non-shiftable appliances. The simulation results showed that adopting a quadratic pricing strategy by the utility company and activating the QP scheduler at the users' SM successfully shaves the PAR.

For future research, binary quadratic programming scheduler that can switch the appliances only on or off, without any power control mechanism, deserves further investigation.

Acknowledgment. The research leading to these results has received funding from the FEDER through Programa Operacional Factores de Competitividade COMPETE - Fundacão para a Ciência e a Tecnologia and the ENIACs JU and ARTEMIS through projects E2SG (ENIAC/0002/2011 Grant Agreement n° 296131) and ACCUS (ARTE MIS/0005/2012, Grant Agreement n° 333020). Firooz Bashashi Saghezchi would also like to acknowledge his PhD grant funded by the Fundacão para a Ciência e a Tecnologia (FCT-Portugal) with reference number SFRH/BD/79909/2011.

References

1. Saad, W., Han, Z., Poor, H.V., Basar, T.: Game-theoretic methods for the smart grid: an overview of microgrid systems, demand-side management, and smart grid communications. IEEE Signal Process. Mag. **29**(5), 86–105 (2012)
2. Mohsenian-Rad, A.H., Leon-Garcia, A.: Optimal residential load control with price prediction in real-time electricity pricing environments. IEEE Trans. Smart Grid **1**(2), 120–133 (2010)
3. Palensky, P., Dietrich, D.: Demand side management: demand response, intelligent energy systems, and smart loads. IEEE Trans. Industr. Inf. **7**(3), 381–388 (2011)
4. Albadi, M.H., El-Saadany, E.F.: A summary of demand response in electricity markets. Electr. Power Syst. Res. **78**(11), 1989–1996 (2008)
5. Li, N., Chen, L., Low, S.H.: Optimal demand response based on utility maximization in power networks. In: IEEE Power and Energy Society General Meeting, pp. 1–8 (2011)
6. Samadi, P., Mohsenian-Rad, A.H., Schober, R., Wong, V.W.S., Jatskevich, J.: Optimal real-time pricing algorithm based on utility maximization for smart grid. In: IEEE 1st International Conference on Smart Grid Communications (SmartGrid-Comm), pp. 415–420 (2010)
7. Samadi, P., Mohsenian-Rad, A.H., Schober, R., Wong, V.W.S.: Advanced demand side management for the future smart grid using mechanism design. IEEE Trans. Smart Grid **3**(3), 1170–1180 (2012)
8. Mohsenian-Rad, A.H., Wong, V.W., Jatskevich, J., Schober, R., Leon-Garcia, A.: Autonomous demand-side management based on game-theoretic energy consumption scheduling for the future smart grid. IEEE Trans. Smart Grid **1**(3), 320–331 (2010)
9. Saghezchi, F.B., Saghezchi, F.B., Nascimento, A., Rodriguez, J.: Game theory and pricing strategies for demand-side management in the smart grid. In: IEEE/IET 9th International Symposium on Communication Systems, Networks & Digital Signal Processing (CSNDSP), Manchester, pp. 883–887, (2014)

Towards an Advanced PKI-Based Security Solution for Next Generation e-Passport and Associated Applications: The NewP@ss Approach

Joaquim Bastos[✉], Georgios Mantas, José C. Ribeiro, and Jonathan Rodriguez

Instituto de Telecomunicações - Aveiro,
Campus Universitário de Santiago, 3810-193 Aveiro, Portugal
{jbastos,gimantas,jcarlosvgr,jonathan}@av.it.pt

Abstract. The electronic passport, introduced not long ago, in 2005, is continuing to evolve in order to provide higher levels of authentication for citizens crossing international borders, while respecting their privacy. A brief overview of the whole e-passport architecture is presented, as well as the key aspects and changes that this document has been going through in its evolution. In this paper we present a promising novel PKI-based security solution that could be integrated in the next generation (4G) of electronic passports, namely in its supporting overall architecture, in the ambit of the NewP@ss project.

Keywords: Electronic passport · ICAO · LDS · PKI · BAC · EAC · SAC · Authorization · Authentication · Verification · CSCA · CVCA · DVCA · NewP@ss

1 Introduction

The electronic passport (e-passport) is a machine-readable travel document (MRTD) enhanced with its holder biometric information, based on specifications defined by ICAO (International Civil Aviation Organization) [1, 2]. This kind of document and its inherent technology has been introduced with the main purpose of strengthening security at international borders, preventing illegal immigration, reducing threats of identity theft, as well as any sort of related international trans-border crime.

Not long after the dramatic incidents occurred on September 11th 2001, the USA decided to strengthen the requirements for entering the country. In that way, all countries participating in USA's *Visa Waiver Program* (no entry visa needed for citizens from such countries) were obligated to start issuing electronic passports from late October 2006 onwards, for their citizens to be allowed to enter USA, according with ICAO's specifications. Additionally, in December 2004, the European Commission (EC) approved specific regulations for the establishment of common technical specifications to allow and support the usage of biometric information, or markers, in MRTDs such as e-passports [3].

In October 2005, Sweden and Norway became the first countries to start issuing e-passports fully compliant with ICAO's and EC's criteria and specifications, using

© Institute for Computer Sciences, Social Informatics and Telecommunications Engineering 2015
S. Mumtaz et al. (Eds.): WICON 2014, LNICST 146, pp. 105–112, 2015.
DOI: 10.1007/978-3-319-18802-7_15

facial biometric markers. By late August 2006, there were 25 countries from USA's *Visa Waiver Program* issuing e-passports to their citizens.

In the remaining sections of this paper, a general overview of the e-passport general architecture, as well as its evolution, is made in Sect. 2, while the proposed PKI (Public Key Infrastructure) based security solution for next generation e-passport is described in Sect. 3. Finally, Sect. 4 concludes the paper.

2   Electronic Passport Architecture and its Evolution

The technology of e-passports, as MRTDs to be read by machines, involves a whole architecture, which includes, e.g., contactless reading devices, also known as PCD (Proximity Coupling Device), in this case integrated in inspection systems (IS). Such architecture is composed of specific hardware and software to allow, establish and assure secured short range contactless communications with a personalised electronic chip embedded in the e-passport, also known as PICC (Proximity Integrated Circuit Card), securely containing the holder's required identification data, stored at e-passport issuance, and non-modifiable [4]. The architecture is also responsible for providing authentication of both chip and contactless reader/IS as well.

The e-passport holder's information is included in the chip memory in a specific format, known as Logical Data Structure (LDS) [2]. This data structure duplicates most of the printed data in the e-passport's Machine Readable Zone (MRZ), in an OCR (Optical Character Recognition) prone font, but most importantly it also includes additional sensitive data, such as holder's biometrics [5]. The latter data is securely encoded inside the chip due to its sensitive nature and it is only disclosed outside once the reader/IS, and the chip itself, are successfully authenticated, namely complying with privacy aspects, for all necessary biometric matching [6]. A very succinct illustration of the general e-passport architecture is shown in Fig. 1.

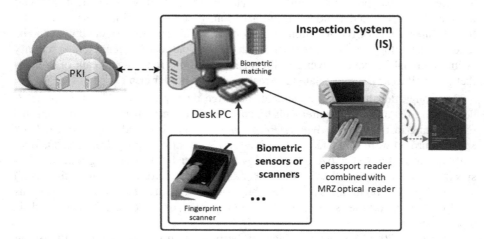

Fig. 1. Overall e-passport architecture.

The e-passport holder's biometric data released by the chip and read by the IS after mutual authentication, is then compared, using biometric matching/recognition algorithms, against the holder's biometrics scanned at the time of actual inspection, e.g., at an airport border control, immediately preceding the respective person to be allowed (or not) to enter a particular country [7]. Since its debut, the e-passport, as a MRTD, but also the whole architecture and systems supporting it, have been evolving in terms of security in order to be always a few steps ahead of malicious actors once potential security threats are identified, and any eventual consequential attacks are made [8, 9]. In that evolution most of the involved technology adds improved security mechanisms, which overlay on the preceding ones, also allowing backward compatibility, including with the conventional passport without chip, with printed booklet only.

The European project NewP@ss focuses on the technical development of advanced secured platforms, namely of nanoelectronics hardware, software and overall supporting architecture, appropriate for the upcoming 3rd, and future 4th, generations of e-passports complying with the requirements and specifications established by ICAO [10]. Those requisites concern mostly the involved security aspects, but also possible features and functionality to provide additional electronic services to dedicated applications, both in public and private domains, such as electronic visas or electronic travel stamps (e-government), and electronic boarding tickets or frequent flyer services from airline companies, respectively.

In the following subsections are introduced the main key aspects, and distinctions, between the several e-passport generations as outcome of its evolution, which nonetheless continue to also comply with the specifications of the conventional passport. The latter, namely include the holder's face photo and further detailed identification information printed in a booklet with a MRZ, providing conventional document security by implementing appropriate printing technologies, and with several blank pages for adding border control travel stamps and visas when necessary.

2.1 1st Generation (ICAO BAC) e-Passport, 2005

The first issued e-passports essentially include a contactless smartcard chip embedded in a booklet that complies with the conventional passport specifications, namely concerning security assurance through specific printing technologies. The chip, composed by a microprocessor/controller and 32 kB memory, stores a copy of the e-passport holder's identification information, as also printed in the MRZ, including the holder's photo as facial biometrics.

The holder's data stored in the e-passport chip is digitally signed by the issuing country, which allows for its authentication when read by an inspection system. For this, it is necessary to have a basic PKI (Public Key Infrastructure) implementation for the e-passport personalisation (issuance) and verification, at the issuing country administration and at inspection systems, respectively.

The access to the data contained in the chip, to be read by the IS, follows BAC (Basic Access Control) security mechanism, in which all communications between chip and IS are encrypted using a symmetric key derived from MRZ data [2, 3]. This data is available to both parties, in electronic and printed format, to chip and IS (through OCR), respectively. This basic security mechanism offers already some level of security, namely against eavesdropping, but it lacks in a few aspects, e.g., it does not secure the chip against cloning.

The communication between IS and chip is made through NFC (Near Field Communication) technology, according with ISO/IEC 14443 standard to be more precise, and can achieve a throughput of 424 kbps [4].

2.2   2nd Generation (EU EACv1) e-Passport, 2009

In the second generation of e-passport, the main addition in terms of data stored on the chip refers to the holder's fingerprints as additional biometric information, adding up to facial biometric markers. For that, chip's memory is also increased to 64 kB. The same technology continues to be used for communications, at similar speed.

Since the new biometric information is of very sensitive nature, namely concerning holder's privacy, the access to that specific information, by the IS, follows more advanced security mechanisms implemented as EAC (Extended Access Control), on top of the already existing security mechanisms in the first generation, such as BAC, not replacing it. EAC is simply the mechanism for securing the sensitive biometric data. The holder's facial image, as well as any other regular identification data, can still be read via BAC, also encrypted. The EAC mechanism includes both chip authentication and terminal (IS) authentication [2, 7].

Pairs of public and private keys are used in EAC to allow the required mutual authentication of chip and IS, increasing significantly the level of involved security, namely in the communications related with the sensitive biometric data. For this, it is necessary to have a much more complex PKI implementation in the overall e-passport architecture, which is responsible for signing and verifying certificates, as well as managing public and private keys, that are used in the referred mutual authentication process. Figure 2 briefly illustrates the overall involved parties and security flows in such PKI.

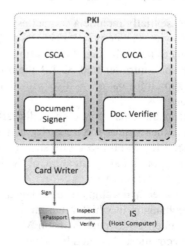

Fig. 2. EAC e-passport two-layer PKI.

The main entities in this two-layer PKI scheme are the CSCA (Country Signer Certificate Authority), which provides certificates to the DS (Document Signer) that forwards them to a smartcard writer, which in turn will write the necessary information on the e-passport chip. On the other hand, the CVCA (Country Verifier Certificate Authority) provides certificates to the DV (Document Verifier), which are used at the IS, in a host computer/PC, for authentication and verification procedures during e-passport inspection.

2.3   3rd Generation (ICAO/EU EACv2.10/SAC) e-Passport, 2014/2015

In order to accommodate more holder's biometric information, such as iris markers, the chip should have a further increased memory, close to 100 kB. It should also be as harmonised as possible, namely in terms of security, with other electronic documents, such as *eID* or *eResidence*. The same technology continues to be used for contactless (NFC) communications, but throughput should now be up to 848 kbps in order to, at least, maintain low global transaction time at inspection, taking into account the bigger payload to be transmitted.

An evolution of EAC, EACv2.10, is now the enhanced security mechanism to control access to the highly sensitive biometric information [11]. On the other hand, to overcome the limitations of BAC, SAC (Supplemental Access Control) is now introduced [12]. SAC is based on PACE (Password Authenticated Connection Establishment) protocol [13].

Just as BAC, SAC assures the e-passport can only be read when there is physical access to the document itself, and generates session keys used for the communication between the chip and IS. What makes SAC significantly more secure than BAC is that it uses asymmetric cryptography (Diffie-Hellman key agreement) to generate the required symmetric session keys. Using BAC, the session key is derived straight from the MRZ of the e-passport, with low entropy, while SAC uses a six-digit password, CAN (Card Access Number), with eventually low entropy as well, to generate the necessary session keys. Nevertheless, the quality of the session key resultant from SAC is independent from CAN's entropy, while BAC is dependent on MRZ's entropy.

This e-passport generation also includes further advanced cryptography technologies, such as more robust/long RSA cryptosystem, AES (Advanced Encryption Standard) and ECC (Elliptic curve cryptography) [12, 13]. On the other hand, it is not required to make any significant changes in the mandatory PKI already used in the second-generation e-passport.

2.4   4th Generation e-Passport, Before 2020

Standardisation bodies, ICAO and industry are already actively discussing the fourth generation e-passport. Its main innovation will be directly linked with the intended additional information to be stored in the chip, which this time will be, for the first time, possible to add after the e-passport personalisation by the authorised entities. Such information includes additional biometrics, border control travel stamps and electronic visa records. Obviously, this will require larger memory capacity in the chip, typically around 600 kB is to be expected, and data throughput in communications should also grow at similar ratio, being expected to reach 6.8 Mbps using NFC/VHBR (Very High Bit Rate), in order to allow reasonable global transaction time during inspection.

All information stored in the chip will be structured according with the second version of LDS (LDS2), at least, which includes new DGs (Data Groups) to accommodate the additional readable/writable (non-erasable, though) information.

There should be no significant changes concerning security and access mechanisms, such as SAC, EAC, etc., in relation to the previous generation. On the other hand there should be very significant updates on the required multi-layer PKI, which must also assure appropriately secured functionality with regard to the new post-personalisation writing operations, and eventual associated applications. In the next section, a PKI solution is proposed for the forth-generation (4G) e-passport.

3   The Proposed PKI-Based Security Solution

We present here a PKI-based security solution to support 4G e-passports applications in a reliable and secure way. In the design phase of the proposed security solution, we took into consideration the following three factors: (a) due to the adoption of LDS2, the 4G e-passports will not only support the legacy applications based on the data provided by the Logical Data Structure version 1.0 (LDS1), but also applications based on the travel stamps, visa records and additional biometrics provided by the LDS2, (b) the upcoming 4G e-passports will allow States to write data related to travel stamps and visa records on them after their personalization through ISs, and (c) the future 4G e-passports will allow States to read the LDS2 additional biometrics data stored on them through ISs. The proposed solution extends the legacy PKI-based security solution integrating the ICAO e-Passport PKI or Personalization PKI and the EAC e-Passport PKI or Authorization PKI by adding an additional PKI and enhancing the authorization functionality of the EAC e-Passport PKI.

The new PKI of our proposed security solution is used by States to write LDS2 data (i.e., travel stamps, visa records and additional biometrics) on 4G e-Passports and is responsible to ensure data integrity and authenticity for these data by using digital signatures. In the rest of the paper, the new PKI is referred to as LDS2 Data Signing PKI. The key elements of the LDS2 Data Signing PKI are the CSCA and the LDS2 Data Signer. The CSCA is the same entity that we have met in the ICAO e-Passport PKI and it plays the role of the root CA for the new PKI as well. However, in the context of the proposed PKI-based security solution, it does not only issue a self-signed certificate (i.e., CSCA Cert) and certificates for the DS (i.e., DS Cert), but also certificates for the LDS2 Data Signer (i.e., Signer Cert) within its own State. The Signer Cert contains an indication about the type of the LDS2 data that will have to be signed. To check the validity status of the Signer Cert, the CRL of the ICAO e-Passport PKI, which is issued by the CSCA and located at the Public Key Directory (PKD), is extended in order to include also revocation notices for the Signer Cert. On the other hand, the LDS2 Data Signer is the new entity that is responsible to digitally sign the LDS2 data, which are going to be written on the e-passport.

The enhanced Authorization PKI is based on the EAC e-Passport PKI and extends its functionality in order to provide mutual authentication between the IS and the e-Passport as well as enable a State issuing e-Passports to authorize the writing/reading of LDS2 data to/from its e-Passports. Specifically, the e-Passport issuing State is able to control domestic ISs (i.e., ISs belong to the issuing State) and foreign ISs (i.e., ISs belong to foreign States) to write data related to travel stamps, visa records and additional biometrics to its e-Passports after their personalization. Moreover, the issuing State is able to control the domestic and foreign ISs to read additional biometrics stored on its e-Passports. Thus, each IS which has to prove that is authorized to write/read LDS2 data to/from any future e-Passport should store three different certificates; (a) CVCA certificate (i.e., CVCA Cert), (b) DVCA certificate (i.e., DVCA Cert), and (c) IS certificate (i.e., IS Cert).

The CVCA is the root CA for the enhanced Authorization PKI of the State that allows the writing/reading of LDS2 data to/from its e-Passports. Each CVCA determines the access rights to its e-Passports for all DVCAs (i.e., domestic and foreign) and issues certificates (i.e., DVCA Certs) for these DVCAs including their corresponding access rights for the LDS2 data. The communication between a given CVCA with foreign DVCAs (i.e., DVCAs that belong to another State) is realized through an additional entity that plays the intermediary role of a contact point. Thus, each State should set up a contact point for authentication and authorization purposes. In addition, each CVCA of an issuing State issues a self-signed certificate (i.e., CVCA Cert), which is distributed to all ISs that belong to the domestic and foreign DVCAs of the given CVCA. This certificate is stored on ISs and is used to update the stored CVCA Cert on e-Passports issued by the State of the given CVCA in case that it has been expired.

Furthermore, each DVCA is responsible to manage a group of ISs, which belong to its domain, and issues certificates (i.e., IS Certs) for them including their granted access

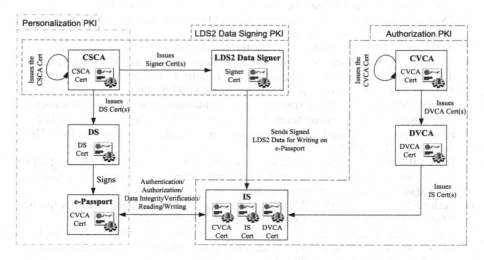

Fig. 3. Overview of the proposed PKI-based security solution architecture for 4G e-passports and associated applications.

rights related to the LDS2 data. Only after a DVCA has received its own certificate (i.e., DVCA Cert) from the root CVCA does it issue the IS Certs for the ISs within its domain. It is allowed the IS Certs issued by a DVCA to inherit all the access rights from the DVCA Cert or a subset of them. An overview of the architecture of the proposed PKI-based security solution is given in Fig. 3 depicting its key elements and the interaction among them.

4   Conclusion

The overall architecture of e-passport must be ready to support evolving standards for security, as well as new kinds of data, including biometrics and additional post-person-alisation writable information, and new applications.

In this paper a PKI-based security solution is proposed for the 4th e-passport generation, which takes into account the intended additional holder's data and records to be written after e-passport personalisation. Upcoming implementation is envisaged and further security analysis and optimisation should also eventually be carried out.

Acknowledgments. The authors would like to acknowledge the project N. 23183 - NEWPASS, co-financed by the European Funds for Regional Development (FEDER) by COMPETE – Programa Operacional Factores de Competitividade (POFC) of QREN - Quadro de Referência Estratégica Nacional, and labelled as CA206-NewP@ss by the European EUREKA-CATRENE programme.

References

1. ICAO website. http://www.icao.int
2. ICAO, Machine Readable Travel Documents - Part 1 & 3, ICAO Doc 9303
3. BSI-CC-PP-0055 (v1.10) - Protection Profile for Machine Readable Travel Document with "ICAO Application", Basic Access Control
4. ISO14443-2:2010, ISO14443-3:2011, and ISO14443:4:2008
5. Atanasiu, A., Mihailescu, M.I.: Biometric passports (ePassports). In: Communications (COMM), 8th International Conference at Bucharest, 10–12 June 2010
6. Jain, A.K.: Biometric authentication. Scholarpedia 3(6), 3716 (2008)
7. BSI-CC-PP-0056-V2-2012 - Protection Profile for Machine Readable Travel Document w/ "ICAO Application" Extended Access Control with PACE (EAC PP) – v1.3.1, 22/03/2012
8. Brömme, A.: A risk analysis approach for biometric authentication technology. Int. J. Netw. Secur. 2(1), 52–63 (2006)
9. Jeng, A.B., Chen, L.-Y.: How to enhance the security of ePassport, In: Proceedings of the 8th International Conference on Machine Learning and Cybernetics, Baoding, 12–15 July 2009
10. NewP@ss project website. http://newpass.av.it.pt
11. Technical Guideline – BSI - TR03110 v2.10- Advanced Security Mechanisms for Machine Readable Travel Documents – Extended Access Control (EAC v2.10)
12. ICAO Technical Report - Supplemental Access Control (SAC) for MRTDs v1.01 final2
13. BSI-CC-PP-0068-V2-2011 - Protection Profile for MRTD using standard inspection procedure with PACE (PACE PP) – SAC

UTTB FDSOI Back-Gate Biasing for Low Power and High-Speed Chip Design

Wael Dghais[✉] and Jonathan Rodriguez

Institute of Telecommunications, Department of Electronics, Telecommunications, and Informatics, University of Aveiro, Aveiro, Portugal
{waeldghais,jonathan}@av.it.pt

Abstract. The paper presents the advantage of the Ultra-thin body and buried-oxide (BOX) (UTTB) fully depleted silicon-on-insulator (FDSOI) as an enabling transistor technology through effective back-gate biasing schemes to overcome the challenges that arises from downscaling bulk CMOS technology for low power and high-speed design tradeoff. The effects of the back-gate bias methodologies that can vary or modulate the substrate bias to adapt the transistor's threshold voltage are detailed. The design schemes that can be used with this technology are described to illustrate their applications with UTTB FDSOI transistor.

Keywords: Back-gate biasing · Low power and high-speed design · Threshold voltage modulation · UTTB FDSOI

1 Introduction

The reduction of the power/energy consumption while maintaining high-speed in system-on-chip (SoC) performance has become the most important design concerns due to the increased use of handheld portable and wireless devices [1]. In facts, the transistor geometry shrinking and the downscaling of applied voltages have increased the transistor's short channel effects (SCE) and therefore the leakage power dissipation at nanoscale bulk CMOS technology which has made the end of its downscaling process [2]. Moreover, leakage power dissipation not only affects the battery life performance but also has a large impact on packaging, reliability, and heat removal costs. For instance, a modest leakage current around 100 nA per transistor, can cause a smartphone chip containing one hundred million transistors to consume a standby current of 10 A, thus, the battery would be drained in minutes without receiving or transmitting any signals. Therefore, new transistor architectures along with novel design methodologies that manage the low power circuits are required to boost green communication by taking advantage of the new energy-harvesting technology which recharge batteries by scavenging power from motion, wireless power transfer, and solar cells [3].

Even though handled devices designed based on nanometer scale transistor technology dissipate minimal dynamic energy, the leakage power becomes a significant contributor in their power equation [4–6]. Therefore, the leakage power reduction techniques play an important role for handheld devices such as cell phones, which are "on",

© Institute for Computer Sciences, Social Informatics and Telecommunications Engineering 2015
S. Mumtaz et al. (Eds.): WICON 2014, LNICST 146, pp. 113–121, 2015.
DOI: 10.1007/978-3-319-18802-7_16

but not active most of the time or in the sleep mode when the cellphone state is held in RAM, then cuts power to unneeded subsystems and places the RAM into a minimum power state, just sufficient to retain its data.

Since, the leakage current strongly depends on the threshold voltage V_{TH}, different V_{TH} transistors can be used for speed and power tradeoff. Therefore, high speed and low leakage current device could be optimized through fixing or modulating the V_{TH} [6]. This work presents low static power design techniques through back-gate biasing design methodologies enabled by the UTTB FDSOI technology at the sub-28 nm node without sacrificing chip's speed. The remaining of this paper is organized as follows. Section 2 describes the bulk technology downscaling challenges. Section 3 details the back-gate biasing mechanisms and effects. Section 4 presents the fundamental techniques to reduce leakage power. Finally, conclusions are drawn in Sect. 5.

2   Downscaling Challenges in Bulk Technology

Transistor dimensions have been scaled to design higher density chips with improved performance. This is achieved by reducing cost per transistor, minimizing the capacitance, and the power supply voltage, V_{dd}. Moreover, the V_{dd} and V_{TH} voltages tend to scale by same factor to limit drive-current degradation. Nevertheless, the SCE such as gate-induced drain leakage, gate oxide tunneling, drain-induced barrier lowering have a direct impact on the V_{TH} which has resulted in an exponential increase of the off-state leakage current [1–3]. Therefore, the most significant trend in bulk CMOS technology is the increasing contribution of leakage power in the total power dissipation of a bulk electronic designed system as shown in Fig. 1(a) [1] where is it illustrated how the total power has increased due to the standby leakage power. This downscaling consequences have moved the bulk CMOS technology to a power constrained condition and to balance the trading off between speed and standby power. This has led to the development of different circuit design techniques to optimize the delay and leakage which are becoming the key enabler for further CMOS downscaling.

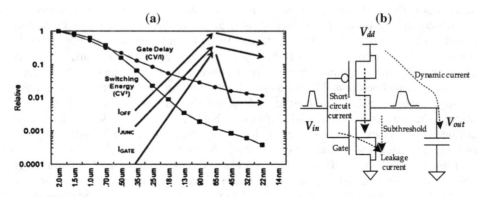

Fig. 1. (a) Ratio of active, leakage powers, and the gate delay over the CMOS technology [1]. (b) The dynamic and static (leakage) currents associated with a CMOS device.

The CMOS power consumption can be divided into three components. The dynamic and short-circuit power are consumed while the input logic state switches. The static leakage power is consumed due to the transistor's sub-threshold, gate and diode junction's currents while the input is kept at high or low logic state of a CMOS inverter as shown in Fig. 1(b). The main current of concern in limiting leakage power consumption is the sub-threshold flow.

$$P_{total} = \alpha \cdot C \cdot V^2 \cdot f_{clk} + V_{dd} \cdot I_{sc} + V_{dd} \cdot I_{Leakage}. \tag{1}$$

The first and second terms in (1) refer to the dynamic power which represents the switching and short circuit power, P_{sw}, P_{sc}, respectively. P_{sw} is determined by the activity factor, α which is the the the fraction of the circuit that is switching under the supply voltage V_{dd}, the clock speed, f_{clk}, and the equivalent switching capacitance, C. P_{sc} is consumed when both the pull up and pull down network of the logic gate circuit partially conduct as illustrated in Fig. 1(b).

3   Body Biasing

3.1   Threshold Voltage and Current

The V_{TH} is a fundamental parameter in circuit design and testing, as well as in technology characterization, and modeling. In fact, the V_{TH} represents the minimum voltage needed to invert the channel between the source and drain terminals which leads to a current flow I_{DS} as it goes from weak to strong inversion. Since this transition is very gradual, the V_{TH} can be directly identified from the I_{DS} vs. V_{GS} characteristic. Based on the inversion condition of the channel, these regimes are called weak inversion, moderate inversion, and strong inversion as shown in Fig. 2 for an n-channel MOSFET.

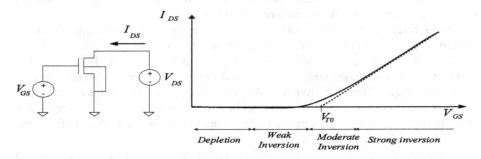

Fig. 2. Different regimes of operation identified from the I_{DS} vs. V_{GS} NMOSFET characteristics.

The transistor sub-threshold output current is the undesirable leakage current, I_{DS}, which is observed at $V_{GS} < V_{TH}$ (i.e. off-state (I_{OFF})) of an n-channel transistor. This is the main contributor to the MOSFET, I_{OFF} which is the I_{DS} measured at $V_{GS} = 0$ and $V_{DS} = V_{DD}$. It is important to keep it very small in order to minimize the static power that a circuit consumes even when it is in the standby (i.e. sleep) mode. The leakage current gradually became a limiting factor for down-scaling the V_{TH} since it determines the power consumption of a chip in its idle state that describes the device behavior in the so-called sub-threshold (e.g. weak-inversion) regime. Moreover, the drain current increases exponentially on the V_{GS} in this regime [7].

$$I_{DS,sub} \propto \exp\left(\frac{q.V_{GS}}{n.K.T}\right). \tag{2}$$

where K is the Boltzmann constant, T is the absolute temperature, q is the electron charge, and the sub-threshold slope factor n depends on the capacitance of the CMOS technology (i.e. Bulk, FDSOI, FinFET). It is worth to note that the V_{TH} influences the $I_{ds,sub}$ and I_{ON} (i.e. saturation) currents. For instance, a higher I_{ON} maximizes the circuit speed because it reduces the charging time of the pad output capacitances of the logic cells. This higher I_{ON} can be achieved by a lower V_{TH}. However, lowering V_{TH} increases exponentially the leakage current. This is the compromise between speed and power that the designer should balance.

3.2   UTTB FDSOI Body Biasing Effect

The transistor V_{TH} can be controlled by the potential of the body terminal contact [3].

$$V_{TH} = V_{TH0} + \gamma\left(\sqrt{|-2\phi_F + V_{SB}|} - \sqrt{|2\phi_F|}\right). \tag{3}$$

where γ is the body effect coefficient, ϕ_F is the Fermi potential, and V_{TH0} is the zero threshold voltage while source-bulk bias is equal to 0 ($V_{SB} = 0$). The body effect describes the changes (e.g. shifting) in the V_{TH} by modulating or varying the V_{SB} voltage. It can be consider as a second gate and is sometimes referred to as the "back gate" that helps to determine how fast the transistor turns on and off.

Strong body effect enables a variety of effective body biasing techniques that were effectively used in older process generations. However, body effect has diminished with Bulk transistor scaling, and conventional deep-nanometer transistors have very little body effect. For this reason body bias is not widely used for 65 nm and smaller process Bulk technologies. Thus, the strength of the body effect, γ is crucial in the effectiveness of this dynamic body-biasing approach [8]. For this reason, there is need of a reasonable body effect for post silicon tuning techniques which is essential for compromising the low power and high performance.

Consequently, an enabler process technology to the innovative low-power design techniques is required for a better V_{TH} control. From transistor architecture and materials (e.g. metal, oxide, and semiconductors) perspectives, breakthroughs were needed to reduce the SCE and the leakage currents in sub-28 nm bulk CMOS technology process and to decrease the capacitance factor.

The Fin-type field-effect transistors (FinFET) and fully depleted silicon-on-insulator (FDSOI) technology provides the promising new transistor technology to do back-gate biasing effects. The FDSOI MOSFET structure has been proposed for scaling CMOS technology to sub-28 nm nodes. This is because leakage currents are well suppressed in a FD-SOI MOSFET when the body thickness (T_{Si}) is less than or equal to one-fourth of the gate length (L_G) [5, 6].

In addition, the SCE in an ultra-thin body FDSOI MOSFET can be suppressed by thinning down the silicon body and buried oxide (BOX) thickness. Furthermore, scaling down the BOX thickness of a FDSOI MOSFET below 5 nm can lead to a double-gate device structure on SOI substrate. This Ultra-thin body and BOX (UTBB) FDSOI transistor architecture has a stronger body effect than conventional transistors and therefore enables effective V_{TH} management through body biasing. This strong body effect is a key enabler of low-power and high-speed circuit operation for deep submicron CMOS technologies by fixing or modulating the V_{TH} voltage. It is worth to note also that double-gate transistor structures such as the vertical (3D) FinFET are more challenging to manufacture than the planar (2D) FD-SOI MOSFET structure as shown in Fig. 3. The range of back-gate biasing in UTBB FDSOI is quite wider (i.e. $-3V < V_{SB} < 3V$) by a factor of 10 compared to the bulk technology (i.e. $-300\,mV < V_{SB} < 300\,mV$) due to the transistor structure as shown in Fig. 4.

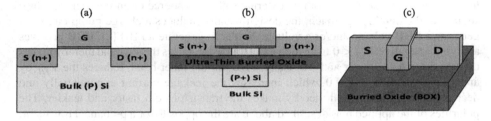

Fig. 3. Structure of different transistor technology: (a) Conventional planar bulk transistor, (b) Planar single-or double gate FDSOI, (c) Vertical multiple-gate FinFET SOI [4].

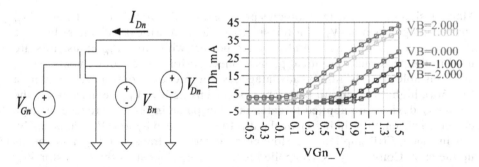

Fig. 4. Shifting effects on the V_{TH} introduced by the back-gate biasing n-channel UTTB FDSOI.

Back-biasing consists of applying a voltage just under the BOX target of the UTTB FDSOI transistors. This changes the electrostatic control of the transistors and shifts their V_{TH}, as shown in Fig. 4, to either get more drive current (hence higher speed) at the expense of increased leakage current or reduce it at the expense of speed degradation. While back-bias in planar FD is somewhat similar to body-bias implemented in bulk

CMOS technology, it offers a number of key advantages in terms of level and efficiency of the bias that can be applied. Back-biasing can be utilized in a dynamic way, on a block-by-block basis. It can be used to boost performance during the limited periods of time when maximum peak performance is required from that block. It can also be used to cut leakage during the periods of time when limited performance is not an issue. In other words, back-bias offers a new and efficient trade-off on the speed/power [6].

4   Static Low Power Design

Leakage power minimization has prompted various chip manufacturers to employ dual-/multi-V_{TH} and adaptive and dynamic body biasing processes [3]. All of these body bias methodologies, circuits and design techniques take advantage of the increased body effect provided by the UTBB FDSOI transistors to reduce power consumption by managing V_{TH} more effectively than the conventional bulk transistors.

The V_{TH} can be adjusted by applying forward body biasing (FBB) or reverse body biasing (RBB). Back-gate bias involves connecting the transistor bodies to a bias network. It can be supplied from an external (off-chip) source or an internal (on-chip) source. In the on-chip approach, the design usually includes a charge pump circuit to generate a RBB voltage and/or a voltage divider to generate a FBB [8]. RBB involves applying a negative $V_{SB} < 0$ to an n-channel transistor, raises the V_{TH} and thereby makes the transistor both slower and less leaky. FBB, on the other hand, reduces the V_{TH} by applying a positive $V_{SB} > 0$ which increases the leakage current exponentially and decrease the gate delay and thereby makes the transistor both faster and leakier. The polarities of the applied bias described above are the opposite for a p-channel transistor.

4.1   Dual V_{TH} Partitioning

Many design kit process technologies provide dual-V_{TH} transistors. The dual V_{TH} partitioning uses high-V_{TH} for transistors in the non-critical paths to reduce the static power (minimizing overall leakage power) while low-V_{TH} transistors are used in the performance-critical paths to meet performance requirements. Thus, an adjustable V_{TH} is highly advantageous for process control. As shown in Fig. 5(a), high speed circuit paths are designed using low-V_{TH} devices, while the high-V_{TH} devices are applied to gates in other paths in order to reduce leakage current. This enables timing-critical paths to be swapped by low-V_{TH} cells easily. For instance, FBB applied to a slow chip, lowers the transistor V_{TH} and speeds up the chip. Conversely, RBB applied to a fast chip, increases the transistor V_{TH} and reduces the excess leakage current of the chip. This enables the chip designer to balance the tradeoff between the speed and power [8].

4.2   Multiple Threshold Biasing

The multiple threshold biasing technique employs the low-V_{TH} transistors to design the logic gates for which the switching speed is essential, and the high-V_{TH} transistors (also

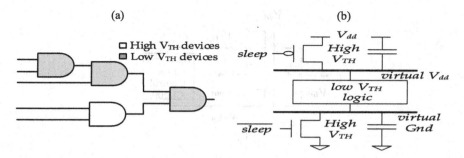

Fig. 5. (a) Dual-V_{TH} partitioning and (b) Multiple threshold design scheme [9].

called sleep transistors) to effectively isolate the logic gates in the standby state and reduce the leakage dissipation. The generic circuit structure of the multiple threshold design circuit is offered in Fig. 5(b).

The sleep transistors are controlled by the sleep signal. During the active mode, the sleep signal is enabled, causing both high-V_{TH} transistors to turn on and provide a virtual power and ground to the low-V_{TH} logic. When the circuit is inactive, sleep signal is disabled which forces both high-V_{TH} transistors to cut-off and disconnect the power lines from the low-V_{TH} logic. This results in a very low sub-threshold leakage current from power to ground when the circuit is in standby mode.

4.3 Adaptive and Dynamic Back-Gate Biasing

Rather than employ multiple threshold voltage process options, a more advanced body bias methodology is to apply an adaptive body bias, where for each chip a different fixed body bias value is calibrated at production test. Adaptive body bias is a valuable tool for overcoming systematic manufacturing variation, which is usually manifested in the handled devices as leakage or timing variation between chips. This undesirable current can be controlled adaptively through a body-bias circuit generator that is connected to the back-gate of the low-V_{TH} SOI nMOS and pMOS transistors as shown in Fig. 6. This dynamic control enable to continuously shift device V_{TH} during its operation, rather than setting the body bias just once either during design or at production test, in order to either lower the V_{TH} when needing more speed, or raise it when running at lower speeds to optimize the leakage power. Consequently, dynamic body bias can be used to compensate the process variation related to the temperature and aging effects as well as to efficiently manage power modes [8].

During the active mode the transistors circuit of Fig. 6 work as conventional CMOS transistors without back-gate biasing. As the circuit enters to the standby state, the back-gate bias control circuit generates a lower $V_{SB,n}$ for the SOI nMOS transistor and a higher $V_{SB,p}$ for the SOI pMOS transistor. As a result, the magnitudes of the respective threshold voltages $V_{TH,p}$ and $V_{TH,p}$ both increase in the standby mode due to the back-gate effect. Therefore, the leakage power dissipation in the standby state can be significantly reduced with this circuit design technique.

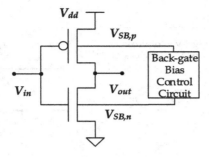

Fig. 6. Adaptive biasing scheme of low-V_{TH} and low-V_{DD} UTTB FSOI inverter.

5 Conclusion

This paper has analyzed the mechanisms behind the back-gate biasing effects and the friendly design methodologies in order to achieve low power and high-speed logic cells performances. Moreover, the back-gate biasing challenges faced with the conventional bulk at nanometers scale has been described along with the breakthrough of the UTBB FD-SOI technology.

The UTBB FDSOI revives the ability of higher back-gate bias effect by enabling wider range of back voltage to adjust the V_{TH} according to the circuit specifications. Also, it brings a significant improvement in terms of speed, dynamic power saving and flexibility to static leakage power management design techniques for energy efficiency optimization during early silicon stage design or at the post-silicon stage by tuning the chip's bias for process compensation.

Acknowledgments. The research leading to these results has received funding from the Fundação para a Ciência e Tecnologia and the ENIAC JU (THINGS2DO–GA n. 621221).

References

1. Bohr, M.: Silicon technology leadership for the mobility era. In: Intel Developer Forum (2012)
2. Saijets, J.: MOSFET RF Characterization Using Bulk and SOI CMOS Technologies. Helsinki University of Technology, Finland (2007)
3. Vitale, S.A., Wyatt, P.W., Checka, N., Kedzierski, J., Keast, C.L.: FD-SOI process technology for subthreshold-operation ultralow-power electronics. Proc. IEEE **98**, 333–342 (2010)
4. Pelloux-Prayer, B., Blagojevic, M., Thomas, O., Amara, A., Vladimirescu, A., Nikolic, B., Cesana, G., Flatresse, P.: Planar fully depleted SOI technology: the convergence of high performance and low power towards multimedia mobile applications. In: IEEE Conference Faible Tension Faible Consommation, pp. 1–4 (2012)
5. Magarshack, P., Flatresse, P., Cesana, G.: UTBB FD-SOI: a process/design symbiosis for breakthrough energy-efficiency. In: IEEE Design, Automation & Test in Europe (DATE), pp. 952–957 (2013)

6. Noel, J.-P., Thomas, O., Jaud, M., Weber, O., Poiroux, T., Fenouillet-Beranger, C., Rivallin, P., Scheiblin, P., Andrieu, F., Vinet, M., Rozeau, O., Boeuf, F., Faynot, O., Amar, A.: Multi-Vt UTBB FDSOI device architectures for low-power CMOS circuit. IEEE Trans. Electron Devices **58**(8), 2473–2482 (2011)
7. Panda, P.R., Silpa, B.V.N., Shrivastava, A., Gummidipudi, K.: Power-Efficient System Design, ch. 2, pp. 11–39. Springer, Heidelberg (2010)
8. Suvolta. Body Effect and Body Biasing, Technology Brief (2011)
9. Bailey, A., Zahrani, A.A., Fu, G., Di, J., Smith, S.C.: Multi-threshold asynchronous circuit design for ultra-low power. J. Low Power Electron. **4**, 337–348 (2008)

An Architectural Framework for Delivering SIP-AS Multimedia Services Based on JADE/OSGi Technology

Renato B. Cabelino Ribeiro[1(✉)], Magnos Martinello[1],
Celso Alberto Saibel Santos[1], and Rosane Bodart Soares[2]

[1] Departamento de Informática, UFES, Vitória, Brasil
renato@ifes.edu.br, {magnos,saibel}@inf.ufes.br
[2] Departamento de Engenharia Elétrica, UFES, Vitória, Brasil
rosane@ele.ufes.br

Abstract. This paper proposes a scenario of service-oriented architecture based on OSGi technology, in combination with multi agents systems developed using JADE environment. A key part of the scenario is the new architecture for SIP application server as part of the IMS Core network. As a proof of concept, a simulated environment for a televoting service was implemented. The major contributions of this work are the identification and analysis of jitter, variation of jitter, packet loss, load capacity and CPU utilization of the JADE/OSGi SIP-AS. Test results validate the approach and show good overall performance.

Keywords: IMS · SIP-AS · JADE · OSGi · Multimedia services · Televoting

1 Introduction

The world of digital communications is quickly moving away from a dependence on access methods to service-oriented providers. This paper introduces a service-oriented architecture combined with multi-agents systems as a hosting platform for telecommunication supplementary services on IP Multimedia Subsystem (IMS).

The JADE platform, integrated with the OSGi framework, is the proposed agent-based development environment [1, 2]. This approach allows for a more flexible and dynamic form of service provisioning over the IMS architecture, allowing services to be negotiated on demand according to the current environment requirements (services rules, QoS requirements, interaction parameters, etc.).

This article presents the implementation of a SIP Application Server (SIP-AS) on OSGi service-oriented architecture, integrated with JADE framework for the creation and provision of multimedia services on IMS. In Sect. 2, the related works are described. The technology is presented in Sect. 3. Section 4 describes the design and implementation of the televoting service, and the result analysis. Conclusions are described in Sect. 5.

© Institute for Computer Sciences, Social Informatics and Telecommunications Engineering 2015
S. Mumtaz et al. (Eds.): WICON 2014, LNICST 146, pp. 122–128, 2015.
DOI: 10.1007/978-3-319-18802-7_17

2 Related Works

This section analyzes exclusively SIP approaches that have correlation with customized telecommunications services (for example, additional services, toll free phone services, Televoting, local number portability) or with the framework presented in this work. Oliveira et al. [8] propose two approaches for implementing number portability service in IMS networks, tested on an AS (Application Server) according to the standards of the General Regulations of Portability. In the first approach, the AS performs the function of local number portability without call states control, routing every call originated by IMS to AS, or those based on a numeric phone context through an Initial Filter Criteria (IFC). In the second approach, the number portability service acts as a back-to-back user agent (B2BUA), i.e. in a leg termination call aimed to a ported user, configures an IFC to conduct the call routing for an AS, which acts on behalf of the user ported and initiates a new call to the correct destination. For the implementation of AS, SIP Servlet technology was created by the authors.

Munadi et al. [9] propose the design and implementation of VoIP services with OpenIMS and ASTERISK, interconnected by an ENUM server which develops numerical mapping function between the two servers. The authors observed the proposed environment according to: (a) performance measures for each server; (b) the Post Dial Delay (PDD) and (c) of the same CPU consumption. The values measured and analyzed in (a) identify the service time consumption on the part of the SIP signaling system. In (b), three scenarios were tested where the Traffic Analyzer WIRESHARK was used in order to capture and analyze traffic from the User Agent Caller from its application until its acceptance by the counterparty in the call, which allowed the analysis of the PDD in each test performed. For (c), were used the TOP utility from the operating system itself in order to obtain the maximum CPU value throughout the experiments.

Li et al. [10] implement two IMS services – a chat room (SIP-IM) and Presence services, in a SIP-AS. SIP-AS architecture used is based on Mobicents SIP Servlet component (MSS). In addition, we used the OpenIMS Core to IMS Core Network implementation. The authors have developed a use case diagram and class diagram for the services analyzed. For the test scenarios, XML templates were made to present the requirements and the design of both services.

3 Technology Base: IMS and JADE/OSGi Integration

IMS is an evolving definition of an architecture that addresses the continuing demands and frustrations of users and enterprises. The ultimate goal of the architecture is to define a model that separates the services offered by fixed-line, mobile, and converged service providers from access networks used to carry those services [3].

The layered approach proposed by IMS increases the importance of the application layer as services are designed to work independently of the access network. IMS is designed to bridge the gap between them [4]. It offers more flexibility for telecom operators to manage different services with distinct requisites (e.g.: bandwidth, latency, jitter, etc).

JADE is a middleware for the development and execution of peer-to-peer applications based on the agent paradigm that can easily work and interoperate on traditional or wireless network environments. JADE internal architecture is currently the only architecture entirely compliant with FIPA standards [5]. According to [6] and [1], the JADE platform can offer the following: Graphical interface which allows monitoring, debugging and logging; Components which can be distributed over the network; Mobility and cloning of agents as well as multi-tasking scheduling; Lifecycle management, name and yellow pages services, point-to-point message transport service, speech-act message structure and ontology service; Interoperability with other platforms that offer support to FIPA standards.

The development of applications using OSGi can be accomplished through the combination of collaborative, reusable modules associated with descriptive information on their metafiles which include service-related input that must be instantiated/imported to achieve a consistent execution of the modules [7]. Also, the services provided by OSGi implement a JAVA interface for registering on local service registries. Through this centralized control model, the modules (or bundles) can verify their service dependencies.

Furthermore, the OSGi services platform offers developers the means to maximize the use of platform independent resources and dynamic updating of JAVA modules, allowing development of services for devices with limited computing resources, widely used in corporate environments. New services registration as well as research and maintenance of pre-existing services (including their uninstallation from the system), services status notifications and follow-ups on bundles lifecycle can be carried out in a simple and efficient way.

4   Design and Implementation

Figure 1 introduces the scenario for implementation Televoting service (or another multimedia service) through the utilization of the JADE platform along with the OSGi framework, running on SIP-AS.

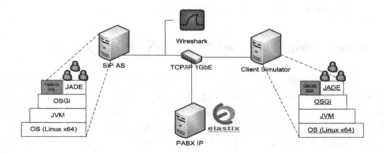

Fig. 1. Network Topology.

4.1   Televoting Service Lifecycle

Upon start, the OSGi Televoting service bundle loads its configuration parameters from a file named televoto.conf and automatically creates a number of attendant agents on the JADE platform. Each agent registers itself on IP PBX as an extension and become operational. All registered agents are grouped in a unique number. When a call arrives at that unique number, the IP PBX redirects it to one of the registered agents and the call is then processed. The rules for redirection (first available, ring all, last called, etc.) depend on the IP PBX distribution. In the proposed scenario the programmed rule is first available. As described above, televoting agent register along IP PBX and became ready to work. Once created, they turn visible on JADE GUI (inside MAIN container) and your control is now managed by JADE framework.

4.2   Validation Tests

We have developed a sequence of tests to validate integration of JADE/OSGi as a SIP-AS. The parameters observed in the experiment are: jitter, variation of jitter, packet loss and CPU load of the SIP-AS. To support this scenario, the equipment presented in Fig. 2 and detailed in Table 1 below, were used.

Table 1.   Test equipment's specification.

ITEM	EQUIPMENT
SIP-AS, Client Simulator	Dual Intel Xeon with 4 core/processor, 20 GB RAM, Intel Gigabit Ethernet, OS Linux Server 12.04 x64
IP PBX	Single Intel Xeon with 4 core, 8 GB RAM, Intel Gigabit Ethernet, ELASTIX Custom Distro
Switch	H3C-2928 24 ports Gigabit Ethernet
Network Analizer	Intel Core2 Duo, 4 GB RAM, Atheros Gigabit Ethernert, OS Microsoft Windows XP SP3

In each test, the client simulator performed a load of calls to its counterpart in the televoting service (a client for each service agent). This load of calls was parameterized in the configuration file of client simulator such that it is executed one or more times, depending on the amount of redials parameter set.

With this approach, we identified the capacity of the SIP-AS in handling calls faster without the need of integration with the IMS Core. During testing, all network traffic was captured by the Analyzer for subsequent analysis.

The methodology used in the tests was developed according to the following profile: (a) the whole SIP-AS infrastructure is initialized; (b) the packet capture is initialized in the WIRESHARK; (c) the client Simulator is initialized, running 100 concurrent calls to the Televoting service and (d) at the end, the entire environment is shutdown. In each test, the client Simulator is reconfigured to generate additional concurrent calls as shown in Table 2, up to a total of 1000 calls, in order to identify its impact with respect to jitter

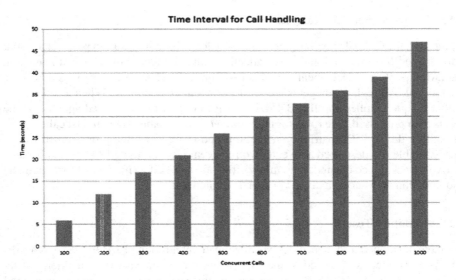

Fig. 2. Time interval for handling *n* calls.

and jitter variation. Note that the average value of jitter, as well as your variation (MAXDELTA), increases as the load of concurrent calls grows.

Table 2. Mean values of Jitter and its MAXDELTA.

Concurrent Calls	Jitter (ms)	MAXDELTA (ms)
100	0,72	111,80
200	1,74	213,07
300	3,03	354,79
400	3,96	401,76
500	4,94	485,36
600	5,93	522,16
700	7,29	629,50
800	9,71	784,57
900	9,91	716,44
1000	11,98	853,66

In the jitter column, we observe that even with a high load of concurrent calls, the values remain at an acceptable threshold. However, the same does not occur with the MAXDELTA values, because the higher the value presented more occurrences of gaps in the audio message from the televoting were perceived on the Wireshark RTP-analysis.

About CPU usage analysis, the minimum and maximum load values were between 60 and 80 percent. When added more processing resources to SIP-AS, the average value was reduced by half, leaving around 30 to 35 percent.

The values of packet loss measured were insignificant in all tests and did not influence the communication on media plan of televoting service. As noted in Fig. 2, the time spent to attend the n concurrent calls in Televoting service presented a behavior near the linearity, while the average of call handled (per second) showed practically stable after the amount of 400 concurrent calls.

5 Conclusions

We present the design and the development of a service oriented architectural framework to support the provisioning of IP Multimedia Services (IMS). Specifically, we follow a totally different approach from the already existing approaches, presented in the literature, which are about the design and the development of functional solutions based on the combination of the OSGi and JADE technologies, by focusing in the same time to the deployment of innovative techniques/solutions that enable the multimedia sharing over IP between IP enabled devices that are able to participate a televoting service.

The tests performed indicate good performance results in concurrent call handling. In addition, the system response time in the processing of televoting calls is close to those found in the same service offered in PSTN Intelligent Network (IN). Server CPU consumption is high and can be attenuated with the vertical scaling (provisioning of more hardware resources, already tested as shown in subsection 4.2) or horizontal (distribution of the service on a clustered JADE/OSGi). In a future work, we are programming the system for automatic scaling calls (load balancing, etc.) as well as the mobility of service agents and model integration with OpenIMS Core.

References

1. Bellifemine, F., Caire, G., Greenwood, D.: Developing MultiAgent Systems with JADE. Wiley, Inglaterra (2007)
2. OSGi Alliance. OSGi Service Platform: Core Specification, Release 4, Version 4.2. Technical report (2009). Disponível em http://www.osgi.org/download/r4v42/r4.core.pdf
3. Salchow Jr., K.: Introduction to the IP Multimedia Subsystem (IMS): IMS Basic Concepts and Terminology. http://www.f5.com/pdf/white-papers/ims-introduction-wp.pdf
4. Poikselkä, M., Mayer, G.: The IMS: IP Multimedia Concepts and Services, 3rd edn. Wiley, Chichester (2009)
5. Bellifemine, F., Caire, G., Poggi, A., Rimassa, G.: JADE White Paper, disponível em: http://jade.tilab.com/papers/2003/WhitePaperJADEEXP.pdf
6. Wooldridge, M.: An Introduction to MultiAgent Systems, 2nd edn. Wiley, Chichester (2009)
7. Ribeiro, R.B.C., Soares, R.B.: The application of JADE and OSGi technologies in the telecommunications services architecture. In: EUROCON 2011 (2011)

8. Oliveira, R.G., et al.: An application server approach for number portability in IMS networks. In: IEEE - SBrT - ITS 2010 - International Telecommunications Symposium, 6–9 September, Manaus, Amazonas, Brazil (2010)
9. Munadi, R., et al.: Design and implementation VoIP service on open IMS and asterisk servers interconnected through enum server. Int. J. Next-Gener. Netw. (IJNGN) 2(2) (2010)
10. Li, K., et al.: Two exploring experiments on IMS service based on SIP AS. Int. J. Multimedia Ubiquit. Eng. 9(4), 375–386 (2014)

Easily Guiding of Blind: Providing Information and Navigation - SmartNav

Karen Duarte[✉], José Cecílio, and Pedro Furtado

Department of Informatics Engineering, University of Coimbra,
Coimbra, Portugal
kduarte@uc.pt, {jcecilio,pnf}@dei.uc.pt

Abstract. This work intends to provide an assistive technology that helps blind persons to independently navigate inside public spaces. Blind persons often travel through known routes as they already know some features of it. Our technology helps users to travel through unknown spaces and find products or services available there. It is supported by personal smartphones running Android OS and beacons deployed in the space.

Keywords: Blind people · Guiding the blind · Assistive technology · Assisted navigation

1 Introduction

Blind people often have to learn to navigate through new routes, usually those that best fit daily needs. As they have limited perception of what is happening, they are advised to take known routes and to use points of reference (e.g. sounds, textures) to localize their selves. Commonly, blind persons firstly rely on others to learn routes, and then have to ask for help whenever they want to go through another way.

The assistive technology proposed in this paper intends to provide, for blind users, the information and assistance needed to safely navigate inside public spaces, therefore enabling them to navigate to unknown spaces/routes and providing an extra assurance when navigating through known spaces. Besides providing assistance during navigation, SmartNav also helps the user to get information about spaces, such as the services, products or promotions that may be of interest for he/she.

One of the main objectives of SmartNav is to equalize the access to information from everyone. As there is a strong amount of information accessed by visual means, there is also a strong amount of information inaccessible to blind people. The technology intends to replace the visual mean of receiving information with a voice channel robust enough to smartly interact and be trusted by blind users. Smart interaction is achieved by a keyword-based process that enables the blind user to promptly find the desired information.

The document is structured as follows: the next section reviews the related work on this field, the third section presents the SmartNav with more detail, the forth exposes the testing process and its results and the fifth concludes the paper.

© Institute for Computer Sciences, Social Informatics and Telecommunications Engineering 2015
S. Mumtaz et al. (Eds.): WICON 2014, LNICST 146, pp. 129–134, 2015.
DOI: 10.1007/978-3-319-18802-7_18

2   Related Work

Some technologies were studied and developed concerning the issue of assisting the navigation of blind persons. The literature review enables to identify RFID and GPS as the technologies more often used.

BlindAid [5], is an RFID-based technology developed to assist blind people on navigation, by guiding them to desired destinations. Other works based in RFID technology are presented in [1, 3, 8]. This technologies use maps representations of the environment and the RFID sensors to locate the person. System [9] uses RFID technology for indoor navigation and GPS for outdoor. As known GPS has the problem of being extremely inaccurate for pedestrian navigation.

Regarding the issue of finding specific products/services, ShopTalk [6], BlindShopping [4] and RoboCart [2], are technologies developed to assist blind persons using blind-friendly mechanisms, such as the communication of information by voice or vibration.

In what concerns the level of assistance provided to blind people, the study presented in [7] concludes that the navigation skills acquired by blind persons should be included in the navigation system. Therefore, technologies intended to assist the blind during navigation does not require the utilization of complex sensors, as they are already aware of detecting structures, danger and moving objects or persons. Our work is based in this premise, SmartNav just instructs the user to navigate through the path, detecting objects and other structures rely on user abilities.

3   SmartNav

Taking into account features of the technologies revised in the literature (e.g. localization techniques, portable devices for blind persons), we defined the major features for the SmartNav. First of all, it must perform user positioning with enough accuracy to generate the correct instructions that can guide the user. The system must also comprise the information needed to help users concerning navigation and space, such as the services and products available. Additionally, the system intends to be a supplement of navigation techniques already used by users (for example, white cans and dogs). At the same time, the system must have low weight and size to be wearable by anyone.

Thus, we decided that the SmartNav must not force the user to carry another device, therefore it would be entirely developed to a smartphone (yet only developed for Android OS).

The SmartNav comprises four main functions: Interact, Inform, Guide and Position. Positioning is performed by placing beacons on the environment. Those beacons must be strategically placed in order to cover the entire space with radio signal. The technology can accurately position the user as long as there is signal surrounding he/she. The systems also uses GPS signal to guide the user in outdoor environments. Concerning indoor location, the type of beacons that can be used rely on the capacity of the user's device to identify them. At this moment we developed the SmartNav based on Bluetooth beacons, because a wide range of smartphones already have incorporated the Bluetooth technology.

Interactions and Information play a special role in this system, as the target users are blind, there must be smart and efficient interaction methodologies. Similarly, in order to access and deliver the desired information, the information is treated in an intelligent and effective way. In the next two subsections we explained the interaction methodology and information treatment mechanisms.

3.1 Interaction

The mechanisms of Interaction play a special role in technologies designed from blind people. Once the SmartNav is intended to be used during navigation, it was developed without requiring any touch interaction (buttons). All changes of information are made by voice: both from the user and application.

Speech synthesis and speech recognition used are based on the Google API's available for Android programming. Voice instructions (speech synthesis) are supported by the Android Text-To-Speech API, which enables to store or immediately play the speech. Since storing ASCII information is easily to be searched, SmartNav does not store information in voice format. Text-To-Speech API has several languages available (e.g. English, French, German, Italian and Spanish), not all languages or idioms are supported. The latest update on the API enables more a few languages, like Portuguese (Brazilian accent). The SmartNav was designed to accommodate new languages as soon as they are available.

The Text-To-Speech API uses a central queue to convert from text to voice instructions. That queue acts like a waiting list. There are two main methods of enter messages in the queue: place the text to convert on the last position of the queue and wait for its time, or forcing to convert and deliver it at the moment. The first method is used to deliver information about the environment surrounding the user, while the second method is used to deliver navigation instructions (e.g. "Turn left."), which require a tight relation between generation of instructions and its deliver to user.

Speech recognition is performed by Google Speech Input API, which is factory installed on most Android devices. This API supports some more languages than the Text-To-Speech API, but once again, the SmartNav will be able to understand more languages as soon as the API is updated.

3.2 Information

SmartNav is able to inform the user of the available spaces and/or services surrounding he/she. This information contains the name of the points-of-interest available (e.g. spaces or services), a brief description of each one, and the promotions available at the moment (if he is navigating inside a shopping center).

Regarding the limitations of the target users, we designed a keyword-based approach to assist the user in finding the wanted information. The user is asked to introduce a keyword associated to the desired point-of-interest. This approach is used either to get information about the point-of-interest (service/place), either to select it as destination point and start assisted navigation (Fig. 1).

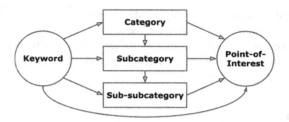

Fig. 1. Designed information handling approach.

The above figure represents a diagram flow of the approach. Available points-of-interest are categorized into categories, subcategories and sub-subcategories. For example, the Fashion category can have the subcategories Clothing and Shoes, and subcategory Clothing can have Woman, Man and Children sub-subcategories. Every category, subcategory, sub-subcategory and point-of-interest is labeled with some keywords.

The introduced keyword is used to search for associated categories, subcategories, sub-subcategories or points-of-interest. Then a short list of associated categories (or subcategories, or sub-subcategories) or points-of-interest is delivered to user, referring first the points-of-interest. This list is labeled with numbers to easy selection of the user's choice. For example, considering the keyword "Tennis", the returned list would be "1 – Converse, 2 – Nike, 3 – Reebok, 4 - More choices". The user is now able to choose one of the options, by saying its number. We opt by using numbers because they are easily understood by Recognizer part.

When a user chooses a point-of-interest, he/she can listening a short description of the point-of-interest, its latest promotions or defining it as destination point. If the uses chooses a category, the associated points-of-interest or subcategories are delivered the same way. To assist the understanding of information storage, Fig. 2 schematizes structures created and their relations. C1, C2, Cn are the categories available, SC1 to SCn the subcategories, SSC the sub-subcategories and the K's are the recognized keywords. Each Category keeps its relation with associated subcategories and keywords. A similar relation is established for subcategories and sub-subcategories.

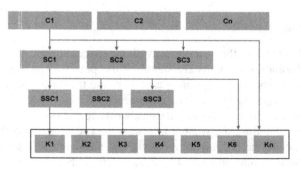

Fig. 2. Organization of information in SmartNav.

Similarly, points-of-interest have some particular keywords that are added to the keywords' structure. When the user introduces a keyword this structure is used to search for what is the interest of the user and what is available in the information system. At any time the user can introduce a new keyword and reset the informing process to the beginning. For example, after select a category and a subcategory, and received a list of the associated points-of-interest, the user can say a new keyword (instead of a number, used to select options from the list).

Since a destination point is defined, this informing cycle gives place to the assisted navigation.

4   Testing and Results

As referred before, the current version of SmartNav was developed for Android OS. Since it was designed to help blind people, it shows a simple visual interface with two big buttons: one at the top and other at the bottom of the screen (half size of the screen is used by each button). The button at the top is used to ask for help: either during navigation (to ask for navigation instructions to reach the defined destination) or just to request information about the space nearby. The button at the bottom is used to explore the information about the environment (this information is organized according to the specification detailed in Sect. 3.2). This can lead to the assisted navigation (as long as the user defines a destination point).

In order to evaluate the capabilities of SmartNav, a set of tests were performed. This tests intends to evaluate each function of the application: positioning, guiding, inform and interact. To test the positioning process, two scenarios were created. Fifty different positions were tested and in all of them, the position was delivered correctly. The guiding process was tested by defining 30 different routes and checking if the navigation instructions were correctly generated (giving the correct instruction in the right moment). Interaction was tested by extensively performing conversions from text to speech. Portuguese sentences and Portuguese sentences with loanwords were tested. The informing function was tested by navigating through the information process.

The testing phase showed the correct functioning of the positioning process, presenting maximum error of 20 cm from the correct position, and therefore, the guiding process is able to correctly generate navigation instructions in the right moment. Concerning to interaction tests, both Text-To-Speech and speech synthesis API used are robust enough to convert Portuguese words (form text to speech and versus), but some loanwords cannot be recognized or correctly converted to speech. Tests performed to the informing function showed its correct functioning, enabling the user to find any of the points-of-interest available.

5   Conclusion and Future Work

Blind people are deprived from a great amount of information because it is commonly delivered by visual marks. Usually locations, news and promotions are indicated with visual signs, so the blind person is incapacitated of being aware of any change made to his/her already known environment. They usually rely on others to receive this information.

SmartNav is a system specially designed for blind users, whose main objective is to assist on going and navigate inside public spaces. The system is supported by the user's smartphone, thus enhancing its ability to use it (SmartNav is just another installable Android application). Interactions with the user are mostly performed by voice exchanges. In order to use the SmartNav, spaces must be provided with beacons, which allow determining user positioning based on radio signals.

The development of SmartNav's prototype opened horizons to what it could be, as future work. We have assigned, as future work, the utilization of some sensors of smartphones, such as the gyroscope and accelerometer, and the creation of an online server with information about several public spaces. It will enable the user to be informed of available services and promotions without leaving the comfort of home.

References

1. Chumkamon, S., Tuvaphanthaphiphat, P., Keeratiwintakorn, P.: A blind navigation system using RFID for indoor environments. In: 2008 5th International Conference on Electrical Engineering/Electronics, Computer, Telecommunications and Information Technology, pp. 765–768 (2008)
2. Gharpure, C.P., Kulyukin, V.A.: Robot-assisted shopping for the blind: Issues in spatial cognition and product selection. Intel. Serv. Robot. **1**, 237–251 (2008)
3. Kulyukin, V., Gharpure, C., Nicholson, J., Pavithran, S.: RFID in robot-assisted indoor navigation for the visually impaired. In: 2004 IEEE/RSJ International Conference on Intelligent Robots and Systems (IROS) (IEEE Cat. No.04CH37566), vol. 2 (2004)
4. López-de-Ipiña, D., Lorido, T., López, U.: Indoor navigation and product recognition for blind people assisted shopping. In: Bravo, J., Hervás, R., Villarreal, V. (eds.) IWAAL 2011. LNCS, vol. 6693, pp. 33–40. Springer, Heidelberg (2011)
5. Mau, S., Melchior, N., Makatchev, M., Stein, A.: BlindAid: An Electronic Travel Aid for the Blind (2008)
6. Nicholson, J., Kulyukin, V., Coster, D.: ShopTalk: independent blind shopping through verbal route directions and barcode scans. Open Rehabil. J. **2**, 11–23 (2009)
7. Nicholson, J.: Generation and analysis of verbal route directions for blind navigation. ProQuest Dissertations Theses **3409234**, 211 (2010)
8. Varpe, K., Wankhade, M.P.: Survey of visually impaired assistive system. Int. J. Eng. Innovative Technol. (IJEIT) **2**(11), 161–166 (2013)
9. Yelamarthi, K., Haas, D., Nielsen, D., Mothersell, S.: RFID and GPS integrated navigation system for the visually impaired. In: Midwest Symposium on Circuits and Systems, pp. 1149–1152 (2010)

Intelligent and Efficient Car Management Application for Advanced Green Routing

Ioannis Loumiotis$^{(\boxtimes)}$, V. Asthenopoulos, Evgenia Adamopoulou,
Konstantinos Demestichas, and E. Sykas

National Technical University of Athens, Athens, Greece
i_loumiotis@cn.ntua.gr

Abstract. The tremendous growth of the transportation systems during the last decades has created a significant environmental impact. As a result, in order to reduce the atmospheric pollution many attempts have been employed, including eco-driving systems. However, the scope of such systems is only to attempt to inform the user about his driving behaviour. In the current paper, a novel system targeted for supporting green daily commuting habits, with a particular focus on helping the user save on fuel expenses and time on a regular daily basis is proposed and its functional architecture is fully presented.

Keywords: Road transport services · Green routing · Energy efficiency

1 Introduction

During the last decades there has been a tremendous growth in the transportation systems. The technology advancements have allowed the penetration of cars in our daily lives. However, this comes at a certain cost. Though cars are now more environmentally friendly in contrast to previous years, the general environmental impact of cars is considered significant. To this end, governments are using fiscal policies in order to promote cars with low CO_2.

However, it is noted that the most significant cause of the air pollution in metropolitan areas is due to transportation sector. Specifically, the transportation problems in big metropolitan areas further deteriorate the impact of vehicles on the environmental pollution. In general, the transportation sector is responsible for the 14 % of the global Greenhouse gas emissions, and its impact is expected to be 28 % by 2030 [1].

The increased demand in the transportation sector is considered one of the main issues of the atmospheric pollution. In the last few years a new trend has been introduced for the reduction of the emitting pollutants based on ecological driving methods (eco-driving)[1]. Towards this direction, approaches such as [2] have been proposed, which study the green vehicle routing problem. A more general approach is proposed in [3], where the dynamic traffic routing is investigated. However, the scope of the proposed scheme is to maximise the network utilisation and not the individual's payoff.

---

[1] The term eco-driving is used to describe energy efficient use of vehicles.

© Institute for Computer Sciences, Social Informatics and Telecommunications Engineering 2015
S. Mumtaz et al. (Eds.): WICON 2014, LNICST 146, pp. 135–140, 2015.
DOI: 10.1007/978-3-319-18802-7_19

In the current transportation landscape there are many eco-driving systems either embedded in the vehicles or portable that provide feedback to the driver in order to optimise his driving behaviour and reduce the fuel consumption. In the former category, such systems are adopted by many companies such as SCANIA [4] and Honda [5], while the latter category includes after market applications such as GreenRoad [6] and GreenMeter [7]. However, the current driver assistance systems lack the capability of allowing the combination of data sources in order to provide the driver with accurate measurements and predictions of trip parameters, such as fuel consumption and monetary cost.

In this paper, the authors propose an innovative system architecture targeted to support and promote green daily commuting habits, with a particular focus on helping the user save on fuel expenses, time, and greenhouse gas emissions, on a regular and daily basis. The proposed system, called CARMA, provides reliable feedback to the users on how much fuel, money, time, and CO_2 they spend when driving their way to their destinations. In order to achieve this, CARMA employs a green decision support system, which helps users make the best road commute choices both pre-trip and on-trip, by combining several traffic data sources collected by heterogeneous sources, including anonymous bulk location data provided by network operators, mobile end-user data, fleet data, and legacy road traffic monitoring data. A visual representation of the proposed system is depicted in Fig. 1. According to the authors' best knowledge the proposed functionality, described below in detail, is innovative and not yet integrated in existing commercially available products.

2   System Architecture

The proposed system consists of a central platform that collects and processes the heterogeneous data, and many advanced driver assistant systems (ADAS) that are used by the drivers and they are responsible for the routing process.

2.1   Central Platform

An overview of the proposed architecture of the central platform is depicted in Fig. 2 by means of the ArchiMate modelling [8]. Below, all the involved functional entities are described in detail.

Message Exchange System. The Message Exchange System comprises the main entity through which the central platform communicates with the ADAS and collects all the necessary heterogeneous data in order to employ green routing. Specifically, the Message Exchange System is responsible for the reception of road data, vehicle fleet data, mobile network data and data from the advanced driver assistant system (ADAS). Furthermore, it informs the administrator when an alert has been issued by the Emergency Situations Addressing System and dispatches the routing graph and the road usage patterns to the individual users and to the road operator, respectively.

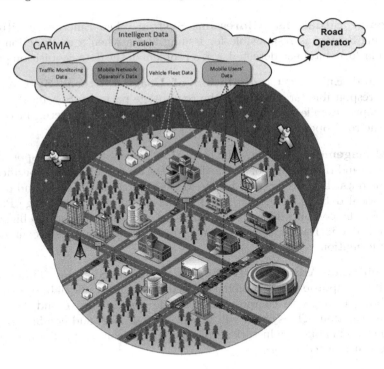

Fig. 1. The CARMA concept.

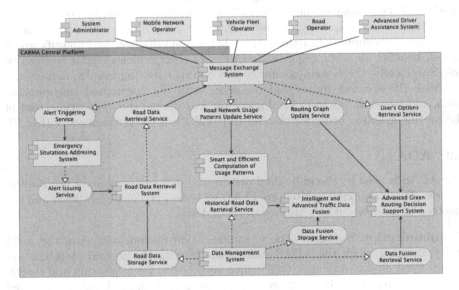

Fig. 2. Functional architecture of the central platform of CARMA.

Emergency Situations Addressing System. The Emergency Situations Addressing System is responsible for issuing alerts when a malfunction in the central platform has been detected, e.g. a problem in the data acquisition process.

Smart and Efficient Computation of Usage Patterns System. This entity is responsible for computing the road usage patterns. Specifically, it uses the appropriate collected data and calculates the usage patterns in order to inform the road operator.

Data Management System. The Data Management System is responsible for the storage and the retrieval of all the data in the central platform. Specifically, it stores the data that are received by the Message Exchange System and provides the historical data to the Smart and Efficient Computation of Usage Patterns System for the computation of the road usage patterns and the Intelligent and Advanced Traffic Data Fusion System in order to appropriately compose the traffic information.

Intelligent and Advanced Traffic Data Fusion System. This entity is responsible to appropriately combine the heterogeneous traffic data sources identified above, in order to compose and provide comprehensive and dependable traffic information. The system will intelligently process and combine not only real-time (recent) but also historical (past) heterogeneous traffic data, employing machine-learning techniques.

Advanced Green Routing Decision Support System. This entity is responsible for predicting the routing graph, taking into account the dependable fused traffic knowledge of the platform. The scope of this system is to enable the end-users to be significantly assisted in choosing the greenest and most economical route. This support function, which helps users discover and identify green routes, benefits all users, regardless of whether their vehicles engine is green or not. Specifically, the system computes two different routing graphs, namely the one with the shortest routes and the other with the normalised consumption costs, and based on the individual users' options it send the appropriate part of the routing graph in order for the ADAS to calculate the optimal route (Fig. 3).

2.2   ADAS

The ADAS is used by the individual drivers and it is responsible for the routing process. The functional architecture of ADAS is depicted in Fig. 4. Below, all the involved functional entities are described in detail.

Communication System. The Communication System comprises the main entity through which the ADAS communicates with the central platform and the optional on-board device (OBD). It is responsible for requesting and receiving the routing graph from the central platform and dispatching the collected data concerning the traversed route. Apart from that, the Communication System receives the information by the OBD regarding the data collected from the vehicle through the driving process, e.g. fuel consumption.

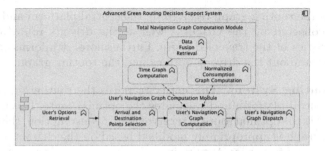

Fig. 3. Functional architecture of the advanced green routing decision support system.

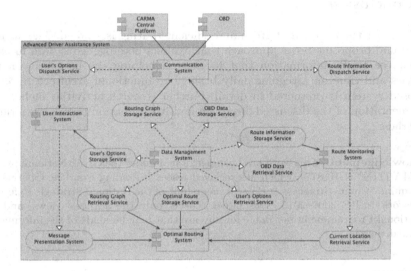

Fig. 4. Functional architecture of the advanced driver assistant system (ADAS).

User Interaction System. The User Interaction System is responsible for the communication between the ADAS and the driver.

Route Monitoring System. The Route Monitoring System is responsible to retrieve at real time the position of the vehicle from the GPS and associate its position with the information collected by the OBD. At the end of the route, the system informs the driver about the characteristics of the followed route through the User Interaction System. Furthermore, the Route Monitoring System informs at real time the Optimal Routing System in order to calculate an updated optimal route if the driver deviates from the optimal course.

Data Management System. This entity is responsible for the storage and the retrieval of all the information in the ADAS. Specifically, the Data Management

System stores the routing graph received by the central platform and the vehicle information collected by the OBD, as well as the driver's route options and the characteristics of the traversed route. Furthermore, it informs the Optimal Routing System about the driver's options and the routing graph.

Optimal Routing System. This entity retrieves the routing graph that was sent by the central platform and calculates the optimal route. It is noted that if the driver selects the optimal route in terms of lowest consumption, the normalised consumption graph is appropriately modified based on the characteristics of the vehicle itself. Apart from that, the Optimal Routing System is responsible for the recalculation of the optimal route when a deviation is detected.

3 Conclusion

In this paper the problem of green and efficient routing is studied. The authors discuss and propose a novel approach that exploits heterogeneous data in order to compose traffic information that focuses on helping the user save on fuel expenses and time on a regular daily basis. The functional architecture of the proposed system is presented in detail. Further research activities include the implementation of the discussed approach and its evaluation through a series of field trials.

Acknowledgement. This work has been performed under the Greek National project CARMA (11ΣΥΝ_10_877), which has received research funding from the Operational Programme "Competitiveness & Entrepreneurship" of the National Strategic Reference Framework NSRF 2007–2013. This paper reflects only the authors' views, and the Operational Programme in not liable for any use that may be made of the information contained therein.

References

1. United States Climate Action Report 2014 (2014), www.state.gov
2. Jovanovic, A., Pamucar, D., Pejcic-Tarle, S.: Green vehicle routing in urban zones - a neuro-fuzzy approach. Expert Syst. Appl. **41**(7), 3189–3203 (2014)
3. Sadek, A., Basha, N.: Self-learning intelligent agents for dynamic traffic routing on transportation networks. In: Minai, A., Braha, D., Bar-Yam, Y. (eds.) Unifying Themes in Complex Systems, pp. 503–510. Springer, Heidelberg (2008)
4. Scania Driver active prediction. http://www.scania.com/products-services/trucks/safety-driver-support/driver-support-systems/active-prediction/
5. HONDA Ecological Drive Assist System. http://world.honda.com/news/2008/4081120Ecological-Drive-Assist-System/
6. Greenroad website. http://greenroad.com
7. Greenmeter application. http://hunter.pairsite.com/greenmeter/
8. Archimate 2.1 Specification. http://www.archimate.nl

Artificial Neural Networks for Traffic Prediction in 4G Networks

Ioannis Loumiotis[✉], Evgenia Adamopoulou, Konstantinos Demestichas, Pavlos Kosmides, and Michael Theologou

National Technical University of Athens, Athens, Greece
i_loumiotis@cn.ntua.gr

Abstract. The increasing proliferation of 4G mobile technologies is expected to satisfy the constantly growing demand for wireless broadband services. However, the high data rates provided by 4G networks at the air interface raise the need for more efficient management of the backhaul resources especially if the backhaul network has been leased by the mobile operator. In the present work, the authors investigate on the backhaul resource allocation problem at the side of the base station (BS) and a novel distributed scheme is proposed that can efficiently forecast the aggregated traffic demand at the BS using artificial neural networks. It is shown that the proposed scheme provides a mean absolute percentage error of about 10 % for the downlink traffic and about 19 % for the uplink traffic.

Keywords: Resource management · Backhaul network · Prediction · Artificial neural networks

1 Introduction

During the last decade, the mobile communications scenery is characterized by the proliferation of new bandwidth consuming applications leading to a growing demand for higher end-user data rates [1]. The advent of 4G network access technologies which offer low latency, seamless mobility and high capacity, aims to meet this demand [2]. In this direction, the convergence of optical and wireless networks has been proposed. Specifically, in [3] the authors propose a passive optical network (xPON) as a backhaul solution for the next generation mobile networks. The high data rates supported by the optical network can potentially satisfy the end-users' needs in the converged scheme.

Traditionally, mobile operators have used empirical methods for network planning which resulted in a flat commitment of the backhaul resources so that possible worst-case scenarios could be satisfied. Further reconsiderations about the allocated resources were sparse and only arose at times of network expansion. Although the results of such methods were acceptable in early networks (2G), packet-based 4G networks require more efficient approaches, which are consistent with the self-organisation [4] trend in communication networks.

© Institute for Computer Sciences, Social Informatics and Telecommunications Engineering 2015
S. Mumtaz et al. (Eds.): WICON 2014, LNICST 146, pp. 141–146, 2015.
DOI: 10.1007/978-3-319-18802-7_20

In the literature, many schemes concerning the forecasting of network traffic are studied. These schemes can be classified into two major categories, namely approaches that propose linear methods [5] and approaches that propose non-linear methods [6, 7]. Specifically, in [5], the authors combine wavelet multiresolution analysis with an autoregressive integrated moving average model to predict the Internet backbone traffic. The proposed scheme results in an absolute relative forecasting error which is less than 15 % for a period of 6 months in the future and 17 % across a year. In [6], the authors propose a back propagation (BP) neural network based on artificial bee colony algorithm and particle swarm optimisation in order to optimise the weight and threshold value of the BP neural network. In [7], the predictability of network traffic using artificial neural networks (ANNs) is studied and the authors showed that a preprocessing of the collected data improves the accuracy of the forecasting model.

In the current paper, the authors propose a new dynamic scheme for the management of the backhaul resources in 4G networks. The proposed scheme is based on the deployment of an Intelligent Agent at the BS, which is responsible for monitoring and collecting the necessary data from its environment, predicting the forthcoming bandwidth requirements and requesting the appropriate resources from the backhaul network in advance. In the current approach, ANNs are employed for the forecasting process. The ability of ANNs to learn a target function by means of a training set consisting of input and output data constitutes them ideal for forecasting problems. Furthermore, the ANNs can accurately capture the nonliniarities of the network traffic, providing them with a comparative advantage over the widely used autoregressive models for the forecasting process. In this direction, the authors investigate two types of ANNs for the implementation of the proposed scheme and compare their performance using real data collected by a BS in Greece.

The rest of the paper is organized as follows. In Sect. 2, the proposed scheme is described in detail and an analysis of the collected data is presented. The experimental results of the ANNs under investigation are provided in Sect. 3. Finally, Sect. 4 concludes the paper.

2   Dynamic Backhaul Resource Allocation

2.1   Intelligent Agent

The proposed scheme is depicted in Fig. 1. The Intelligent Agent is able to monitor the traffic between the BS and the backhaul network and store all the necessary data that are, subsequently, used for the forecasting process. Specifically, the agent monitors, using the Simple Network Management Protocol (SNMP), and stores the aggregated demand of the BS each time period, and based on the collected data, it is able to predict the forthcoming bandwidth demand using ANNs and request the commitment of the necessary backhaul resources from the resource management system of the PON in advance.

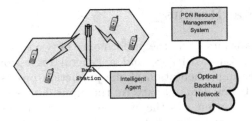

Fig. 1. Graphical representation of the Intelligent Agent.

2.2 Collected Measurements

In order to validate the proposed scheme, a set of training data collected by a fully operational BS located in Athens, capital of Greece that supports HSPA+ connectivity is used. The collected data consist of 3866 hourly averaged measurements and refer to partly sparse data that correspond to the aggregated demand experienced by the BS.

Intuitively, it is reasonable to expect that there are certain periodicities in the traffic pattern, which correspond to the habitual behaviour of the subscribers. Towards this direction, the Fourier transformation is employed. It is noted that because the data were sparsely collected, only a consecutive portion of them is used for the Fourier transformation. The results are depicted in Fig. 2 for the downlink and the uplink traffic. It becomes clear that there is a dominant period of twenty-four hours in the collected data for both the uplink and the downlink case.

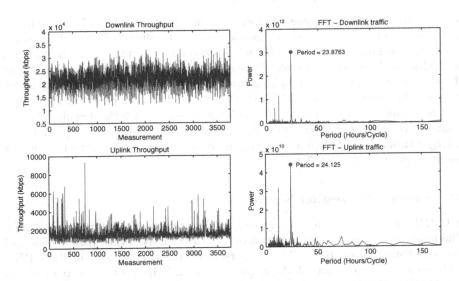

Fig. 2. The downlink and the uplink traffic of the BS and the corresponding fast Fourier transformation.

3   Experimental Results

In this section, the authors study the performance of two types of ANNs, namely a multilayer perceptron (MLP) [8] and a general regression neural network (GRNN) [9], for the implementation of the prediction process. Because of the periodicities in the traffic demand pattern, the input data $\mathbf{x}$ of the ANN is time associated, while the output y is the averaged bandwidth demand. In order to increase the efficiency of the prediction model, special days (e.g. holidays or other special events) that can have an influence on the bandwidth demand are also considered. Hence, the input variable $\mathbf{x}$ is expressed as

$$\mathbf{x} = (D, DT, M, Y, H, SE) \tag{1}$$

where D denotes the day (e.g. Sunday), DT is the sequence number of the day (e.g. 20), M denotes the month, Y is the year, H denotes the hour and SE is a binary variable that designates a special event.

Furthermore, in order to investigate on the impact of the training set size on the performance of the ANNs, three different scenarios are studied. In the first scenario, the training set contains the first 1288 measurements (Sample 1). In the second scenario, the training set contains the first 2576 measurements (Sample 2), while, in the third scenario, all the collected measurements are used (Sample 3). Finally, the authors employ the 10-fold cross validation technique for the validation of the model, whilst the mean absolute percentage error (MAPE) is used to compare the performance of the ANNs.

3.1   Multilayer Perceptron Neural Network

MLP neural networks [8] are the most commonly used ANNs. In the current approach, a 3-layered feedforward neural network is studied. The authors investigate the performance of the MLP with respect to the number of the neurons in the hidden layer. From the results presented in Fig. 3, it becomes evident that the number of neurons in the hidden layer does not have a significant impact on the MAPE, which is about 10.8 %–11.6 % for the downlink case and 24 %–30 % for the uplink case. Furthermore, it can be deduced that for the downlink traffic, a smaller training set (Sample 1) yields better results, while for the uplink traffic a larger training set (Sample 3) seems more appropriate. A discussion on this result is provided in Sect. 3.3.

3.2   General Regression Neural Network

A GRNN [9] is also examined for the implementation of the Intelligent Agent. The most crucial part in the construction of the GRNN is the optimal choice of the smoothing parameter σ. The authors study the performance of the GRNN with respect to the value of the σ parameter and the results are depicted in Fig. 4 where the MAPE of the validation process is depicted with respect to the value of the σ parameter for the cases of downlink and uplink traffic. It is

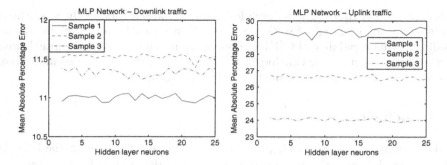

Fig. 3. MAPE of an MLP neural network for the cases of downlink and uplink traffic with respect to the number of the hidden layer neurons.

obvious that a choice of $0.05 < \sigma < 0.3$ provides a MAPE of 9.5 %–10.5 % for the case of downlink traffic. Similarly, for the case of uplink traffic, a choice of $0.05 < \sigma < 0.3$ provides a MAPE of 18 %–26 %. Furthermore, like in the case of the other two ANNs, a smaller training set (Sample 1) provides more accurate results for the downlink traffic, while a larger training set (Sample 3) is required for the uplink traffic.

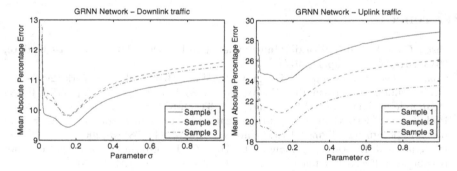

Fig. 4. MAPE of a GRNN for the cases of downlink and uplink traffic with respect to parameter σ.

3.3   Discussion of the Results

According to the above results, it becomes apparent that the uplink traffic is more difficult to be accurately predicted. The main reason for this inefficiency lies in the peaks of the pattern in Fig. 2, which greatly vary from the mean value. As a result, a larger training set is required in the uplink case, in order to improve the forecasting process and make the prediction model more accurate. On the other hand, for the downlink traffic a smaller training set that is characterised by smaller variations around the mean value can provide more accurate results.

Finally, concerning the performance of the ANNs, it may be observed that the GRNN outperforms the MLP, providing significantly better results for both the downlink and the uplink traffic, even for non-optimal selection of the smoothing parameter σ in the range of $0.05 < \sigma < 0.3$. Consequently, based on the above results and the capability of GRNN networks to handle sparse data in real-time environments [9], it can be concluded that they constitute the optimal and safest choice for the implementation of the Intelligent Agent.

4 Conclusion

In the current paper, the problem of backhaul resource allocation at the BS side is investigated. Due to the periodicities in the traffic demand pattern experienced by BSs, the authors propose an ANN approach that can efficiently predict the forthcoming demand. Real data collected from a BS were used and two types of ANNs were investigated under different scenarios concerning the size of the input data. It was found that a GRNN outperforms the MLP neural network providing a mean absolute percentage error of about 10 % for the downlink traffic and about 19 % for the uplink traffic. Finally, it has been observed that a smaller size of input data can yield better results for the case of consistent traffic patterns like the downlink traffic, while a larger size of input data is required for traffic patterns that experience significant fluctuations like the uplink traffic.

References

1. Cisco: Cisco Visual Networking Index: Global Mobile Data Traffic Forecast Update, 2013–2018. White Paper (2014)
2. Cox, C.: An Introduction to LTE, 2nd edn. Wiley-Blackwell, New York (2014)
3. Orphanoudakis, T., Kosmatos, E., Angelopoulos, J., Stavdas, A.: Exploiting PONs for mobile backhaul. IEEE Commun. Mag. **51**(2), S27–S34 (2013)
4. Prehofer, C., Bettstetter, C.: Self-organization in communication networks: principles and design paradigms. IEEE Commun. Mag. **43**(7), 78–85 (2005)
5. Papagiannaki, K., Taft, N., Zhang, Z.L., Diot, C.: Long-term forecasting of internet backbone traffic. IEEE Trans. Neural Netw. **16**(5), 1110–1124 (2005)
6. Zhu, Y., Zhang, G., Qiu, J.: Network traffic prediction based on particle swarm BP neural network. J. Netw. **8**(11), 2685–2691 (2013)
7. Loumiotis, I., et al.: On the predictability of next generation mobile network traffic using artificial neural networks. Int. J. Commun. Syst. (2013). doi:10.1002/dac.2728
8. Haykin, S.: Neural Networks: A Comprehensive Foundation. Prentice Hall, Upper Saddle River (1999)
9. Specht, D.F.: A general regression neural network. IEEE Trans. Neural Netw. **2**(6), 568–576 (1991)

Pros and Cons of Software Standards Use

Michal Žemlička[1]([⊠]) and Jaroslav Král[2,3]

[1] The University of Finance and Administration, Estonská 500,
101 00 Praha 10, Czech Republic
michal.zemlicka@post.cz
[2] Faculty of Mathematics and Physics, Charles University, Malostranské nám. 25,
118 00 Praha 1, Czech Republic
kral@sisal.mff.cuni.cz
[3] Faculty of Informatics, Masaryk University, Botanická 68a,
602 00 Brno, Czech Republic
kral@fi.muni.cz

Abstract. The number of standards and recommendations in IT grows. The requirements on applying them are of growing strength and frequency. Application of the standards is felt as a good solution. We show that if there are too many standards to apply or if they are too big, they can be sources of issues. We also discuss some of such issues like document size and error proneness.

Keywords: IT standards · Complexity of IT standards · Advantages and issues of IT standards use

1 Introduction

Railroad is a technology existing for centuries. It must now and in the future integrate information technologies (IT) existing for decades or even a few years only. The development rates of the technologies and, what is more important, their "cultures" are very different. The lifetime of a typical IT product is several years whereas the lifetime of railway vehicles is often several decades.

Software engineering attitudes and tools develop very quickly. Main software engineering paradigms change at least every ten years. Software development practices, tool, techniques, and overall software engineering knowledge have half lifetime from 3 to 5 years. The railway software system must therefore be able to cooperate with (to integrate) subsystems of various age and philosophy. It is an extremely difficult problem. We will discuss the following issues:

- obstacles of the adaptation and use of software standards in given context;
- consequences of the IT standards size;
- reasons and consequences of the quick changes of standards.

This paper is inspired by the experience of authors being active as software engineers – they take part among others in the development of software for trains.

© Institute for Computer Sciences, Social Informatics and Telecommunications Engineering 2015
S. Mumtaz et al. (Eds.): WICON 2014, LNICST 146, pp. 147–152, 2015.
DOI: 10.1007/978-3-319-18802-7_21

The paper is structured as follows: Sect. 2 discusses significant difference in software and railroad vehicle products lifecycle. Section 3 focuses on differences in the development of standards for various disciplines as well as modern and traditional approach. Recommendations are collected in Sect. 4, conclusions in Sect. 5.

2   Product Lifecycle

The lifecycle of most IT products is quite short. Commercial communication devices (like mobile phones or tablets) are developed, produced, and sold during a few months only. For such devices it is often expected that they will be considered obsolete (or at least not fashionable) before their legal warranty end. The products are manufactured in huge series. Their development costs can be paid by millions of users. Their certification is usually quite fast and simple. It makes the products relatively cheap.

What is substantially more important, is the fact that IT principles (paradigms) do change more frequently – at least with the period of 10 years.

Maintenance of such products is rare (who will give lot of money for repairing an out-of-mode device, if it is possible to get for a bit more money a new fashionable one?), not well supported (vendors want to sell new products, not to support the old ones). Their reliability need not be, from the view of other industrial products, good enough.

The domain of business IT behaves similarly – with the difference that some products are manufactured and supported for several years. But even there after some 5–7 years most devices are obsolete. At least there is a big market push to be so. Buying a product-specific spare part for a three years old device is often a very hard task.

Railroad vehicles are expected to be used for decades. Their development and certification takes sometime years, sometimes a decade. It is therefore reasonable to expect that some spare parts can be reasonably used several decades after their development.

One can say that it is possible to replace entire IT support after several years (when there will be no spare parts). The issue is that the vehicle must be recertified for the use of the new IT – especially if it is used for the vehicle control or safety. The development of new IT support and its recertification can again take years. It can happen that the used device can be retired before its use is certified. It is known as a permanent obsolescence or reorg cycle [1]. The problem with IT is that Reorg Cycle Antipattern is for the very complex software systems unavoidable unless appropriate software architecture is used.

We therefore need either IT products with extremely long lifecycle (what is hard to expect) or standards and protocols with long time support and with quite fast and simple (but still safe and reliable) certification of the replaced software and hardware. Such standards could positively influence interoperability of the vehicles produced by different vendors or for use in different countries – compare the case of the international standard WTB (Wire Train Bus, [2]) and the Austrian vehicles that even "WTB compliant" are interoperable only with other vehicles produced for Austria; most of the communication is running in a specific national extension of the standard.

It generally holds that if something is large and complex then it is likely that there is at least one error. It holds for standards too. As many of them have hundreds of pages and as there are usually multiple standards handling some (usually complex) situation, it is very likely that there is something important stated improperly, or missing. It is, everyone, who wants to follow the standards, must read and adopt hundreds or thousands of pages. There is therefore a lot of space for misunderstanding:

– There can be errors in the standards.
– The standards can be improperly understood.
– The solution could be improperly implemented.

Moreover, there are two additional issues:

– The standards can omit something important necessary for their application. A nice example is how web services should contact each other: using "a well-known address" [3] As a full specification it is at least suboptimal.
– At least some of the standards are now built as good idea instead of as good practice. It means that the standards are first coded and then only implemented. It can lead to discovery that the standard is not implementable and must be changed. If the issue is in design, it can lead to efficiency, security, or safety issues. A chance that once accepted ill-designed standard will be completely redesigned (and within reasonable time – most of the standards are created when they appear to be necessary) is not very high.

Standards designed as a best practice usually describe practically usable solution. Standards designed from scratch are more likely to follow the antipattern "Designed by Committee" [4]. It is, they can contain many good ideas but the ideas may not fit together.

Such issues concern consumer or business IT standards as well as control ones.

3   Consumer vs. Control IT Standards

Although IT can be felt as a single domain, there are three big subdomains having their own technology, business models, and standards:

1. consumer IT,
2. business IT,
3. embedded/control IT.

The first two domains are developing quite quickly and make a lot of money. The third domain must care more about quality, safety, and reliability of the products. The first two domains are slightly more tolerant to failures, if they are not too frequent or too annoying: if the device is responding time to time too slowly, people can usually wait; if the device responds time to time in a strange way, it is possible to recognize it and to enter the request again. It is no good behavior but it is still possible to use the device.

If an improper behavior occurs in a control, it can harm someone's health or even life. It can also cause big loss (e.g. a damage of a production line).

Such conditions cause longer development time and costs (for corresponding functionality). It is moreover often required to handle multiple requests at the same time what requires additional effort and design complexity. In control it is common to use harder testing and often also code proving.

It results in longer development time (often longer than entire lifecycle in the consumer electronic field). The use of control IT is often planned for many years, sometimes even multiple decades. It is therefore reasonable to keep the lifecycle of many control-specific products significantly longer.

There is still one issue: even if a producer is willing to support its products for a long time, situation on the market may cause it to stop the support.

It is therefore reasonable to set up the testing and certification processes so that they can be done within a reasonable time, if necessary. Otherwise there can be many real-world issues.

Application of control and office standards together may lead to logical inconsistences: each group of standards is based on some experience and on some way of thinking. In software development mixing multiple paradigms is a source of many issues. It appears that standards that share many features with software may behave the same way. It is therefore reasonable that any dependencies between standards based on various paradigms should be checked very carefully.

4   Recommendations

Summarizing the above issues and recommendations we get to the following hints:

– Full separation of operating and additional train services and communication.
  – Separation of these two application groups allows reduction of the certification load. If additional services failures cannot influence operating ones, it could be enough to certify just the operating ones. It can speed up the refreshing of the additional services (typically on-board entertainment) on to keep it up-to-date (i.e. compatible with the quickly changing consumer electronics). This part can use business or consumer standards with all its advantages and disadvantages.
  – The control part can be standardized in the way to simplify certification of its parts and to reduce the number of required standards. (The standards that must be fulfilled are described on thousands of pages. It alone makes from their fulfillment a very hard task.)
  – Separation of control and application groups allows the use of different standards and technologies in the mentioned parts. It is, we can use cheaper and faster updated devices and software for the consumer part

and more stable and hardly certified technology for the control part. It will be no more necessary to support quickly developing constructs like web services [5] requiring many quite complicated standards (at least XML [6], WSDL [7], and SOAP [8]); but usually many others (XSchema [9], WS-Addressing [10], WS-Discovery [3], WS-Eventing [11], . . .).

– Properly defined connectivity standards (how the vehicles of various vendors should cooperate).

We have introduced some ideas for improvement of the development in the railway vehicular IT domain. We provided discussion of their advantages and disadvantages.

We suppose that it could be reasonable to return back to the use of standards developed as "best practice". Sometimes the use some standards may be contra-productive: using web technologies and browsers in vehicles may significantly increase their complexity and vulnerability to attacks. Such opportunity is strengthened by the fact that there is a trend to connect vehicles to internet and its services. It could be therefore reasonable to let control physically separated from information and entertainment services although current standards allow providing all these kinds of services at one network at once.

5   Conclusions

The integration of software systems into Railway technologies is an extremely complicated task. The standards to be used are so large that they are very difficult to be applied. The standards are moreover complicated by the fact that they must coordinate the philosophies and processes of two very different domains: computer science and railways ones. The standards are changed frequently. A successful application of the standards in industrial railway projects will need yet an enormous effort and a long time. The overgrown standards must contain many ambiguous or simply erroneous places. It is therefore likely that the first successful system implementing the standards will be used as a de facto standard.

Acknowledgement. The paper was supported by The institutional funding of long-term conceptual development of research organization, the University of Finance and Administration in the 2014.

References

1. Armour, P.: The reorg cycle. Commun. ACM **46**, 19–22 (2003)
2. International Electrotechnical Commission: (IEC 61375-2-1 electronic railway equipment - train communication network (TCN) - wire train bus)
3. Beatty, J., Kakivaya, G., Kemp, D., Kuehnel, T., Lovering, B., Roe, B., John, C.S., Schlimmer, J., Simonnet, G., Walter, D., Weast, J., Yarmosh, Y., Yendluri, P.: Web services dynamic discovery (WS-Discovery) (2005)

4. Brown, W.J., Malveau, R.C., Hays, W., McCormick, I., Mowbray, T.J.: AntiPatterns: Refactoring Software, Architectures, and Projects in Crisis. Wiley, New York (1998)
5. W3 consortium: web of services (2013). http://www.w3.org/standards/webofservices/
6. W3 consortium: extensible markup language (XML) 1.1, 2nd edn. (2006). http://www.w3.org/TR/2006/REC-xml11-20060816
7. W3 consortium: web services description language (WSDL) version 2.0 (2007). http://www.w3.org/TR/#tr_WSDL
8. W3 consortium: SOAP version 1.2 part 1: messaging framework, 2nd edn. (2007). http://www.w3.org/TR/soap12-part1/
9. W3 consortium: XML schema (2012). http://www.w3.org/TR/#tr_XML_Schema
10. W3 consortium: web services addressing 1.0 - core (2006). http://www.w3.org/TR/2006/REC-ws-addr-core-20060509
11. Box, D., Cabrera, L.F., Critchley, C., Curbera, F., Ferguson, D., Graham, S., Hull, D., Kakivaya, G., Lewis, A., Lovering, B., Niblett, P., Orchard, D., Samdarshi, S., Schlimmer, J., Sedukhin, I., Shewchuk, J., Weerawarana, S., Wortendyke, D.: Web services eventing (WS-Eventing) (2006). http://www.w3.org/Submission/2006/SUBM-WS-Eventing-20060315/

Storm: Rateless MDS Erasure Codes

Pedro Moreira da Silva$^{(\boxtimes)}$, Jaime Dias, and Manuel Ricardo

INESC TEC, Faculdade de Engenharia, Universidade do Porto,
Rua Dr. Roberto Frias, 378, 4200-465 Porto, Portugal
{pmms,jdias,mricardo}@inesctec.pt

Abstract. Erasure codes have been employed in a wide range of applications to increase content availability, improve channel reliability, or to reduce downloading time. For several applications, such as P2P file sharing, MDS erasure codes are more suitable as the network is typically the most constrained resource, not the CPU. Rateless MDS erasure codes also enable to adjust encoding and decoding algorithms as function of dynamic variables to maximize erasure coding gains. State-of-the-art MDS erasure codes are either fixed-rate or have practical limitations. We propose Storm erasure codes, a rateless MDS construction of Reed-Solomon codes over the finite field $\mathbb{F}_{p^2}$, where p is a Mersenne prime. To the best of our knowledge, we are the first to propose a rateless construction (n can be increased in steps of k) with $\Theta\left(n \log k\right)$ encoding time complexity and $\min\left\{\Theta\left(n \log n\right), \Theta\left(k \log^2 k\right)\right\}$ upper bound for decoding time complexity. We provide the complexity analysis of encoding and decoding algorithms and evaluate Storm's performance.

1 Introduction

Erasure codes have been employed in a wide range of applications to increase content availability, improve channel reliability, or to reduce downloading time. An erasure code generates a set of n symbols, from a set of k symbols at a rate given by $^k/_n$, so that any subset of $k\left(1 + \epsilon(k)\right)$ is enough to reconstruct the original information, where $\epsilon(k)$ is the erasure coding overhead. Erasure codes are usually classified according to three orthogonal properties: (1) systematicity, (2) rate fixedness, and (3) coding overhead. An erasure code is systematic if the input symbols are embed into output symbols, and non-systematic otherwise. If n is static and need to be known before encoding, the erasure code is fixed-rate. If n can be dynamically increased and the amount of symbols that can be generated does not impose any practical limitation, the erasure code is rateless. Finally, an erasure code is said MDS (Maximum Distance Separable) if any k symbols out of n are enough to reconstruct the original information [$\epsilon(k) = 0$], or non-MDS if additional symbols are required [$\epsilon(k) > 0$]. Non-MDS erasure codes introduce coding overhead for reducing significantly the encoding and decoding time complexities. LT codes [1] and Raptor codes [2] are the most prominent examples of non-MDS erasure codes because they are rateless and asymptotically optimal [$\epsilon(k) \to 0$ as $k \to \infty$], and the latter is able to achieve linear coding and decoding time complexities.

© Institute for Computer Sciences, Social Informatics and Telecommunications Engineering 2015
S. Mumtaz et al. (Eds.): WICON 2014, LNICST 146, pp. 153–158, 2015.
DOI: 10.1007/978-3-319-18802-7_22

For several applications, such as P2P file sharing, MDS erasure codes are more suitable as the network is typically the most constrained resource, not the CPU [3]. Rateless MDS erasure codes also enable to set n as a function of dynamic variables, such as peer participation dynamics and content popularity, to maximize erasure coding gains. Classic Reed-Solomon (RS) codes [4], the most well-known class of MDS codes, are systematic, fixed-rate and have $\Theta\left(nk\right)$ encoding, and $\Theta\left(k^2\right)$ decoding time complexities, which limits their practical application to 255 symbols. ROME [5] is a rateless MDS construction but one with equivalent time complexity and practical limitations. To overcome these limitations, Didier [6] proposed encoding and decoding algorithms for RS codes over the binary finite field $\mathbb{F}_{2^m}$ with, respectively, $\Theta\left(n\log n\right)$ and $\Theta\left(n\log^2 n\right)$ time complexities, where $n = 2^m$ and is fixed to the size of the binary finite field. Soro [7] presented encoding and decoding algorithms with $\Theta\left(n\log n\right)$ time complexity over a finite field $\mathbb{F}_p$, where p is a Fermat prime $\left(p = 2^{2^m} + 1\right)$. Lin [8] extended the work of Didier [6] and proposed $\Theta\left(n\log k\right)$ encoding and $\Theta\left(n\log n\right)$ decoding algorithms over $\mathbb{F}_{2^m}$ with n also fixed to the finite field size.

Despite their merits, [6–8] still create fixed-rate codes because all encoding symbols must be generated at once for achieving such encoding time complexities. Also, their practical use is limited to about 2^{16} symbols: $2^{16} + 1$ is the largest Fermat number prime up to $2^{2048} + 1$; multiplications over binary finite fields are performed using a lookup table, as carry-less multiplication is not as efficient on current CPUs, and large lookup tables severely degrade performance.

We propose a rateless MDS construction of Reed-Solomon codes over the finite field $\mathbb{F}_{p^2}$, where p is a Mersenne prime $\left(p = 2^m - 1\right)$, which we name Storm. Although the construction of RS codes over such field has already been proposed [9], to the best of our knowledge, we are the first to propose a rateless construction (n can be increased in steps of k) with $\Theta\left(n\log k\right)$ encoding time complexity and $\min\left\{\Theta\left(n\log n\right),\Theta\left(k\log^2 k\right)\right\}$ upper bound for decoding time complexity. We provide the complexity analysis of encoding and decoding algorithms and evaluate Storm's performance.

The remaining of this paper is structured as follows. Storm erasure codes are presented in Sect. 2. The performance assessment is conducted on Sect. 3. Section 4 concludes this paper and presents the future work.

2   Storm Erasure Codes

Let $s = (s_0, s_1, \ldots, s_{k-1})$ be a source vector of size k, $s(x) = \sum_{i=0}^{k-1} s_i \cdot x^i$ its associated polynomial, and $e = (e_0, e_1, \ldots, e_{n-1})$ an encode vector of size n. The transformation $(s_0, \ldots, s_{k-1}) \xrightarrow{\mathcal{F}} (e_0, \ldots, e_{n-1})$ over $\mathbb{F}_p^n$, with $e_j = \sum_{i=0}^{k-1} s_i \cdot x_j^i$, can be performed as a multipoint polynomial evaluation at the points (code locators) x_j, i.e., $e_j = s(x_j)$. The inverse transformation, $\mathcal{F}^{-1}$, given that a polynomial of degree $<k$ is uniquely determined by any k unique pairs (x_i, e_i), can be performed as a polynomial interpolation. Let the Lagrange basis polynomial be $L(x) = \prod_{i=0}^{k-1} x - x_i$, the barycentric weights be $w_i = \left(\prod_{j=0,j\neq i}^{k-1} x_i - x_j\right)^{-1}$,

and $s(x)$ is defined by

$$s(x) = \sum_{i=0}^{k-1} e_i \cdot \prod_{j=0,\ j\neq i}^{k-1} \frac{x - x_j}{x_i - x_j} = L(x) \cdot \sum_{i=0}^{k-1} \frac{e_i \cdot w_i}{x - x_i} . \qquad (1)$$

Let $M(k)$ represent the time complexity of multiplying two polynomials of degree $<k$ over a finite field $\mathbb{F}_p$. The encoding and decoding algorithms at arbitrary points takes $M(k) \log k$ time. We refer the reader to [10] for a description of the multipoint evaluation and interpolation algorithms at arbitrary points.

Let r be an nth root of unity of a non-binary finite field $\mathbb{F}_p$, i.e., $n \mid p - 1$ so that $r^n \equiv 1 \mod p$ and $r^i \not\equiv 1 \mod p$, $0 < i < n$. Let r^{z_j} be the power representation of x_j, it follows that $e_j = s(r^{z_j}) = \sum_{i=0}^{k-1} s_i \cdot r^{i \cdot z_j}$. As so, the fast Fourier transform (FFT) is an efficient method for evaluating a polynomial of degree $<n$ at all of the n roots of unity in $\Theta(n \log n)$ time. The FFT can also be used to perform efficient multiplication of polynomials in $\Theta(k \log k)$ time $[M(k) = \Theta(k \log k)]$: multiplying two polynomials of degree $<k$ takes two FFTs of size $2k$ and one inverse FFT (IFFT) of size $2k$.

2.1 Finite Field

The finite field $\mathbb{F}_{p^2}$, where p is a Mersenne prime $(p = 2^m - 1)$, can be constructed as $\mathbb{F}_{p^2} = \{a + b\hat{\imath} \mid a, b \in \mathbb{F}_p\}$, where $\hat{\imath} = \sqrt{-1}$, given that every irreducible quadratic polynomial over $\mathbb{F}_p$ must split over $\mathbb{F}_{p^2}$ [9]. Moreover, in $\mathbb{F}_{p^2}$ there is always a multiplicative group of size 2^{m+1}, as $2^{m+1} \mid p^2 - 1$, whose root, r, is $2^{2^{m-2}} + (-3)^{2^{m-2}}$ [11], and the components of the 8th unity roots are fixed powers of two, only involving additions and circular shifts, enabling efficient radix-8 FFTs. Let $c = 2^{(m-1)/2}$, the set of 8th roots of unity is $\{1, -1, \hat{\imath}, -\hat{\imath}, c(1+\hat{\imath}), c(1-\hat{\imath}), c(-1+\hat{\imath}), c(-1-\hat{\imath})\}$. For improved performance, when performing FFT and IFFT, the unity roots must be pre-calculated. Given that in $\mathbb{F}_{p^2}$ the inverse of a unity root z is its complex conjugate $(z \cdot z^{-1} = z \cdot \overline{z} = 1)$, the set of unity roots can be shared by the FFT and the IFFT. Finally, there is no known file size limit for $\mathbb{F}_{p^2}$, being $2^{57885161} - 1$ the largest known Mersenne prime.

2.2 Mapping

Elements of $\mathbb{F}_{p^2}$ are pairs of $\mathbb{F}_p$ elements. Therefore, we map each m bits of source data into an $\mathbb{F}_p$ element. Yet, 0 has to be distinguished from $2^m - 1$ as $2^m - 1 \equiv 0 \mod p$. A transformation on $\mathbb{F}_{p^2}^{p/2-1}$ has, at most, $p - 2$ elements of $\mathbb{F}_p$ $[2 \cdot (p/2 - 1)]$. Thus, for the set of source elements, s, there is at least one element of $\mathbb{F}_p$, a, that is not in the set: $\forall s \in \mathbb{F}_{p^2}^{p/2-1}, \exists a \in \mathbb{F}_p : a \notin s$. This element can be used to replace $2^m - 1$ in the source data whenever it occurs, before encoding, and do the reverse after decoding. A transformation on $\mathbb{F}_{p^2}^n$, where $n \geq p/2$, can be treated the same way by dividing it in several $\mathbb{F}_{p^2}^{p/2-1}$ transformations.

2.3   Encoding

Let $s = (s_0, s_1, \ldots, s_{k-1})$ be a source vector of size k, and $e = (e_0, e_1, \ldots, e_{n-1})$ an encoded vector of size n. Extending s with $n - k$ zeros to make it of size n, $s = (s_0, s_1, \ldots, s_{k-1}, 0, \ldots, 0)$, enables n symbols to be generated, at once, using a size n FFT (FFT_n). However, this approach does not enable e to increase as needed, at least not efficiently. To make Storm rateless, we developed an encoding algorithm that enables e to increase in steps of k elements. Let r_n be the nth root of unity in $\mathbb{F}_{p^2}$, i.e., $r_n = r^{\frac{2^{m+1}}{n}}$, $\forall n : n \mid 2^{m+1}$. Considering that,

$$e_{j' = g + (^n/k)j} = \sum_{i=0}^{k-1} s_i \cdot r_n^{i(g + (^n/k)j)} = \sum_{i=0}^{k-1} \left(s_i \cdot r_n^{ig} \right) \cdot r_k^{ij} \qquad (2)$$

k innovative symbols can be generated using an FFT_k by applying r_n^{ig} factors to each s_i, $0 \leq i < k$, where $0 \leq g < {}^n/k$. The generation of n symbols can be performed in $^n/k$ independent steps, and has $\Theta\left(n \log k\right)$ time complexity. Let $R_n = \left\{ r_n^0, \ldots, r_n^{n-1} \right\}$ be the set of nth roots of unity. Given that $R_{n/2} \subset R_n$, increasing n has no impact on the previously encoded symbols. A transmission data unit of d symbols, such as an IP packet or a P2P chunk, is composed by the evaluation of d source vectors of size k at a given code locator x_i.

2.4   Decoding

The decoding algorithm consists in five main steps: (1) calculate $L(x)$; (2) compute $L'(x)$; (3) evaluate the barycentric weights as $w_i = L'(x_i)$; (4) compute all $y_i = e_i \cdot w_i$; (5) perform the interpolation. Given that any set of k points is a subset of a set of n roots of unity, the interpolation can be performed either at k arbitrary points or at n unity roots. Let $Y(x) = \sum_{i=0}^{k-1} y_i \cdot x^{z_i}$, and using the Taylor series of $^1/(x - r^{z_i}) = -\sum_j r^{z_i(-j-1)} \cdot x^j$, Lagrange's interpolation formula becomes [7]

$$s(x) = -L(x) \cdot \sum_{i=0}^{k-1} \left(\sum_{j=0}^{n-1} y_i \cdot (r^{z_i})^{-j-1} \cdot x^j \right) = -L(x) \cdot \sum_{j=0}^{n-1} Y(r^{-j-1}) \cdot x^j . \quad (3)$$

Considering $FFT_{2k} \approx 2FFT_k$, step 1) takes $M(k) \log k$ time: $\log k$ stages each taking $3FFT_{2k} \approx 6FFT_k$. Step 2) takes $\Theta(k)$ time. Step 3) takes $M(n)$ time at n roots of unity – $1FFT_n$ – or $M(k) \log k$ time at arbitrary points – $\log k$ stages of $6FFT_k$. Step 4 has also linear time complexity. Step 5), using Eq. 3, takes $M(n)$ time at n unity roots because evaluating $Y(x)$, evaluating $\sum_{j=0}^{n-1} Y(r^{-j-1}) \cdot x^j$, and multiplying the result by $L(x)$ are all performed in $M(n)$ time: $1FFT_n + 3FFT_{2n} \approx 7FFT_n$. At arbitrary points, step 5) takes $M(k) \log k$ time: $\log k$ stages of $6FFT_k$. Therefore, step 5) has $\min \{M(n), M(k) \log k\}$ time complexity. The overall time complexity is $M(k) \log k + \min \{M(n), M(k) \log k\}$. However, in practice, the overall time complexity is just $\min \{M(n), M(k) \log k\}$ because steps 1–3, since they only depend on x_i, are only performed once, while steps 4 and 5 are performed several hundreds or thousands of times for an IP packet or a P2P file sharing chunk. $L(x)$ also depends only on x_i and only needs to be computed once per packet or chunk, thus step 5) can be performed in $5FFT_n$ at n roots of unity. Therefore, the decoding has min $\{M(n), M(k) \log k\}$ practical time complexity: min $\{5FFT_n, \log k \cdot 6FFT_k\}$.

3 Results

Complexity analysis is important to understand how an algorithm behaves as the input grows; still, it hides constant factors that may alter significantly the algorithms real performance. To assess Storm erasure codes performance, and to compare them with Soro's [7] – the only ones with $\Theta(n \log n)$ time complexity that admit any power of two for n and k, $k \le n$ –, we implemented them in C++, and ran them on an Intel Core i5-560M under Ubuntu 13.10 64 bits. For evaluation, the Fermat field is $\mathbb{F}_{2^{16}+1}$ and the Mersenne extension field is $\mathbb{F}_{(2^{31}-1)^2}$. The results shown are for a single thread.

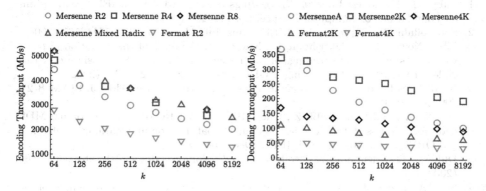

Fig. 1. Encoding throughput for radix-2, radix-4, radix-8, and mixed radix over Mersenne extension field, and for radix-2 over Fermat field [left]. Decoding throughput using interpolation at arbitrary points (A suffix), and at roots of unity with $n = 2k$ and $n = 4k$ over Mersenne and Fermat fields [right].

It can be seen in Fig. 1 the performance improvement provided by radix-8 FFT in comparison to radix-2 FFT. The mixed radix FFT over $\mathbb{F}_{p^2}$, which uses higher radices whenever possible, nearly doubles the throughput provided by radix-2 FFT over Fermat fields. When comparing only radix-2 FFTs, the larger symbols of $\mathbb{F}_{p^2}$ (62 vs 16 bits) improve performance despite multiplications being slightly more expensive (four integer multiplications and two additions). Identical results were obtained for decoding: the throughput for $n = 2k$ over Mersenne extension field, which is about twice the throughput for $n = 4k$ over that field, is slightly greater than twice the throughput for $n = 2k$ over $\mathbb{F}_{2^{16}+1}$. The decoding algorithm at arbitrary points is more advantageous for small values of k and, for k up to 8192 when $n/k > 2$.

4   Conclusions

We presented Storm erasure codes, rateless MDS erasure codes based on RS codes with $\Theta(n \log k)$ encoding time complexity and $\min\{M(n), M(k) \log k\}$ upper bound for decoding time complexity, and assessed their practical performance. These codes are able to saturate a Gigabit interface on a four years old CPU, and are able to provide nearly twice the throughput of equivalent codes defined over Fermat fields. Unlike Fermat fields, there is no known field size limit for $\mathbb{F}_{p^2}$. For evaluation, we only considered a single thread, so we intend to create a parallel multi-core CPU and GPU implementation.

Acknowledgments. This work was supported by Fundação para a Ciência e Tecnologia (FCT) under grant SFRH/BD/69388/2010.

References

1. Luby, M.: LT codes. In: 2002 Proceedings of the 43rd Annual IEEE Symposium on Foundations of Computer Science, pp. 271–280 (2002)
2. Shokrollahi, A.: Raptor codes. IEEE Trans. Inf. Theory **52**(6), 2551–2567 (2006)
3. Liben-Nowell, D., Balakrishnan, H., Karger, D.: Analysis of the evolution of peer-to-peer systems. In: Proceedings of the Twenty-First Annual Symposium on Principles of Distributed Computing, PODC 2002, pp. 233–242. ACM (2002)
4. Reed, I., Solomon, G.: Polynomial codes over certain finite fields. J. SIAM **8**(2), 300–304 (1960)
5. He, N., Xu, Y., Cao, J., Li, Z., Chen, H., Ren, Y.: ROME: rateless online MDS code for wireless data broadcasting. In: Global Telecommunications Conference (GLOBECOM 2010), pp. 1–5. IEEE, December 2010
6. Didier, F.: Efficient erasure decoding of Reed-Solomon codes. CoRR, abs/0901.1886 (2009)
7. Soro, A., Lacan, J.: FNT-based Reed-Solomon erasure codes. In: Proceedings of the 7th IEEE Conference on Consumer Communications and Networking Conference, CCNC 2010, Piscataway, NJ, USA, pp. 466–470. IEEE Press (2010)
8. Lin, S.-J., Chung, W.-H., Han, Y.S.: Fast encoding/decoding algorithms for Reed-Solomon erasure codes. CoRR, abs/1404.3458 (2014)
9. Reed, I., Truong, T., Welch, L.: The fast decoding of Reed-Solomon codes using number theoretic transforms. To The Deep Space Network Progress Report, pp. 42–35 (1976)
10. Crandall, R.E., Pomerance, C.: Prime Numbers: A Computational Perspective, 2nd edn. Springer, New York (2005)
11. Creutzburg, R., Tasche, M.: Parameter determination for complex number-theoretic transforms using cyclotomic polynomials. Math. Comput. **52**(185), 189–200 (1989)

A Framework for Object Classification in Farfield Videos

Insaf Setitra[1,2](✉), Slimane Larabi[1], and Takeaki Uno[3]

[1] Research Center on Scientific and Technical Information Cerist, Algiers, Algeria
isetitra@cerist.dz, slarabi@ustb.dz
[2] University of Science and Technology USTHB, Bab Ezzouar, Algeria
[3] National Institute of Informatics NII, Tokyo, Japan
uno@nii.jp

Abstract. Object classification in videos is an important step in many applications such as abnormal event detection in video surveillance, traffic analysis is urban scenes and behavior control in crowded locations. In this work, propose a framework for moving object classification in farfield videos. Much works have been dedicated to accomplish this task. We overview existing works and combine several techniques to implement a real time object classifier with offline training phase. We follow three main steps to classify objects in steady background videos : background subtraction, object tracking and classification. We measure accuracy of our classifier by experiments done using the PETS 2009 dataset.

Keywords: Background subtraction · Feature extraction · Object tracking · Object classification · Video analysis

1 Introduction

Over the last decades, much work has been dedicated to object recognition in images and videos. This research area is concerned with 3 main problems: Object Categorization, object recognition and object detection [1]. Object classification is more assimilated to the first problem gender i.e. Object categorization. Among manifold conditions of classification robustness, three fundamental necessities for an object classifier in videos must be verified: [2,3] (1) performing under real-time constraints; (2) being robust to illumination changes and shadow effects and efficient in both indoor and outdoor environments; and (3) solving a multiclass problem [4–6]. In performing under real-time constraints, the current systems have significant limitations since classification may be a result of several steps including movement segmentation, feature extraction and classification for which, each step is time consuming. More limited systems in time saving perform classification after getting entire tracks of objects which leads to a non-real time processing [3,7]. Current systems suffer also of condition changes which affects both movement segmentation and classification. In this work, we aim to solve several of concerns depicted bellow by developing a complete framework

© Institute for Computer Sciences, Social Informatics and Telecommunications Engineering 2015
S. Mumtaz et al. (Eds.): WICON 2014, LNICST 146, pp. 159–166, 2015.
DOI: 10.1007/978-3-319-18802-7_23

for object classification. We contribute on developing a robust non-parametric tracker which processes tracking in real time while using pairs of consecutive frames to perform tracking. We conduct several experiments using our framework and discuss results at each step. The remaining of the paper is organized as follows: We first, overview in Sect. 2 state of the art on object classification. Section 3 is concerned with describing our framework, Sect. 4 presents our results and we conclude in Sect. 5 with our accomplishments and future works.

2   State of the Art

The prevalent research topics which have potential for improving object classification in videos are: Background subtraction, feature extraction, feature selection, classification and evaluation/benchmarking. The core problem of background subtraction is to identify the set of pixels that are significantly different between the last image of the sequence and the previous ones. Background subtraction algorithms can be recursive and non-recursive techniques. Recursive techniques use a unique value to account for background while non-recursive techniques use an entire buffer to represent it [8]. Recursive techniques are most often used because of their fast processing time and the non-need for defining a buffer size. Feature extraction refers to the process of extracting meaningful features that best represent the object. Because of low resolution of videos, perspective distortion and occlusion, feature selection is a tricky task. Features can be instance features and temporal features [7]. They can be scene dependent and scene independent [2]. Features are extracted to be used in tracking and/or classification. Algorithms of tracking are processed in several steps; the prediction of the object position with respect to its previous position and movement using a model; the mapping of the predicted position to the actual one; and the update of the model parameters. Tracking algorithms have two distinct components: the prediction phase and the matching phase. The first component contains particularly algorithms based on the prediction of the next position of the object based on its motion parameters [9–12]. The second component focuses on mapping elements by measuring minimum distance between them. Approaches aim to locate a 2D or 3D model of the target [13,14] and/or match primitives such as color or edges [15,16]. classification predicts the class membership of an unknown object based on previous observations. In [17] authors use 3 classifiers SVDD (Support Vector Data Descriptor) SVM (Support vector machine) with one vs. all strategy and NN (Neural Network) based classifiers to classify human and vehicles, [3] use a Maximum A posteriori problem of tracked objects to classify Human (including groups of people) and Vehicles, [18] combines a discriminative Support vector machine classifier with one vs. all strategy with an RBF (radial basis kernel) with a generative Gaussian Mixture Distribution classifier. The classification was improved since it combines strength of both classifiers, [2] used an SVM with an RBF kernel and one vs. all strategy, a feed backpropagation, a Bayesian network, a Decision tree, and a K Nearest Neighbor to compare classification of each classifier. Authors classified 5 classes: human, body organs, bag, group of people and clutter, [19] used an SVM to classify bicycle, car, motorbike and people, [20] used a novel Contextualized SVM with a Kernel function based on χ^2 distance for each feature, kernels are then combined to an average kernel for kernelized Context-SVM. Authors classified over 15 classes but using a set of images not videos, in [21] Adaboost was used to classify Vehicle and people. State of the art on classification of objects in videos usually do not classify more than 6 classes.

3 Our Framework

Our framework consists of three main modules: background subtraction module, tracking module and classification module. We explain each module in the following sub-sections.

3.1 Background Subtraction

We use Gaussian mixture model [22] for background subtraction where we model each background pixel as a mixture of Gaussian. In the frame F_t at time t, the probability of having the pixel X_t at time $t+1$ (the background model of the pixel) is given by:

$$p(X_t) = \sum_{i=1}^{N_k} w_i^t \eta(X_t, \mu_i^t, \Sigma_i^t) \qquad (1)$$

where $X^t = X_1; X_2..X_t$ is the history of the pixel X at time t, w_i^t is the weight of the gaussian at time t, μ_i^t and Σ_i^t are the mean and the covariance matrix of the gaussian i at time t respectively and η is a Gaussian probability density function. Initialization of the model occurs at some frames after the first frame of the sequence. The pixel X_t belongs to one of the k background distributions if it falls within 2.5 standard deviations of a distribution. If none of the K distributions match the current pixel value, the least probable distribution is replaced with a distribution with the current value as its mean value, an initially high variance, and low prior weight and weights of other distributions are adjusted. If the pixel X falls under 2.5 standard deviation of one of the k distributions then the latter is updated as follows:

$$\mu_t = (1 - \rho)\mu_{t-1} + \rho X_t \qquad (2)$$

$$\sigma_t^2 = (1 - \rho)\sigma_{t-1}^2 + \rho(X_t - \mu_t)^T(X_t - \mu_t) \qquad (3)$$

where $\rho = \alpha\eta(X_t \mid \mu_k, \sigma_k)$ is the learning factor for adapting current distributions.

3.2 Object Tracking

We use only the second component defined defined in Sect. 2 to track objects in the scene, i.e. we use primitive features to make correspondence between objects in the different frames of the video. We thus avoid computing model parameters and gain time. Features used for tracking are: Centroid C, area A, gray level histogram H and bounding box B. We use each feature separately and then combine all features as follow: Combinations for the tracking are then: each feature alone, each two features together, each three features together and all four features grouped. Number of combinations is then:

$$Combinations = C_4^1 + C_4^2 + C_4^3 + C_4^4 \qquad (4)$$

where C_n^p is the number of possible combinations of p over n and

$$C_n^p = \frac{n!}{p!(n-p)!} \qquad (5)$$

To form the possible 12 combinations we use a probability tree for each combination, we give the example of C_4^2 in what follows and process with the same rational for all combinations:

$$
\begin{array}{ccc}
C & A & H \\
\overset{\uparrow}{\frown} & \frown & | \\
A\ H\ B & H\ B & B
\end{array}
$$

In this case, the tracking will be done using the couple: (C,A), (C,H), (C,B), (A,H), (A,B), (H,B). To explain our tracker, let us take a tracking using only the centroid of objects. The centroid is a two dimensional vector representing the position of an object in the scene. Let O_1: be Object 1 detected in frame 1, O_2 the Object 2 in frame 2 and O_3 the Object 3 detected in the frame 2. O_1 is O_2 (with a certain displacement) if the distance between C_1 (centroid of O_1) and C_2 (centroid of O_2) is minimum. In this case, the distance between C_1 and C_2 is less than the distance between C_1 and C_3 (centroid of O_3). Distance between two centroids is computed using the Euclidean distance:

$$Dist(C_1, C_2) = \sqrt{(x_1 - x_2)^2 + (y_1 - y_2)^2)} \qquad (6)$$

where C_1 is represented by its Euclidean vector $\binom{x_1}{y_1}$ and C_2 is represented by its Euclidian vector $\binom{x_2}{y_2}$.

When the scene contains several objects, the correspondence is given to the vector which gives the minimum distance. We use the tracking primarily to label objects tracked in the video since the database is not already labeled. Once we have all objects tracked, we label only one object of each class and the class label is automatically propagated to the whole set of the same object. We do this by putting tracks of each object in a separate folder. Tracking is also useful for having movement features of objects such as velocity and time derivative moments [7].

3.3   Object Classification

We choose in our experiments a basic classifier based on modeling; the Quadratic Bayes. Quadratic Bayes classifier makes an assumption that the data distribution is normal, hence each class follows a multivariate normal distribution:

$$P(x|\omega_j) = \frac{1}{(2\pi)^{\frac{d}{2}} |\Sigma_j|^{\frac{1}{2}}} \exp\left(-\frac{1}{2}(x - \mu_j)^T \Sigma_j^{-1}(x - \mu_j)\right) \qquad (7)$$

where x is the feature vector, Σ_j and μ_j are the covariance matrix and the mean vector of class data ω_j and d is the feature vector dimension.

The learning phase then use the training data to estimate for each class, the mean and covariance matrix. These parameters will then be used to classify test examples using the Bayes rule by estimating the posterior probabilities:

$$P(\omega_j|x) = \frac{P(x|\omega_j)P(\omega_j)}{P(x)} \tag{8}$$

where $P(\omega_j)$ is the prior probability of class ω_j and $p(x)$ is probability of having the feature x and is defined by:

$$p(x) = \sum_{j=1}^{C} P(x|\omega_j)P(\omega_j) \tag{9}$$

where C is the number of classes of the problem.

The decision about class membership is taken by looking for the maximum probability value among discriminant functions associated with each class.

4   Results and Discussions

This section provides experimental results and analysis for the classification accuracy. Background subtraction was implemented in C++ and using the open library OpenCv, tracking and classification were both implemented using matlab 2010. First, we divide features into groups and evaluate the classification accuracy achieved by each classifier for each group. Data are comprised of videos from Pets 2009 dataset. The class variable can have one of 8 class values, which are distributed as shown in Fig. 1.a.

Data are divided into two datasets, where the first dataset, comprising 50 % of each class is used in the training phase, and the second dataset, is used for evaluating the classification accuracies.

Accuracy of background subtraction is measured visually as the Pets 2009 do not contain any ground truth. Best results of background subtraction are given

Class	Abbreviation	Number of images
human	H	30
group of human	GOH	84
small vehicle	SV	4
big vehicle	BV	17
human and car	HC	10
small human	SH	100
part of a vehicle	PV	13
other	Other	2045
Total	-	2303

(a)

	H	GOH	SV	BV	Other	HC	SH	PV
H	12	0	2	0	0	0	0	1
GOH	20	3	6	0	0	13	0	0
SV	0	0	2	0	0	0	0	0
BV	0	3	0	5	0	0	0	0
Other	28	35	4	1	906	17	0	20
HC	0	2	3	0	0	0	0	0
SH	0	0	0	0	49	0	0	1
PV	5	0	0	0	1	0	0	0

(b)

Fig. 1. Data for classification and classification results, (a): Classes used, (b): Confusion matrix

using the parameters:Number of Gaussians = 3, Background threshold = 0.2, Standard deviation threshold = 0.75, Variance initialization = 30, Weight initialization = 1. As results of background subtraction are sometimes unsatisfying where parts of an abject or several objects are sometimes split and/or merged, we use some morphological operators to group split parts [8], merged objects are detected in the classification phase to be either a group of people if the two objects are human and the class other in all remaining cases. Operations used are a closing described in [23] and filling holes.

In the tracking step, an object i_j in a frame is the $j^t h$ object of the frame i. The following example explains better the tracking process:

Let an object 1 of frame 1 be represented by 1_1. Practically, the object 1_1 is a box of dimension $n \times m$ including the object where n is the height of the bounding box which is smaller than the height of the frame, and m is the width of the bounding box which is smaller than the width of the frame. If the object 1_1 corresponds to the object 2_1 (first object of the second frame) then both objects (images) are stored in the same folder called 1_1 (the tracking of the first object which appeared first in the frame 1). If the distance between 1_1 and all objects of a new frame is above a certain threshold, which means that 1_1 is probably not any of the objects detected in the new frame, then 1_1 is considered disappearing from the scene and its tracking is stopped. If a new object say 5_7 appears the first time in the frame 5 then a new folder with the name 5_7 (tracking of the $7^t h$ object of image 5 which appeared for the first time in the image 5) for that object is created and will contain all tracks of it.

In tracking features separately, best results were obtained by tracking the centroid. Experiments showed also that the tracking fails for almost all features when we depict a split or a merge. Tracking using histogram was the worst tracking since no a priori knowledge about the position of objects is known. Histogram combined to centroid gives better results than histogram alone however, accuracy is smaller than the one of tracking with only centroid because histogram feature has the same weight as the centroid feature. Combinations of features explained in Sect. 3.2 and using a majority vote did not improve the results and in many cases downgraded them. In this case adding weight or a regarding features would improve results.

Classification accuracy is measured using the confusion matrix. Figure 1.b presents classification accuracy using confusion matrix. As shown therein, accuracy is not perfect, this is due to the fact that the Quadratic Bayes classifier is not an exact classifier even in the since it adopts a probability model to model classes and then based on this model classify observations. Also, since videos contain much clutter and unnecessary objects like swaying cords, and resemblance between classes and clutter is very present, classification is confused. Another bad point is the unbalanced number of classes where the class "other" is the predominant with a number of tracks of 2045.

5   Conclusion

We presented in this work our framework for object classification in farfield videos. Videos used are considered farfield because they are put outdoor and in a certain distance from region of interest. Results are encouraging, and allow us to better focus on improvements of our classifier. We also proposed a real time non-parametric tracker which use simple feature to make correspondence between objects in a scene. We aim in a further work to focus on the classification phase by choosing more suitable features scene independent and scale invariant, and integrating motion features and use more sophisticated classifiers such as SVM and Neural Network classifiers.

References

1. Gouet-Brunet, V., Lameyre, B.: Object recognition and segmentation in videos by connecting heterogeneous visual features. Comput. Vis. Image Underst. **111**(1), 86–109 (2008)
2. Gurwicz, Y., Yehezkel, R., Lachover, B.: Multiclass object classification for real-time video surveillance systems. Pattern Recognit. Lett. **32**(6), 805–815 (2011)
3. Chen, L., Feris, R., Zhai, Y., Brown, L., Hampapur, A.: An integrated system for moving object classification in surveillance videos. In: IEEE Fifth International Conference on Advanced Video and Signal Based Surveillance, AVSS 2008, pp. 52–59, Sept 2008
4. Moeslund, T.B., Hilton, A., Krger, V.: A survey of advances in vision-based human motion capture and analysis. Comput. Vis. Image Underst. **104**(23), 90–126 (2006). Special Issue on Modeling People: vision-based understanding of a persons shape, appearance, movement and behaviour
5. Hu, W., Tan, T., Wang, L., Mayban, S.: A survey on visual surveillance of object motion and behaviors. IEEE Trans. Syst. Man Cybern. Part C: Appl. Rev. **34**(3), 334–352 (2004)
6. Lew, M.S., Sebe, N., Djeraba, C., Jain, R.: Content-based multimedia information retrieval: state of the art and challenges. ACM Trans. Multimed. Comput. Commun. Appl. **2**(1), 1–19 (2006)
7. Bose, B., Grimson, E.: Improving object classification in far-field video. In: Proceedings of the 2004 IEEE Computer Society Conference on Computer Vision and Pattern Recognition, CVPR 2004, vol. 2, pp. II-673–II-680, June 2004
8. Setitra, I., Larabi, S.: Background subtraction algorithms with post processing a review. In: 2014 22nd International Conference on Pattern Recognition (ICPR), Aug 2014
9. Kalman, R.E.: A new approach to linear filtering and prediction problems. ASME J. Basic Eng. **82**, 35–45 (1960)
10. Jazwinski, A.H.: Stochastic Processes and Filtering Theory. Mathematics in science and engineering, vol. 64. Academic Press, New York (1970)
11. Arulampalam, M.S., Maskell, S., Gordon, N.: A tutorial on particle filters for online nonlinear/non-gaussian bayesian tracking. IEEE Trans. Signal Process. **50**, 174–188 (2002)
12. Forsyth, D.A., Ponce, J.: Computer Vision: A Modern Approach. Prentice Hall Professional Technical Reference, Upper Saddle River (2002)
13. Lowe, D.G.: Robust model-based motion tracking through the integration of search and estimation. Int. J. Comput. Vision **8**(2), 113–122 (1992)
14. Drummond, T., Cipolla, R.: Real-time tracking of complex structures with on-line camera calibration. Image Vis. Comput. **20**(56), 427–433 (2002)

15. Comaniciu, D., Ramesh, V., Meer, P.: Real-time tracking of non-rigid objects using mean shift. In: Proceedings of the IEEE Conference on Computer Vision and Pattern Recognition, vol. 2, pp. 142–149 (2000)
16. Jepson, A.D., Fleet, D.J., El-Maraghi, T.F.: Robust online appearance models for visual tracking. IEEE Trans. Pattern Anal. Mach. Intell. **25**(10), 1296–1311 (2003)
17. Hota, R.N., Venkoparao, V., Rajagopal, A.: Shape based object classification for automated video surveillance with feature selection. In: Proceedings of the 10th International Conference on Information Technology, ICIT 2007, pp. 97–99. IEEE Computer Society, Washington (2007)
18. Deselaers, T., Heigold, G., Ney, H.: Object classification by fusing svms and gaussian mixtures. Pattern Recogn. **43**(7), 2476–2484 (2010)
19. Han, S., Vasconcelos, N.: Complex discriminant features for object classification. In: 15th IEEE International Conference on Image Processing, ICIP 2008, pp. 1700–1703, Oct 2008
20. Song, Z., Chen, Q., Huang, Z., Hua, Y., Yan, S.: Contextualizing object detection and classification. In: 2011 IEEE Conference on Computer Vision and Pattern Recognition (CVPR), pp. 1585–1592, June 2011
21. Zhang, Z., Li, M., Huang, K., Tan, T.: Boosting local feature descriptors for automatic objects classification in traffic scene surveillance. In: 19th International Conference on Pattern Recognition, ICPR 2008, pp. 1–4, Dec 2008
22. Stauffer, C., Grimson, W.E.L.: Learning patterns of activity using real-time tracking. IEEE Trans. Pattern Anal. Mach. Intell. **22**(8), 747–757 (2000)
23. Bradski, G., Kaehler, A.: Learning OpenCV: Computer Vision with the OpenCV Library. O'Reilly Media, Sebastopol (2008)

Positioning-Protocol-Based Digital Signature

Qingshui Xue[1(✉)], Fengying Li[2], and Zhenfu Cao[1]

[1] Department of Computer Science and Engineering,
Shanghai Jiao Tong University, Shanghai 200240, China
{xue-qsh,zfcao}@cs.sjtu.edu.cn
[2] School of Continuous Education,
Shanghai Jiao Tong University, Shanghai 201101, China
fyli@sjtu.edu.cn

Abstract. Position-based cryptography has attracted many researchers' attention. In mobile Internet, there are lots of position-based security applications. In the paper, one new conception, positioning-protocol-based digital signature is proposed. Based on a secure positioning protocol, one model of positioning-protocol-based digital signature is proposed. In the model, the positioning protocol is bound to digital signature tightly, not loosely. Further, we propose one concrete positioning-protocol-based digital signature scheme and its correctness is proved.

Keywords: Positioning protocol · Digital signature · Model · Scheme

1 Introduction

In the setting of mobile Internet, position services and position-binding security applications become one key requirement, especially the latter. Position services include position inquiring, secure positioning and so forth. Position inquiring consists of inquiring your own position and positioning of other entities. The technology of inquiring your own position has Global Positioning System (GPS) and other satellite service systems. The technology of positioning of other entities has radar and so on [2–6]. As we all know, the positioning of other entities is a more challenging one. Position-binding security applications such as position-based encryption and position-based signature and authentication are increasingly necessary for us. For example, when one mobile user sends messages to one specific position, which is one either physical or logical address (such as Internet Protocol address), it is desirable for us that only the user who is at that address can receive and decrypt messages encrypted. Even if other mobile users at that position receive messages, but they can't decrypt them. Or the specified receiver at that position due to some reasons temporarily leaves his/her address, it will be unable to receive or decrypt messages any more. In addition, if the

Q. Xue — The paper is supported by NSFC under Grant No. 61170227, Ministry of Education Fund under Grant No. 14YJA880033, and Shanghai Projects under Grant No. 2013BTQ001, XZ201301 and 2013001.

© Institute for Computer Sciences, Social Informatics and Telecommunications Engineering 2015
S. Mumtaz et al. (Eds.): WICON 2014, LNICST 146, pp. 167–172, 2015.
DOI: 10.1007/978-3-319-18802-7_24

original receiver at that place moves to another place, he/she maybe hope he/she can receive and decrypt messages at the new place. Take one application about position-based signature and authentication as an example. One mobile or fixed user signs messages at one place and sends them to another mobile user. The receiver can receive the signed message and verify whether or not received messages are truly signed where the signer signed on them. Even if the signer moves to another address, it will not affect the receiving and verifying of signed messages.

Currently, the research on position-based cryptography focuses on secure positioning, about which some works had been proposed [1]. These positioning protocols are based on one-dimension, two-dimension or three-dimension spaces, including traditional wireless network settings [1], as well as the quantum setting [7–9]. It seems to us that position-based cryptography should integrate secure positioning with cryptographic primitives. If only or too much concentrating on positioning protocols, perhaps we will be far away from position-based cryptography. In other words, nowadays positioning is bound loosely with related security applications, not tightly, as results in slow progresses of position-based cryptography and applications. Relying on the thoughts, in the paper, our main contributions are as follows.

(1) We propose one model of positioning-protocol-based digital signature. First, positioning-protocol-based digital signature is one kind of digital signature, but a novel one. The definition is given and its model is constructed.
(2) To realize the kind of digital signature, one positioning-protocol-based digital signature scheme is proposed and its correctness is proved as well.

We will organize the rest of the paper as follows. In Sect. 2, we will introduce the function of positioning and one secure positioning protocol. In Sect. 3, one model and definition of positioning-protocol-based digital signature are constructed. We will propose one positioning-protocol-based digital signature scheme in Sect. 4. The correctness of the scheme is proved in Sect. 5. Finally, the conclusion is given.

2 Positioning Protocols

2.1 Function of Positioning Protocols

The goal of positioning protocols is to check whether one position claimer is really at the position claimed by it. Generally speaking, in the positioning protocol, there are at least two participants including position claimers (prover) and verifiers, where the verifiers may be treated as position infrastructure. According to aims of the positioning, there are two kinds of positioning protocols, i.e., your own position positioning protocols and others' positions positioning protocols. As of now, lots of work on your own position positioning protocols have been done [2–6]. Nevertheless, the research on others' position positioning protocols is much less and there are still many open questions to solve. In our model and scheme, we will make use of the former positioning protocols.

2.2   One Secure Positioning Protocol

In the section, we will review N. Chandran et al.'s secure positioning protocol in 3-dimension spaces [1], which can be used in mobile Internet. In the protocol, 4 verifiers denoted by $V_1, V_2, \ldots, V_4$, which can output string X_i, are used. The prover claims his/her position which is enclosed in the tetrahedron defined by the 4 verifiers. Let $t_1, \ldots \ldots, t_4$ be the time taken for radio waves to arrive at the point P from verifier $V_1, V_2, \ldots, V_4$ respectively. When we say that $V_1, V_2, \ldots, V_4$ broadcast messages such that they "meet" at P, we mean that they broadcast the messages at time $T - t_1, T - t_2, T - t_3$ and $T - t_4$ respectively so that at time T all the messages are at position P in space. The protocol uses a pseudorandom generator namely an $\varepsilon-$ secure $PRG : \{0, 1\}^n \times \{0, 1\}^m \rightarrow \{0, 1\}^m$. They select the parameters such that $\varepsilon + 2^{-m}$ is negligible in the security parameters. X_i denotes a string chosen randomly from a reverse block entropy source. The protocol is stated as follows:

Step 1. $V_1, \ldots, V_3$ and V_4 pick keys $K_1, \ldots, K_3$ and K_4 selected randomly from $\{0, 1\}^m$ and broadcast them through their private channels.
Step 2. For the sake of enabling the device at P to compute K_i for $1 \leq i \leq 4$, the verifiers do as follows. V_1 broadcasts K_1 at time $T - t_1.V_2$ broadcasts X_1 at time $T - t_2$ and meanwhile broadcasts $K_2' = PRG(X_1, K_1) \oplus K_2$. Similarly, at time $T - t_3$, V_3 broadcasts $(X_2, K_3' = PRG(X_2, K_2) \oplus K_3)$, and V_4 broadcasts $(X_3, K_4' = PRG(X_3, K_3) \oplus K_4)$ at time $T - t_4$.
Step 3. At time T, the prover at position P calculates messages $K_{i+1} = PRG(X_i, K_i) \oplus K_{i+1}'$ for $1 \leq i \leq 3$. Then it sends K_4 to all verifiers.
Step 4. All verifiers check that the string K_4 is received at time $(T + t_i)$ and that it equals K_4 that they pre-picked. If the verifications hold, the position claim of the prover is accepted and it is supposed to be indeed at position P. Otherwise, the position claim is invalid.

3   The Model of Positioning-Protocol-Based Digital Signature

3.1   The Basic Idea

In the model, there are three parties including the sender, the receiver and position infrastructure (PI). The sender takes responsibility of confirmation of position of his own and generation of digital signature of messages; the receiver is responsible for the verification of positioning-protocol-based digital signature. As far as the sender is concerned, it is unnecessary for him/her to have the knowledge of the receiver's position. As for the receiver, he/she need check that the positioning-protocol-based digital signature was generated by the sender at the sender's valid position. It should be noted that here we use "valid", not "real", since the receiver only cares the fact that the sender or signer was at his/her claimed position when the sender signs the message. That's to say, if the sender finishes his/her signing and moves to another position, the receiver doesn't care it. PI which is one trusted third party, is used to verify or provide services of positions.

3.2   Definition

Positioning-Protocol-Based Digital Signature. Simply speaking, the kind of digital signature combines traditional digital signature and positioning protocols as one single scheme. It is mainly composed of two modules of sender signing and receiver verifying. In the course of sender signing, the sender first confirms the position of his/her own by running positioning protocols with PI and gets the corresponding signing private key. By using the signing private key, the sender can sign one message only once and then sends the signature to the receiver. At the side of the receiver, the receiver uses the sender's identity and position to verify the signature.

In the model, the positioning-protocol-based digital signature consists of three primitives: Initialization, PropSign and PropVerify.

Initialization. PI takes as input secure parameter and outputs system master key and public parameter, meanwhile, the system distributes users' identities for users.

PropSign. When the sender wants to sign one message based on position, he/she first sends his/her identity and claimed position to PI and runs the positioning protocol with PI. If and only if PI can confirm the validity of the sender's identity and claimed position, as means the sender is really at the claimed position, the sender can obtain his/her signing private key to sign one message for only once. The sender can sign the message by any ID-based or attribute-based signing algorithm using the signing private key.

PropVerify. After receiving the signature from the sender, the receiver takes as input the identity and position of the sender to run the signature verification algorithm. If the signature passes the verification, as means that the message had been signed by the sender at the position, it is valid; otherwise, the receiver will reject it.

3.3   Security Properties of Positioning-Protocol-Based Digital Signature

(1) Positioning Protocol Binding. In the course of PropSign, the sender is requested to confirm the position of his/her own by communicating with PI. If and only if the sender is indeed at his/her claimed position, he/she is able to acquire his/her signing private key, which will be used to sign one message for only once. That's to say, if the sender wants to sign another message, he/she has to run the positioning protocol with PI once again. During the course of PropVerify, the model's goal is to guarantee that the receiver can confirm the message received is signed by the sender at the claimed position. If the sender finishes signing one message and moved to another place, the receiver will not care it.

4   One Positioning-Protocol-Based Digital Signature Scheme

The scheme mainly has three kinds of participants: the sender, the receiver and PI. PI will utilize the secure positioning protocol mentioned in Sect. 2.2 to provide services of position authentication for the sender. In addition, PI serves as GPS for positioning users' own positions. The scheme consists of three primitives of Initialization, PropSign and PropVerify.

4.1   Initialization

PI takes as input secure parameter 1^k and outputs system master key mk and public parameter pp. Meanwhile the system distributes user identity ID_i for user i.

4.2   PropSign

The sender randomly chooses one nonce n_{sender} and sends n_{sender}, his/her identity ID_{sender} and position Pos_{sender} to PI. PI runs the secure positioning protocol with the sender and checks that the sender is at the claimed position Pos_{sender}. If the sender is really at the position, PI generates one signing private key sk corresponding to n_{sender}, ID_{sender}, and Pos_{sender}. Meanwhile, PI stores the tuple $(sk, n_{sender}, ID_{sender}, Pos_{sender})$ in his database and sends sk to the sender by secure channel. Then the sender can use sk to sign the message m for only once and generates the signature s. The sender sends $(m, s, pp, ID_{sender}, Pos_{sender})$ to the receiver.

4.3   PropVerify

After receiving the signature $(m, s, pp, ID_{sender}, Pos_{sender})$, the receiver uses ID_{sender} and Pos_{sender} to check that s is one valid signature on message m. If yes, the receiver can be certain that the message m is from the sender and is signed at the position Pos_{sender} by the sender; otherwise, the receiver rejects it.

5   Correctness of Above Scheme

Theorem 1. If the scheme runs according to the phases above, the receiver can confirm that the message received is from the sender and is signed at the sender's claimed position.

Proof. In the course of PropSign, the sender first selects one nonce n_{sender} at random and sends n_{sender}, his/her identity ID_{sender} and position Pos_{sender} to PI. After PI runs secure positioning protocols with the sender, If the sender is really at the position Pos_{sender}, PI generates one signing private key corresponding to n_{sender}, ID_{sender}, and Pos_{sender}, and sends it to the sender by secure channel. The sender uses it to sign the message m to generate the signature s. At the side of the receiver, the receiver can verify the validity of $(m, s, pp, ID_{sender}, Pos_{sender})$ accordingly.

6 Conclusions

In the paper, according to security requirements of mobile Internet, we construct a model of positioning-protocol-based digital signature. Its definition, security properties and construction are given. Meanwhile, we propose one positioning-protocol-based digital signature scheme. We will further improve relevant models and schemes, as well as positioning-protocol-based hybrid encryption. It is believed by us that the research on positioning-protocol-based cryptographic models or schemes will become one focus in the setting of mobile Internet.

References

1. Chandran, N., Goyal, V., Moriarty, R., Ostrovsky, R.: Position based cryptography. In: Halevi, S. (ed.) CRYPTO 2009. LNCS, vol. 5677, pp. 391–407. Springer, Heidelberg (2009)
2. Sastry, N., Shankar, U., Wagner, D.: Secure verification of location claims. In: Proceedings of the 2003 ACM Workshop on Wireless Security, WiSe 2003, pp. 1–10 (2003)
3. Singelee, D., Preneel, B.: Location verification using secure distance bounding protocols. In: IEEE Conference on Mobile Adhoc and Sensor Systems Conference (2005)
4. Bussard, L.: Trust establishment protocols for communicating devices. Ph.D. thesis, Eurecom-ENST (2004)
5. Capkun, S., Hubaux, J.P.: Secure positioning of wireless devices with application to sensor networks. In: IEEE INFOCOM, pp. 1917–1928 (2005)
6. Capkun, S., Cagalj, M., Srivastava, M.: Secure localization with hidden and mobile base stations. In: IEEE INFOCOM (2006)
7. Buhrman, H., Chandran, N., Fehr, S., Gelles, R., Goyal, V., Ostrovsky, R., Schaffner, C.: Position-based quantum cryptography: impossibility and constructions. In: Rogaway, P. (ed.) CRYPTO 2011. LNCS, vol. 6841, pp. 429–446. Springer, Heidelberg (2011)
8. Buhrman, H., Chandran, N., Fehr, S., Gelles, R., Goyal, V., Ostrovsky, R., Schaffner, C.: Position-based quantum cryptography: impossibility and constructions. In: CoRR abs/1009.2490 (2010)
9. Buhrman, H., Fehr, S., Schaffner, C., Speelman, F.: The Garden-Hose game: a new model of computation, and application to position-based quantum cryptography. In: CoRR abs/1109.2563 (2011)

Verification of Various Attack Approaches Against CSI-Based Secret Key in Different Types of LOS Channels

Michał Pilc[✉] and Jędrzej Stańczak

Faculty of Electronics and Telecommunications, Poznan University of Technology,
ul. Polanka 3, 60-965 Poznań, Poland
{michal.s.pilc,jedrzej.r.stanczak}@doctorate.put.poznan.pl

Abstract. Exploiting random fluctuations of radio channel for key agreement has been investigated for several years; however, these methods of key reconciliation in wireless LANs are vulnerable to attacks especially in case of Line-of-Sight (LOS) channels. In the following paper we will verify whether applying antenna arrays with reconfigurable antennas reduces the number of key bits leaking to the eavesdropper by utilizing two types of attack: Nearest Neighbour Excursion (NNE) and Average RSSI.

1 Introduction

Providing secure data transfer in wireless LANs has been a formidable task since 1990's, when IEEE 802.11 standard was established. Cryptographic protocols like WEP, WPA and WPA2 applied in WiFi devices and E0 protocol applied in Bluetooth technology were supposed to provide confidentiality, integrity and authenticity of the data sent over radio channel based on the assumption that breaking the secret key is computationally difficult problem. However, this assumption must be reviewed nowadays in the light of rapidly increasing computational power and the appearance of quantum computers. Therefore, information-theoretic approach must replace cryptographic approach to provide security in modern radio systems. Exploiting random fluctuations of radio channel can help to generate information-theoretically secret keys (i.e. Eve's computational resources are unlimited). Theoretical fundamentals of information-theoretic security originate from the seminal papers by Shannon, Wyner and Maurer [1–3]. Based on these assumptions several proposals of secret key agreement treating the channel state information (CSI) as a source of common randomness were formulated in the following 20 years. In [4] Wallace and Sharma showed the way of extracting secret bits from reciprocal time-varying channel by applying low complexity quantization algorithms. In [5] a level-crossing algorithm of key extraction from fading wireless channels was developed. Unfortunately, both methods have limited applicability in static and LOS channels (typical for indoor environment). In such case the number of secret bits per second tends to zero with increasing coherence time of the channel. Moreover, in LOS and almost static channels the location of transmitter's (i.e. Alice) and legitimate receiver's (i.e. Bob) antennas brings additional side information for an intruder (i.e. Eve), which can extract transmission parameters (e.g. direction of arrival) allowing him to discover the key. Additionally, MIMO LOS channels are highly correlated when the

© Institute for Computer Sciences, Social Informatics and Telecommunications Engineering 2015
S. Mumtaz et al. (Eds.): WICON 2014, LNICST 146, pp. 173–179, 2015.
DOI: 10.1007/978-3-319-18802-7_25

spacing between antennas at one side does not exceed 2λ, where λ is the carrier's wavelength [6, 7].

Laboratory experiments proved that the extended Saleh-Valenzuela model with spherical wave propagation describes the LOS channel with higher fidelity than other models [6]. Recent studies by Wallace et al. have shown that introducing artificial variability to a static or LOS radio channel by applying reconfigurable antenna arrays (the so called RECAPs) increases Eve's equivocation about the Alice-Bob channel [8].

In the following paper we try to verify whether applying RECAPs increases the immunity to two types of attack in indoor LOS channels with different K-factors.

In Sect. 2 we present the model of the simulated system and describe the assumptions we have made. In Sect. 3 simulation results are discussed. Section 4 summarizes the results and brings conclusions for future research.

2   System Model

In Fig. 1 a typical wireless indoor environment is depicted (a large room of size 12 m × 10 m × 4 m). The location of Alice, Bob and Eve is given in 3D coordinates.

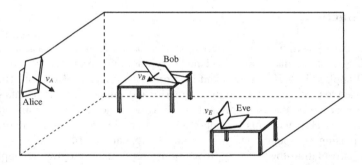

Fig. 1. Access point (Alice) exchanges messages with a legitimate mobile terminal (Bob), transmission is overheard by an eavesdropper (Eve)

Alice is a wireless access point hanging at the ceiling, whereas Bob and Eve are mobile terminals lying at a desk. The location of transceivers are as follows: Alice(0.13 m, 0.18 m, 3.7 m), Bob(3.6 m, 4.8 m, 1.1 m) and Eve(7.8 m, 2.1 m, 1.2 m). Alice utilizes a 4 × 5 array of microstrip antennas, Bob utilizes a 3 × 4 antenna array and Eve overhears the transmission with 2 fixed antennas (Fig. 2). Vectors perpendicular to antenna arrays are: $v_A = [8;6;-3]$, $v_B = [-2;-0.5;-0.3]$ and $v_E = [-1;-0.5;-0.1]$. The parameters given above were chosen arbitrarily to reflect a typical real-life situation. The distances between communicating nodes are: $d_{AB} = 5.85$ m, $d_{AE} = 8.30$ m and $d_{BE} = 5.05$ m.

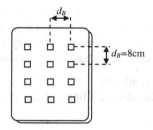

Fig. 2. Bob's antenna array with microstrip antennas

2.1   Parameters of the System Under Consideration

The carrier frequency f_c equals 5 GHz, hence the carrier's wavelength, λ is equal to 6 cm. The separation of antennas within a column or a row of the array equals $d_A = 8$ cm for Alice, $d_B = 6$ cm for Bob and $d_E = 10$ cm for Eve (Fig. 2). A TGn channel model, type E with modified LOS terms according to spherical wave propagation is used. By K factor we denote the ratio of two values: the power of LOS term to the total power of Non-Line-of-Sight (NLOS) terms. The maximum speed of obstacles equals 0.5 m/s. Physical layer parameters describing OFDM modulation are similar to those used in IEEE 802.11n standard, i.e.: time of orthogonality $t_{ort} = 3.2\mu$s, cyclic prefix length $t_{CP} = 0.8\mu$s, IFFT/FFT size is 64; 52 QPSK data symbols and 4 pilot symbols are assigned to the entries of IFFT for each OFDM symbol. One transmit frame consists of 100 OFDM symbols per antenna preceded by a preamble and the frames are exchanged between Alice and Bob in Time Division Duplex (TDD) mode.

The antenna reconfiguration mechanism we emulate is similar to the one presented in [8]. In each iteration two active antennas are selected at random from Alice's and Bob's antenna array. The receiver estimates the value of CFR (channel frequency response) between the m-th transmitting ($m = 1$ or 2) and the n-th ($n = 1$ or 2) receiving antenna at 4 pilot subcarriers. The CFR values are estimated every two OFDM symbols because we exploit a 2×2 MIMO scheme in space division multiplexing mode, which is chosen on purpose. Capacity achieving codes like Turbo or LDPC codes should be applied for error correction instead of space-time codes.

When reconfigurable aperture antennas are used the following operations are performed in every iteration prior to key reconciliation:

- Alice selects two active antennas out of 20 and with the aid of these antennas she sends Bob a frame, which consists of 100 OFDM symbols per transmit antenna;
- Eve receives the frame from Bob with her antennas and estimates the CFR values for pilot subcarriers;
- Bob selects two active antennas out of 12 for reception and for transmission;
- upon receiving the frame Bob estimates the CFR for pilot subcarriers;
- Bob sends Alice a frame of 100 OFDM symbols with his active antennas;
- Alice receives the frame with her active antennas and estimates the CFR
- Eve receives the frame from Alice with her antennas and estimates the CFR

In order to accumulate the estimated values of CFR for longer period and observe variability of radio channel the steps above were repeated 7200 times, which lasted 5.9 s. The accumulated values of CFR were later used for key-reconciliation with the level-crossing algorithm developed in [5]. It is based on two assumptions:

- Channel fluctuations occur randomly
- Observations of wireless channels at different locations are uncorrelated.

2.2 Key Reconciliation with the Level-Crossing Algorithm and Attack Methods

We collected 360000 samples of estimated CFR values between the m-th active transmitting and the n-th active receiving antenna at the k-th subcarrier ($k = -21, -7, +7$ or $+21$) and calculated their magnitude for further processing. The spacing between two consecutive samples was 8 μs. After subtracting a moving average with a window of length 20000 samples the level-crossing algorithm was applied. An excursion is valid if at least m consecutive samples of series X cross the threshold. In order to obtain uncorrelated bits the latter parameter was fixed such that $m = 1000$. Hence, a secret bit is extracted from an excursion if its duration is longer than 16 ms. The threshold levels are given by the following formulae:

$$q^+ = \bar{x} + \alpha \cdot \sigma$$
$$q^- = \bar{x} - \alpha \cdot \sigma \tag{1}$$

where σ is the standard deviation of the samples collected in the series X and $\alpha = 1$ is a modifiable parameter. Hence, if at least m consecutive terms of X are greater than q^+ then the key bit value is assigned 1. Similarly, if at least m consecutive samples of X are lower than q^- the key bit value is assigned 0. The operation of key exchange is repeated for every pilot subcarrier and for every pair of Tx-Rx antenna baseband units. Thus, $4 \times 4 = 16$ keys are merged to form one secret key of length L.

The authors of [9] noticed a strong correlation of signals observed by adversaries located at much bigger distance from two communicating parties than $\lambda/2$. They gave several proposals of compromising the key exchanged with a level-crossing algorithm. Two of these proposals were implemented by us in Monte Carlo simulations, i.e. the NNE algorithm and the Average RSSI method.

3   Simulation Results

We performed Monte Carlo simulations described in Sect. 2 for the following scenarios:

- Case 1 – antenna reconfiguration in each iteration, denoted as RECAP;
- Case 2 – no antenna reconfiguration; fixed antenna positions during the whole simulation period, denoted as no_reconf.

We consider two scenarios of Case 2: with low (i.e. Low Antenna Spacing) and with large spacing (i.e. Large Antenna Spacing) between the antennas of one terminal. In the first scenario two neighbouring antennas are active and in the latter – two most distant antennas for both Alice and Bob.

First and foremost we have taken into account such straightforward quality indicator as key compliance between K_{AB} (a valid key agreed between Alice and Bob), K_{AE} and K_{BE} (key estimated by Eve based on channel observations from Alice and Bob, respectively), i.e. $K_{AB}(i) = K_{AE}(i) = K_{BE}(i)$, $i \in \{1, \ldots, L\}$. Figure 3 illustrates the relationship between these parameters for Low Antenna Spacing scenario. It is clearly visible that irrespective of the K-factor value at most a quarter of bits captured by Eve match the bits of K_{AB} for both methods of attack.

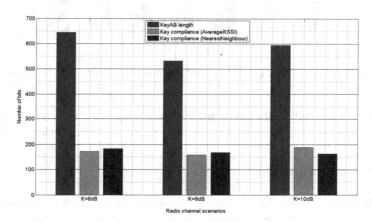

Fig. 3. Key length versus the number of bits estimated by Eve that match "overall compliance" criteria (Low Antenna Spacing scenario).

The results for Large Antenna Spacing scenario were comparable. Such alteration does not invoke any major deviations from the behaviour shown in Fig. 3. A distinctive tendency that can be noticed is the increase of key length with ascending K factor. Furthermore, K_{AB} has a slightly longer duration for $K = 6$ dB in Large Antenna Spacing scenario (573 bits compared to 532 bits for Low Antenna Spacing). However, the percentage of bits that have been correctly estimated on the basis of A-E and B-E channel observations remain nearly equal (for Average RSSI: 161 bits, 155 bits and 181 for 6 dB, 8 dB and 10 dB, respectively).

The constraint that K_{AE} bits must consent with K_{BE} observations is quite severe, resulting in just a quarter of bits fulfilling "overall compliance" requirements. Figure 4 presents less rigid outcome when just a single estimation (either K_{AE} or K_{BE}) was taken into account. One can notice what is the ratio of correctly estimated bits in case Average RSSI attack has been conducted.

The highest efficacy (reaching almost 60 %) is achieved for $K = 6$ dB, Low Antenna Spacing with no reconfiguration scenario. Nevertheless, most calculations fluctuate around 0.5 with the lowest number of evaluated bits for K_{AE} in RECAP system. The results put forward in Fig. 4 are comparable to those obtained for NNE. Those two

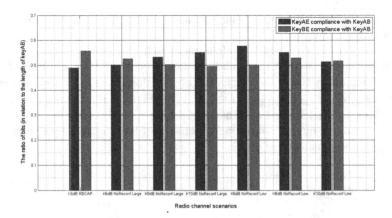

Fig. 4. The ratio of correctly estimated key bits by applying the Average RSSI attack in relation to the length of K_{AB}.

methods of attack yield similar performance. The average ratio of correctly estimated key bits is approximately 52 % for both Average RSSI and NNE attack.

4   Final Conclusions

In the following paper we have verified two techniques of attack against secret key agreed between two legitimate parties. None of them prevails over the other. Approximately 52 % of key bits were correctly estimated by Eve regardless of the spacing between antennas at one side (Low Antenna Spacing vs Large Antenna Spacing) and of the K-factor. This outcome is only slightly better than the result of guessing key bits in a random way, (i.e. 50 %). Thus, immunity to more sophisticated methods of attack should be seriously considered. Applying blind deconvolution methods (i.e. ESPRIT algorithm) may help to verify whether reducing the K-factor or applying RECAP antennas reduces the number of secret bits leaking to Eve for indoor LOS channels.

References

1. Shannon, C.E.: Communication theory of secrecy systems. Bell Syst. Tech. J. **28**, 656–715 (1949)
2. Wyner, A.D.: The wire-tap Channel. Bell Sys. Tech. J. **54**, 1355–1387 (1975)
3. Maurer, U.M.: Secret key agreement by public discussion from common information. IEEE Trans. Inf. Theory **39**(3), 733–742 (1993)
4. Wallace, J., Sharma, R.: Automatic secret keys form reciprocal MIMO wireless channel: measurement and analysis. IEEE Trans. Inf. Forensics Secur. **5**(3), 381–392 (2010)
5. Ye, C., Mathur, S., Reznik, A., Shah, Y., Trappe, W., Mandayam, N.: Information-theoretically secret key generation for fading wireless channels. IEEE Trans. Inf. Forensics Secur. **5**(2), 240–254 (2010)

6. Hofman, C.A., Knopp, A., Ogermann, D., Schwarz, R.T., Lankl, B: Deficiencies of common MIMO channel models with regard to indoor line-of-sight channels. In: IEEE 19th Symposium on Personal, Indoor and Mobile Radio Communications (2008)
7. Kolmonen, V.-M., Haneda, K., Hult, T., Poutanen, J., Tufvesson, F., Vainikainen, P.: Measurement-based evaluation of interlink correlation for indoor multiuser MIMO channels. IEEE Antennas Wirel. Propag. Lett. **9**, 311–314 (2010)
8. Mehmood, R., Wallace, J.: Wireless security enhancement using parasitic reconfigurable aperture antennas. In: Proceedings of the 5th European Conference on Antennas and Propagation (2011)
9. Edman, M., Kiayias, A., Yener, B.: On passive inference against physical-layer key extraction. In: EUROSEC 2011, European Workshop on System Security, Salzburg, Austria (2011)

A Method for Localization of Computational Node and Proxy Server in Educational Data Synchronization

Süleyman Eken[✉], Fidan Kaya, Ahmet Sayar,
Adnan Kavak, and Suhap Şahin

Computer Engineering Department, Kocaeli University,
Umuttepe Campus, 41380 Izmit, Turkey
{suleyman.eken,fidan.kaya,ahmet.sayar,akavak,suhapsahin}
@kocaeli.edu.tr

Abstract. Localization methods enable location estimation accurately and provide location information about mobile devices, people, cars, data and equipment. Accurate location detection is a vital process for most of location-based applications such as emergency rescue, in-building guidance, security services, and product tracking in hospitals. This paper addresses localization of student/ teacher tablets and school level proxy servers for educational data synchronization. For this purpose, locations of proxy servers and tablets are detected using Android Location API. After localization, if tablets are outside of school, they could access cloud server directly to get educational data and if tablets are in school, they could access data via proxy server. Experimental results show that the proposed technique increases the efficiency in data transfers between the end users and cloud servers.

Keywords: Localization · Distributed file synchronization · Position estimation · Network traffic

1 Introduction

Location estimation based services require computing and detection the position of mobile devices. These services enable the development of various applications such as resource management, navigation and mapping [1, 2], people monitoring [3], instant messaging [4], emergency rescue [5], buddy finder [6], travel and tourist guides [7], localized advertising and shopping [8]. Recent location detection techniques can be classified into two classes. The first type requires additional hardware connection such as A-GPS (Assisted Global Positioning System). This type has two disadvantages. First, GPS based localization needs at least clear sighted four satellites in order to work which is not suitable for indoors and urban areas hindered geographically. The second disadvantage is uncertainty of localization in case of closed nodes in small area. It results imprecision of the localization. The second type, GPS-free, requires proprietary units to wireless operators' network.

We propose proxy server based solution approach to both decreasing network traffic and increasing the efficiency in data transfers between the end users (tablets) and cloud

© Institute for Computer Sciences, Social Informatics and Telecommunications Engineering 2015
S. Mumtaz et al. (Eds.): WICON 2014, LNICST 146, pp. 180–190, 2015.
DOI: 10.1007/978-3-319-18802-7_26

servers [9, 10]. In concept of this system, location detection of tablet users and proxy servers is very important process. So, we mainly focus on localization of these actors in this paper.

This paper is structured as follows: In the second section, relevant works are given for localization techniques. Third section clarifies proxy server based data management synchronization architecture. Fourth section explains location detection of proxy servers and student tablets using Android Location API. Conclusion and some future enhancements are given at the conclusion section.

2 Related Works

In the literature, a number of localization techniques have been proposed. Each of them has advantages, as well as drawbacks. The best unambiguous can be obtained using positioning systems based on signals emitted by satellites [11, 12]. It is not possible to use this method of localization because lack of satellite signals and lack of required signal receiver in the device. In this paper, we imply mobile localization with location detection, because, we use Android Location API to find positions of proxy servers and tablets. So, mobile location techniques can be categorized according to the measurements employed by algorithms.

There are number of positioning mechanisms: (i)Time of Arrival (TOA), (ii) Observed Time Difference of Arrival (OTDOA), (iii) Timing Advance (TA), (iv) Angle of Arrival (AOA), (v) Received Signal Strength (RSS)and (vi) General navigation system assisted. TOA is a procedure in which the information is based on triangulating the propagation time delay. This delay reclines between mobile terminal and minimum three Base Stations (BSs) [13]. Similarly it measures signals transmitted by the mobile terminal. The properties of BSs which are capable to receive signals from the mobile terminals, and contribute to a suitable reference time. The arrival time of signal can be measure from the mobile terminal. As a result these times-of-arrival may be used to calculate to the approximate distance of the mobile terminal and consequently derive a location estimate [14]. In Observed Time Difference of Arrival (OTDOA) technique, terminal calculates differences between the downlink signals sent by the nearby BSs. The efficient accuracy of the location estimates made by this procedure depends on the two main scenarios. Firstly the precision of the timing measurements and secondly the comparative position of the BSs involved [15]. TA method is based on the TA parameter for uplink transmissions. The TA measurement describes a circle along which the mobile terminal may be located [16]. AOA information is measured at the BS using complicated antenna array, but generally two BSs are sufficient to obtain unique location. This technique utilizes Line of Bearing (LoB) of the terminal's signal and determines terminal location by acquiring point of intersection of these LoBs. As we approach for the best case this method produces efficient results in rural areas, because in rural areas the line-of-sight (LoS) paths between the BSs and mobile terminal are predominant. This method assists the handover process, as part of its standard functionality the RSS measurements are gathered by mobile terminal. There are two kinds of RSS which are proper propagation model and fingerprint technique. The proper propagation model converts the RSS values to the distance from their nearby BSs and determines the position with the help of standard trilateration techniques [17]. The other kind of RSS is fingerprint techniques which apply a fingerprint measured database inside the area where the terminal is to be placed [18] Some GPS enabled Smartphones, are able to navigate the location. Satellite transmission is used for this purpose.

Localization can be obtained from a cellular network or through algorithms provided by operating system vendors.W3C Gelocalization API was [19] proposed by World Wide Web Consortium (W3C) [20] as the uniform way to access mobile device location from the Web browser. The API defines programmatically access to localization data. Taking available information as input data, dedicated algorithms are able to calculate position of the mobile device. The most commonly used data sources include: Wi-Fi connection parameters, device's IP address used for mobile communication, list of sensed GSM/CDMA cells, radio communication signal strength.

Location providers continuously collect data from mobile devices being used worldwide and improve quality of localization accuracy. However, any major change in it may cause drop in the quality of information obtained through the API, because they do not control configuration of the infrastructure which is used for mobile communication.

Cell-Id based localization is one of the most common methods used by mobile networks. Its popularity comes from the fact that it relies on the mechanisms already in place which are required for basic voice and data communication [21]. In this study, locations of proxy servers and tablets are detected using Android Location API. The proposed architecture will be explained in the following sections in detail.

3   Data Management and Synchronization Architecture

According to the concept of most important educational projects in Turkey, Movement of Enhancing Opportunities and Improving Technology, abbreviated as FATIH, students and teachers can use their tablet PCs to get educational data (text, images, media, etc.) stored in cloud services, but, the limited network bandwidth and highly increased the number of users and the educational data sizes degrade the system performance and even negatively affect the overall usability of the system. In order to solve these problems, we propose to install a client-side proxy server in schools and an extension framework for integrating it into the cloud system.

Overall structure of proxy server-based approach is showed in Fig. 1. Tablets are connected with cloud from school or outside of the school. Tablets which are outside of the school access cloud server directly to access educational data. Tablets which are in school access data via proxy server. Educational data will be shared among tablets, will be organized according to the following scenarios with proxy server:

- Getting the educational data that published via cloud server.
- Getting educational data from cloud server when the network traffic is low.
- Organizing the educational data that will be shared among student's tablets.
- Organizing the data requests when the network traffic is high at school.
- Transmitting the educational data updates from proxy server to cloud server.

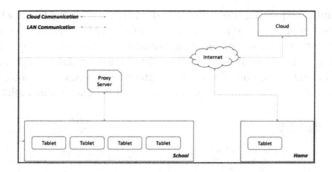

Fig. 1. High level communication between inter-components

Proxy server-based approach has generally two types of communication: (i) tablet-cloud server communication and (ii) tablet-proxy server communication.

3.1   Status of Tablet-Cloud Server Communication

This scenario includes situations when tablet is used outside of the school and inside of the school without connected with proxy servers. If tablets are connected with the internet will also be connected to cloud, it does not matter whether tablets are in school or outside of the school. Cloud server always determines whether tablets will access educational data from cloud server or proxy server by identifying from where the tablet is connected. In other words, cloud server is decisive actor.

Figure 2 shows a flow diagram depicting that a tablet is connected to cloud server from outside of the school and accessing educational data from cloud server. Communication between tablet and cloud server will be provided via ARCSPXP (ARDIC Cloud Service Platform Extension Protocol) [22] protocol in this scenario. If tablet has internet connection, this communication would always be active. Downloading data from cloud server would be active only during content transfer, and the system has a structure which does not require continuous connection between cloud server and tablet.

3.2   Status of Tablet-Proxy Server Communication

The tablets which are connected with internet first time would be connected directly to the cloud server. For each new connection, a control will be started via cloud server. With this control, cloud server will decide whether tablet is an educational tablet or not. The cloud server will also decide whether tablet needs any adjustment or not. If a tablet wants to get any service from cloud server, it must be defined on cloud server with the following information before connection:

- Tablet's unique identity,
- User information assigned to the tablet,
- If the tablet assign a pre-defined group (e.g. group Istanbul), group assignment must be done,
- School ID, class and so on, which the tablet belonged.

After definition of required information, cloud server controls the tablet whether tablet is an educational tablet or not. If tablet is an educational tablet, cloud server will progress predefined operations. These operations are shown in Fig. 3. Detecting the location of the tablet (in school or outside of school) is one of these predefined operations. Later, if the tablet is in school, cloud server sends signalling message, including information about its proxy server to be able to upload and download data to this tablet.

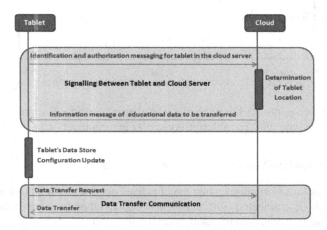

Fig. 2. Flow diagram of cloud signalling and data transfer when tablet is outside of the school

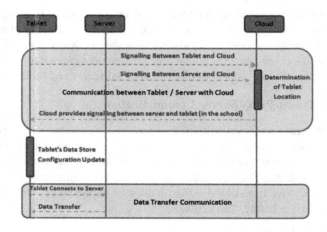

Fig. 3. Flow diagram of cloud signalling and data transfer when tablet is in the school

4 Location Detection of Tablet Users and Proxy Server

In our developed model, the locations of two different system devices should be determined. These are proxy servers which are placed in schools and student's tablets. In these both systems, Android Location API is used to get the location information. Many Android terminals are capable of detection of the recent location by using GPS module, Cell Tower Triangulation or Wi-Fi Networks. To determine the recent position, Android contains the android.location package.

Android API has a Location Manager class. This class provides access to location services of Android, and these services allow to access location providers to register location update listeners and proximity alerts and more. There are many sub-classes under Location Provider class. Location Provider class reads location information from these sub-classes. Android devices have too many Location Provider class in their own structure. Device location can be found using one of these classes. In Table 1, location provider types and their properties are listed. These three types are general types and every Android device contains these types [23].

Table 1. Location provider properties [23]

Location provider	Description
Network	Mobile network or Wi-Fi is used to detect the best location.
GPS	GPS receiver in the Android device is used to determine the best location via satellites.
Passive	Allows to participate in location of updates of other components to save energy

The method developed for both cases is explained in detail below.

4.1 Determination of the Proxy Servers' Location

The proposed model is developed for schools to share educational data. We can connect too many schools to the system and the network traffic could increase. The most important aim of the system is to reduce the network traffic. To reduce the load on the cloud server, a proxy server is placed in every school. But we don't have information about these proxy servers, and we also don't know which proxy server is placed in which school. During initial setup we must found the proxy server's location. For this purpose, an admin tablet is used to detect server exact location. Location information of proxy server identified by using admin tablet's location application and this location information is sent to the proxy server. In this scenario, we suppose that admin tablet and proxy server should be in the same network and also the information transfer between proxy server and tablet is provided via UDP connection. Because IP address of proxy server is unknown. Location detection application working on admin tablet uses Android Location API to detect location. Figure 4 shows this process in detailed.

As seen in Fig. 4, we suppose that admin tablet is near (or sufficiently close) to the proxy server. Admin tablet broadcasts a message including its location information and physical address to all nodes in the network. These are tablet's MAC address, longitude and latitude. Proxy server takes this information and sends cloud server via TCP connection. Since proxy server must be sure that information is sent. Cloud server sends a response message like "ACK" to proxy server. After proxy server receives "ACK" message, it realizes that information was send and proxy server closes connection. This process should be performed only once during the initial setup of each proxy server. Thus position detection of proxy server would be automatic. Figure 5 depicts message flow diagram while proxy server localization.

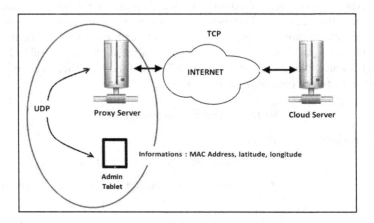

Fig. 4. Proxy server localization

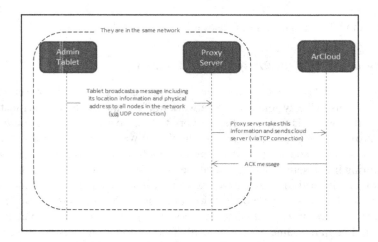

Fig. 5. Message flow diagram of proxy server localization

4.2   Determination of the Tablets' Location

To detect the position of student tablet is a process that would be repeated each time whenever application is open. The location of the student tablet could be (i) inside of the school or (ii) outside of the school. In these both cases student tablet would communicate with the cloud server. According to the cloud server decision, the student tablet would connect with proxy server if it is inside of the school, otherwise the student tablet would directly connect to cloud server through internet. This scenario is explained in detailed in Fig. 6.

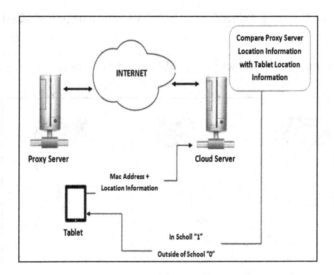

Fig. 6. Student tablet localization

As seen in Fig. 6, initially the tablet sends its location information (lat, long) and MAC address to cloud server, the same approach is also used to find out the proxy server. Cloud Server compares received student's tablet location information with the data already stored in cloud server database (see Table 2). The comparison process is done according to Eq. (1). When tablet is opened, its distance with near proxy server is measured. If the distance "d" is less than desired interval/meters, student tablet can communicate with that proxy server (in case of tablet in school), otherwise it must communicate with cloud server (in case of tablet is outside of school). After comparison process, cloud server sends "1" message to tablet to connect proxy server or sends "0" message to tablet to connect cloud server. Figure 7 depicts message flow diagram while tablet localization.

$$d = \sqrt{\left(\text{lat}_{Sm} - \text{lat}_{Tn}\right)^2 + \left(\text{long}_{Sm} - \text{long}_{Tn}\right)^2} \qquad (1)$$

Table 2. Location information about proxy servers and tablets in cloud server

Proxy servers	Tablets	Info about proxies and tablets
Server 1	Tablet 1	$[MAC_{S1} + lat_{S1}, long_{S1} + MAC_{T1}]$
Server 1	Tablet 2	$[MAC_{S1} + lat_{S1}, long_{S1} + MAC_{T2}]$
Server 2	Tablet 3	$[MAC_{S1} + lat_{S2}, long_{S2} + MAC_{T3}]$
Server 2	Tablet 4	$[MAC_{S2} + lat_{S2}, long_{S2} + MAC_{T4}]$
Server 2	Tablet 5	$[MAC_{S2} + lat_{S2}, long_{S2} + MAC_{T5}]$
..	..	..
Server n	Tablet m	$[MAC_{Sn} + lat_{Sn}, long_{Sn} + MAC_{Tm}]$

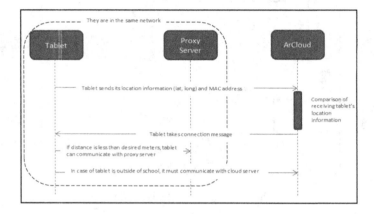

Fig. 7. Flow diagram of tablet localization

Where $\left(lat_{Sm}, long_{Sm}\right)$ and $\left(lat_{Tn}, long_{Tn}\right)$ indicate latitude-longitude of Server$_m$ and Tablet$_n$ respectively.

In Table 2 it is shown that cloud server stored the information after localization of proxy servers and tablets. In Table 2, MAC_{Sn}, MAC_{Tm}, and $(lat_{Sn}, long_{Sn})$ indicate MAC of Server$_n$, MAC of Tablet$_m$, and latitude-longitude of Server$_n$ respectively. As a result, the number of devices connecting with cloud server would decrease and the network traffic will be reduced.

5   Conclusion and Future Works

All local events and facts related to the area seem to be more important to find out the location of remote devices. Localization data is used in all types of services. One of the most important applications is detection of student tablets' locations for educational data synchronization. In this paper, we utilize Android Location API to find location of proxy servers and tablets. This proposed technique is not application specific, so it could be used in various applications requiring location information.

In future, we plan to enhance the system with some other location techniques and optimize results to obtain more accurate outcomes.

Acknowledgments. This work is supported by the TUBİTAK under grant EEEAG 113E033 within 1003 Fatih Project Call.

References

1. Jokinen, K.: Usability in location-based services: context and mobile map navigation. In: Stephanidis, C. (ed.) UAHCI 2007 (Part II). LNCS, vol. 4555, pp. 401–410. Springer, Heidelberg (2007)
2. Richter, K.-F., Dara-Abrams, D., Raubal, M.: Navigating and learning with location based services: a user-centric design. In: G. Gartner, Y. Li (Eds.), Proceedings of the 7th International Symposium on LBS and Telecartography, pp. 261–276 (2010)
3. Marco, A., Casas, R., Falco, J., Gracia, H., Artigas, J.I., Roy, A.: Location-based services for elderly and disabled people. Comput. Commun. **31**(6), 1055–1066 (2008)
4. Patinge, S.A., Soni, P.D.: A survey on instant message and location sharing system for android. Int. J. Appl. Innov. Eng. Manage. (IJAIEM) **2**(10), 219–221 (2013)
5. Kamarudin, N., Salam, S.: Enabling mobile location based services for emergency cases. In: 2011 International Conference on Research and Innovation in Information Systems (ICRIIS), Kuala Lumpur, pp. 1–6 (2011)
6. Ndakunda, S.T., Wright, M., Terzoli, A.: Composing a simple friend-finder application using the sip location-based services toolkit. In: Southern Africa Telecommunication Networks and Applications Conference (SATNAC), South Africa, pp. 1–6 (2011)
7. Chang-jie, M., Jin-yun F.: Location-based mobile tour guide services towards digital dunhuang. In: International Society for Photogrammetry and Remote Sensing, vol. XXXVII, Part B4, pp. 949–954. Beijing (2008)
8. Steinfield, C.: The development of location based services in mobile commerce. In: Preissl, B., Bouwman, H., Steinfield, C. (eds.) Elife After the Dot Com Bust, pp. 177–197. Springer, Berlin (2004)
9. Eken, S., Kaya, F., İlhan, Z., Sayar, A., Kavak, A., Kocasaraç, U., Şahin, S.: Analyzing distributed file synchronization techniques for educational data. In: 10th International Conference on Electronics, Computer, and Computation, Ankara, Turkey, pp. 318–321 (2013)
10. Kaya, F., Eken, S., Ilhan, Z., Kavak, A., Sayar, A., Kocasarac, U., Sahin, S.: A comparative study of signaling protocols for data management and synchronization in fatih project with school level cloud proxy server deployment. In: IEEE 3rd Symposium on Network Cloud Computing and Applications (NCCA 2014), Rome, Italy, pp. 133–136 (2014)
11. Harvey, B.: The Rebirth of the Russian Space Program: 50 Years After Sputnik, New Frontiers. Springer, Berlin (2007)
12. Prasad, R., Ruggieri, M.: Applied Satellite Navigation Using GPS, GALILEO, nd Augmentation Systems. Mobile Communication Series. Artech House, Boston (2005)
13. Snaptrack, Location Techniques for GSM, GPRS and UMTS Networks. White Paper (2003)

14. Fischer, S., Kangas, A.: Time-of-arrival estimation for e-otd location in geran. In: 12th IEEE International Symposium on Personal, Indoor and Mobile Radio Communications, vol. 2, pp. 121–25 (2001)
15. Zhao, Y.: Standardization of mobile phone positioning for 3G systems. IEEE Commun. Mag. **40**(7), 108–116 (2002)
16. Silventoinen, M., Rantalainen, T.: Mobile station emergency locating in GSM. In: IEEE International Conference on Personal Wireless Communications, pp. 232–238 (1996)
17. Caffery, J., Stuber, G.: Overview of radiolocation in CDMA cellular systems. J. IEEE Commun. Mag. **36**(4), 38–45 (1998)
18. Laoudias, C., Kemppi, P., Panayiotou, C.G.: Localization using radial basis function networks and signal strength fingerprints in WLAN. In: IEEE Global Telecommunications Conference (GLOBECOM 2009), pp. 1–6 (2009)
19. Popescu, A. (ed.): Geolocation API Specification, W3C Proposed Recommendation, 10 May 2012
20. World Wide Web Consortium. http://www.w3.org/. Accessed 25 July 2014
21. Sabak, G.: Tests of smartphone localization accuracy using W3C API and cell-id. In: Proceedings of the 2013 Federated Conference on Computer Science and Information Systems, pp. 845–849 (2013)
22. http://www.ardictech.com/. Accessed 25 July 2014
23. http://www.vogella.com/tutorials/AndroidLocationAPI/article.html. Accessed 25 July 2014

Social Networks and Internet of Things, an Overview of the SITAC Project

Celestino Monteiro[1(✉)], Manuel Oliveira[1], Joaquim Bastos[2],
Tipu Ramrekha[2], and Jonathan Rodriguez[2]

[1] GS LDA, Aveiro, Portugal
capitcha@gmail.com, info@gs-lda.pt
[2] Instituto de Telecomunicações, Campus de Santiago,
3810-193 Aveiro, Portugal

Abstract. Two of the most promising paradigms for the next decade are the Social Networks (SN) and Internet of Things (IoT). The challenge will be enabling autonomous interaction among humans and devices when these two paradigms converge. The ITEA2 SITAC project proposes to undertake the challenge of creating a unifying architecture and 'ecosystem' comprising platforms, tools and methodologies that enable the seamless connection and cooperation of many types of network-connected entities, whether systems, machines, devices or humans with personal devices. Beyond the state of the art challenges on big data management, management of large number of number of entities and advanced context management are specific role of the SITAC proposed unified architecture. In this scope is also described in detail a project a use case, the *Intouch*, which is an energy aware clustering application for social networking applications, scope of the Portuguese partnership within the project.

Keywords: Iot · Clustering · Energy-aware

1 Introduction

Social Networks (SN) and Internet of Things (IoT) are two of the most promising paradigms of the next decade. Enabling autonomous interaction among humans and devices is the main objective when these two paradigms converge.

The Internet is expected to ultimately interconnect billions of people and trillions of devices. For several years, "Web-of-Objects" and "Internet-of-Things" initiatives have emerged primarily aimed at machine-to-machine or device-to-device interactions using standard communications protocols. But, as of yet, their rate of adoption in commercial products and services is fairly low.

The challenge undertaken by the SITAC project [1] is to create a unifying architecture and "ecosystem" – comprising platforms, tools and methodologies – that enables seamless connection and cooperation of many types of network-connected entities, whether systems, machines, devices or humans equipped with handheld devices. This ecosystem must make business sense and therefore cover the needs of various types of

© Institute for Computer Sciences, Social Informatics and Telecommunications Engineering 2015
S. Mumtaz et al. (Eds.): WICON 2014, LNICST 146, pp. 191–196, 2015.
DOI: 10.1007/978-3-319-18802-7_27

industrial stakeholders: device manufacturers, telecom operators, service providers and companies acting as users.

Thus, sensors and actuators will be seamlessly connected amongst each other and with different types of smart spaces. Mobile devices will assist users in managing their everyday tasks. New breeds of smart services will emerge, e.g., context sharing between family members, adapting residential facilities to the needs of new tenants, interactions with and between home devices optimizing home energy consumption, etc. Intelligent buildings and smart grids will provide enabling technologies required for smart cities.

SITAC will exploit the appropriate related works done so far in the area of Internet-of-Things (IoT): reference architectures and models [2], patterns, protocols and software development methodologies and practices [3].

This paper is presented as follows: in the Sect. 2 is presented the IoT and SN joint scenario where the SITAC will cover. In the Sect. 3 is presented the platform neutral reference architecture proposed. In the Sect. 4 we present the role of the Portuguese consortium, in the project and architecture and in the Sect. 5 the conclusions are taken.

2 The SITAC Scenario and Functional Architecture

For SITAC, IoT is an enabler for new and exciting social and crowd services. The big data that is created by IoT enablers will have value for a new set of uses and users.

The Internet of Things is all about convergence, from connected computing using RFID, NFC and sensor technology to digital content and context-aware services. The success of the Internet of Things will not so much depend on the development of new technologies, but more so on connecting and integrating existing resources, ranging from small-scale objects, such as RFID tags, up to large-scale software systems that serve thousands of clients at a time. The goal is to create a software architecture that enables objects to exchange information through the Internet to achieve nonintrusive behavior and customized services. Part of the architecture's responsibility is to make sure that relevant information arrives at the right place in a way that the recipient understands what it receives.

SITAC aims to go beyond the state of the art devoting its effort to the next key technology areas:

Management of "Big Data" for Enhanced Services and System Performance – Currently, the amount of information on the Internet/Web is doubled every 8–12 months. As IoT proliferates, a boom of continuous data generation can be expected. Due to the pure volumes, redundancy and limited data actuality period, a state of the art advance is required when it comes to "in-flow management of big data".

Embracing Paradigms from Bio/Eco/Socio Systems for Robustness, Scalability and Manageability – As the number of entities and system complexity grow, aspects such as manageability, scalability and robustness become increasingly challenging. A following approach is required addressed by "nature" in biological, ecological and societal systems. In particular, a study and learn is required from the emerging Internet based social media/communities.

Advanced Context Management for Proactive and Supportive IoT Solutions – Most of the approaches at "context awareness" do not very well address the need for proactive system/service behaviour, e.g., instrumented by forecasting of context changes. An approach is required not focus on context awareness per se, but as well keep track of, and contribute to advancements when it comes to context awareness enablers. Advancements in context awareness are highly desired in order to enable best-effort automatic (re)configuration of large scale IoT systems.

"Super-Generalised" Entity Types for Reuse and Simplicity – In most initiatives up to now, families of actually very "similar" entities – e.g., "actors" like people, vehicles, phones and computers or "address identifiers" like fixed phone number, mobile phone number, URL, e-mail address, home address and work address – have been viewed and treated as too much separate type of entities. It is necessary definition and construction of a reference model on a carefully chosen set (vital few) of "super-generalized" entities. SITAC approach attempt to propose super-generalised entity types (classes) which can be; "actors", "spaces", "flows" and "data".

3 SITAC Functional Architecture

General Description. The SITAC project aims to develop a reference architecture with enabling technologies for creating a common platform for heterogeneous networks capable of addressing the challenges of scalability, adaptability and security. This architecture will support distributed and heterogeneous environments and address a spectrum of network-based configurations spectrum of network-based configurations and-control style of resource-constrained sensor-actuator networks. This architecture will also allow for heterogeneous networks (and infrastructure) to be exposed to make it tangible for a device owner to consciously select (or build) a relevant network infrastructure according to specific needs. Furthermore, the use of semantic interoperability and context awareness techniques will facilitate the delivery of information at the right place and at the right time. In this respect, SITAC will focus on dynamic and behavioural interoperability and meeting quality requirements in dynamic situations, with design time support of configuration, scalability and optimisation.

The Reference Architecture. A functional view of the proposed architecture is depicted in the Fig. 1. In terms of functions the architecture can be represented by: - **Core**, where the main and generic functions are required which consists mainly on the computing and processing, storage, device and identity management, service layer and communication management (these functions should be available in the format of API, in order to allow inter-relation); - **Front-end**, where core services are placed together to provide features to the users. These includes mainly the applications itself, a Marketplace where the services can be accessed and capabilities for data analysis.

The actors in this architecture are the applications and functionalities designers, the users and administrators which are the responsible of the management of the system. All can be based in a Cloud based perspective. Moreover, the Data sources, Sinks and

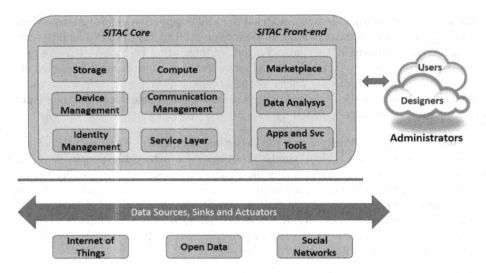

Fig. 1. SITAC project functional view, including data and actors.

Actuators can include: a variety of inter-connected things, including sensors, devices; a variety of collected data that can be used by the applications; and the Social networks, where variable data from social networks can be used in order to create somehow add-value.

The work that is proposed in the scope of the project can be placed in terms of SITAC architecture, mainly on three aspects in the core part of the SITAC architecture:

- Communication Management;
- Device Management;
- Identity Management;

4   GS and IT Role in the Project

The role of the Portuguese partners GS and IT in the scope of this project is the development of the *Intouch* application which is basically an energy aware clustering for social networking applications. The application should be able to allow terminal devices to exchange common interest data both using direct communication without the need of infrastructure when devices are in the range of others. If common interest devices are not in the range of each other, an available infrastructure should be used. The idea is to provide an energy aware solution, where several work have been published related to the energy efficiency in ad hoc wireless networks [4, 5].

The mapping of the proposed work on the logical functional view of the SITAC project presented in the Fig. 1, is in the SITAC core side and has both components of Communication Management and Device Management.

The work is based the study and implementation of ad hoc and cellular networking topologies that can provide energy savings and security based on the notion of cooperation. The case study is based on terminal devices aiming to exchange common interest data, where communication is made optimally either through short range, saying device-to-device direct communication or through the long range, where the communication is made through using the infrastructure and cross the cloud. In this last case, a M2M based architecture should be adopted.

As presented before, two modes of communication can be established in the multi-mode terminal devices. When the devices are in the range of each other, common interest social data can be exchanged through a direct communication. A cluster has to be established, and then communication is performed based on clustering paradigm. Cluster based communication is normally based in cluster head which coordinates the data exchange. This topology is presented in the left side of the Fig. 2. The method of selection of the cluster head can be based in various principles. Our idea is to optimize the energy consumption in the cluster.

When the terminals are not in the direct communication range, infrastructure based communication is then selected, and the communication will cross the cloud. This is the topology presented in the right side of the Fig. 2. In this case an architecture based in M2M can be used for the common data exchange among the end-to-end terminals.

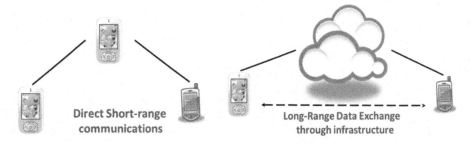

Fig. 2. Two approaches proposed for use case implementation for the Portuguese partners use-case, when short-range is possible (left) and when long-range/infrastructure only is possible

The use case is implemented based on the WiFi-direct for the short-range, and the cluster head, the main node that coordinates the communication, is selected in each selection period, based on the overall cluster energy consumption primitives. For long-range, although the long range access communication technology can be xDSL, HFC, satellite, GERAN, UTRAN, eUTRAN, W-LAN or WiMAX in our implementation we will consider the LTE (eUTRAN) and the M2M support architecture.

5   Conclusions and Future Work

In this work we presented the SITAC project where a unified architecture is proposed to support the paradigm of both Social Networks and Internet of things. For this project a platform neutral reference architecture capable of addressing the challenges of scalability, adaptability and security required for an unifying architecture and 'ecosystem' that enable the seamless connection and cooperation of many types of network-connected entities, whether systems, machines, devices. The logical view of the architecture, both in the core part and in the front-end is presented with all identified components. It was also presented the *Intouch* application, which is an energy aware clustering application for social networking applications, scope of the Portuguese partnership within the project.

Future Work in the project include among other tasks, a full demonstration of the crowd based and IoT paradigm with a Solar Energy Production Managed by Users and a Crowd Based Building Management Expert System both including participation of the international partners established both in the industry and in the academic world.

References

1. ITEA 2 SITAC, 11020 SITAC. https://itea3.org/project/sitac.html
2. IoT-A/FP7-IP, Internet-of-Things Architecture. (http://www.iot-a.eu/public)
3. SOFIA/Artemis, Smart Objects for Intelligent Applications. (http://www.sofia-project.eu/)
4. Cardei, M., Thai, M. T., Li, Y.: Energy-efficient target coverage in wireless sensor network. In: Proceedings of Infocom 2005, May 2005
5. Dargie, W., Chao, X., Denko, M.K.: Modelling the energy cost of a fully operational wireless sensor network. Springer Telecommun. Syst. J. **44**(1–2), 3–15 (2010)

Community Discovery Topology Construction for Ad Hoc Networks

Ahlem Drif[1]([✉]), Abdallah Boukerram[2], and Yacine Slimani[3]

[1] Computer Science Department, University of Setif 1, Sétif, Algeria
adrif.univsetif@gmail.com
[2] Computer Science Department, University of Bejaia, Béjaïa, Algeria
boukerram@hotmail.com
[3] Laboratory of Intelligent Systems, University of Setif 1, Sétif, Algeria
slimani_y09@univ-setif.dz

Abstract. One of the most obvious features of ad hoc communication is the analyze of the relationships between the ad hoc network users and their need for communication. On that point, the determination of topologies for efficient broadcast based on property of users of ad hoc networks has attracted a growing interest. In the current work, we propose a method to build a virtual topology that exploits the property of community structure in ad hoc network. The first phase of the proposed method constructs a clustering tree based on structural weight of nodes, while maintaining capacity-efficient links. In the second phase, the algorithm determines a community backbone in order to ensure efficient transmission coverage. Results confirm the generation of a good topology.

Keywords: Graph algorithms · Structural equivalence · Topology algorithm · Ad Hoc networks · Discovering communities

1 Introduction

A mobile ad hoc network is collection of autonomous wireless mobile units that move freely using their wireless interfaces for communication without the aid of an existing infrastructure [1]. This mobile network don't require a centralized administration entity to manage the operation of the different mobile nodes. A very significant characteristic of ad hoc networks is the presence of community structure which can be represented by a group of mobile devices that carried by humans that share common interest. The communication of such devices is, then, necessarily based on socialisation behaviour, so a community organization is paramount and a number of social and technical barriers must be overcome in order for mobile ad hoc communities to self-organize cooperatively [2]. Community structure proprieties, very current in recent years, appears to be common to many real-world networks and allows us to understand the relationship between a single node in microscopy and a groups in the macroscopic [3].

© Institute for Computer Sciences, Social Informatics and Telecommunications Engineering 2015
S. Mumtaz et al. (Eds.): WICON 2014, LNICST 146, pp. 197–208, 2015.
DOI: 10.1007/978-3-319-18802-7_28

Communities (or clusters or modules) are groups of vertices that probably share common properties and/or play similar roles within the graph [7]. The aim of this work is to construct an efficient topology that realistically establishes communication links according to the relevant communities for the users of the ad hoc network. The efficient use of the scarce energy resources available to ad hoc network nodes is one of the fundamental goals of constructing topology, we note that there are two different types of topologies as is proposed in [8]: topology of sets spanning nodes (MPR, k-CDS, DS/IS...) and that of structures based links (DAGs, spanning tree, cliques...). Nodes covering set is based on spanning subsets of nodes, usually independent, covering all other network nodes that includes Multipoint relay (MPR sets), connected dominated set(Dominating Sets), sets of independent nodes (Independent Sets),... etc. Independent sets dominant CDS can be used for building clusters. CDSs have several advantages in network applications such as ease of dissemination and construction of virtual backbones [9], however, connected dominated set may generate an undesirable number of clusterheads. Hence, several studies focus on the decision problem of the minimum connected dominating set. Guha et al. [10] have proposed two algorithms for centralized finding dominant sets connected sub optimal. To minimize the number of cluster heads the WCDS can be used to construct clusters [11]. Several methods have been proposed to construct a Minimum independent set of a graph. These methods extract a maximal set of nodes such Minimum independent set noted that no two nodes of the Minimum independent set are found adjacent in the graph, and no independent set of the graph contains it. The work presented in [12] surveys a comprehensive review of the available to construct MIS and CDS solutions in ad hoc networks. Structures based links are based on the subgraph modeling the network. It includes the directed acyclic graphs (DAG), spanning trees, rings, etc. Looking for solutions to better construct virtual dynamic topology for ad hoc network allows their organization for addressing problematic, routing, data aggregation, discovery community,... etc. Thus, our work consists of creating a virtual topology that discovers communities. The remainder of this paper is organized as follows. The second section describes the constructing topology phase in which the nodes in a cluster form a tree with the root as the cluster-head. Section 3 presents the methodology of discovering the backbone of users communities in ad hoc networks. In Sect. 4 the results of our method are presented. Finally, the last section concludes the paper.

2   Constructing Topology Based on Structural Equivalence

The proposed approach ensures that a mobile can reach all members of its community based on an efficient virtual backbone of community. In this fact, we have proposed a distributed algorithm to construct a clustering tree topology based on structural equivalence. In the first phase, the algorithm identifies a sets of nodes that cover all nodes of the graph, regardless of their belonging to communities in order to build a set of privileged nodes and their clusters. In the second phase, the algorithm connects only nodes in the clustering tree to nodes that are either in the same community or they are covering at least one node of this community by creating virtual backbone of community in order to ensure the nodes community discovery and manage efficiently the routing requests.

2.1   Preliminary and Definitions

Let's consider an ad hoc wireless network modeled by a graph $G = (V, E)$, with V is the set of nodes and $E \subseteq V^2$ is the set of communication edges, according to the unit disk graph (UDG). We suppose that the nodes have the same range transmission and the radio signal propagates according to the free space model. We define

n: the number of nodes in the network, $n = |V|$
k_u: the degree of node u.
Γ: the maximum degree of graph.
$N(u)$: the set of neighbors of node u, $N(u) = \{v \in V/v \neq u \wedge (u, v) \in E\}$
$A_{u,v}$: is the adjacency matrix of the network. It is defined as 1 if nodes u and v are connected, otherwise it is 0.

Each node u belongs to a community of interest which is denoted by C_u. The goal of this work is to enable a node to reach all members of its community through an optimal route of the graph of communication. So, the proposed algorithm analysis similarity between nodes using the information contained in the network structure in order to design an efficient backbone and ensure sufficient coverage of nodes in one community. Similarity can be determined in many different ways. Here, we focus on the topological structure measure [4]. Two nodes in a network are structurally equivalent if they share many of the same network neighbors [6]. The idea of our contribution is to take advantage of the positional perspective of the structural equivalence measure. In an intuitive way, the nodes that have high structural weight maintain high nodes coverage in the constructed topology and the nodes that are members in the same community have a high tendency to have neighbors in common which offer an efficient backbone of all members that belongs to same community. Thus, we define the structural equivalence.

Definition. Two nodes in a network are structurally equivalent if they are connected and share many of the same network neighbors. Formally, the structurally equivalent between two connected nodes u and v can be written

$$\sigma_{vu} = \frac{\sum(A_{u,} * A_{,v}) * A_{uv}}{\sqrt{k_u k_v}} A_{u,v} \tag{1}$$

We define the structural weight for each node. Thus

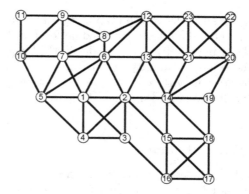

Fig. 1. Initial network

$$S_u = \sum_v \sigma_{uv} \tag{2}$$

Figure 1 shows an example of structural equivalence between two nodes 1 and 2. They have a direct wireless link and share two same neighbors, but both also have neighbors that are not shared. Noting that $\delta_{12} = 0.40$, that means both has a high tendency to being members in the same cluster.

2.2   Determination of Neighbors

We assume that the node u wants to send a message to node v, in case of direct transmission, the minimum power required to send the message is written as follows

$$P_t(u,v) = \tau d_{u,v}^\alpha \tag{3}$$

Where $\tau d_{u,v}^\alpha$ is the power transmission from node u to node v, α is the path loss exponent, $2 \leq \alpha \leq 4$, it depends on the characteristics of communication medium [5]. We assume that all the nodes have the same maximum transmit power and that the wireless medium is symmetric. The proposed algorithm allows to identify the list of neighbor with minimum transmit power. Initially, each node u send a control message at maximum power, upon receiving the beacon from a certain neighbor v, the node can compute the transmit power needed to reach v by comparing the received power of the beacon with the maximum transmit power. Our algorithm selects the neighbor of node u according to the transmit power and eliminates the neighbor node which requires a transmit power upper than a given threshold of transmit signal strength in order to reduce the number of coordination and the energy consumption.

2.3   Constructing a Clustering Tree Algorithm

In this section, we propose a clustering mechanism, clustering tree algorithm, exploiting the set of privileged nodes to ensure sufficient coverage and constructing a virtual topology able to support efficiently the messages exchange for community discovery backbone construction. The algorithm is composed of three steps like representing in algorithm 1: first, node u broadcasts a beacon message containing its ID and position at maximum transmit power, then, when beacon messages of other nodes are received, every node in the network checks whether it has efficient power link $P_t(u, v)$ between its neighbors. If so, it adds them to the set of its neighbors, in the last step, every node updates the matrix adjacency, computes and broadcasts its structural weight in local way, then, a clusters construction phase is initiated to determine the clustering tree, which is a subgraph of G.

In clusters formation phase, we define nodes state as follows:cluster member (SN) and

$state_u = CH$, cluster head (CH).
$state_u = SN$, cluster member (Simple Node).
$state_u = LN$, cluster member (Leaf Node).

Several clustering approaches have been proposed. The Lowest-ID algorithm [13] gives each node a separate ID "identification" and periodically broadcasts a list of its neighbors. This algorithm has been improved in [14]. Basu et al. [15] introduced a metric for mobility for ad hoc mobile networks witch is based on the ratio of the received power levels of successive transmissions measured at any node of all its neighboring nodes. The definition of a cluster should not be defined a priori by some fixed criteria, but should reflect the density of the network [16]. In our work, the idea is that nodes have highest structural weight are the best candidates for cluster head covering larger number of nodes and constructing a clustering tree. Therefore, the proposed cluster head selection process is as follows: each node u compares its structural weight with its 1-neighbors $N(u)$, let $v \in N(u)$, if the node u has the highest structural weight $(S(u) > S(v))$, it is selected as cluster head $L(u) = u$, otherwise the algorithm chooses as a parent of node u the highest structural weight neighbor $D(u) = z$, so we have defined three cases to allow the node u to join the cluster:

- If u's parent is a cluster head, u will join it $(D(u) = L(w) = w)$.
- If u's parent is not a cluster head, the node compares its structural weight with that of its neighbors except its parent w (this set is defined $M(u) = u \cup N(u) \cap w$), in order to join the nearest cluster head, so the node u selects a new parent, the process will be iterated until that u will join its cluster head.
- When node u has low degree $(k_u = 2)$ or is a leaf node it will join its parent node w, then a branch of a tree extends in height until it joins its cluster head.

Note that the procedure for constructing the topology, $Construct(T, u, w)$ builds a clustering tree gradually in which every node belongs to a cluster and the designed inter-clusters allow the nodes to exchange data.

3   Construction of Community Discovery Backbone

We proposed a distributed algorithm to build a community discovery virtual backbone which is presented in algorithm 2. Discovering this underlying structure allows us to understand how network topology and user communities are related.

In the second phase of our method, a node s sends a search request (s, C_r) to its members of cluster to discover in-demand community C_r. We assume that a request sent by a node is received correctly in a finished time by all its members of cluster. The cluster head nodes are coverage nodes, it serves as a relay, and consequently they are part of the backbone. Upon receiving of such request by a node u, it should respond by sending a request reply according to its state in the cluster (NS, NF). When the node u is a simple node, the steps of the algorithm is as follows: if this node belongs to the in-demand community, it responds then by sending a request reply $RRep(u, M = 1, Mem = \{(u, L(u))\}, LB = \{\})$ to $D(u)$, where u is the node identifier, the parameter $M = 1$ indicates that the node belongs to the in-demand community, the set $Mem = \{(u, L(u))\}$ contain the cluster head of node u, and the set LB indicates all nodes identified as a member of the backbone. Then, the node u is added to the local backbone that is connected to the cluster head $L(u)$ calling the construction function $LocalBackbone(L(u))$. After, node u will broadcast the search request to the list of node u 's child $NC = \{v \in N(u)/D(v) = u\}$ even if it does not belong to the in-demand community in order to find the bakcbone members by sending $Req(u, C_r)$ to $NC(u)$. Let v belongs to NC. Node u processes all received requests $RRep(v, M(v), Mem, LB)$ from a node $v \in NC(u)$, so, the algorithm adds node v to the local backbone if $M(v) = 1$. However, if the node u and the list of node u's child is not a member of the in-demand community, u and its child will not be selected as a member of the virtual backbone. If a leaf node u belongs to the in-demand community, it will send the responds to its parent.

4   Discussion

The proposed approach discovers and describes an efficient backbone for communication between the users of the ad hoc networks according to their communities of interest. The first method is a clustering topology phase, where all the nodes get its neighborhood information, update its own data structure (adjacency matrix, structural equivalence, structural weight), and construct a clustering tree topology which ensures connectivity and result of an efficient coverage of community members.

Data: $G(E, V), P_{max}$ the maximum node transmit power.

1. Initialization
begin
 | $N(u) = \{\}$; $D(u) = \{\}$; $L(u) = \{\}$; $M(u) = \{\}$;
end

2. Information exchange
begin
 | u sends beacon message at transmit power P_{max}
end

3. Neighbors detection
begin
 | upon receiving message from node v
 | Compute the $P_t(u, v)$
 | **if** $P_t(u, v) < P_{threshold(u,N(u))}$ **then**
 | | $N(u) = N(u) \cup \{v\}$
 | **end**
end

4. Clusters Construction
begin
 | u broadcasts locally the list of its neighbor
 | Wait for stabilization time
 | Update A_{uv}
 | Compute structural equivalence neighbors $list(u)$
 | Node u broadcast its structural weight in beacon message
 | **while** $L(u) = \{\}$ **do**
 | | **if** $(\forall v \in N(u), S(v) < S(u))$ **then**
 | | | $L(u) = u$
 | | | $Statut_u = CH$
 | | | $Construct(T, (u, N(u)))$
 | | **end**
 | | **else**
 | | | $(\exists w \in N(u), (\forall v \in \{u\} \cup N(u), S(v) < S(w))$
 | | | $D(u) = \{w\}$
 | | | $L(u) = L(w)$
 | | | **if** $D(w) = L(w) = w$ **then**
 | | | | $Statut_u = SN$
 | | | | **if** $deg(u) = 1$ **then**
 | | | | | $Statut_u = LN$
 | | | | **end**
 | | | | $Construct(T, u, w)$
 | | | **end**
 | | | **else**
 | | | | begin
 | | | | | **if** $D(w) = L(w) \neq w$ and $deg(u) >= 3$ **then**
 | | | | | | $M(u) = u \cup N(u) \cap w$
 | | | | | | order(list(M(u)))
 | | | | | | $(\exists z \in M(u), (z = first(list(M(u)))$
 | | | | | | **if** $u=z$ **then**
 | | | | | | | $L(u) = u$
 | | | | | | | $Statut_u = CH$
 | | | | | | | $Construct(T, u, M(u))$
 | | | | | | **end**
 | | | | | | **else**
 | | | | | | | $D(z) = x, x \in N(z)$
 | | | | | | | $L(u) = L(z) = L(x)$ Iterated until that u is joined to its
 | | | | | | | cluster head
 | | | | | | **end**
 | | | | | **end**
 | | | | | **else**
 | | | | | | **if** $deg(u) < 3$ **then**
 | | | | | | | $D(w) = k, k \in N(w)$
 | | | | | | | $Statut_u = SN$
 | | | | | | | **if** $deg(u) = 1$ **then**
 | | | | | | | | $Statut_u = LN$
 | | | | | | | **end**
 | | | | | | | $Construct(T, u, w)$
 | | | | | | | $L(u) = L(w) = L(k)$ Iterated until that u is joined to its
 | | | | | | | cluster head
 | | | | | | **end**
 | | | | | **end**
 | | | | **end**
 | | | **end**
 | | **end**
 | **end**
end
return $ConstructClusteringTree(T, D(u), L(u))$

Algorithm 1. Construction of clustering tree - phase 1

Data: $T, L(u), D(u)$
Procedure CommunityDiscoveryBackbobne ()
begin

    M: variable indicating whether the node u belongs to the searched community or not.
    $Cache$: caching of node u
    $LB = \{\}$
    Upon receiving the request packet $Req(s, C_r)$ from u node
    if $(statut_u = NS)$ **then**
        if $(C_u = C_r)$ **then**
            Send $RRep(u, M = 1, Mem = \{(u, L(u))\}, LB = \{u\})$ to $D(u)$
            Add u to $LocalBackbone(L(u))$
        end
        $NC = \{v \in N(u)/D(v) = u\}$
        Send Request packet $Req(u, C_r)$ to $NC(u)$
        time stabilization
        for *each received* $RRep(v, M(v), Mem, LB)$ *from* $v \in NC(u)$ **do**
            if $(M(v) = 1)$ **then**
                $LB = LB \cup \{v \in NC(u)/M(v) = 1 \wedge D(v) = u\}$
                $LocalBackbone = true$
            end
        end
        if $(LocalBackbone = true) and (C_u = C_r)$ **then**
            Send $RRep(u, M = 1, Mem = \{(u, L(u))\}, LB)$ to $L(u)$
            Add all nodes in LB to LocalBackbone(L(u))
        end
        if $(C_u \neq C_r) and (LocalBackbone = true)$ **then**
            Send $RRep(u, M = 0, Mem = \{(u, L(u))\}, LB)$ to $L(u)$
            Add u to $LocalBackbone(L(u))$
            Add all nodes in LB to $LocalBackbone(L(u))$
        end
    end
    else
        if $(statut_u = NF)$ **then**
            if $(C_u = C_r)$ **then**
                Send $RRep(u, M = 1, Mem = \{(u, L(u))\}, LB = \phi)$ to $D(u)$
                Add u to $LocalBackbone(L(u))$
            end
        end
    end
end
begin
    Broadcast $Req(s, C_r)$ to node member of cluster for 1 hop
    $CommunityDiscoveryBackbobne()$
    Send information for Update caching of node s
end
return $GlobalBackbone(C_r)$

Algorithm 2. Constructing Global Backbone Algorithm phase 2

In Fig. 1, the network contains 23 nodes and 54 links. After eliminating the non-efficient power link, we have obtained 43 links. Table 1 gives the structural equivalence between nodes and the structural weight of each node. The algorithms selects the leaders 1, 9,15, and 23 because they have the highest structural weight (2.19, 1.63, 1.64, and 1.83) respectively or they prefer to become cluster head if the neighbor node owns the highest structural weight has joined a parent node that is not in their direct neighbors. During the construction of clusters the algorithm selects the inter-cluster links with a good link quality (red lines in Fig. 2a). The obtained clustering tree topology is shown in Fig. 2a. The second phase selects the members of the virtual backbone. Figure 2b shows an example about how to discover a community backbone (the backbone of community (1) is presented by red line), for example, the node $s(id = 8)$ sends a request for discovering its community members, upon receiving this request from the cluster

Table 1. Structural equivalence and structural weight of the studied network.

Nodes	$\sigma_{i,j}$						S
1	$\sigma_{1,2(0,40)}$	$\sigma_{1,3(0,47)}$	$\sigma_{1,4(0,47)}$	$\sigma_{1,5(0,47)}$	$\sigma_{1,6(0,18)}$	$\sigma_{1,7(0,18)}$	2, 19
2	$\sigma_{2,1(0,40)}$	$\sigma_{2,3(0,28)}$	$\sigma_{2,6(0,22)}$				0, 90
3	$\sigma_{3,1(0,47)}$	$\sigma_{3,2(0,28)}$	$\sigma_{3,4(0,33)}$				1, 08
4	$\sigma_{4,1(0,47)}$	$\sigma_{4,3(0,33)}$	$\sigma_{4,5(0,33)}$				1, 13
5	$\sigma_{5,1(0,47)}$	$\sigma_{5,4(0,33)}$	$\sigma_{5,7(0,26)}$				1, 06
6	$\sigma_{6,1(0,18)}$	$\sigma_{6,2(0,22)}$	$\sigma_{6,8(0,22)}$	$\sigma_{6,12(0,45)}$	$\sigma_{6,13(0,20)}$		1, 28
7	$\sigma_{7,1(0,18)}$	$\sigma_{7,5(0,26)}$	$\sigma_{7,8(0,22)}$	$\sigma_{7,9(0,45)}$	$\sigma_{7,10(0,26)}$		1, 37
8	$\sigma_{8,6(0,22)}$	$\sigma_{8,7(0,22)}$	$\sigma_{8,9(0,25)}$	$\sigma_{8,12(0,25)}$			0, 95
9	$\sigma_{9,7(0,45)}$	$\sigma_{9,8(0,25)}$	$\sigma_{9,10(0,58)}$	$\sigma_{9,11(0,35)}$			1, 63
10	$\sigma_{10,7(0,26)}$	$\sigma_{10,9(0,58)}$	$\sigma_{10,11(0,41)}$				1, 24
11	$\sigma_{11,9(0,35)}$	$\sigma_{11,10(0,41)}$					0, 76
12	$\sigma_{12,6(0,45)}$	$\sigma_{12,8(0,25)}$	$\sigma_{12,13(0,5)}$	$\sigma_{12,23(0,22)}$			1, 37
13	$\sigma_{13,6(0,20)}$	$\sigma_{13,12(0,45)}$	$\sigma_{13,14(0,18)}$	$\sigma_{13,21(0,45)}$	$\sigma_{13,23(0,40)}$		1, 68
14	$\sigma_{13,14(0.18)}$	$\sigma_{14,15(0,20)}$	$\sigma_{14,18(0,41)}$	$\sigma_{14,19(0,24)}$	$\sigma_{14,21(0.20)}$		1.23
15	$\sigma_{15,14(0,20)}$	$\sigma_{15,16(0,35)}$	$\sigma_{15,17(0,58)}$	$\sigma_{15,18(0,50)}$			1, 64
16	$\sigma_{16,15(0,35)}$	$\sigma_{16,17(0.41)}$					0, 75
17	$\sigma_{17,15(0,58)}$	$\sigma_{17,16(0,41)}$	$\sigma_{17,18(0,29)}$				1, 27
18	$\sigma_{18,14(0,41)}$	$\sigma_{18,15(0,50)}$	$\sigma_{18,17(0,29)}$	$\sigma_{18,19(0,29)}$			1, 49
19	$\sigma_{19,14(0,24)}$	$\sigma_{19,18(0,29)}$					0, 52
20	$\sigma_{20,21(0,25)}$	$\sigma_{20,22(0,35)}$	$\sigma_{20,23(0,45)}$				1, 05
21	$\sigma_{21,13(0,45)}$	$\sigma_{14,21(0.20)}$	$\sigma_{21,20(0,25)}$	$\sigma_{21,23(0,45)}$			1, 35
22	$\sigma_{22,20(0,35)}$	$\sigma_{22,23(0,32)}$					0, 67
23	$\sigma_{23,12(0,22)}$	$\sigma_{23,13(0,40)}$	$\sigma_{23,20(0,45)}$	$\sigma_{23,21(0,45)}$	$\sigma_{23,22(0,32)}$		1, 83

Fig. 2. Results of the proposed algorithm. (a) a clustering tree network topology. (b) the community backbone (Color figure online).

head 9, it will broadcasts the search request to its cluster members, so, if the leaf nodes 10 and 11 belong to the in-demand community $C_r = 1$, they will send a responds to its parent 9 and so on. The clustering tree algorithm is cost in term of messages overhead. We have proposed a distributed algorithm in the construction phase of the discovering community backbone, all nodes are searching community members, a node looks for its community by sending a research request to its cluster head which send the research request to its members, so the complexity message is $(n\Gamma^2)$, where Γ is the maximum degree of graph. The constructed structures are planar, bounded degree and ensures connectivity.

In order to simulate the community backbone construction, we have proposed a second modified clustering scheme using a Minimum Independent Dominating Set algorithm defined in [17]. The dominating independent set based clustering scheme ensures that the entire network is covered. To this end, we have constructed the set of MIS nodes of the graph $G(V, E)$, and then we focus on the construction of covering graph of a community C_r, we have employed the method for constructing a Minimum-Degree Spanning Tree proposed in [18]. In this MIS backbone method, we have retained the same principle manner for exchanging messages between each MIS node and its dominated nodes that we have defined in algorithm 2. We have built our own simulator to evaluate the performances of our clustering tree backbone and compare it with the results given when using MIS backbone algorithm. The following scenario is fixed: all nodes have the same transmission range of $50m$ and all nodes are deployed uniformly and randomly in a square area of $100\,\text{m} \times 100\,\text{m}$. We compare both algorithms in terms of the number of backbone nodes, and network lifetime, which is defined as the time duration until the first backbone node runs out of energy. We can see in Fig. 3 the number of backbone nodes that construct the virtual backbone of the in-demand community C_r, when the total number of nodes is changing from 50 nodes to 100 nodes, the number of backbone nodes is increasing as the network size increases, we remark that clustering tree structure uses less backbone

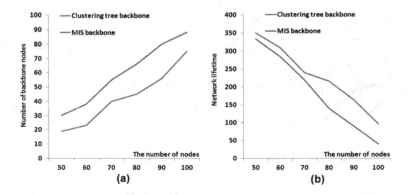

Fig. 3. Comparaison between MIS backbone and Clustering tree backbone. (a) The number of backbone nodes. (b) Network lifetime.

nodes than the MIS backbone. This is because it selects the best candidates for cluster head covering larger number of nodes by using the structural weight metric which take into consideration the relationship between the users of the ad hoc networks. The simulation results show that our algorithm has a good performance because of the smaller virtual backbone performs better in network lifetime prolonging.

5   Conclusion

This paper describes the construction of a virtual backbone to ensure an efficient communication between nodes that share the same community of interest. That for we propose a topology based on the reduction of the set of nodes that provide the coverage of the community members, so when a cluster head received an information addressed to a given community members, it relays this information, only, via a link belonging to a backbone. Therefore, the number of data exchange is optimized. Future work includes improving backbone schemes metrics such as mobility, rate of broadcast messages and stability.

References

1. Ilyas, M.: The Handbook of Ad Hoc Wireless Networks. CRC PRESS LLC, Boca Raton Florida (2003)
2. Rheingold, H.: Smart Mobs: The Next Social Revolution. Macquarie University, Sydney (2002)
3. Flake, G.W., Lawrence, S., Giles, C.L., Coetzee, F.M.: Selforganization and identification of web communities. Computer 35(3), 6670 (2002)
4. Lorrain, F., White, H.C.: Structural equivalence of individuals in social networks. J. Math. Sociol. 1(1), 49–80 (1971)
5. Rappaport, T.S.: Wireless Communications: Principles and Practices. Prentice Hall, New York (1996)
6. Mark, N.: Networks an introduction. Oxford University Press, New York (2010)
7. Boccaletti, S., Latora, V., Moreno, Y., Chavez, M., Hwang, D.-U.: Complex networks: Structure and dynamics. Phys. Rep. 424(4), 175–308 (2006)
8. Haddad, M., Kheddouci, H.: Discussion on virtual dynamic topologies in Ad Hoc networks. In: META 2010, Hammamet, Tunisia (2010)
9. Stojmenovic, I., Seddigh, M., Zunic, J.: Dominating sets and neighbor elimination-based broadcasting algorithms in wireless networks. IEEE Trans. Parallel Distrib. Syst. 13(1), 14–25 (2002)
10. Guha, S., Khuller, S.: Approximation Algorithms for Connected Dominating Sets. Springer, New York (1998). LLC, ISSN: 0178–4617
11. Chen, Y.P., Liestman, A.L.: A zonal algorithm for clustering Ad Hoc networks. Int. J. Found. Comput. Sci. 14(2), 305–322 (2003)
12. Liu, Z., Wang, B., Guo, L.: A survey on connected dominating set construction algorithm for wireless sensor networks. Inf. Technol. J. 9, 1081–1092 (2010)
13. Gerla, M., Tsai, J.T.-C.: Multicluster, Mobile Multimedia Radio Networks, Wireless Networks. Wireless Netw. 1, 255–265 (1995)

14. Chiang, C.-C., Wu, H.-K., Liu, W., Gerla, M.: Routing in clustered networks with fading channel. In: Proceedings of SICON (1997)
15. Basu, P., Khan, N., Little, T.: A mobility based metric for clustering in mobile Ad Hoc networks. In: DCS Workshop (2001)
16. Mitton, N., Busson, A., Fleury, E: Self-organization in large scale Ad Hoc networks. In: 3rd Med-Hoc-Net, June 2004
17. Goddard, W., Hedetniemi, S.T., Jacobs, D.P., Srimani, K.: Self-Stabilizing protocols for maximal matching and maximal independent sets for Ad Hoc networks. In: Proceedings of IPDPS, pp. 162–162 (2003)
18. Blin, L., Gradinariu, M. Butucaru, P., Rovedakis, S.: Self-stabilizing minimum-degree spanning tree within one from the optimal degree. In: Proceedings of the 23rd IEEE International Conference on Parallel and Distributed Processing Systems (IPDPS), Rome, Italy, pp. 1–11 (2009)

Applied MMAS Algorithm to Optimal Resource Allocation to Support QoS Requirements in NGNs

Dac-Nhuong Le[✉]

Hai Phong University, Hai Phong, Vietnam
Nhuongld@hus.edu.vn

Abstract. In this paper, we proposed a novel Min-Max Ant System algorithm for dynamic resource allocation with many of service classes while maximizing the provider's utility in service-oriented networks. The model considers a pricing scheme for the offered services and the quality of service (QoS) requirements of each service class, which operates under a probabilistic delay bound constraint. The goal is to investigate how the utility function and the resource allocation respond to changes of various parameters given the QoS requirements of each service class. Our algorithm performance is evaluated through numerical studies and our solution is approximated the optimal solution. The computational results showed that this approach is currently among the best performing algorithms and much better than previous studies for this problem.

Keywords: Pricing model · Resource allocation · Quality of service · Next Generation Network · Min-max ant system

1 Introduction

The Next Generation Network (NGN) architecture based on IP network to supporting different access network technologies, handle diverse types of traffics. NGN will provide advanced services, such as QoS guarantees, to users and their applications. As a result of, these enhancements, it is expected that service providers will face an increasing number of users as well as a wide variety of applications. Under these demanding conditions, network service providers must carefully provision and allocate network resources for their customers. Provisioning is the acquisition of large end-to-end network services/connections over a long time scale. In contrast, allocation is the distribution of these provisioned services to individual users over a smaller time scale [1]. Determining the optimal amounts to provision and allocate remains a difficult problem under realistic conditions. Service providers must balance user needs in the short-term while provisioning connections for the long-term. Furthermore, this must be done in a scalable fashion to meet the growing demand for network services, while also being adaptable to future network technologies. In [2], P. Xu et al. proposed a measurement-based resource allocation scheme based on a linear pricing model

© Institute for Computer Sciences, Social Informatics and Telecommunications Engineering 2015
S. Mumtaz et al. (Eds.): WICON 2014, LNICST 146, pp. 209–216, 2015.
DOI: 10.1007/978-3-319-18802-7_29

and average queue delay guarantees. This scheme has the disadvantage of not being scalable to large number of service classes. Moreover, average queue delay is not always an appropriate QoS constraint. The authors in [3] perform maximization over a utility function provided from the network users and resources are shared based on the solution of that optimization problem. In [4], the authors study the problem of resource allocation with dynamic pricing in which the network administrator controls the price of the resources that users demand based on the demand the prices are dynamically changed over different time periods so as to maximize the revenue of the administrator. Measurement-based resource allocation has also been studied in different contexts in [5,6]. The online traffic control part of this work utilizes the EWMA control scheme [7,8] monitoring traffic intensities so as to optimally allocate the resources of a Switched Processing System. Traffic measurements play also a key-role in [9] for setting the optimal pricing scheme that maximizes social welfare using traffic monitoring. Similarly, an optimal measurement-based pricing scheme for M/M/1 queues, where the total charge depends on both the mean delay at the queue and arrival rate of each customer is presented in [10]. H. Yeganeh et al. consider the problem of pricing for optimal resource allocation service using engineering optimization with Particle Swarm algorithm (PSO) that ensures efficient resource allocation that provides guaranteed quality of service while maximizing profit in multiservice networks in [11]. In [12], we proposed Ant Colony Optimization (ACO) [13] algorithm to solve this problem.

2   Problem Formulation

The pricing model introduced in [9], whose solution yields the optimal allocation of resources to the network service node. Suppose that the node can provide N different types of services. The proportions of these services to be allocated are denoted by $s = (s_1, s_2, ..., s_N)$. The profit of a provider is the difference between the revenue $r(s)$ that is obtained for providing these services and the cost $c(s)$ that incurs from producing them. The aim of this provider is to maximize the profit function subject to the feasibility constraints. If the system is already highly utilized and the reallocation of resources cannot alleviate the incurred cost, the provider should consider acquiring more resources. It should be noted that prices cannot by a specific QoS performance. Prices are used as a priority parameter for each service s_i and the intuition is that service that pays more will get more bandwidth. Allocation also depends on the QoS ε_i and the delay threshold d_i. In other words, our utility function represents the level of user satisfaction at the allocated rate and according to the desired QoS. We have a SLA violation if at given traffic conditions $\bar{\alpha}$, σ_i and H_i, the stochastic delay bound $D_i(s_i)$, for the agreed QoS $\varepsilon_i \geq d_i$. A stricter QoS implies a small value of ε_i that generates a larger $D_i(s_i)$. Hence, the SLA is more likely to be violated for a given delay threshold d_i and, therefore, the provider is motivated to allocate more resources to that service class.

Putting the revenue and cost components together, the resource allocation to support QoS requirements to maximize the profit function subject to the feasibility constraints [15] following notation in Table 1 is defined beblow.

Table 1. Definition notation

Notation	Mean
$s = \{s_i\}_{i=1..N}$	Set of N different types of services in each node
$r_i(s_i)$	The profit of a provider received from services $s_i \forall i = 1..N$
$c_i(s_i)$	The cost of a provider is obtained for providing these services $s_i \forall i = 1..N$
p_i	The price that the provider charges for the ith service s_i
b_i	The amount the provider has to reimburse the users whenever the service level agreement (SLA) are not satisfied. A higher priority class u requires better service than a lower one v and thus it is charged accordingly $p_u > p_v$ and $b_u > b_v$
$D_i(s_i)$	Denotes the value of the performance metric experienced by users of service s_i
d_i	The delay threshold, target level under the service level agreement
β_i	The parameter controls the steepness of the cost function
ε_i	The QoS required (e.g. $\varepsilon_i = 10^{-6}$)
$\bar{\alpha}_i$	The traffic conditions of service s_i
$s_i C$	The resources (*e.g., bandwidth, CPU,...*) dedicated to this particular class s_i
H	The Hurst parameter

Definition 1. (Resource allocation support QoS requirements problem)

$$f = \max_{S} \left\{ \sum_{i=1}^{N} p_i s_i C - \sum_{i=1}^{N} d_i D_i(s_i) e^{\beta_i(D_i(s_i)-d_i)} \right\} \tag{1}$$

subject to:

$$\begin{cases} s_i \geq 0, \ \forall i = 1..N \\ \sum_{i=1}^{N} s_i \leq 1 \\ s_i > \bar{\alpha}_i, \ \forall i = 1..N \end{cases} \tag{2}$$

3   Our Algorithm

The Max-Min Ant System (MMAS) [14] based on several modifications to Ant System [13]. The configuration of ant k is encrypted by a real array $k = \{s_1, s_2, ..., s_N\}$, where s_i is the proportions of these services to be allocated and $s_i \in [0,1]$ is generated as uniformly distributed random number corresponding sets of N different types of services. We use fully random initialization in order to initialize the ant population, the pheromone matrix $A_{N \times N}$ is generated to represent a location for ant movement, and possible receiver location. We use real encoding to express an element of matrix $a_{ij} = [r_i(s_i) - c_i(s_i)] - [r_j(s_j) - c_j(s_j)]$ is the profit distance of two providers. Each ant can move to any location according to the transition probability defined by:

$$p_{ij}^k = \frac{[\tau_{ij}]^\alpha [\eta_{ij}]^\beta}{\sum\limits_{l \in N_i^k} [\tau_{ij}]^\alpha [\eta_{ij}]^\beta} \tag{3}$$

where, τ_{ij} is the pheromone content of the path from vertical s_i to s_j; N_i^k is the neighborhood includes only locations that have not been visited by ant k when it is at vertical s_i; η_{ij} is the desirability of service s_j, and it depends of optimization goal so it can be our cost function. The influence of the pheromone concentration to the probability value is presented by the constant α, while constant β do the same for the desirability. Let τ_{min}, τ_{max} are lower and upper bounds on pheromone values. We initialize all pheromone trails to $\tau_{max}, \forall \tau_{ij}$. The ants deposit pheromone on the locations they visited according to the relation.

$$\tau_{ij} \leftarrow (1 - \rho)\tau_{ij} + \Delta\tau_{ij}^{best} \tag{4}$$

with parameter ρ is the trail evaporation rate ($0 \le \rho < 1$). Pheromone updates are performed using a strong elitist strategy: only the best solution generated is allowed to update pheromone trails. This can be the *iteration-best* solution (I_{best}), that is, the best in the current iteration, or the *global-best* solution (G_{best}).

In fact, the I_{best} and G_{best} ants can be used alternately in the pheromone update. $\Delta\tau_{ij}^{best} = \frac{1}{f(G_{best})}$ or $\Delta\tau_{ij}^{best} = \frac{1}{f(I_{best})}$ is the amount of pheromone that ant k exudes to the service s_j when it is going from vertical s_i to vertical s_j. If a trail gets smaller than the minimum trail limit, the trail is set to the minimal value and if a trail gets bigger than the maximum trails limit, the trail is set to the maximal value. After pheromone update, τ_{ij} is set in $[\tau_{min}, \tau_{max}], \forall \tau_{ij}$ defined by:

$$\tau_{ij} = \begin{cases} \tau_{max} & \text{if } \tau_{ij} > \tau_{max} \\ \tau_{max} & \text{if } \tau_{ij} \in [\tau_{min}, \tau_{max}] \\ \tau_{min} & \text{if } \tau_{ij} < \tau_{min} \end{cases} \tag{5}$$

After the trails update, ants construct a new population of solutions and the process repeats, the cost function for the ant k is the provider's profit given by (1). The complexity of algorithm is $O(N^2.N_{Max}.K)$ where, N is the number of services, K is ant population size, N_{Max} is number of iterations respectively. We have already implemented and applied variants as follows:

The performance of MMAS is evaluated in 3 case studies to verify the effects of parameter to utilities function and compare the optimal solution of PSO [11], ACO [12] and results in [15]. The experiment was conducted on Genuine Intel CPU Duo Core 3.0 GHz, 2 GB of RAM machine.

4 Experimental Evaluations

Our goal is to investigate how the utility function $f(\bar{x})$, and the resource allocation vector $\bar{x}$ respond to changes of various parameters, including the mean arrival rate ($\bar{\alpha}_i$), price (p_i), delay threshold (d_i) and Hurst parameter (H_i). We start analysis our experiences with a simple system of two service classes

Algorithm 1. Min-Max Ant System-MMAS

```
BEGIN
    INITIALIZATION:
        Algorithm parameters: α = 1, β = 10, ρ = 0.5. Pheromone trails: τ_min = 0.01, τ_max = 0.5
        Ant population size: K = 100. Maximum number of iteration: N_Max = 500;
    GENERATION:
        Initialize pheromone trails τ_ij = τ_max, ∀τ_ij; i = 1; I_best ⇐ ∅; G_best ⇐ ∅;
        Repeat
            For each ant k = 1...K do
                Construct solution s^k;
                If (I_best = ∅) then I_best ⇐ s^k;
                If f(I_best) < f(s^k) then
                    I_best ⇐ s^k; Update pheromone trails follows I_best by (4) and (5);
                end if
            end for
            If (G_best = ∅) then G_best ⇐ I_best;
            If (f(G_best) < f(I_best)) then
                G_best ⇐ I_best; Update pheromone trails follows G_best by (4) and (5);
            end if
        Until (i > N_Max) or (optimal solution found);
        s* ⇐ G_best; Compute cost function f(s*) according to (1);
END
```

$s_i(i = 1, 2)$, the parameters of each service class are $p_i = 1$, $b_i = 0.1$ (price_unit/ Mbps), $d_i = 0.01$, QoS(ε_i)=10^{-6}, $\beta_i = 10$, $\bar{\alpha}_i = 0.2$, $\sigma_i = 0.01$, $H_i = 0.7$. The traffic parameters $\bar{\alpha}_i, \alpha_i$ are normalized to the capacity $C = 10$ Mbps.

Case study 1: Table 2(a) is shown a comparison the optimal allocations and utilitites functions of ACO, PSO and MMAS when change the arrival rates $(\bar{\alpha}_1, \bar{\alpha}_2)$ varies while all other parameters are held fixed. Figure 1(a) show that when the arrival rate varies the optimal solution can be observed. In the equal arrival rates case the resource are equally shared. Moreover, the system becomes more stressed when the overall profit of the provider decreases substantially.

Case study 2: Comparison the optimal allocations and utilitites functions of ACO, PSO and MMAS when change the delay thresholds (d_1, d_2) varies while

Table 2. Comparison the optimal solutions when change the parameters $\bar{\alpha}_i, d_i, p_i$

(a) Comparison the optimal solutions when change the arrival rates

			PSO [11]		ACO [12]		MMAS		Optimal* [15]		Δf(s*)
Test	ᾱ₁	ᾱ₂	(s₁*, s₂*)	f(s*)	(s₁*, s₂*)	f(s*)	(s₁*, s₂*)	f(s*)	(s₁*, s₂*)	f(s*)	(%)
#1	0.2	0.2	(0.5, 0.5)	9.962	(0.5, 0.5)	9.962	(0.5, 0.5)	9.962	(0.5, 0.5)	9.962	0.00%
#2	0.3	0.2	(0.5462, 0.4538)	9.931	(0.5446, 0.4554)	9.936	(0.5446, 0.4554)	9.936	(0.5446, 0.4554)	9.936	0.00%
#3	0.4	0.2	(0.5911, 0.4089)	9.869	(0.5893, 0.4107)	9.815	(0.5718, 0.4282)	9.885	(0.5873, 0.4127)	9.897	0.12%
#4	0.4	0.3	(0.5215, 0.4785)	7.872	(0.5198, 0.4802)	7.822	(0.5213, 0.4787)	8.214	(0.5275, 0.4725)	8.238	0.29%
#5	0.4	0.5	(0.4532, 0.5467)	6.782	(0.4803, 0.5197)	6.725	(0.4532, 0.5467)	6.782	(0.4516, 0.5484)	6.796	0.21%

(b) Comparison the optimal solutions when change the delay threshold

			PSO [11]		ACO [12]		MMAS		Optimal* [15]		Δf(s*)
Test	d₁	d₂	(s₁*, s₂*)	f(s*)	(s₁*, s₂*)	f(s*)	(s₁*, s₂*)	f(s*)	(s₁*, s₂*)	f(s*)	(%)
#1	0.2	0.2	(0.5, 0.5)	9.962	(0.5, 0.5)	9.962	(0.5, 0.5)	9.962	(0.5, 0.5)	9.962	0.00%
#6	0.01	0.03	(0.5158, 0.4842)	9.956	(0.5217, 0.4673)	9.961	(0.5327, 0.4673)	9.965	(0.5327, 0.4673)	9.969	0.04%
#7	0.01	0.06	(0.5195, 0.4805)	9.968	(0.5187, 0.4813)	9.965	(0.5195, 0.4805)	9.968	(0.5195, 0.4805)	9.968	0.00%
#8	0.01	0.09	(0.5076, 0.4924)	9.858	(0.5102, 0.4898)	9.881	(0.5231, 0.4769)	9.881	(0.5265, 0.4735)	9.978	0.17%
#9	0.01	0.12	(0.5293, 0.4707)	9.982	(0.5375, 0.4625)	9.975	(0.5375, 0.4625)	9.975	(0.5488, 0.4512)	9.982	0.07%

(c) Comparison the optimal solutions when change the pricing factors

			PSO [11]		ACO [12]		MMAS		Optimal* [15]		Δf(s*)
Test	p₁	p₂	(s₁*, s₂*)	f(s*)	(s₁*, s₂*)	f(s*)	(s₁*, s₂*)	f(s*)	(s₁*, s₂*)	f(s*)	(%)
#1	1	1	(0.5, 0.5)	9.96	(0.5, 0.5)	9.96	(0.5, 0.5)	9.96	(0.5, 0.5)	9.96	0.00%
#10	1	2	(0.3049, 0.6951)	16.27	(0.3108, 0.6892)	16.34	(0.3108, 0.6892)	16.34	(0.3083, 0.6917)	16.52	1.08%
#12	2	1	(0.6951, 0.3049)	16.27	(0.6892, 0.3108)	16.34	(0.6892, 0.3108)	16.34	(0.6917, 0.3083)	16.52	1.08%
#13	3	2	(0.6527, 0.3473)	39.05	(0.6534, 0.3466)	39.17	(0.6534, 0.3466)	39.17	(0.6534, 0.3466)	39.17	0.00%
#14	4	1	(0.7298, 0.2702)	30.15	(0.7231, 0.2769)	30.66	(0.7183, 0.2817)	30.69	(0.7183, 0.2817)	30.69	0.00%
#15	4	3	(0.5723, 0.4277)	45.63	(0.5748, 0.4252)	45.75	(0.5748, 0.4252)	45.75	(0.5748, 0.4252)	45.75	0.00%
#16	4	4	(0.5, 0.5)	39.96	(0.5, 0.5)	39.96	(0.5, 0.5)	39.96	(0.5, 0.5)	39.96	0.00%
#17	4	8	(0.245, 0.755)	64.81	(0.257, 0.743)	65.72	(0.257, 0.743)	65.72	(0.276, 0.724)	67.90	3.21%

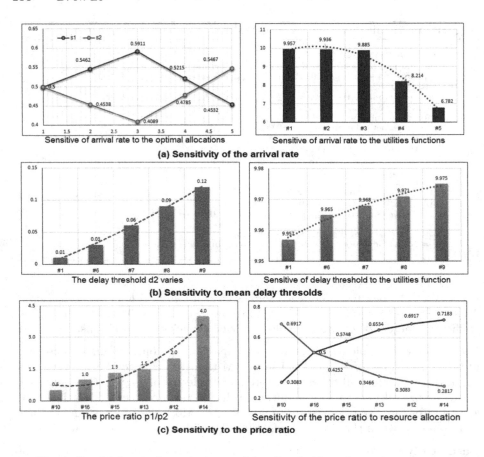

Fig. 1. Sensitivity to the arrival rate, delay thresholds, price ratio parameters

all other parameters are held fixed are shown in Table 2(b). Figure 1(b) show the sensitivity of the model with respect to the delay threshold d_i. We can see when the threshold increases, the profit of the provider also increases which is due to the fact that $\frac{\partial f}{\partial d_i} = b_i \beta_i D_i \beta_i (D_i - d_i) > 0$. And, it is also worth notice that, the class with stricter QoS requirements is allocated more resources.

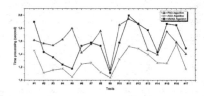

Fig. 2. Comparison of time processing of PSO, ACO and MMAS algorithms

Case study 3: The optimal resource allocations when change the pricing factors (p_1, p_2) varies while all other parameters are held fixed are shown in Table 2(c). If equal prices we obtain equal allocation, while the allocation of resources exhibits a strong sensitivity to the price ratio $\frac{p_1}{p_2}$ are shown in Fig. 1(c).

The comparison of time processing of each algorithm are shown in Fig. 2. This proves that the performance of our algorithm is better than PSO and ACO.

5 Conclusions

In this paper, we proposed a MMAS algorithm for dynamic resource allocation with manny of service classes. Our algorithm performance is evaluated through numerical studies and our solution is approximated the optimal solution. The computational results are compared to PSO [11], ACO [12] to evaluate the effects of the arrival rate, delay thresolds, pricing factors parameter to the optimal allocations and utilities functions show that our approach is currently among the best performing algorithms and much better than previous studies. The optimal available resources allocations dynamically in a network of multiple service intermediaries and multiple types of resources will be our next research goals.

References

1. Nahrstedt, K., et al.: Qos and resource management in distributed interactive multimedia environments. Multimedia Tools Appl. **51**(1), 99–132 (2010)
2. Xu, P., et al.: Profit-oriented resource allocation using online scheduling in flexible heterogeneous networks. Telecommun. Syst. **31**(3), 289–303 (2006)
3. Kalyanasundaram, S., et al.: Optimal resource allocation in multi-class networks with user-specified utility functions. Comput. Netw. **38**(5), 613–630 (2002)
4. Savagaonkar, U., et al.: Online pricing for bandwidth provisioning in multi-class networks. Comput. Netw. **44**(6), 835–853 (2004)
5. Chandra, A., Gong, W., Shenoy, P.D.: Dynamic resource allocation for shared data centers using online measurements. In: Jeffay, K., Stoica, I., Wehrle, K. (eds.) IWQoS 2003. LNCS, vol. 2707, pp. 381–400. Springer, Heidelberg (2003)
6. Knightly, E.W., Shroff, N.B.: Admission control for statistical QoS: theory and practice. IEEE Netw. **13**(2), 20–29 (1999)
7. Lucas, J.M., et al.: Exponentially weighted moving average control schemes: properties and enhancements. Technometrics **32**(1), 129 (1990)
8. Hung, Y., et al.: A measurement based dynamic policy for switched processing systems. In: IEEE International Conference on Communications, pp. 301–306 (2007)
9. Courcoubetis, C., Weber, R.: Pricing Communication Networks. Wiley, New York (2003)
10. Hayel, : Optimal measurement-based pricing for an M/M/1 queue. Netw. Spat. Econ. **7**(2), 177–195 (2007)
11. Yeganeh, H., et al.: Optimal resource allocation in ngn services using engineering optimization with linear constraint particle swarm. IJCSNS **8**, 238–334 (2008)
12. Le, D.N.: Optimizing resource allocation to support qos requirements in next generation networks using aco algorithm. IJCSIT **2**(5), 931–938 (2012)

13. Stutzle, T., Ibanez, M.L., Dorigo, M.: A Concise Overview of Application of Ant Colony Optimization. Wiley, New York (2010)
14. Stutzle, T., Hoos, H.H.: Improving the ant system: a detailed report on the maxmin ant system. Technical report AIDA-96-12, FG Intellektik (1996)
15. Kallitsis, M.G.: Optimal resource allocation for next generation network services. Ph.D. Dissertation, Raleigh, North Carolina (2010)

Sub-Optimum Detection Scheme for Distributed Closed-Loop Quasi Orthogonal Space Time Block Coding in Asynchronous Cooperative Two Dual-Antenna Relay Networks

Abdulghani Elazreg$^{(\boxtimes)}$ and Ahmad Kharaz

Institute for Innovation in Sustainable Engineering, University of Derby,
Derby DE1 3HD, Derby, UK
{A.Elazreg,A.Kharaz}@derby.ac.uk

Abstract. In this paper, a sub-optimum detection scheme is proposed for distributed closed-loop quasi orthogonal space time block (D-CL QO-STBC) for two dual antenna relay nodes in decode-and-forward (DF) asynchronous cooperative relay network. The direct transmission (DT) link connection among the source node and the destination node is considered in this network. The proposed scheme is robust against synchronization error and it reduces the receiver complexity as compared to previous work. Furthermore, the maximum available cooperative diversity gain and full transmission rate between the relay nodes and the destination node, and symbol-by-symbol decoding are all achieved. Simulation results are demonstrated to show the proposed scheme for various synchronization errors and effectively eliminate the interference components induced by intersymbol interference (ISI) among the relay nodes.

Keywords: Distributed space time block coding · Closed-loop method · Asynchronous cooperative relay networks · Sub-optimum detection scheme

1 Introduction

Recently, a new communication scheme, so-called cooperative diversity techniques has been proposed in order to gain the benefits of multi-input multi-output (MIMO) communications systems in a wireless network [1–3]. In particular, distributed space time block coding (STBC) is combined with distributed wireless system, such as an ad-hoc or a wireless sensor network. This kind of application is commonly known as cooperative relay node transmission since the distributed relay nodes in the network will cooperate with each other and apply STBC to provide an effective way of improving system performance [4–7]. In fact, synchronization in distributed wireless system is very essential, it allows for successful communication among relay nodes within the wireless cooperative relay network. There have been a number of reported research works based on

© Institute for Computer Sciences, Social Informatics and Telecommunications Engineering 2015
S. Mumtaz et al. (Eds.): WICON 2014, LNICST 146, pp. 217–228, 2015.
DOI: 10.1007/978-3-319-18802-7_30

implemented distributed (D-STBC) over distributed wireless systems. In these systems perfect synchronization is assumed assuming among cooperating relay nodes in which all the signals transmitted from the cooperating relay nodes will arrive effectively at the destination node simultaneously [6,7]. Nevertheless, due to the distributed nature of cooperative relay nodes and their different local oscillators, the received signals from the relay nodes at the destination node are not continuously aligned in symbol level. Therefore, this lack of synchronization in time results in intersymbol interference (ISI) between the received signals at the destination node, which will damage the orthogonally of the D-STBC and thus makes the conventional D-STBC linear decoding method fail and this will lead to performance degradation [8–10].

In [8], the equalization technique was mainly employed at the destination node to overcome the issue of imperfect synchronization among the transmitted relay nodes at the destination node, however, this leads to increased receiver complexity at the destination node. While in [9], the distributed orthogonal STBC (D-OSTBC) in DF asynchronous cooperative relay networks with parallel interference cancellation (PIC) detection scheme for the case of four relay nodes, each relay equipped only with one antenna is proposed and shown to be a very effective approach to eliminate the timing error at the destination node also the assumption of DT link connection between the source node and the destination node is considered in this work. Nevertheless, the schemes in [9] are limited since complex OSTBC with data transmission rate 3/4 is used between the relay nodes and the destination node. On the other hand, the approach that was introduced in [10] for eliminating the effect of imperfect synchronization issue has achieved the full cooperative diversity order and full data transmission rate between the relay nodes and the destination node by using D-CL QO-STBC and PIC detection scheme in DF asynchronous cooperative relay networks utilizing four relay nodes, each relay node equipped with only one antenna with the assumption there is a DT link connection between the source node and the destination node. However, the PIC detection scheme has the disadvantage that their computational complexity is dependent upon the number of PIC detection iterations which lead to receiver complexity.

In this paper, a sub-optimum detection scheme in DF asynchronous cooperative relay networks using D-CL QO-STBC for two relay nodes, each of which is equipped with two dual antenna and with the assumption there is a DT link connection between the source node and the destination node is proposed. It is shown that the proposed scheme does not require multiple iterations and the detection complexity at the destination is only dependent upon the constellation size. Furthermore, reducing timing error among the relay nodes when using two dual antennas on each relay node will lead to reducing the detection process at the destination node as compared in previous work in [9,10]. Finally the proposed scheme has achieved the full cooperative diversity order and full data transmission rate between the relay nodes and the destination as compared to previous work in [9].

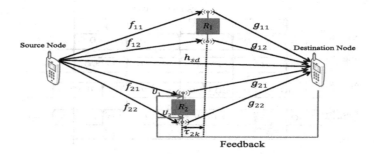

Fig. 1. Asynchronous wireless cooperative relay network with a single antenna at source and destination nodes, and two dual-antenna relay nodes

The paper is structured as follows; Sect. 2 describes the signal model of cooperative two dual antenna relay node network. In Sect. 3 the proposed D-CL QO-STBC under imperfect synchronization for two dual relay nodes is introduced. A sub-optimum detection is presented in Sect. 4 to mitigate the ISI at the symbol level at the destination node. Simulation results are shown in Sect. 5. The final section summarizes this paper.

Notations, $[.]^T$, $[.]^*$, $|.|$, $\Re\{.\}$, $\{.\}^H$ and $CN(0, \sigma_n^2)$ denote transpose, conjugate, absolute value, real part of a complex number, Hermitian (complex conjugate transpose) operations and stands for circularly symmetric Gaussian random vector with zero mean and covariance σ_n^2.

2   Signal Model

In this work, we consider a general two-hop asynchronous cooperative relay network scenario with single source node communicating to destination node via a stage of two wireless relay nodes randomly located within the network region and they are assumed to operate in half-duplex mode. As depicted in Fig. 1, it is assumed that the source node and the destination node are equipped with only one antenna, while the relay nodes are equipped with two dual antenna and the distance between each pair of antenna in each relay node is assumed to be equal to half of transmitted wavelength[1] [11]. Also, the channel state information (CSI) is assumed to be estimated without error at the destination node.

The relay nodes are assumed to be regenerative, i.e., they perform decoding operations on the received signals and forward the re-encoding signals to the destination node, this protocol so-called DF transmission type. The DT link connection between the source node and the destination node is assumed to be available as shown in Fig. 1. Throughout this paper all links are modelled as Rayleigh fading frequency flat channels. We assume that the channel coefficients are constant during the transmission of a signal code block (quasi-static), where

---

[1] The received signal becomes practically uncorrelated, if the antennas at the relay nodes are spaced equal to half of transmitted wavelength signals.

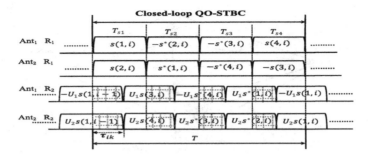

Fig. 2. Received signals misalignment representation at the destination node inducing ISI in the case of two dual-antenna relay nodes

the channel between the source node and each antenna of each relay node is represented as f_{mk}, the relaying channel gain between each antenna of each relay node and the destination node is represented as g_{mk}, $m, k \in 1, 2$, and the channel gain between the source node and the destination node is represented as h_{sd}.

In this paper, a feedback method in [12] is utilized to orthogonalize the QO-STBC and achieve full diversity order with full data transmission rate for four transmission antenna, it is achieved by rotating the transmitted symbols from the first antenna and the second antenna of the second relay node with particular angles [12], while the other two antennas of the first relay node are kept unchanged as shown in Fig. 1. Moreover, the antennas of the first relay node R_1 is assumed to be synchronized to the destination node, while the antennas of the second relay node R_2 is assumed to be asynchronous to the destination node as depicted in Fig. 2.

3   Distributed Closed-Loop QO-STBC in Asynchronous Cooperative Two Dual-Antenna Relay Networks

As in almost all cooperative wireless relay networks, the transmission process can be divided in two orthogonal phases. In the first phase, the source node broadcasts the sequence of information bits, after modulating and mapping to the destination node and the antennas of cooperative relay nodes. The transmitted symbols are grouped into number of symbols pairs and denoted by vector $\mathbf{s}(i) = [s(1, i), ..., s(4, i)]^T$, where i denotes the discrete pair index. Therefore, the signal received $\mathbf{r}_{sd}(i) = [r_{sd}(1, i), ..., r_{sd}(4, i)]^T$ at the destination node through the DT link connection during four different time slots $T_{s1}, ..., T_{s4}$ can be represented as

$$\mathbf{r}_{sd}(i) = h_{sd}\mathbf{s}(i) + \mathbf{n}_{sd}(i) \tag{1}$$

where $\mathbf{n}_{sd}(i) = [n_{sd}(1, i), ..., n_{sd}(4, i)]^T$ is a noise vector containing independent circularly-symmetric complex additive Gaussian random variables at the destination node, each having distribution $CN(0, \sigma_n^2)$. The structure of maximum likelihood (ML) detector is used at the destination node to detect which symbol was actually transmitted from the source node through DT link connection, the least squares (LS) method can be used as follows

$$\hat{\mathbf{s}}_{sd}(i) = arg \min_{s_t \in S} |h_{sd}^* \mathbf{r}_{sd}(i) - |h_{sd}|^2 \, s_t|^2 \qquad (2)$$

where S denotes the set of all possible transmitted vector symbols and $\hat{s}_{sd}(i) = [\hat{s}_{sd}(1,i), ..., \hat{s}_{sd}(4,i)]^T$ is the detected symbols which are actually transmitted from the source node. Even if the DT link connection described in (2) provides limited end-to-end performance is still contains information which can be used to initialize further processing as will be shown in the next section [9,10]. Also the received signal vector $\mathbf{r}_{mk}(i) = [r_{mk}(1,i), ..., r_{mk}(4,i)]^T$ at each antenna of each relay node is given by

$$\mathbf{r}_{mk}(i) = f_{mk}\mathbf{s}(i) + \mathbf{n}_{mk} \quad \text{for} \quad m, k \in 1, 2 \qquad (3)$$

where $\mathbf{n}_{mk}(i) = [n_{mk}(1,i), ..., n_{mk}(4,i)]^T$ is a noise vector containing independent circularly-symmetric complex additive Gaussian random variables at each antenna at each relay node, each having distribution $CN(0, \sigma_n^2)$. In the second phase, it is assumed that the relay nodes are set to work in the DF transmission type. As such, a sufficient level of cyclic redundancy check (CRC) can be included into the signals at the source node, therefore the relaying will happen if the signals are correctly detected at the relay nodes [9]. Therefore, the relay node can successfully decode the signal $\mathbf{s}(i)$ using a DF transmission type, then all the antennas on the relay nodes R_1 and R_2 preform D-QO-STBC encoding on their received vector in (3). However, before transmitting the encoded signal from the antennas on the relay nodes in four different time slots, the modulated signals from the first and the second antennas on the second relay nodes are respectively rotated by two phases $U_1 = e^{j\phi}$ and $U_2 = e^{j\theta}$ as shown in Fig. 1, to provide full cooperative diversity between the relay nodes and destination node in proportion to the number of transmitting antenna on the relay nodes. This is discussed further in [10,12]. Therefore, the transmitted signal matrix from the antennas for both relay nodes can be expressed as

Table 1. Represented the code matrix of D-CL QO-STBC.

	T_{s1}	T_{s2}	T_{s3}	T_{s4}
Ant$_1R_1$	$s(1,i)$	$-s^*(2,i)$	$-s^*(3,i)$	$s(4,i)$
Ant$_2R_1$	$s(2,i)$	$s^*(1,i)$	$-s^*(4,i)$	$-s(3,i)$
Ant$_1R_2$	$U_1s(3,i)$	$-U_1s^*(4,i)$	$U_1s^*(1,i)$	$-U_1s(2,i)$
Ant$_2R_2$	$U_1s(4,i)$	$U_1s^*(3,i)$	$U_1s^*(2,i)$	$U_1s(1,i)$

As shown in Fig. 2, for many practical STBC application such as cooperative transmission, it is impossible to achieve accurate synchronization level between the transmitted signals from the antennas on the first and the second relay nodes at the destination node. This is due to timing misalignment, τ_{2k}, $k \in 1, 2$ between the received versions of these signals at the destination node. As mention in the previous section and shown in Fig. 2, in this model it is assumed that the received signal at the destination node is perfectly synchronized to the relay node R_1 i.e. $\tau_{1k} = 0$. Therefore the received signal $\mathbf{r}(i) = [r(1, i), ..., r(4, i)]^T$ at the destination node in four independent time slots are expressed as follows

$$r(1, i) = \sum_{k=1}^{2}(g_{1k}s(k, i)) + \sum_{k=1}^{2}(U_k g_{2k}s(k + 2, i))$$
$$\underbrace{- U_1 g_{21}^{-1}s(2, i - 1) + U_2 g_{22}^{-1}s(1, i - 1)}_{I_{int}(1,i)} + n(1, i)$$

$$r(2, i) = -g_{11}s^*(2, i) + g_{12}s^*(1, i) - U_1 g_{21}s^*(4, i)$$
$$+ U_2 g_{22}s^*(3, i) + \underbrace{U_1 g_{21}^{-1}s(3, i) + U_2 g_{22}^{-1}s(4, i)}_{I_{int}(2,i)}$$
$$+ n(2, i)$$

$$r(3, i) = -g_{11}s^*(3, i) - g_{12}s^*(4, i) + U_1 g_{21}s^*(1, i)$$
$$+ U_2 g_{22}s^*(2, i) - \underbrace{U_1 g_{21}^{-1}s^*(4, i) + U_2 g_{22}^{-1}s^*(3, i)}_{I_{int}(3,i)}$$
$$+ n(3, i)$$

$$r(4, i) = g_{11}s(4, i) - g_{12}s(3, i) - U_1 g_{21}s(2, i)$$
$$+ U_2 g_{22}s(1, i) + \underbrace{U_1 g_{21}^{-1}s^*(1, i) + U_2 g_{22}^{-1}s^*(2, i)}_{I_{int}(4,i)}$$
$$+ n(4, i) \tag{4}$$

where $n(1, i), ..., n(4, i)$ are additive Gaussian noise terms with distribution CN $(0, \sigma_n^2)$ at the destination node and $I_{int}(1, i), ..., I_{int}(4, i)$ are ISI terms at destination node in each transmission period. Due to asynchronism issue between the relay nodes the channel coefficients g_{2k}^{-1} reflects the ISI from previous symbols as shown in Fig. 2. Therefore, the relative strength of g_{2k}^{-1} is represented by ratio as follows

$$\beta = \frac{|g_{2k}^{-1}|^2}{|g_{2k}|^2} \quad \text{for} \quad k \in 1, 2 \tag{5}$$

Due to co-located both antenna in the same relay node R_2, $\beta = \beta_{21} = \beta_{22}$. By taking the conjugates of $r(2, i)$ and $r(3, i)$ in (4), the received signal at the destination node from relay nodes can be expressed as follows

$$\mathbf{r}(i) = \mathbf{H}\mathbf{s}(i) + \mathbf{I}_{int}(i) + \mathbf{n}(i) \tag{6}$$

where

$$\mathbf{H} = \begin{bmatrix} g_{11} & g_{12} & U_1 g_{21} & U_2 g_{22} \\ g_{12}^* & -g_{11}^* & U_2^* g_{22}^* & -U_1^* g_{21}^* \\ U_1^* g_{21}^* & U_2^* g_{22}^* & -g_{11}^* & -g_{12}^* \\ U_2 g_{22} & -U_1 g_{21} & -g_{12} & g_{11} \end{bmatrix}$$

and $\mathbf{I}_{int}(i) = [I_{int}(1,i), I_{int}^*(2,i), I_{int}^*(3,i), I_{int}(4,i)]^T$ contains the interference terms at the destination node from the relay node R_2 and can be modelled as follow

$$I_{int}(1,i) = -U_1 g 21^{-1} s(2, i-1) + U_2 g_{22}^{-1} s(1, i-1)$$
$$I_{int}^*(2,i) = U_1^* g 21^{*-1} s^*(3, i) + U_2^* g_{22}^{*-1} s^*(4, i)$$
$$I_{int}^*(3,i) = -U_1^* g 21^{*-1} s(4, i) + U_2^* g_{22}^{*-1} s(3, i)$$
$$I_{int}(4,i) = -U_1 g 21^{-1} s(1, i) + U_2 g_{22}^{-1} s(2, i) \tag{7}$$

From (6), it is well-known from estimation theory that the matched filter is the optimum front-end receiver to obtain sufficient statistics for detection in the sense it preserves information [13]. Assuming the CSI at the destination node, the conventional CL QO-STBC can be carried as follows

- By multiplying the signal received from the relay nodes in (6) by $\mathbf{H}^H$. Therefore, the estimated signals can be represented as

$$\mathbf{y}(i) = \mathbf{H}^H \mathbf{H} s(i) + \mathbf{H}^H \mathbf{I}_{int}(i) + \mathbf{H}^H \mathbf{n}(i) \tag{8}$$

- Applying LS detection at the destination node to estimate the transmitted signals from the source node through the DT channel h_{sd} and relay nodes channels g_{ik}, $i, k \in 1, 2$ as follows

$$\hat{\mathbf{s}}(i) = arg \min_{s_t \in S} |(\mathbf{y}(i) - \mathbf{H}^H \mathbf{H}\ s_t) + (h_{sd}^* \mathbf{r}_{sd}(i) - |h_{sd}|^2\ s_t)|^2 \tag{9}$$

where S denotes the set of all possible transmitted vector symbols. Therefore, as will be seen in the simulation section the above conventional procedure will suffer from significant detection error, because the interference component $\mathbf{H}^H \mathbf{I}_{int}(i)$ in (8) will damage the orthogonality of D-CL QO-STBC scheme (Table 1).

4   Sub-Optimum Detection for D-CL QO-STBC Using Dual-Antenna Relay Nodes

In this section, the proposed sub-optimum detection scheme for the D-CL QO-STBC utilizing two dual antenna relay nodes is used to eliminate the effect of $\mathbf{I}_{int}(i)$ in (6), where $s(1, i-1)$ and $s(2, i-1)$ are in fact already known if the detection process has been initialized properly [9]. Therefore, the interference component $I_{int}(1,i)$ can be removed before applying the matched filter in (8). This Yields

$$\hat{\mathbf{y}}(i) = \mathbf{H}^H \mathbf{r}_{rd} = \mathbf{H}^H \mathbf{H} s(i) + \mathbf{z}(i) + \mathbf{H}^H \mathbf{n}(i) \tag{10}$$

where

$$\mathbf{z}(i) = \begin{bmatrix} z(1,i) \\ z(2,i) \\ z(3,i) \\ z(4,i) \end{bmatrix} = \mathbf{H}^H \begin{bmatrix} 0 \\ I_{int}^*(2,i) \\ I_{int}^*(3,i) \\ I_{int}(4,i) \end{bmatrix} \tag{11}$$

Therefore,

$$z(1,i) = g_{12}I_{int}(2,i) - g_{21}I_{int}^*(3,i) + g_{22}^*I_{int}(4,i)$$
$$z(2,i) = -g_{11}I_{int}(2,i) + g_{22}I_{int}^*(3,i) - g_{21}^*I_{int}(4,i)$$
$$z(3,i) = U_1g_{22}I_{int}(2,i) - U_1g_{11}I_{int}^*(3,i) + U_1^*g_{12}^*I_{int}(4,i)$$
$$z(4,i) = -U_2g_{21}I_{int}(2,i) + U_2g_{12}I_{int}^*(3,i) + U_2^*g_{11}^*I_{int}(4,i) \tag{12}$$

As mention early the received signals through the DT link connection between the source node and the destination node h_{sd} is available. Therefore, the detection signals of DT link connection in (2) is utilized to initialize

$$\begin{bmatrix} s(1,i) \\ s(2,i) \\ s(3,i) \\ s(4,i) \end{bmatrix} = \begin{bmatrix} \hat{s}_{sd}(1,i) \\ \hat{s}_{sd}(2,i) \\ \hat{s}_{sd}(3,i) \\ \hat{s}_{sd}(4,i) \end{bmatrix} \tag{13}$$

Hence, (7) can be rewritten as

$$\dot{I}_{int}^*(2,i) = U_1^*g21^{*-1}\hat{s}_{sd}^*(3,i) + U_2^*g_{22}^{*-1}\hat{s}_{sd}^*(4,i)$$
$$\dot{I}_{int}^*(3,i) = -U_1^*g21^{*-1}\hat{s}_{sd}(4,i) + U_2^*g_{22}^{*-1}\hat{s}_{sd}(3,i)$$
$$\dot{I}_{int}(4,i) = -U_1g21^{-1}\hat{s}_{sd}(1,i) + U_2g_{22}^{-1}\hat{s}_{sd}(2,i) \tag{14}$$

Substituting (14) in (12) by replacing

$$I_{int}^*(2,i) \Rightarrow \dot{I}_{int}^*(2,i)$$
$$I_{int}^*(3,i) \Rightarrow \dot{I}_{int}^*(3,i)$$
$$I_{int}(4,i) \Rightarrow \dot{I}_{int}(4,i) \tag{15}$$

Then $\dot{z}(1,i) = z(1,i)$, $\dot{z}(2,i) = z(2,i)$, $\dot{z}(3,i) = z(3,i)$, and $\dot{z}(4,i) = z(4,i)$. Finally $\mathbf{s}(i)$ can be detected by utilized the LS detection method at the destination node to estimate the transmitted signals from the source node through the DT channel h_{sd} and relay nodes channels g_{ik}, $i,k \in 1,2$ as follows

$$\hat{\mathbf{s}}(i) = arg \min_{s_t \in S} |(\mathbf{y}(i) - \mathbf{H}^H s_t - \dot{\mathbf{z}}(i)) + (h_{sd}^*\mathbf{r}_{sd}(i) - |h_{sd}|^2 s_t)|^2 \tag{16}$$

Therefore, as will be seen in simulation results, the above procedure totally mitigates the interference induced by different time delays from the antennas of the second relay node at the destination node. Moreover, the above analysis has shown that the detection complexity of this approach is only dependent upon the constellation size as compared with detection schemes presented in [9,10] and does rely on the detection result of the DT link connection between the source node and the destination node.

5   Simulation Results

In this section, simulation results of the proposed scheme under imperfect synchronization are demonstrated. We assume that all channels are quasi-static

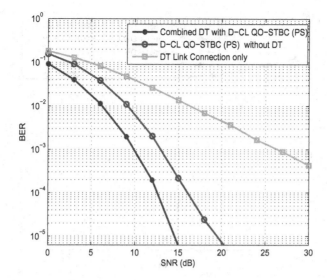

Fig. 3. The BER performance of D-CL QO-STBC using conventional detection under perfect synchronization (PS) with and without DT link combining as well as the performance of DT only.

Rayleigh fading frequency flat channels. The bit error rate (BER) performance is evaluated as a function of the signal-to-noise ratio (SNR) using the quadrature phase shift keying (QPSK) mapping scheme, where the x-axis represents SNR, while the y-axis represents the average BER. For fair comparison with a non-relay scheme, each antenna on the relay nodes transmit at $1/4$ power that is $\sigma_r^2 = \sigma_s^2/4$.

Figure 3, shows the comparisons of BER performance with the proposed D-CL QO-STBC combined with and without DT link connection link under perfect synchronization (PS). The performance of D-CL QO-STBC combined with DT link connection is greatly improves the system performance due to the higher diversity order as compared to D-CL QO-STBC without DT link connection with approximately 3 dB improvement at the value of BER = 10^{-3}. However, Fig. 4, shows the impact of imperfect synchronization by changing the value of $\beta = 0, -3, -6$ dB, which means β reflects the impact of time delay between transmission from the antennas on the first relay and the antennas on second relay nodes. The conventional detector of D-CL QO-STBC is included as reference, as can be seen in the figure, the performance of D-CL QO-STBC scheme utilizing conventional detector is severely degraded with timing error and an error floor appears in the BER curves even under small time misalignments $\beta = -6$ dB.

On the other hand, Fig. 5, illustrates the performance of the sub-optimum detection which it is able to deliver the desired performance and approach to that perfect synchronized case when the timing error $\beta = -3, -6$ dB. Also when $\beta = 0$ dB, the sub-optimum approach requires approximately 19 dB of power to get a BER of 10^{-4} as compared to convectional detector in Fig. 4.

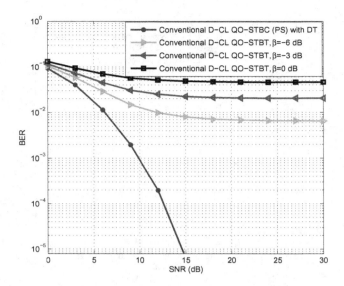

Fig. 4. The BER performance of D-CL QO-STBC using conventional detection under imperfect synchronization $\beta = 0, -3, -6$ dB with DT link combining.

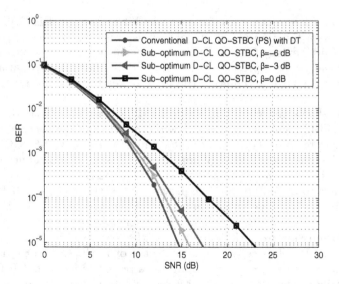

Fig. 5. The BER performance of D-CL QO-STBC using the proposed sub-optimum detection scheme under imperfect synchronization $\beta = 0, -3, -6$ dB with DT link combining.

Table 2. Comparison of proposed detection scheme with previous detection scheme in [9,10].

Detection scheme	Scheme in [9]	Scheme in [10]	Proposed scheme
Number of relay nodes	4	4	2
Number of antennas at relay nodes	1	1	2
Number of time misalignments	3	3	2
Detection complexity	High	High	Low
DT link	Needed	Needed	Needed
Data rate between relay and destination	3/4	1	1

Therefore, it can be observed that there a large improvement on the performance over the convectional detector even for large time misalignments and significantly eliminates the effect of the interference components due to asynchronism with no computational detection complexity as compared with the pervious work in [10].

Table 2, illustrates the comparison between the proposed detection scheme with previous detection scheme in [9,10], it can be seen that the full data transmission rate can be obtained by using the proposed scheme and the detection scheme in [10]. All detection scheme require the DT link between the source node and the destination node. However, the detection complexity process at the destination node utilizing the proposed scheme is low compared to the detection schemes in [9,10].

6   Conclusion

Synchronization error is always expected in distributed space time cooperative relay networks. Hence, in this paper a sub-optimum detection scheme has been proposed to reduce the detection complexity at the destination node. It's complexity is only dependent upon the constellation size unlike the previous work in [10]. It has also been proved to be robust against synchronization error. Furthermore, by co-locating two dual antennas on each relay node, this will reduce the timing error as compared to previous work in [10], which will lead to simplify the detection process at the destination node. It has been shown through simulation results that the proposed sub-optimum detection scheme works well for various synchronization error levels.

Acknowledgment. The authors would like to thanks Professor Richard Hall, Director of Institute for Innovation in Sustainable Engineering, University of Derby for his much appreciated support.

References

1. Nosratinia, A., Hunter, T., Hedayat, A.: Cooperative communication in wireless networks. In: IEEE Communications Magazine, vol. 42, pp. 74–80 (2004)
2. Laneman, L., Tse, D., Wornell, G.: Cooperative diversity in wireless networks: Efficient protocols and outage behaviour. IEEE Trans. Inf. Theory 50, 3062–3080 (2004)
3. Lin, K., Sadek, A., Su, W., Kwasinski, A.: Introduction in cooperative communications and networking, 1st edn., pp. 3–44. Cambridge University Press, New York (2009)
4. Nabar, R., Bokskei, H., Kneububler, F.: Fading relay channels: Performance limits and space-time signal design. IEEE J. Sel. Areas Commun. 22(6), 1099–1103 (2004)
5. Mitra, P., Ochiai, H., Tarokh, V.: Space-Time diversity enhancements using cooperative communications. IEEE Trans. Inf. Theory 51(6), 2041–2057 (2005)
6. Jing, Y., Hassibi, B.: Distributed space-time coding in wireless relay networks. IEEE Trans. Commun. 5(12), 3524–3536 (2006)
7. Jing, Y., Jafarkhani, H.: Using orthogonal and quasi-orthogonal designs in wireless relay networks. IEEE Trans. Inf. Theory 53(11), 4106–4118 (2007)
8. Li, X.: Space-time coded multi-transmission among distributed transmitters without perfect synchronization. IEEE Signal Process. Lett. 11(12), 948–951 (2004)
9. Zheng, F., Burr, A., Olafsson, S.: Signal detection for distributed space-time block coding: 4 relay nodes under quasi-synchronization. IEEE Trans. Commun. 57(5), 1250–1255 (2009)
10. Elazreg, A.M., Abdurahman, F.M., Chambers, J.A.: Distributed closed-loop quasi-orthogonal space time block coding with four relay nodes: overcoming imperfect synchronization. In: IEEE International Conference on Wireless and Mobile Computing, Networking and Communications (WiMob 2009), pp. 320–325 (2009)
11. Harshan, J., Rajan, B.: Co-ordinate interleaved distributed space-time coding for two-antenna-relays networks. IEEE Trans. Wireless Commun. 8, 1783–1791 (2009)
12. Toker, C., Lambotharan, S., Chambers, J.: Closed-loop quasi-orthogonal STBCs and their performance in multipath fading environments and when combined with turbo codes. IEEE Trans. Wireless Commun. 3, 1890–1896 (2004)
13. Alamouti, S.: A simple transmit diversity technique for wireless communications. IEEE J. Sel. Areas Commun. 16, 1451–1458 (1998)

Transferring Data via Dropped Calls

Balwinder Sodhi[✉]

Department of Computer Science and Engineering,
Indian Institute of Technology Ropar, Rupnagar, PB 140001, India
sodhi@iitrpr.ac.in

Abstract. A cheaper alternative to conventional data communication services is desirable in several scenarios involving mobile devices such as phones. We propose a system for transmission of information over an existing telephony network. This system makes use of "dropped" calls as a transmission medium for carrying data. Since subscribers typically do not incur any charges for dropped calls, our system eliminates the cost associated with conventional methods of mobile data communication.

A "data link" layer implementation, herein called Dropped Call Data Link (DCDL), has been described that uses the above transmission medium. In order to send data using this system an application can define its own information encoding rules, or alternatively, use system-generated encoding rules. Communicating application makes use of the DCDL client-side interface provided by this system to send data. We show that reduction in data communication cost with our system is proportional to the number of mobile clients.

Keywords: Communication channel · Data link layer · Dropped call · Data transfer · Information encoding · Telephony

1 Introduction

Exchange of data between different application tiers has become a defining feature of modern applications. Regardless of whether it is an instant messaging application or a callback based mobile app for information retrieval, one or the other form of client↔server data exchange is always present in such systems. A large number of mobile apps depend on availability of data communication services to the subscriber.

As such, finding cost effective data communication methods has always been an important goal for developers. Particularly, ability to transfer information without subscribing to any conventional data services on mobile or fixed telephone systems has been a major motivation for developers of data communication systems.

1.1 Related Work

Sharing communication resources/infrastructure has been a widely explored technique by solution developers. There have been solutions that allow a subscriber

© Institute for Computer Sciences, Social Informatics and Telecommunications Engineering 2015
S. Mumtaz et al. (Eds.): WICON 2014, LNICST 146, pp. 229–234, 2015.
DOI: 10.1007/978-3-319-18802-7_31

of a data service to share/lend bandwidth. For instance, Android app AirMobs developed at MIT [1] allows an Andriod based device to share data plan bandwidth with neighbouring devices via Wifi.

However, use of such solutions as AirMob assumes that the device which is lending its bandwidth has itself subscribed to a data plan or has access to a Wifi network. Often such bandwidth sharing is prohibited by most data service providers. In addition, there exist several scenarios where subscribing to a conventional data service directly or indirectly (such as via bandwidth sharing apps) can be an overkill or is not feasible technically or financially. Technique presented here is aimed at providing a cost-effective solution for data communication without subscribing to a conventional data service.

Motivating Example Scenarios: Examples of such scenarios include: (1) Short data packets transmissions. For example, a mobile phone periodically sending sensor data, such as GPS location, to a central server. (2) An application receiving user poll or opinions with predefined choices as answer options. (3) Service receipt or delivery confirmations.

2   Design of the Proposed System

The system proposed here allows transmitting information over a telephony network without requiring an end user/application to subscribe to a conventional data plan.

When designing a mechanism for transmitting information via a physical medium, typically one needs to first choose a unique property of the medium through which information will be sent. Then by using suitable encoding scheme, the information symbols to be transmitted are mapped onto suitable values of the chosen property of physical medium. The line coding [2, Ch.6] mechanism used in digital data transport systems is an example.

Key design choices that are made in the proposed system are: (a) Use of "dropped" calls as a medium for transmitting information. (b) Use of a pool of receiving-side phones to capture "dropped" calls. Patterns of dropped calls are used to suitably encode information.

Since the information is transmitted via dropped calls (which are typically free), no data service is required to be subscribed by users. This results in a cost-effective system for transmitting information over an existing telephony network.

A sending-side communicating entity transmits data by directing suitable patterns of dropped calls onto a pool of phones (which are part of the proposed system).

Let,

$$S = \text{Set of } n \text{ information symbols, } \{s_i : i = 1, 2, \ldots n\}$$
$$P = \text{Set of } m \text{ receiving phones in the system, } \{p_i : i = 1, 2, \ldots m\}$$
$$R = \text{Set of encoding rules, defined by a function, } f : S \to P$$
$$f(s) = \{p \in P\}, \forall s \in S$$

A client can call a set of m phones, taken m at a time, in $m!$ different sequences. That is, m phones can be used to represent $m!$ unique information *symbols*. Each phone in the receiving pool P logs necessary information about dropped calls in a database, so that with given encoding rules one can decode the transmitted data/message. It is possible to make use of existing suitable information encoding scheme, such as a variant of Huffman coding [3,4], for encoding input symbols.

2.1   Architectural Components

Major components that are required to implement the proposed data communication system are shown in Fig. 1.

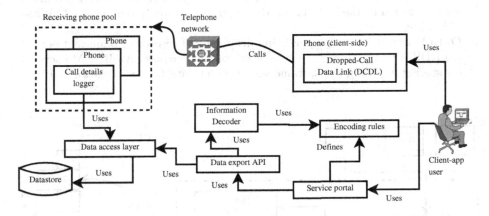

Fig. 1. Component diagram

1. **Receiving Phone Pool.** It comprises of a suitable number of programmable phones. These phones, each with a unique number, can be of any type such as GSM, CDMA, Fixed-line PSTN or even VoIP based soft phones. The client applications direct the dropped calls into these phones.
2. **Encoding Rules** define how the sequence of dropped calls that are received by phones in phone pool P are mapped onto information symbols. A trivial mapping example: $Car \mapsto (p_1, p_2, p_3), Bus \mapsto (p_2, p_1, p_3)$ etc., where p_i denotes a phone number.
3. **Call Details Logger** is deployed into each phone of the receiving phone pool P. Its main function is to log call details (such as caller's phone number, time of call and receiving phone's identity etc.) into a persistent datastore.
4. **Information Decoder** makes use of encoding rules to decode the information symbols from a set of stored call records of receiving-end phones.
5. **Service Portal** is provided for allowing the clients to perform various configuration and reporting tasks. Configuration tasks may include defining custom channel encoding rules, defining data extraction rules and reporting etc.

6. **Dropped Call Data Link (DCDL).** This component acts as a *data link layer* [5, Ch. 3] service (Fig. 2 shows its internal details). It provides necessary API for allowing user applications to send data via dropped calls. It comprises of four main sub-modules that allow this component to perform its service. A *framing module* breaks input data into suitable *frames*. The *Symbol Encoder* encodes data into suitable patterns (i.e. symbols) of dropped calls using *Encoding rules*. Finally it generates dropped calls by using *Call Generation* sub-module.

DCDL frames can be of variable length. Frame structure is shown in Fig. 2. Two frames are separated by a *frame delimiter* (FD). The first symbol in a frame is always the application's ID. Symbols inside a frame are separated by a *symbol delimiter* (SD). Both FD and SD are normally two distinct phone numbers chosen from the receiving pool. For a given client device FD and SD are configured at the installation time and will normally remain fixed for rest of the life.

7. **Data Store** is meant for persisting dropped-call records of phones of pool P. An RDBMS (e.g. MySQL) can be used for this purpose. An RDBMS schema for storing encoding rules, frame settings and data frames is shown in Fig. 3.

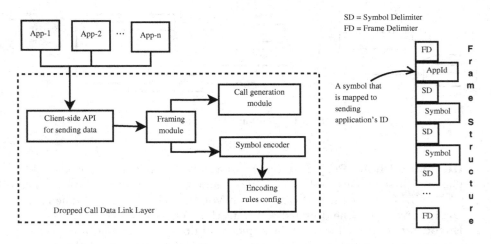

Fig. 2. DCDL (Dropped Call Data Link) implementation

3   Evaluation and Analysis

Let's say that we have a pool, P, of m phones which can receive "dropped" calls from different *client applications*. A client application is a piece of software which has the capabilities to generate "dropped" calls to a set of different phone numbers.

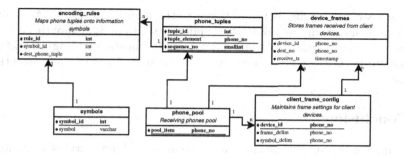

Fig. 3. RDBMS schema for storing encoding rules, frame settings and frames data.

Each client is randomly assigned two phone numbers, from the pool P, as *frame delimiter* (FD) and *symbol delimiter* (SD) signals respectively. That is, a dropped call is made by the client to these two numbers to indicate start of a frame or symbol. From the pool P, we can then make use of remaining $m - 2$ phones for representing (encoding) the symbols comprising the body of a message. These remaining $m - 2$ phones can be used in a variety of ways to define different symbol encoding schemes. Notion of a *symbol* here is quite subjective and depends entirely on the client application which wants to make use of this system for sending messages. For instance, one may map ASCII character set as individual *symbols*, or alternately one could map different words in English dictionary as individual *symbols*.

3.1 Estimating Receiving-Phone Pool Size and Cost Benefit

Let's say there are n distinct symbols to be encoded for transmission using suitable sequences of "dropped" calls to a set P of receiving-end phones. For our system, size of P can be given by:

$$|P| = 2 + min(k) \text{ such that } k! \geq n \tag{1}$$

A common usecase is encoding words from English dictionary. Each word from English dictionary is taken as a unique symbol. A simple encoding scheme can map each symbol (i.e. English word) to a sequence of phone numbers in the set P of receiving phones for making dropped calls to those numbers. For this scheme we can estimate the number of phones required in set P as below.

There are about a quarter million words in English dictionary, i.e., $n \approx 250000$. Solving Eq. (1) by taking $n = 250000$ we get $|P| = 11$, because minimum value of k that satisfies $k! \geq n$ is 9 ($\because 9! \approx 362880$).

Cost Comparison with Conventional Data Services: Let c be the number of mobile application clients, m the number of back-end receiving phones, p_{data} the monthly price of basic data service, and p_{rental} the monthly rental price of basic phone without any data service. The cost comparison ratio of conventional data service subscription based system and our proposed system can be estimated as: $r = (m \times p_{rental}) \div (c \times p_{data})$.

As is clear, cost saving is proportional to the number of clients. Assuming a basic data plan cost and rental of a basic phone each to be $2.5/month, cost comparison for a simple application where 1000 mobile clients send English text data to a remote back-end server comes to be about 0.01 times of the conventional service.

4   Conclusions

Data communication from client devices to remote back-end servers is an integral part of most mobile applications. Despite increased network penetration across the globe, there is still a large section of consumers, particularly in developing economies, where mobile data services are out of reach for many. Cost effective data communication methods are thus quite desirable for such scenarios and several others. A novel technique for transmitting data over dropped calls (which are typically free) has been presented in this paper. This method eliminates the need for client devices to subscribe to any data service in order to send information to remote back-end servers. We have shown that the cost savings are proportional to the number of mobile clients. Taking the example of English dictionary words as symbols, data transfer costs with our system for a 1000 mobile-client application can be reduced up to 1/100 times.

References

1. Hodson, H.: Bandwidth-sharing app brings connectivity to all, NewScientist Magzine. http://www.newscientist.com/article/mg21729015.900-bandwidthsharing-app-brings-connectivity-to-all.html.UxHpLR9qP3x. Retrieved: March 2014
2. Haykin, S.: Digital Communications. Wiley, New York (1988)
3. Huffman, D.A.: A method for the construction of minimum-redundancy codes. In: Proceedings of the I.R.E (1952)
4. "Huffman coding," in A Concise Introduction to Data Compression, pp. 61–91. Springer, London (2008)
5. Tanenbaum, A.: Computer Networks, 4th edn. Prentice Hall Professional Technical Reference, New Jersey (2002)

QoE Assessment of HTTP Adaptive Video Streaming

André Salvador[1], João Nogueira[1,2], and Susana Sargento[1] (✉)

[1] Instituto de Telecomunicações, University of Aveiro,
Campus Universitário de Santiago, 3810-193 Aveiro, Portugal
{andre.salvador,joaonogueira,susana}@ua.pt
[2] Portugal Telecom Inovação e Sistemas, SA, Rua Eng.,
José Ferreira Pinto Basto, 3810-106 Aveiro, Portugal

Abstract. Quality of Experience (QoE) is a crucial characteristic of any multimedia service and must be accounted for during the service development and planning stages. Nonetheless, given its subjective nature, it is extremely difficult to use analytical methods to estimate the average Mean Opinion Score (MOS).

Traditional progressive multimedia streaming is a well researched topic with respect to QoE, however, modern streaming services relying on advanced adaptive video streaming technologies, with specific characteristics, have yet to have an all-encompassing method for QoE estimation, as research work tend to focus on only one, or a small subset, of the technology's aspects, such as the impact of buffering events, bit-rate change frequency, or initial playout delay.

This paper proposes a model for determining the QoE estimate of a playback session of HTTP adaptive video streaming, encompassing its complete range of characteristics. Several key-metrics are extracted throughout the playback session, and then analyzed by an analytical method able to predict the consumers' QoE. A subjective QoE survey is conducted according to industry's best practices and recommendations in order to validate the proposed models. The obtained results show that both subjective and objective estimations produce similar results, hence validating the proposed model.

Keywords: QoE · Quality of experience · Adaptive streaming · Smooth Streaming · Survey

1 Introduction

The Internet is a fundamental commodity that most humanity has come to depend on. It has been growing in features, and complexity ever since it was created, and has evolved to support advanced multimedia services not initially foreseen.

Multimedia streaming has seen an outstanding growth in demand, fueled by ever increasing broadband speeds and community provided content. Streaming technologies, as opposed to *download-and-play* technologies, are characterized

© Institute for Computer Sciences, Social Informatics and Telecommunications Engineering 2015
S. Mumtaz et al. (Eds.): WICON 2014, LNICST 146, pp. 235–242, 2015.
DOI: 10.1007/978-3-319-18802-7_32

by the capability of a receiving device being able to consume the data while it is still being transferred, thus reducing the amount of storage required at the client to that of the playback buffer. Video streaming in particular requires a network connection with adequate performance especially in terms bandwidth, but also with respect to delay, depending on the application.

Regardless of the underlying technologies in multimedia streaming, a factor that has gained importance over that last years is that of Quality of Experience (QoE). QoE is a purely subjective metric, but it is so important that it can make or break the success of streaming service. It is heavily dependent on the underlying Quality of Service (QoS) parameters, but expands on it by taking advantage of human perceptions and focusing on the overall experience.

Adaptive HTTP streaming technologies aim to increase the users' QoE by embracing the natural variations of the underlying networks' performance, along with different terminal characteristics, while taking advantage of the ubiquitous HTTP infrastructure. The technology has gained traction with several implementations, including Microsoft's Smooth Streaming, Apple's HTTP Live Streaming (HLS), and the recently standardized MPEG-DASH. Given the characteristics of these adaptive streaming technologies, previous QoE estimation models do not directly apply, as they fail to encompass the new dynamics of a users' viewing session.

Previous works exist focused on QoE research in the context of adaptive streaming, however, they are restricted to the analysis of specific metrics, such as pause-intensity, or the impact of quality changes in QoE. An overall industry-calibrated approach has not, to best of the authors knowledge, been developed yet, and is thus the focus of this research work.

The remainder of this paper is organized as follows. Section 2 presents the proposed architecture to estimate the QoE. Section 3 presents the implementation aspects of the proposed mechanism, while Sect. 4 describes the tested scenarios and presents the results. Finally, Sect. 5 presents conclusions and points out future work.

QoE may be estimated through subjective and/or objective methods, however, it should be noted that any estimation is merely an approximation, as it varies from user to user [6].

Subjective methods [1,3] do not rely on technical characteristics, given that they are only based on human assessments of a video stream, and instead rely on a large number of surveys to have statistical significance. On the other hand, objective methods require concrete analytical metrics to classify the video stream and required subjective approaches for calibration; databases are usually made available with previously determined reference data, such as OPTICOM's Perceptual Evaluation of Video Quality (PEVq) [4].

Video streaming systems are complex because they can depend on many factors, such as codec, screen size, resolution, and others. For example, "a low bit-rate video displaying on a 17" laptop client with a full High-definition (HD) screen will likely translate into a low QoE, but the exact same video on smartphone client with a 3.5-inch screen will probably provide a higher QoE.

2   QoE Assessment Architecture

In this section, the proposed model for accurate QoE prediction on adaptive HTTP streaming is presented. The goal is to devise a model usable by a streaming service provider, so that proper monitoring of the service performance, and its users' QoE, is performed.

Because the overall experience of a video streaming session up to a given instant is influenced by the previous instants, the model needs to consider a memory effect over the elapsed period.

The proposed algorithm may be decomposed into two phases, illustrated in the building blocks of Fig. 1.

A first one classifies individual video chunks regardless of others. It considers the video codec information, the client's terminal characteristics, and the network's QoS parameters in order to establish a baseline MOS for each individual video chunk, and is calibrated against PEVq.

The second phase builds on the basic classification of video chunks performed on phase 1, with respect to their individual MOS estimates, and considers the impact of the previously reproduced chunks in the current MOS, thus emulating the human memory effect.

2.1   Video Chunk Scoring

Initially, an objective assessment of the video chunks is performed using features that are independent over the time, such as the bit-rate and the FPS of a specific chunk, from a particular quality level - adaptive streaming technologies provide different quality levels, or representations, for the exact same content.

This multi-parameter assessment is performed by carefully and separately analyzing the impact of each particular metric in the MOS estimate. The impact of the variation of each parameter is determined through the use of previously calibrated tools that contain databases of the MOS values, such as PEVq, which provides reliable MOS values, obtained according to ITU recommendations [4].

The selection of metrics is essential to the design of the model given that, for practical reasons, it can only use metrics that are obtainable in the context of video players. Most related studies in this area consider only one or two metrics, as the increase on the number of metrics also increases the complexity of the algorithms, in spite of a reduction in the forecast error. As description of methods used in the video assessment process ensues.

Bitrate: The bit-rate metric contributes largely to the quality of user experience. In adaptive HTTP streaming, the videos are encoded with a constant bit-rate so that each video chunk (of given quality level), has an approximately equal wire size (in bytes). Constant bit-rate encoding is a problem with videos that have highly dynamic scenes, such as sports, because it results in lower compression gains. The encoded bit-rates of adaptive HTTP streaming videos, typically range from 250 Kbps to 3 Mbps.

Frames per Second: The maximum rendered FPS are usually a limitation of the devices' performance, albeit it is also upper limited by the quality of the video chunk, which depending on may reduce the number of frames per second, in exchange of a higher resolution (for a specific average bit-rate). A drop in FPS is most of the times immediately evident to video consumers.

Rebuffering: Rebuffering is characterized by the amount of times elapsed while a player waits for the download of a new chunk after suffering a buffer under-run. This has a crucial impact on QoE and significantly effects the user experience it is lasts over a couple of seconds.

Screen resolution [ratio]: The relation between the screen resolution and the video track is relevant to estimate the users' QoE. Thus, it is possible to differentiate the QoE from a device with a small screen and a device with a large screen. The impact of the screen size is heavily dependent on the users' viewing distance (this effect was studied in work [5]), so it is required that the stream resolution is within range of the devices' screen resolution.

2.2   Human Memory Filter

The previously detailed video chunk scoring approach is based on metrics that do not depend on time, however, in practice the user experience does, as the human memory plays a role in quality of experience perception.

Take as an example a situation where the user is watches a video comprised of two video chunks, with different qualities. If the user first watches the chunk with the highest quality and then the one with the lowest quality, his perception of QoE will be lower than if he had first watched the low quality chunk and then the higher quality one, even if in practice the average chunk quality is the same.

This example illustrates the need of a memory filter able to replicate the impact of past experiences in the current evaluation. The proposed model applies a filter with a sampling frequency of 1 Hz, which updates the current QoE estimation considering the previously displayed chunks.

3   Implementation

The proposed method to estimate the QoE described in the previous section results in a two phase architecture: the first related to individual chunk scoring and a second relating to the perception of chunk sequences by the user.

In the chunk scoring phase, the sampling frequency is crucial to the analysis. Typical chunks contain 2 s of video, but re-buffering events may occur in smaller intervals. The human perception is defined by the eyes, to which 42 ms of the sampling is an acceptable value; thus, the chunk score can be done at 100 ms intervals (Fig. 2), so that in each second 10 quality samples at produced that may be used in the second phase, that of the human memory filter.

An equation is proposed that relates a complete set of technical metrics, previously described, and then outputs a video quality estimation. Equation 1

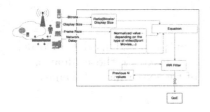

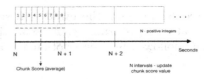

Fig. 1. Adaptive HTTP video streaming QoE estimation architecture.

Fig. 2. Method proposed - sampling frequency.

relates the metrics behavior, and the calibrated equation is obtained by determining the values of $v1$, $v2$, $v3$, $v4$, $v5$, $v6$, $v7$, $v8$.

The calibration of the equation is performed using MOS values obtained by a variation of the video characteristics. In the first phase, the re-buffering and the screen size metrics were not considered ($Rebuffering = 0$ & $Screen_{size} = 1$) in the process to calibrate the other metrics in the equation. The re-buffering and the screen size were considered in the process calibration in a later phase.

$$v_1 = 2.038 \qquad v_2 = 1.027 \qquad v_3 = 1.42^{-6}$$
$$v_4 = 0.3031 \qquad v_5 = 3.064 \qquad v_6 = 0.5407$$
$$v_7 = 0.05652 \qquad v_8 = 1.756$$

$$Score_{chunks} = v_2 \arctan\left(Bitrate \times v_3\right) \times \log\left(v_4 \times FPS\right)$$
$$- \log\left(v_5 \times Rebuffering + v_6\right)$$
$$- \log\left(v_7 \times Screen_{size} + v_8\right) + v_1, \tag{1}$$

This equation outputs a MOS value with respect to the characteristics of the video, and there is the need to measure the evaluation of user experience in a streaming session. Thus, this equation calculates a chunk value that will later be upgraded with a human memory filter.

Initially, in the evaluation of the video stream, the method starts the playback without previous values. There is no history of the session information when the video stream is started, so the lack of previous values is initially a problem, since the last 30 samples (fa = 1 Hz) are necessary for the method to apply the filter of human memory.

The proposed solution adjusts the influence of the samples to 100 percent; for example, the first evaluation (starts at 0 s) of the chunk depends only on the current value. The next evaluation (starts at 2 s) depends only on the previous and current value. These values are adjusted to 100 percent, with the previous value influencing 63.75 %, and the actual value influencing 36.25.

In this architecture, it is necessary to verify the influence of the human memory filter through real scenarios that use subjective methods (surveys), which will be presented in the next section.

4   Results

This section presents the evaluation results of the proposed model, in order to validate its performance. A simulation scenario used for the evaluation is outlined, followed by a description and analysis of the experimental scenarios.

4.1   Simulation Scenario

In the simulation scenario, the proposed model for QoE estimation is compared with PEVq-calibrated results for individual chunks. This scenario is used to verify the impact of memory in a streaming session.

Figure 3 illustrates the time line of a streaming session where network conditions vary significantly and some buffering events occur. Up to 10 s into the streaming session, the video quality rises with the rise of chunk quality, but when a congested network reduces the available bandwidth and causes playback interruptions, the estimated QoE is heavily impacted. This scenario may occur, for example, when a user starts watching television on a tablet and then goes into another room where the wireless network has a weak signal [2].

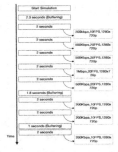

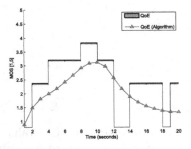

Fig. 3. Scenario - Video session time line.

Fig. 4. Scenario - QoE variation with time (s).

The outcome of this simulation is presented on Fig. 4, where both the individual chunks' expected QoE is presented (in rectangular shapes), and the outcome of the proposed algorithm is displayed as curve with discrete estimates of the QoE value.

A disparity between the assessments is evident. Whereas the individual chunk quality immediately produces a particular QoE, and maintains it while the chunk bit-rate does not change, the proposed model is both dynamic and more conservative in the sense that it considers past experiences, thus not showing instant QoE variations, and outputting lower QoE values representing the negative impact of buffering events and quality transitions.

4.2   Experimental Scenarios

Given that QoE is a subjective concept, a subjective approach to determine MOS values is required so that the proposed model may be benchmarked against real-life results.

In the experimental scenarios, a survey was conducted using real users to assess their quality of experience when watching variations of 2 reference videos: an animation one, and a sports one. The videos were made available in a set of 20 videos streams, with variations in the quality levels usable by the users' adaptive player (different sets of bit-rates per video stream).

ITU recommends that questionnaires should have at least 50 responses in order to have enough confidence in the results, hence we considered 64 users assessing the quality of the 20 video streams available on a web page. Each video stream is classifiable with a MOS score, ranging from 1 to 5. In practice, however, it is difficult to get an average MOS higher than 4.5 or lower than 1.5, because not everyone classifies their experience with the extreme values of 5 or 1.

Figure 5 shows the results of the video qualities questionnaires, indeed demonstrating that the users' MOS estimate does not present values near the extremes (MOS equal 5 or 1).

The results show that MOS estimates produced by the survey are in line with the estimates provided by the QoE model, especially in the case of animation video streams (scenarios 15 to 20). In scenarios 1 to 15 the reference is the sports video, and the QoE model does not perform as good as it does in the animation video. This is likely a general effect of sports videos, whose picture quality is usually harder to estimate due to fast moving scenes.

Overall, it is possible to conclude that the proposed model is able to closely track the subjective results, and does not present results near the extremes. As a side note, scenarios 1 and 11 are the same but are separated by 10 intermediate scenarios. It is expected that when a user is viewing scenario 11 he/she does not remember scenario 1, thus it is used as a user coherence validation test.

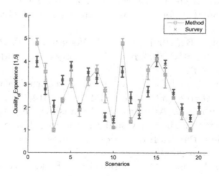

Fig. 5. Survey with 20 scenarios.

5   Conclusion and Future Work

This paper demonstrates a mechanism to estimate the QoE of an adaptive HTTP video streaming service aiming to simulate human video scoring behavior. In order to validate the performance of the developed method, both objective and subjective tests are executed.

In the objective tests, a comparison is performed between the proposed method and PEVq over different network quality scenarios and metrics, such as bit-rate, FPS, re-buffering time and screen size. Furthermore, the maximum deviation was 0.19 in the MOS scale (ranging from 1 to 5). Additional tests evaluating the impact of the video content in the proposed algorithm results lead to the conclusion that the confidence interval is not exceeded in most of the cases, thus demonstrating that the video content does not impact significantly the QoE estimate.

In the subjective assessments, a questionnaire is designed to recreate test scenarios comparable with the ones performed by the objective MOS estimation approach. In the animation video scenario, the results were an almost perfect match to the objective estimate, but the sports video led to small discrepancies caused by the lack of identical submissions.

The all-encompassing approach taken in development of the proposed model enhances the current state of the art by demonstrating the incorporation of the key characteristics of adaptive HTTP streaming in the estimation of the users' QoE. These models will be incorporated in a service provider's QoE probing system.

Acknowledgement. This work was supported by the QREN Initiative, through UE/ FEDER, COMPETE financing, in the Project PANORAMA II.

References

1. Li, D., Cai, M.: A video quality-estimation model for streaming media services based on human visual system. In: International Conference on Computational Intelligence and Software Engineering 2009, CiSE 2009, pp. 1–4, Dec 2009
2. Lui, G., Gallagher, T., Li, B., Dempster, A.G., Rizos, C.: Differences in RSSI readings made by different Wi-Fi chipsets: a limitation of WLAN localization. In: 2011 International Conference on Localization and GNSS, ICL-GNSS 2011, pp. 53–57 (2011)
3. Moorthy, A.K., Choi, L.K., Bovik, A.C., de Veciana, G.: Video quality assessment on mobile devices: subjective, behavioral and objective studies. IEEE J. Sel. Top. Sig. Process. **6**(6), 652–671 (2012)
4. Germany OPTICOM GmbH. Pevq - advanced perceptual evalutoin of video quality (2005). http://www.pevq.com/. Accessed 4 June 2014
5. Sakamoto, K., Aoyama, S., Asahara, S., Yamashita, K., Okada, A.: Evaluation of viewing distance vs. tv size on visual fatigue in a home viewing environment. In: Digest of Technical Papers International Conference on Consumer Electronics, ICCE 2009, pp. 1–2, Jan 2009
6. ur Rehman Laghari, K., Issa, O., Speranza, F., Falk, T.H.: Quality-of-experience perception for video streaming services: preliminary subjective and objective results. In: 2012 Asia-Pacific Signal Information Processing Association Annual Summit and Conference (APSIPA ASC), pp. 1–9, Dec 2012

Congestion Control for Radio Networks

Duarte Santos[1], Susana Sargento[1]([✉]), and Carlos Parada[2]

[1] Instituto de Telecomunicações, Aveiro, Portugal
{djps,susana}@ua.pt
[2] Portugal Telecom Inovação e Sistemas, SA, Rua Eng. José Ferreira Pinto Basto,
3810-106 Aveiro, Portugal
carlos-f-parada@telecom.pt

Abstract. Nowadays, we have witnessed an exponential growth of the traffic generated by users in mobile communications networks. This need for a greater capacity in mobile networks raises problems for operators, because the demand for network capacity is not always accompanied by the evolution of the available technologies. This represents problems in access networks that result in failures in the customer service and losses to the operator. It is quite important that the service is the best possible for both client and the operator: preventing and resolving network congestion is a common interest. The quality of service is also an important point of great concern, that requires to evaluate the service provided in order to achieve the best satisfaction from the user. However, many challenges still need to be surpassed on current mobile networks.

This paper identifies and resolves cases of congestion in mobile networks, as well as it infers the quality of services provided to the customer. It proposes and implements an architecture that is able to identify problems in access networks, through network monitoring, using metrics gathered by a network management system that gives Key Performance Indicators (KPIs) evaluating the network, and through clients' information for a specific cell, obtained through probing. Then, a Call Admission Control (CAC) module in the 3GPP Policy and Charging Rules Function (PCRF) is in charge of applying a rule set designed to resolve the case of the detected congestion. The policies chosen directly affect the users in the congested cell, causing the levels of occupancy to drop, and consequently, the cell resources to become stable. Several congestion use cases are identified and demonstrated, which show the effectiveness of the rules applied to the network, services and users.

1 Introduction

Nowadays, with the development of mobile devices that have functions beyond voice and text communications, providing services like multimedia content, video and online gaming which grow in popularity, there is an exponential growth of traffic in mobile networks. Although the data capacity of networks has increased, the growth of user traffic outpaces the growth in capacity. This exponential growth of cellular data is a big concern to the mobile network operators; therefore, the efficient use of all available resources is extremely important. The

S. Mumtaz et al. (Eds.): WICON 2014, LNICST 146, pp. 243–252, 2015.
DOI: 10.1007/978-3-319-18802-7_33

actions of detecting, avoiding and controlling congestion are important to maximize resources and provide the best service to the users.

To detect and prevent congestion, it is required to take into account two different stages. First of all, it is necessary to detect that there are congestion problems in the network, specifically in the radio access network (where congestion mostly occurs). After this process, it is evaluated the set of actions to be performed. This starts by identifying the main contributors to the problem, and decide on how they will be affected.

There are different clients in the network, and network providers may have different policies to choose the type of clients to be affected when congestion occurs. The first stage must evaluate the network status at its lowest level, directly in the NodeBs and in the Radio Network Controllers (RNCs). At this level, many factors can influence the status of the network. In 3G, for example, factors like the lack of code availability or the lack of power resources can cause congestion. These factors must be chosen and evaluated to deduce a qualitative value for the state of the network. Network providers are also interested in understanding and controlling the quality of the services provided to their services. The second stage consists in identifying the main contributors to the congestion, the called heavy users, and act directly on the services of these users to relieve the load on the congested cell. The actions upon these users must take into account the type of subscribed services by the clients. Clients with a better subscribed service must have a better service than clients with a lower service plan, according to the operator policies.

When the information about the cell status is evaluated and actions have been decided, the result must be transferred to the network element that will force the changes into the costumers' services. To achieve this, it is necessary to create an interface with the existent platform, capable of receiving and analysing the information concerning the network. After that step, new policies are created in the network in the PCRF module, which is in charge of the creation of dynamic rules that can be forced in the network to stop and avoid congestion.

The last step in this operation is the evaluation of the received data. According to the severity of the information received, the rules must adapt the severity of its actions. The new policies that result from the rules will affect the users in the congested cell. The downgrade of the type of service or even drop of low priority clients are some of the actions considered in the rulesets to stop congestion.

Previous solutions, such as [1–7], proposed different mechanisms for congestion and admission control. The solution proposed in this paper considers a congestion control approach grouped with probes and management system to determine the congestion level, and the rules of the PCRF to resolve the network congestion. The paper is organized as follows. This paper shows the proposed solution in Sect. 2. Then, the congestion detection and PCRF policies are presented in Sects. 3 and 4, respectively, and the results of the policies implemented are depicted in Sect. 5. Finally, the conclusions of the paper are presented in Sect. 6.

2   Architecture of the Solution

To accomplish a good CAC solution, PCRF must detect the level of network congestion and receive the maximum information available about the users on the congested cell (ID, throughput, QoS, etc.). This information can be divided in two different types: the information related to network status (the congestion of the cell), and the information related with the subscribers on that cell. The first type of information is taken from RAN components, such as metrics (counters, percentages, etc.) that can describe the number of faults, the percentage of occupation, and the percentage of availability, among other factors. In this solution, a report from the network management system will be evaluated by a module called "Metrics Evaluation" that will transmit data to the PCRF concerning congestion, so it can enforce policies into the subscribers to have the network in a stable state. The proposed solution consists on interpreting the metrics received from the network components and evaluating them to decide whether PCRF must be warned about them or not.

New rule sets are created to include the metrics and the parameters obtained through probing. The CAC interface must be updated to support the new factors received from this external component (the "Metrics Evaluation" module), and the CAC decision must apply specific rule sets depending on the information received. The architecture of the proposed solution is depicted in Fig. 1.

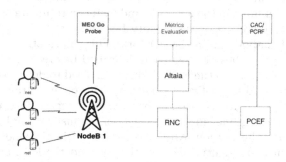

Fig. 1. Architecture of the proposed solution

3   Congestion Detection

The first step in this work is the detection and anticipation of problems that will occur in the radio access network.

To determine these factors, a program was developed in Java programming language to obtain the status of a NodeB. This program reads an Excel file with a report from the network management system which contains a large amount of data concerning a NodeB status that must be processed and analysed. The fields presented in the report must be compared with another set of fields, the fields of interest, to determine the possible problems of the network. When a field in the report matches a field of interest, the value associated with the factor chosen is compared with a threshold defined for that factor. If this value violates the defined threshold, a value of congestion is allocated (based on the algorithm).

With this case, the RAN needs an intervention, therefore the PCRF must be informed to take the right actions to prevent congestion. Before informing the PCRF, the program continues to perform a search in the report to evaluate if any other factor of interest was violated. Every time a field in the received report from the network management system violates a defined threshold, a congestion level is allocated: if it is verified that this case of congestion is worst compared to the previous situation, the value to be sent is the one that represents the worst case of congestion. After checking all the fields referring to one NodeB, it is time to check if it is necessary to inform the PCRF. If any field was considered to be violating the limits defined, the congestion level will be more than 0. The final levels of congestion to be sent to PCRF are described as follows:

- no congestion - level 0;
- low congestion - level 1;
- medium congestion - level 2;
- high congestion - level 3;

The congestion level can also be accessed based on the information coming from a probe. In this solution, it was used a probe that can achieve the state of a streaming service running in the network, and by interpreting its operation (when the video stops to buffering or the quality becomes bad), it can be recognized that congestion is happening in the network. This information is then mapped into one of the three values of congestion described before.

The level 0 is also sent to the PCRF, since it is used to detect that congestion is no more occurring in the network. The simplicity of the parameters transmitted to the PCRF is due to the need to process all events as fast as possible. All complexity of detecting and analysing congestion must be implemented in the module described in this section. After the last evaluation is done, it is generated a XML report with the identification of the cell and the level of congestion in that cell. A HTTP connection with PCRF is created and the report is sent. If no factor was violated and consequently there is no congestion, the program does not report it to the PCRF and it will just wait for another report of the RAN to repeat the process.

4   PCRF Policies

The rule sets are files containing an organized set of rules that will be performed when congestion arises. They are designed in QRE (Quantum Rule Engine) that is a proprietary programming language. This language also supports code written in Java to perform actions of higher complexity. The main feature of QRE is its flexibility that permits changes in the rule sets without needing to compile them, which makes this module very robust in a real time environment.

The rule sets created aim to have impact on the radio access network and mitigate congestion. The actions that PCRF can force into the network are the following three:

- Reduction of the user throughput;
- Increase of the user throughput;
- Drop the user;

With the use of these three actions, PCRF is able to control and decrease congestion levels on the RAN. To reduce/increase the throughput of the user, PCRF has to assign a worst/better service plan to this user. For example, if a user is a gold client (the best service plan with the higher throughput) and the PCRF needs to free some bandwidth, this client service plan may be reduced to the silver type (a service plan with less bandwidth than the gold). The rule sets built aim to evaluate the congestion level received from the "Metrics Evaluation" module on the CAC interface. After this step, the parameters received can be used on the construction of the rule sets, in the CAC decision.

The rule set aims to identify the level of congestion and, based on this parameter, decide the severity of the action to be taken. In the ruleset of the figure it is shown that, if the cell is highly congested, the number of downgrade sessions is higher than if the level of congestion is lower. Depending on the congestion level, the downgrade of sessions can vary, e.g. if the congestion level that arrives in the PCRF has the value 1, the number of sessions to downgrade is x% of all the users in the cell; consequently for value 2, a similar procedure is done but the percentage of downgraded sessions is increased (the same procedure is applied to congestion level 3). From the range of users attached to the problematic cell, some have to be chosen to be affected by the PCRF policies.

The criteria to choose the users to be affected can rely on different factors:

- Operator Options: the operator can have its own preferences to whom it wants to be affected; criteria like the user service plan (the operator may want to "protect" the users that pay more for their service) can be employed. The operator may also want to "protect" the QoS of its applications, and therefore choose users that are using other applications to be downgraded.
- QoS: The QoS can be a factor to take into account when it is needed to affect users; users with low QoS should not be affected first.
- Type of Service: The type of service of the user is one of the factors that can be used to choose who is going to be downgraded; different services have different characteristics, and the decrease of bandwidth affects differently the various types (e.g. the consequences of decreasing the throughput to do the download of an e-mail have less impact than decreasing the throughput available for video streaming);
- Heavy users: The users with higher impact on the network, the main causers of congestion, can be selected (based on their throughput) and be the first to be affected by PCRF.

These rules are going to be applied to the use cases presented in the next section. In this solution, the criteria to choose the users that are going to be downgraded is the type of service. The first users to be downgraded are the Bronze, then the Silver and finally the Gold (with this method, the users that pay more tend to have a better service, since they are the last ones to be downgraded). In the case of having more than one user with the same service plan to be downgraded, the user is chosen randomly. When it is determined that a downgrade must happen, the PCRF sends a RAR (Re-Auth Request) to the PCEF to inform that a package should be installed to the user to downgrade. That package is known by the network and characterises the modifications that must be made to downgrade de user. After the PCEF executes the process, it sends a RAA (Re-Auth Answer) with the acknowledge to the PCRF.

After the congestion stops, it is applied a rule set called "after congestion" that actuates in the users attached to the cell, allocating them their original packages. It starts by verifying if the congestion level is zero (it will only restore the users' original package if there is no congestion), and also verifies if sessions were downgraded (this measure is implemented with a counter that is incremented every time a user is downgraded). If these two conditions are verified, the PCRF is then able to upgrade the users that were downgraded. The upgrade function is called as many times as users were previously downgraded. Due to its internal mechanism, it will only upgrade the users that were downgraded, using the same algorithm to choose users, but in a reverse way.

5   Results

In this section it is described one case of congestion and the situation after congestion, to better understand the operation of the proposed solution. The scenarios consist in simulated network cells that have three clients with different service packages. When congestion occurs, some users are going to be downgraded, and consequently, it is shown in the figures that their throughput is reduced.

Table 1 contains the options that can occur to the users, and also the throughput available for each package. It is worth to note that the user can only be upgraded if it was already downgraded (it is not given a higher throughput than the originally defined).

5.1   Congestion Scenario

In a cell there are three users: one with the Gold package, one with the Silver package and the last one with the Bronze package. It is checked the report from

Table 1. Packages description and possible actions

Type of package	Throughput	Downgrade option	Upgrade option
Gold	7.2 Mbit/s	Silver	No Option
Silver	3 Mbit/s	Bronze	Gold
Bronze	1 Mbit/s	Drop of the cell	Silver

the network management system containing information on the behaviour of a cell. The actuation of "Metrics Evaluation" module can be seen in Fig. 2.

```
START
| ###### Report ######
|There is congestion
|NodeID -> U51004
----------------------------------------------------------------
|Code Tree Usage Mean (%)
|Parameter Value: 88.524167 higher than the minimum threshold: 80.0
|Max Congestion value registed for the cell: 2.0
----------------------------------------------------------------
```

Fig. 2. Metrics Evaluation Module detecting code congestion

With the evaluation of the cell, it is possible to see that there is congestion on the cell and it is due to the code "resource occupation". The value of congestion is 2, and it is then sent to CAC/PCRF so it can apply the correct rules to the users. After running the ruleset that deals with the RAN congestion, since the objective is to "protect" users with higher package, the ones to be downgraded are the ones with lower package. Therefore, the Silver and Bronze users are going to be downgraded.

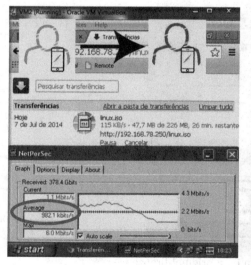

Fig. 3. Original Silver user

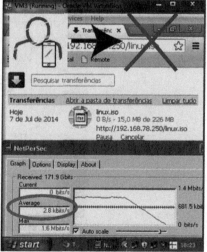

Fig. 4. Original Bronze user

In Figs. 3 and 4, it is possible to observe that the Silver and Bronze users are downgraded, the Silver user was downgraded to the Bronze package (originally from 3 Mbit/s to 1 Mbit/s), while the initial Bronze user was dropped from the cell (originally had a 1 Mbit/s and now bandwidth is cut to 0 Mbit/s). The other user keeps its package and bandwidth without any modification.

5.2   After Congestion Scenario

The following scenario shows a use case that demonstrates the operation of the
"after congestion" ruleset. After receiving a value of congestion for a determined
cell, the next value received is zero, meaning that the cell is no longer congested.
Therefore, it is started the process of allocating the original package of each
client.

In a cell there are three users with the following packages: user 1 with a gold
package, user 2 with a silver package and user 3 with bronze package. Since the congestion value is 1, only one client was downgraded, the bronze client. The actual
configuration of the cell is one gold and one silver clients (the bronze client was
dropped from the cell). The next value received of congestion is 0, meaning that
the cell is no longer congested.

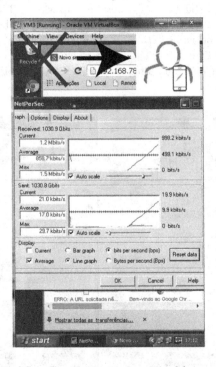

Fig. 5. After Congestion on a original bronze user

Since the value received for the actual congestion level in the cell was 0, PCRF
will upgrade the clients that were downgraded before. In Fig. 5 it is possible to
see that the client was upgraded, allowing him to return to the cell (it goes from
the drop state to the bronze package).

6   Conclusion and Future Work

The work developed in this paper aims to solve a known problem of radio access networks: congestion. For this purpose, several solutions were taken into account, and an architecture that considers both metrics from network management and monitoring systems and probing systems (both passive and active metrics) was specified, developed and tested. Probes can give specific information on users/ services experience on a cell while passive metrics can give the state of the cell. The chosen way to detect congestion was the evaluation of radio access network parameters, while the perception of the QoS experienced in the network for specific services was provided using probes. The metrics evaluation module is capable to connect to a PCRF and warn it that congestion is occurring.

The defined use cases were tested using the integration of the modules with the existing architecture. The metrics evaluation module and PCRF were tested, first using Seagull emulated clients, where it is possible to see the detection of congestion for reports taken from network management system and observe the actions of the PCRF to the users in the case of congestion. Then, tests were performed using clients simulated with virtual machines, that have a behaviour very similar to a real client, being able to generate traffic. It was possible to test the metrics evaluation module working combined with the probes and PCRF, and finally observe the actions taken on the users with real reductions of their bandwidth (proved with the observed reduction of download throughput).

From the obtained results, it is possible to conclude that the solution is capable of solving the congestion problems with a good performance. The metrics evaluation module is able to detect congestion based on the evaluation of specific parameters and combine them to achieve a general qualitative value to congestion. In the case of CAC decision, we showed that it is able to implement the rules defined, with different actions on the users in the cell, according with the received quality and congestion levels, and according to the users and services profiles.

As future work, we plan to extend the apporach to 4G networks, and take the possibility to offload traffic to WiFi networks whenever congestion is detected.

Acknowledgement. This work was supported partly by the QREN Initiative, through UE/FEDER, COMPETE financing, in the Project PANORAMA II, and by the Portugal Telecom Inovação and Sistemas MOB-4G Project.

References

1. Angelos Antonopoulos, L.A., Kartsakli, E., Verikoukis, C.: Dealing with VoIP calls during "Busy Hour" in LTE. In: Recent Advances in Wireless Communications and Networks (2011)
2. Tragos, E.Z., Tsiropoulos, G., Karetsos, G.T., Kyriazakos, S.A.: Admission control for QoS support in heterogeneous 4G wireless networks. IEEE Netw. **22**, 30–37 (2008)

3. Franklin, J.V., Paramasivam, K.: Article: hybrid adaptive call admission control mechanism for ensuring qos in 3g pp: Lte networks. Int. J. Comput. Appl. **42**(21), 36–41 (2012). Published by Foundation of Computer Science, New York, USA
4. Sekercioglu, Y.A., Ivanovich, M., Yegin, A.: A survey of MAC based QoS implementations for WiMAX networks. Comput. Netw. **53**, 2517–2536 (2009)
5. Kong, X., Zhao, J.: Cross-layer-based mapping mechanism in LTE Advanced. IEEE (2011)
6. Lei, H., Yu, M., Zhao, A., Chang, Y., Yang, D.: Adaptive connection admission control algorithm for LTE systems. In: IEEE Vehicular Technology Conference, pp. 2336–2340 (2008)
7. Chadchan, S.M., Akki, C.B.: Priority-scaled preemption of radio resources for 3g pp lte networks. Int. J. Comput. Theory Eng. **3**(6), 743–749 (2011)

The Sensors Are Innovative in Internet of Things

Mohammadreza Rezvan[✉] and Mohammadamin Barekatain

Faculty of Computer Engineering, University of Isfahan, Isfahan, Iran
{mohammadrezarezvan94,amin.5572}@gmail.com

Abstract. The technology is facing enormous changes these days. All the objects and all issues can connect to the internet and announce their locations. This vast science, Internet of Things (IoT), is in progress in this decade. One reason is nowadays IoT is applicable in almost all industries. In addition, sensors are widely used in IoT and the production, service and utility cost of sensors has decreased due to an increase in using and producing the complex sensors. To comprehend IoT, one needs to get all the information about the wireless sensors network and understand all the information about the protocols and sensors used in the IoT that collect the data (receive and transmit). In this paper we are going to introduce some types of the sensors and protocols that are used in IoT and examine RFID tags and NFC sensors. The examination of RFID tags and NFC sensors, demonstrates that among all of the sensors and protocols used in IoT field, the RFID tags and NFC sensors are the best ones.

Keywords: IoT sensors · ZigBee · Bluetooth sensors · RFID tags · NFC sensors

1 Introduction

1.1 The Sensors of IoT

These sensors and protocols of IoT can be organized as follows: Machine to Machine (m2m), Nest (meet the next generation thermostat), Plus Oximeter Sensor, General System for Mobile communication (GSM), Code Division Multiple Access (CDMA), Global Positioning System (GPS), ZigBee, Bluetooth Sensor, Near Field Communication (NFC), Wi-Fi and RFID.

ZigBee (Protocol): It is a high level communication protocol used in creating personal area network based on wave transmission, ZigBee consumes less power and has the ability to transfer data to long distances through passing the data node to node, with the range of about 10−100 m. ZigBee is a wireless standard network design to carry small amount of data over a medium range distance. For longer ranges it requires more power. This sensor is used in smart homes (it is a protocol for personal area network). By passing data through a mesh network of intermediate devices, ZigBee devices are able to transmit data over long distances. The network topology of ZigBee is of mesh network which can be controlled and changed by the users through their devises at their homes regarding any object services. The speed of ZigBee protocol is low; about 250 Kb/s, and it is a safe protocol because, it uses the 128 encryption. Consumption of power in ZigBee

© Institute for Computer Sciences, Social Informatics and Telecommunications Engineering 2015
S. Mumtaz et al. (Eds.): WICON 2014, LNICST 146, pp. 253–261, 2015.
DOI: 10.1007/978-3-319-18802-7_34

protocol is low and can sleep between transmits and a wake up time in ms [4]. ZigBee advantages are [4]:

A. Low cost: every individual or organization can provide it, but the service cost can be expensive.
B. Low power: smartphones use small batteries with these sensors are used.
C. Mesh networking: provide wide range.

Bluetooth Sensor: It is a wireless technology for enchanting data over short distance (2.4 to 2.488 GHz). The features of the sensors are:

A. The range of this sensor is about 3 m unless the power increases, and can carry 3−24 Mb data per second, but most of new devices can transmit data maximum to 3 Mb.
B. The price of this sensor is low so that every phone and other telecommunication devices can contain them.
C. The power consumption of this sensor is low and can sleep between transmissions but the wake up time is about 3 s while the wake up time in ZigBee protocol is about ms.
D. For transfer data between devices such as (video-mp3-film …), connecting headphone to your device and is used in game platform such as Kinect or XBOX.
E. Network distribution of this sensor is node to node (one transmitter to one receiver) One of disadvantages of this sensor is, if one the of devices sleeps between transferring the data, all of the data become omitted and the transmission process should be repeated. The second disadvantage of this sensor is the limited range to transmit the data. There exist four different versions of Bluetooth sensors. Table 1 illustrates them.

Table 1. Different versions of Bluetooth sensors

Version	Data rate
1.2	1 Mb/s
2.0	3 Mb/s
3.0	24 Mb/s
4.0	24 Mb/s

The latest version of Bluetooth sensors is Bluetooth version 4.0. This version has two advantages: The rate of transfer data is faster than the previous version and it consumes less energy, hence maximizing the battery life of the phone [4].

Near Field Communication (NFC): NFC is a form of contactless communication between devices like smartphones or tablets. A user can send data by waving the smartphone over a NFC compatible device by contactless communication. NFC technology is growing fast in the United States and is popular in parts of Asia and Europe for being fast and convenient. "Near field communication maintains interoperability between different wireless communication methods like Bluetooth and other NFC standards including FeliCa - popular in Japan - through the NFC Forum. Founded in 2004 by Sony, Nokia, and Philips, this forum enforces strict standards that manufacturers must meet when designing NFC compatible devices" [3].

Radio Frequency Identification (RFID): One of the useful sensors that is used in IoT is RFID. The function of this sensor is based on electronic and electromagnetic for data transfer. RFID is a part of Automatic Identification Data Capture (AIDC). Three kinds of RFID - the passive, active and battery-assisted passive - are in use.

A. Active: Has an on board battery and periodically transmit, its ID signal
B. Passive: Is activated to start operation it must illuminate with a power level roughly and the passive tags can start to run when three magnetic components run it.
C. A Battery-Assisted Passive (BAP): Has a small battery on board and is active when it is near the RFID reader.

Wi-Fi: Applied as the Local Area Network Technology. This technology is used to exchange data or make a connection among electronic devices. Many devices can use Wi-Fi such as: PC-SP- Video camera console. These devices can be connected to the source by wireless network access point. The access point (or hotspot) has medium range of about 20 meters. Because an intruder (hacker) does not need physical connection, the Wi-Fi is less secure than wired connection [4]. Wi-Fi adopts the following encryption: Wired Equivalent Privacy (WEP) is Using hexadecimal number digit. Wi-Fi Protected Access (WPA & WPA2) are the security protocols to secure wireless computer networks. Wi-Fi Protected Setup (WPS), A network security standard that allows user to easily secure a wireless home network [4].

The Comparison of some sensors are given in Table 2 [2, 5].

2   Specifications of RFID and NFC

With respect to the brief description on the twelve sensors in this discussion, here of the specification of RFID and NFC are present as follows:

2.1   RFID

RFID is short form of radio frequency Identification and this tag has the same technology to bar code Identification. Long checkout lines at the grocery stores are one of the biggest complaints about the shopping experience. The bar code which is a sub section of Universal Product Code (UPC), is replaced by smart labels called Radio Frequency Identification (RFID) tags. The RFID tags are intelligent bar codes able to transmit data to a network system to track every product that the consumer put in his/her shopping cart. For example an RFID tag that is attached to the grocery box can transmit data to a network. You choose some choices and put them in the special place, after that the amounts of choices (the prices) can be detected and this network makes a connection to your bank account, thus a debit for you. RFID system consists of an antenna, a transceiver which read the radio frequency and transfer the information to processing devices, and a transponder or tags, which is an integrated circuit containing the RF circuitry and information to be transmitted [1]. What is RFID? What is its contribution to my business? The RFID is a means of capturing data an object without human interaction in reading data. Using bar code application has 4 disadvantages which should be eliminated: They must be visible, No changes can occur, its appearance cannot be changed, they cover some area on the object [1].

Table 2. Comparison of sensors through tabulation

	Bluetooth	ZigBee	Wi-Fi	RFID
Range	Short range up to 3 m	Medium range up to 100 m.	Medium range up to 100 m	Medium range up to 100 m
Operating frequency	Low and high speed data up to 24 Mbps in version 3	Low speed data up to 250 Kbps	High speed data up to 600 Mbps	High speed data
Power consumption	Low power, it can sleep between transmissions	Low power, it can sleep between transmissions	There are several standards, which include low power	Low power consumption in all three types
Typical applications	Connecting cell phone to computers for peripheral devices	Widely used in industrial and commercial application	Excellent in carrying Ethernet signals wireless. Used to connect electronic devices	Access control, animal tagging, Library books, Laundry identification
Strengths	Designed to replace wires. Good for audio, and can support video	Excellent for very low data rate battery powered applications.	Designed for stationary base station with multiple portable devices.	Excellent for transmitting data to long distances
Weaknesses	Not good at sleeping between transmissions. Limited range	Complicated software to implement. Low safety	Not fit for battery operation	High battery consumption in two types (active and BAP)

2.1.1   The Difference Between RFID and Barcode

RFID eliminates the need for line-of-sight reading that bar coding depends on (we do not need line of sight to read the information)

Scanning in RFID tags can be made at grader distances than that of the bar code. The RFID range is about 90 feet (about 27 m) but in Barcode this range is about 30 cm at the most.

2.1.2   How RFID Works

There are two kinds of Tag which are active and passive. Tag "responds to a signal from the Interrogator (reader/writer/antenna) which in turn sends a signal to the computer" [1]. The tag is consisting of two parts which are an Integrated Circuit (IC) and an antenna. Depending on the application, it may be as a label or engraved in glass or a card [1, 6].

2.1.3   The Differences Between 3 Kinds of RFID Tags

1. Active tags have some form of transmitter in addition to a battery. Thus, the Tag covers a long range. These are two disadvantages in having a battery. It adds to the cost of the tag, are not permanent power supply sources. To decide which type is suitable for you depends on your application [1, 6].
2. Passive tags convert the signal sent by the interrogator into power, while using the signal to transfer the data. All the power of a passive tag is provided by this way. Hence the tag is starts to work when it is exposed to the interrogator beam. For replying the interrogator, The tag uses backscatter technique. "This does not involve a transmitter on the tag, but is the means of "reflecting" the carrier wave and putting a signal into that reflection" [1].
3. Battery assisted tags like passive tags use backscatter however they also use a battery to supply the power. This has a big advantage, because for supplying the power, the tag does not dependent on the signal comes from the interrogator. Therefore it is able to work at a greater distance from the interrogator [1, 6].

2.1.4   The RFID's Frequencies Values

RFID operates on several frequency bands. The Radio Regulatory body controls the exact frequency in each country. RFID has four generic frequencies which are 125–134 KHz, Ultra High Frequency (UHF) 400–960 MHz, 13.56 MHz, 2.45 GHz, 5.8 GHz [1].

The UHF consists of two frequencies: the 400 MHz band and the 860–960 MHz band. For working near water or humans, the lower frequencies (125–134 KHz and 13.56 MHz) are more functional than the higher frequency tags. The range of the lower frequencies tags are less than the passive tags, and also their data transfer rate is slower. From country to country, the higher frequency ranges have more regulatory differences [1].

Examples' regarding the RFID tags are [1]:

1. Low frequency, 100–500 KHz: Applied in access control, animal identification-automobile key

2. High frequency, 13.56 KHz: Applied in smart cardlibrary book tracking, airline baggage tracking
3. UHF, 400–1000 MHz: Applied in management-supply chain
4. Microwave, 2.4–6.0 GHz: Applied in rail road car monitoring, data collection system.

2.1.5 Tag and Reader

Tag is one of the RFID system components. Tags are made of at least two parts, processor and antenna:

1. Processors: Store and process data, modulate the signal and absorb the energy from the reader
2. Antenna: Transmits the signals and data among the tags and readers from long distances.

Some of the tags do not need battery for transmitting signal and data and worked with the voltage that is induced by the electromagnetic field. Figure 1 illustrates tag components. Reader is RFID system is adapted to identify objects by reading the tags attached to their acts. To read data transferred by tag, tag reader is needed which send the signal to the tag and receive data from the tags. Tag readers usually send the data received from tags to the computer for analysis.

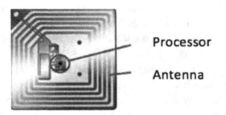

Fig. 1. RFID tag components

2.2 Near Field Communication (NFC)

By creating a radio frequency current, the NFC allows a reader, interrogator, or active device, to communicate with a small NFC tag or another NFC device. Passive devices do not read other devices actively, but communicate with the reader and save the data. In addition, it is possible to have a node-to-node communication through two active devices with NFC. Therefore both devices are able to transmit data [3].

2.2.1 How NFC Works

Devices using NFC may be active or passive. A passive device, such as an NFC tag, contains data that other devices can read but does not read any data itself. Think of a passive device as a sign on a wall; people can read the information, but the sign itself does nothing except exposing the information. Active devices can read information and transmit it. An active NFC device, like a smartphone, would not only be able to collect information from NFC tags, but it would also be able to exchange information with other compatible phones or devices and could even alter the information on the NFC tag if authorized to make such changes [3].

2.2.2   The Differences Between the Types of NFC Tags

In NFC there exist four tag types. Tag types refer to the speed and compatibility between an NFC tag and NFC readers. Most often a Uniform resource locator (URL) will be embedded in a NFC tag. The URLs take up only a small amount of memory, lowering the production cost of the NFC tags since many of them are placed on posters or other items that are eventually thrown away [3]. Tag Types are [3]:

1. Has data collision protection and can be set to either read or rewrite or read-only. Read-only programming prevents the information from being changed or written over, once embedded in the tag. This type is appropriate for a Uniform Resource Locator (URL) or a small amount of data since it has 96 bytes of memory. The tag's memory capacity can expand to a larger size it necessary. The low price makes the type 1 an ideal choice for most near field communication tasks.
2. Also has data collision protection and can be rewritten or read-only. They start at 48 bytes of memory, half of type one, but can expand to be as large as a type 1 tag. Communication speeds are the same for tags types 1 and 2.
3. Is equipped with data collision protection, and has larger memory and faster speeds than tags types 1 and 2. This tag is part of the FeliCa (a nearly Japanese developed system). The bigger size allows it to hold more complex codes, but it costs more to create each tag.
4. Have data collision protection and can use either NFC-A or NFC-B communication. By the time this tag is manufactured, it is set as either rewritable or read-only and this setting is changeable by the user, unlike the other NFC tags which can be altered at a later date. This tag has faster speeds than the other 3 tags and holds 32 Kbytes in memory.

2.2.3   The Advantage of NFC in Businesses

NFC allows your business to provide fast and secure means for customers to pay at the register without digging through their wallets for various credit cards. It also allows the customers to store coupons and redeem customer loyalty points without carrying around extra papers and cards. It also offers means to send information to customers using smart posters and displays with a NFC tag inside. Tourists would be able to swipe their phone to learn more about historic monuments or famous pieces of artwork [3].

2.2.4   The Security of NFC

There are many essential areas for the security of NFC. Each possible vulnerability can be determined. Some of the major NFC security areas represent some of the means where NFC security could be compromised. Though the short range of possible communications reduces the possibility of any threats, it does not guarantee complete NFC security; therefore each NFC security issue must be considered to guarantee that it will not be subject to embranchment [4]. These are consisting of eavesdropping, data distortion, data modification and man-in-middle attack.

1. Eavesdropping: Being a short range technology does not make NFC immune to security attacks. Unwanted users can pick up the signals since NFC uses radio waves for communication, and these propagate not only to the target receiver but also in the vicinity of the transmitter. It is not difficult to create the technology for receiving these signals [4, 7].
2. Data distortion: "This near field communications security issue is essentially a form of denial of service attack. Rather than just listening to the communications, the attacker may try to disturb the communications by sending data that may be valid, or even blocking he channel so that the legitimate data is corrupted." [4, 7].
3. Data modification: "This form of NFC security issue involves the attacker aiming to arrange for the receiving device to receive data that has been manipulated in some form. This data will naturally have to be in the correct format for it to be accepted." [7].
4. Man-in-the-middle: "This form of NFC security issue involves three parties. This form of NFC security issue involves a two party communication being intercepted by a third party. The third party acts as a relay, but using information received and modifying it if required to enable the attacker to achieve their aims. This must obviously be achieved without the two original parties knowing that there is an interceptor between them." [4].

3   Conclusion

Among the twelve sensors addressed in this article RFID and NFC are optimal for our purposes:

1. Consume less energy
2. Ones would fit with high performance
3. High safety
4. Low interference with other data transmitters, between these sensors RFID is more functional
5. Can be made in different sizes
6. The readers can be hidden or unhidden
7. Data on tags is changeable
8. Can transmit data from long distances
9. Have the least Side effects, because of electromagnetic and electronic signal.

Although RFID is very similar to NFC in many aspects, RFID is a much broader technology, NFC is a specific case which is defined by standard enabling it to be interoperable nowadays it is possible to buy everything with mobile phone if the mobile phone has NFC technology like as IPhone 6. In addition, RFID tags used in many fields such as traveling, agriculture, clothes, retail and etc. Moreover it is used for having electronic citizens, smart driver license, electronic passport, and electronic tickets.

References

1. High Tech Aid. http://www.hightechaid.com
2. Altera. http://www.altera.com/technology/system-design
3. NFC. http://www.nearfieldcommunication.org/
4. Radio-electronics. http://www.radio-electronics.com/
5. Voler Systems. http://www.volersystems.com/
6. Understanding RFID. http://www.understandrfid.com/rfid-technology/
7. SECURENFC. http://www.securenfc.com.au/nfc-info-2/
8. Ke-Sheng Wang, M.S.: Intelligent and integrated RFID (II-RFID) system for improving traceability in manufacturing. J. Adv. Manufact. **2**, 106–120 (2014)
9. Urien, P.: LLCPS: a new security framework based on TLS for NFC P2P applications in the internet of things. In: IEEE CCNC 2013, January 2013

Wireless Sensor Networks Lifetime Extension Based on a New Hybrid Hierarchical Routing Mechanism

Hania Aoudia$^{(\boxtimes)}$, Youcef Touati, and Arab Ali-Chérif

Computer Science Lab, LIASD University of Paris 8,
2 Rue de La Liberté, St-Denis, France
{hania,youcef,aa}@univ-paris8.fr

Abstract. Streamline energy consumption in Wireless Sensor Network (WSN) is and stills a topical problem in which several investigations have undertaken. The aim is to develop mechanisms such those based on routing protocols, for prolonging the network lifetime leading to improve its robustness and fluidity of transmissions, and then ensure an overall stable operation. In this paper, we present a robust and hybrid hierarchical multi-hop routing protocol wherein a dynamic clustering mechanism is implemented for optimal clusters construction. The approach combines successfully heterogonous information in terms of residual energy and signal strength of nodes and allows a multipath search by optimizing end-to-end delay and energy consumption. The effectiveness of the proposed approach is illustrated in simulations. For this purpose, a comparative study with LEACH protocol has been carried out for several networks with different densities.

Keywords: Hierarchical routing · Clustering · WSN

1 Introduction

In WSN, routing protocols play an important role to maintain routes and to ensure reliable multi-hop communication by taking into account several constraints transmission range of nodes, their processing and storage capabilities as well as their energy resources. In fact, since sensor nodes use ordinary battery system, they have limited energy capacity. It is a big challenge for network designers in hostile environments where it is impossible to access directly the sensors and replace their batteries. Furthermore, when the energy of a sensor reaches a certain threshold, the sensor will become faulty and will not be able to function properly, which will have a major impact on the network performance. Thus, routing protocols designed for sensors should be as energy efficient as possible to extend their lifetime, and hence prolong the network lifetime while guaranteeing good performance overall. Despite these limitations, several application have been prospected for a variety of fields such as medical monitoring, military operations, rescue missions, climate changes and so on, and obtained results were acceptable [1–4]. In this context, routing algorithms that have been developed may be divided into categories [5].

© Institute for Computer Sciences, Social Informatics and Telecommunications Engineering 2015
S. Mumtaz et al. (Eds.): WICON 2014, LNICST 146, pp. 262–270, 2015.
DOI: 10.1007/978-3-319-18802-7_35

Mobility brings also new challenges to routing protocols in WSN. Sink mobility requires energy-efficient protocols to guarantee data delivery originated from source sensors toward mobile sinks. In hierarchical approach, networks are broken into clustered layers [6]. Nodes are grouped into clusters with a cluster head that has the responsibility of routing from the cluster to the other cluster heads or base stations. Data travel from a lower clustered layer to a higher one. Although, it hops from one node to another, but as it hops from one layer to another it covers larger distances. This moves the data faster to the base station. Clustering provides inherent optimization capabilities at the cluster heads. In this context, designing a routing mechanism using clustering-based approaches provide significant improvements in term of give better results energy consumption optimization and lifetime extension [4]. They present the advantage of minimizing the number of nodes that take part in long distance communication with the base station (BS) through the CH nodes use and, consequently, reduce the energy consumption of the network. In heterogeneity sensor network architecture, there are two types of sensors namely line-powered sensors which have no energy constraint, and the battery-powered sensors having limited lifetime, and hence should use their available energy efficiently by minimizing their potential of data communication and computation. In this work, we are interested by a wide WSN context in which clustering mechanism is an important key to satisfy most constraints cited above. We focus our work on hierarchical approaches particularly on those based on energy and end-to-end delay optimization.

The remainder of this paper is organized as follows: Sect. 2 presents a short background of some WSN routing protocols works and basics. Section 3 describes the robust hierarchical routing protocol HHRP. Section 4 concerns some simulations that have been conducted to show the effectiveness of the proposed approach. A comparative study with a standard routing protocol LEACH [5] is illustrated. We end this paper, in Sect. 5, by dressing some conclusions.

2 Background

As in LEACH, Energy-LEACH consists of several rounds in which CH nodes are elected [7–9]. It improves the CH nodes selection procedure and uses residual energy of nodes as a main metric. In the first round, all nodes have the same probability to become CH nodes. According to a certain probability, the BS proceeds for electing randomly new CH nodes and in the next rounds, knowing that residual energy of each node is different, new CH nodes are determined. It means that nodes having more residual energy become coordinator nodes rather than nodes with less energy. Unlike to LEACH and E-LEACH protocols where communications are ensured in a single-hop whatever the distance between nodes, in Multihop-LEACH protocol, optimal paths between nodes and CH nodes in order to communicate with the BS [10]. Some CH nodes play the role of relay stations and are able to converse each other. Tow-Level-LEACH is a variant proposed in [11] which consists to build a two-level hierarchy for a better consumed energy optimization. The TL-LEACH uses randomized rotation of CH nodes and the corresponding clusters, adaptive and self-configuring cluster formation. Vice-LEACH is a new version proposed in [12]. The objective is to ensure continuously the network operation by electing a vice-CH node within same functionalities as CH node. LEACH-Centralized proposed in [13] is similar to LEACH, but the CH selection is carried out at the BS. During the setup phase, BS receives from other nodes information about their current locations and remaining energy levels. This algorithm attempts to minimize the total energy that non CH nodes use to transmit their data to CH nodes by minimizing the total sum of squared distance between nodes and their cluster head nodes. In [8], authors proposed an improved LEACH protocol called LEACH-M where clusters formation is performed only once, minimizing by this way energy consumption and maximizing in the same time the lifetime of the network. Even if energy consumption gain is 10 % comparatively to LEACH, the main drawback of LEACH-M is that network can stop running once all member nodes (MN) for a given cluster are elected as CH nodes. In other words, only cluster with high number of MN continues to operate in the network by electing other new CH nodes. All other nodes remaining to other clusters set their status to a sleep mode. Thus, the network should reorganize and initialize itself according to LEACH protocol procedure.

In this paper, we present a robust and hybrid hierarchical multi-hop routing protocol (HHRP) wherein a dynamic clustering mechanism is implemented for optimal clusters construction. The approach combines successfully heterogonous information in terms of residual energy and signal strength of nodes and allows a multi-path search by optimizing energy consumption and end-to-end delay.

3 Robust Hybrid Hierarchical Routing Protocol – RHHRP

3.1 Network Architecture

The proposed approach requires a hierarchical topology including a set of clusters automatically built according to residual energy and location of nodes. Each cluster consists of a set of nodes called member nodes NMs with a coordinator called Cluster-Head or CH. It performs treatments and relays information in a single hop between NMs and corresponding CHs, and/or in a multi-hop to the BS via other CH nodes. It depends on coverage area and signal range of nodes. More nodes are distant from the BS, more they use other nodes services to reach the destination. Communication is provided on two hierarchical levels: intra-cluster and inter-cluster. Intra-cluster communications (Intra-Hs communication) concern messages exchanged, in a given cluster, between NMs and their corresponding CH. Such messages may include, for example, slots allocation or simply membership messages of NMs to CHs. In contrast, inter-cluster communications (Inter-Hs communication), concern messages between CHs-CHs-BS or CHs-BS.CH node located so far from the BS can reach the destination via several neighbors, thus it should take into account several constraints imposed by the application for optimal path selection. It can reach the BS on one hop or Multi-hop.

3.2   Energy Model

As described in [13, 14], communication phase requires substantial amounts of energy, which can be expressed by a model including both transmitter and receiver communications. Transmitting k bits of data over a distance d, can be defined as follows:

$$\mathbf{E_{Tx}}(k,d) = \mathbf{E}_{TXelec}(k) + \mathbf{E}_{TXamp}(k,d). \tag{1}$$

where:

$$\mathbf{E}_{TXelec}(k) = k\mathbf{E}_{TXelec}(k,d). \tag{2}$$

and,

$$\mathbf{E}_{TXamp}(k,d) = k\varepsilon_{amp}\,d^2. \tag{3}$$

and the energy required to receive k-bits of data is:

$$\mathbf{E_{Rx}}(k,d) = E_{RXelec}(k) = kE_{elec} \tag{4}$$

Parameters $\mathbf{E}_{elec}$, $\mathbf{E}_{TXamp}$ and ε_{amp} represent respectively transmitter/receiver electronic energy, amplification energy and amplification factor.

Based on (1) and (4), the average energy consumption in each CH node can be computed as follow:

$$\mathbf{E_{moy}} = \mathbf{P}_r[[\mathbf{E}_{TX}(k,d) + \mathbf{E}_{Rx}[(\mathbf{T}_{inter}/\mathbf{T}) - k]] + (1 - \mathbf{P}_r)\,[\mathbf{E}_{Rx}(\mathbf{T}_{inter}/\mathbf{T}) \\ + \mathbf{E}_{Rx}(\mathbf{T}_{intra}/\mathbf{T})\,] \tag{5}$$

$\mathbf{P}_r$ and $\mathbf{T}$ represent respectively the probability that each node has k bits of data to be sent and the required time for transmitting a byte of data. $\mathbf{T}_{inter}$ and $\mathbf{T}_{intra}$ denote respectively the communication time between CHs nodes and the BS, and the communication time between CHs nodes and NMs per round. In the fist term of (5), for a given probability $\mathbf{P}$ corresponding to an inter-CH communication phase, all CHs nodes exchange information with the BS with an energy consumption equivalent to $\mathbf{E}_{Tx}(k,d)$. the rest of the time $(\mathbf{T}_{inter}/\mathbf{T} - k)$ corresponds to the listening time where energy consumption is $\mathbf{E}_{Rx}(\mathbf{T}_{inter}/\mathbf{T} - k)$. The second term of (5) corresponds to a probability $(1 - \mathbf{P}_r)$ where the CH node does not transmit any data to the BS.

He spends all his time for inter-CHs communication in listening mode consuming energy of $\mathbf{E}_{Rx}(\mathbf{T}_{inter}/\mathbf{T})$. During intra-CH communication phase, CH node switches to a receive mode consuming $\mathbf{E}_{Rx}(\mathbf{T}_{intra}/\mathbf{T})$.

3.3   Robust HHRP Approach

The proposed approach consists to classify dynamically nodes into clusters where a coordinator node or CH node with extra privileges is capable to manipulate massages, aggregate data and ensure transmission between nodes and the BS according to TDMA and CDMA schedules. Using the proposed HHRP, the network reconfiguration is carried out dynamically based on a threshold value which is associated to the number of nodes belonging to a smallest cluster. The algorithm is illustrated on Fig. 1.

In round, nodes recognize all their neigbours and according to **RSSI** measures, CHs nodes can build an optimal tree to reach the BS. More **RSSI** value is important, more the coresponding node can be elected to route messages:

$$\text{Message}_{initSB} : \left(\text{ID}_{Ni,} \text{ID}_{Nj,} \textbf{P}, \textbf{R}_d, \text{RSSI}_i^{(j)} \right).$$

Where ID_{Ni} and ID_{Nj} respectively represent identifiers of destination $\textbf{N}_i$ and source $\textbf{N}_j$, $\textbf{P}$ is the probability generated by the BS for electing new CH node.

In TinyOS, a radio component-type CC2420 of a MicaZ sensor, RSSI values provided by the physical layer in ZigBee protocol are single-byte averaged over 8 periods of approximately 128 µs. The power of radio signal is calculated by the following formula:

$$\textbf{P} = \text{RSSI}_{val} + \text{Offset}_{\text{RSSI}} [\textbf{dBm}]. \tag{6}$$

Where **Offset**$_{RSSI}$ is a compensation value defined empirically and estimated approximately to − 45 dBm.

After the first round, in each cluster, the election of a new CH node is computed by the previous CH according to residual energy criterion. Once nodes belonging to the smallest cluster were all elected as CH nodes, the last CH node informs the BS that no other node can be elected as a new CH. Thus, the BS re-organizes dynamically the network by forming new clusters during the phase of initialization. CH nodes are elected according to a random probability given in (7) and all MN inform their memberships for given clusters. During rounds, each CH node elects a new one according to a remaining residual energy until that MN cannot be elected as a CH node. After that, the BS is informed that the cluster is not able to possess a CH for the next round, because all nodes in the cluster have been elected. Therefore, the BS computes a new probability in order to form new clusters.

The energy calculated for each MN can be defined as follows:

$$\textbf{E}_{MN}^{(j)} = \textbf{E}_{MNinit}^{(j)} - \left(k\textbf{E}_i^{(j)} + K\varepsilon_{amp}d_{toCH}^2 \right) \tag{7}$$

Where $\textbf{E}_{MN}^{(i)}$ and $\textbf{E}_{MNinit}^{(i)}$ represent respectively remaining energy and initial energy of **MN** (*i*).

Once determined, energy is compared to minimum energy for transmitting data $\textbf{E}_{TX}$.

Energy of each CH node is computed as follows:

$$\textbf{E}_{CH}^{(j)} = \textbf{E}_{CHinit}^{(j)} - \left(k*(\textbf{N}/\textbf{N}_{CH})*\textbf{E}_{elec} + k\textbf{E}_{tra}^{(j)}d_{toBS}^2 \right) \tag{8}$$

Where $\textbf{E}_{tra}^{(j)}$ is the energy dissipated by the power amplifier.

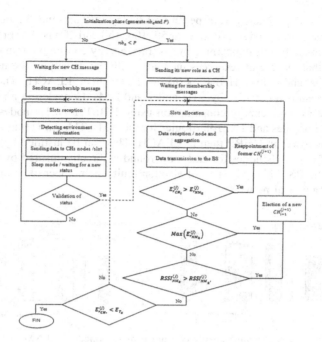

Fig. 1. Robust HHRP Algorithm

For a given round (j), CH node evaluates MN nodes residual energy $\mathbf{E}_{rNMk}^{(j)}$ in order to elect a new CH node. A node having highest energy is elected as a new CH for the next round $(j + 1)$. Thus, based on RSSI measures, we can estimate the optimal path to reach the BS. If $\mathbf{E}_{rNMk}^{(j)}$ is smaller than $\mathbf{E}_{rCHi}^{(j)}$, former CH node is reappointed in his role as a coordinator. If all nodes have been already selected as CH nodes, former CH informs the BS to re-organize the network. It determines a new number of clusters for a new round and the probability of election.

4   Simulations Results and Analysis

To evaluate the efficiency of HHRP, a comparative study has been conducted with LEACH routing protocol. For this purpose, we use dedicated simulators for WSN TOSSIM and POWERTOSSIM [12, 13] with an object-oriented programming language NesC as a development tool. At the beginning, all network nodes have a same level of energy randomly deployed in operational environment over an area of 100×100. The BS is identified as node number 0. Parameters such as dissipated energy of power amplifier, Amplifier parameter, initial energy have been initialized, so that:

$-E_{\text{tra}} = 1.29 \times 10^{-15} \text{J/bit/m}^2$	$-\varepsilon_{\text{amp}} = 10 \times 10^{-12} \text{J/bit/m}^4$	$-E_{init} = 20$ pJoules

A number of experiments were performed taking into account the density of the network. We have proposed networks with 50, 100, 150 and 200 nodes. Figures 2a and b show the obtained results concerning the average energy consumption in the network. One can note that the use of resources increases with the density of the network. The obtained results show that HHRP performs better than LEACH. They illustrate respectively consumed energies by CHs nodes and NMs. Considering a network with 100 nodes, the average energy consumption using HHRP for CHs nodes is approximately 22.7323 pJoules and 17.2148 pJoules for the NMs. Thus, we remark that energy consumption is lower in HHRP than in LEACH. This can be justified by the fact that the election of new CHs nodes for each new round is directly ensured by the old CHs nodes not by the BS. This procedure of election limits the number of control messages and the overloading of network.

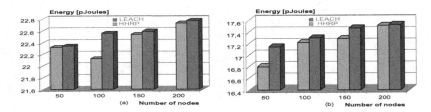

Fig. 2. Average energy consumed by CHs nodes and NMs

These results have a direct impact on the lifetime of the network. In fact, for 50 and 200 nodes, the proposed approach keeps the network operating whereas in LEACH, the network dyes respectively since rounds number 40 and 50 (Fig. 3a). In the same manner, for 200 nodes, HHRP maintains the network active longer than in LEACH (Fig. 3b).

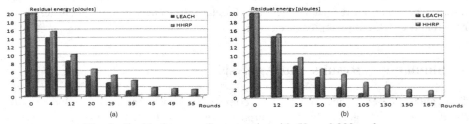

Fig. 3. Residual energy for networks with 50, and 200 nodes

Unlike inter-CHs communication, there are two kinds of intra-CH communications: CH-nodes and all nodes for establishing their membership to a cluster and communication between CH-nodes and MNs. Basically, applying LEACH and HHRP protocols, the number of messages exchanged in intra-CH communication increases according to the network density. The end-to-end delay of a packet is defined as the elapsed time to reach the destination after it is locally generated at the source. HHRP uses an intra-and inter-CHs communication. Based on some assumptions outlined above, data derived from MNs of each cluster moves directly to the corresponding CH-node. Thus, via an inter-CHs communication, aggregated information is transmitted in a single or multi-hop to the BS. The more MNs increases, the greatest time of data aggregation is. The larger the network is the more end-to-end delay increases (Fig. 4). When implementing HHRP, obtained results are better than those of LEACH standard routing protocol. For a network with 100 nodes, end-to-end delays are around of 99,993[ms] and 102,103[ms] respectively for LEACH and HHRP. The same is true for a network with 200 nodes, where end-to-end delays are respectively 100,988[ms] and 103,052[ms] for LEACH and HHRP. The gain in term of elapsed time for any data to reach its destination varies between 2 % to 5 %.

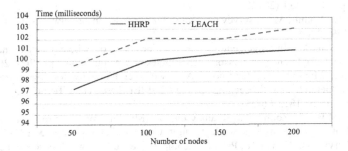

Fig. 4. End-To-End delays

5 Conclusions

In this paper, we propose and study a robust and hybrid hierarchical multi-hop routing protocol wherein a dynamic clustering mechanism is implemented for optimal clusters construction. The aim is to prolong the network lifetime and optimize energy consumption in order to improve its robustness and fluidity of transmissions. The approach combines successfully heterogonous information in terms of residual energy and signal strength of nodes and allows a multipath search by optimizing end-to-end delay and energy consumption. According to the density of the network, obtained results show clearly that HHRP performs better than LEACH.

References

1. Akyildiz, I.F., Su, W., Sankarasubramaniam, Y., Cayirci, E.: Wireless sensor networks: a survey. Comput. Netw. **38**, 393–422 (2002)
2. Akyildiz, I.F., Su, W., Sankarasubramaniam, Y., Cayirci, E.: A survey on sensor networks. IEEE Commun. Mag. **40**, 102–114 (2002)
3. Chong, C.Y., Kumar, S.P.: Sensor networks: evolution, opportunities and challenges. Proc. IEEE **91**, 1247–1256 (2003)

4. Tang, Y., Zhou, M.T., Zhang, X.: Overview of routing protocols in wireless sensor networks. J. Softw. **7**, 410–421 (2006)
5. Singh, S.K., Singh, M.P., Singh, D.K.: Routing protocols in wireless sensor networks – a survey. Int. J. Comput. Sci. Eng. Surv. **1**, 63–83 (2010)
6. Johnson, D.B., et al.: Dynamic source routing in Ad hoc wireless networks. In: Imielinski, T., Korth, H. (eds.) Mobile Computing, Chap. 5, pp. 153–181. Kluwer Academic Publishers, Dordrecht (1996). ISBN: 0792396979
7. Heinzelman, W., Chandrakasan, A., Balakrishnan, H.: Energy-efficient communication protocol for wireless micro-sensor networks. In: Proceedings of the 33rd Hawaii International Conference on System Sciences, vol. 2, pp. 3005−3014 (2000)
8. Aoudia, H., Touati, Y., Ali-Cherif, A., Greussay, P.: Hierarchical routing approach-based energy optimization in wireless sensor networks. In: Proceedings of the 10th ACM International Symposium on Mobility Management and Wireless Access, Paphos (Cyprus Island), pp. 131−134 (2012)
9. Akkaya, K., Younis, M.: A survey on routing for wireless sensor networks. J. Ad Hoc Netw. **3**, 325–349 (2005)
10. Fan, X., Son, Y.: Improvement on LEACH protocol of wireless sensor network. In: International Conference on Sensor Technologies and Applications, pp. 260−264 (2007)
11. Loscri, V., Morabito, G., Marano, S.A.: Two-level hierarchy for low-energy adaptive clustering hierarchy. In: Proceedings of the 62nd IEEE Vehicular Technology Conference, vol. 3, pp. 1809–1813 (2005)
12. Yassein, M.B., Al-Zoubi, A., Khamayseh, Y., Mardini, W.: Improvement on LEACH protocol of wireless sensor network. J. Digit. Content Technol. Appl. **3**, 132–136 (2009)
13. Bhattacharyya, D., Kim, T.H., Pal, S.: A comparative study of wireless sensor networks and their routing protocols. Sensors **10**, 10506–10523 (2010)
14. Levis, P., Lee, N., Welsh, M., Culler, D.: TOSSIM: accurate and scalable simulation of entire TinyOS applications. In: Proceedings of the 1st ACM Conference on Embedded Networked Sensor Systems, pp. 126−137 (2003)
15. Levis, P., Madden, S., Gay, D., Polastre, J., Szewczyk, R., Woo, A., Brewer, E., Culler, D.: The emergence of networking abstractions and techniques in TinyOS. In: Proceedings of the 1st ACM Symposium on Networked Systems Design and Implementation, vol. 1, pp. 1−14 (2004)
16. Yan, H., Sikdar, B.: Optimal cluster head selection in the LEACH architecture. In: Proceedings of IEEE International Conference on Performance, Computing and Communications, New Orleans (LA), pp. 93−100 (2007)

Efficient Dynamic Pricing Scheme for Effective Bandwidth Utilization in Mobile WIMAX IEEE802.16e

Kafilu Barau Danbatta[1(✉)] and Umar Garba Danbatta[2]

[1] Nigerian Communications Commission, Abuja, Nigeria
kdanbatta@ncc.gov.ng
[2] Department of Electrical Engineering, Bayero University Kano, Kano, Nigeria

Abstract. In the next Generation Networks like Mobile WiMAX, it is highly essential to create a market mechanism that would allow the customer to communicate with Network and negotiate a contract based on some QoS parameters like blocking probability, delay, arrival rate, spectral efficiency, resource allocation and price. However, the mechanisms, rather than technical-oriented scheme, that involve the use of economic theories may provide better solutions to accommodate the high demand of mobile services. The purpose of this research work is to propose and validate mathematical model that study the effect of pricing incentives as an additional strategy for encouraging a more efficient usage of limited network resources. An efficient dynamic pricing scheme for optimal network resource utilization in Mobile WiMAX network has been developed and validated. The percentage improvement of the Cumulative Revenue (CR) generated by the proposed model over the existing model ranges between 25 % and 150 % depending on the values of the Price Leveling Factor (PLF).

Keywords: Cumulative Resource Efficiency Index (CRI) · Cumulative Revenue (CR) · Acceptance probability · Utility · Low Priority User (LPU) and High Priority User (HPU) · Bandwidth Utilization (BU)

1 Introduction

WiMAX is wireless technology, based on the IEEE 802.16 standard, for nomadic and mobile data access The IEEE 802.16-2004 standard deals with fixed wireless broadband access, while the IEEE 802.16e standard deals with both fixed and mobile wireless broadband access. WiMAX offers cost-effective and quickly deployable alternative to cable and DSL networks. It provides high bandwidth and various levels of quality of services (QOS) for different classes of traffic [1].

The three QoS classes is considered in order to have a heterogeneous WiMAX environment with real-time and non-real-time users: Unsolicited Grant Service (UGS), rtPS, and Best Effort (BE). The UGS and rtPS classes support real-time service flows that have fixed-size and variable size data packets on a periodic basis, respectively. The IEEE 802.16e standard considers five QoS classes in order to have a heterogeneous WiMAX environment with real-time and non-real-time users: Unsolicited Granted Service (UGS), Real-Time Polling Service (rtPS), Extended Real-Time Polling Service (ertPS), Non-Real

© Institute for Computer Sciences, Social Informatics and Telecommunications Engineering 2015
S. Mumtaz et al. (Eds.): WICON 2014, LNICST 146, pp. 271–277, 2015.
DOI: 10.1007/978-3-319-18802-7_36

Time Polling Service (nrtPS), and Best Effort (BE). The UGS supports real-time traffic that periodically generates packets of fixed length, such as Voice over IP without silence suppression. The rtPS supports real-time traffic that periodically generates packets of variable length, such as MPEG video. The ertPS supports real-time traffic that periodically generates packets of variable length, such as Voice over IP services with silence suppression. The nrtPS supports non-real time traffic that generates packets of variable length and tolerant to delay, such as FTP. The BE service supports traffic that does not require throughput or delay guarantees, such as HTTP [2]. The BE class, designed for non-real-time applications, has no QoS guarantees and then should be identified as LPU and they are evidently be the cheapest one. The other three QoS classes in this paper shall be identified as HPUs [3].

In WDCRS, the total bandwidth is divided among the service classes. The choice of division is to be an optimization problem to get the maximum utilization of the bandwidth [6]. The three higher-priority classes (UGS, rtPS, ertPS) can be studied separately, since each class has fixed channel allocation pattern. For two lower-priority classes (nrtPS and BE), they are treated as two separate cognitive radio users, and the analysis is based on the fact that nrtPS scans the resources first, followed by the BE class [3, 5].

2   System Model

In this section, a mathematical model of price, utility and partitioned based resource CAC for static and dynamic congestion control is developed. Firstly, the CAC algorithm completely partitioned the users according to the five WiMAX classes and prioritizes the traffic into Low Priority Users and Higher Priority Users [4]. The nrtPS and BE are the two lower-priority classes while the UGS, rtPS, and ertPS are the three higher priority classes, each with different price, utility and acceptance probability functions. Secondly, each class is attended independently. The overall revenue, the total allocated resources and resource efficiency indices are developed for final performance analysis. LPUs (Low Priority Users) are charged based on the current HPU (High Priority Users) utilization, like 30%, 40%, 50% etc. The higher the HPU utilization, the higher the price quoted to the LPUs. The lower the HPU utilization the lower the price quoted to the LPUs. When the LPU utilization is above the incentive cut-off point, then, the charging scheme imposes a monetary penalty by charging LPUs above incentive HPU reference prices. This induces negative incentive to utilize the network at this point [5].

2.1   Additional Revenue Generated

To alleviate the shortcoming of the two models already presented in [8], the following scheme is established. The p_{inct}^{LPU} incentive price payable by admitted low priority user and p_{cong}^{LPU} congestion price payable by admitted low priority user can be computed as:

$$P_{ncong}^{LPU} = \left[P_{acces}^{HPU} + \left(P_{inct}^{HPU} - P_{acces}^{HPU} \right) * \left(\frac{\alpha(t) - \alpha_{i,w}^{HPU}}{\alpha_{i,w}^{ic} - \alpha_{i,w}^{HPU}} \right)^{\delta} \right]^{w_{b4}^{ncong}} \tag{1}$$

$$P_{cong}^{LPU} = \left[P_{inct}^{HPU} + \left(P_{cong}^{HPU} - P_{inct}^{HPU} \right) * \left(\frac{\alpha(t) - \alpha_{i,w}^{ic}}{\alpha_{i,w}^{th} - \alpha_{i,w}^{ic}} \right)^{\delta} \right]^{w_{b4}^{cong}} \tag{2}$$

And the additional revenue generated by admitting LPUs for both the proposed modified Dixit, Dixit and the proposed models can be computed as:

$$R = \sum_{i=1}^{N_{LPU}} \alpha(t)_{i-inct}^{LPU} * P_{util}^{LPU} \tag{3}$$

$$p_{inct}^{LPU} = p_{l,inct}^{nrtps} = p_{q,inct}^{BE} \tag{4}$$

$$P_{inct}^{HPU} = p_{i,inct}^{UGS} = p_{i,inct}^{rtps} = p_{k,inct}^{ertps} \tag{5}$$

$$\alpha(t)_{i-inct}^{LPU} = \alpha(t)_{l,inct}^{nrtps} = \alpha(t)_{q,inct}^{BE} \tag{6}$$

Where,

$p_{i,inct}^{UGS}$, $p_{i,inct}^{rtps}$, $p_{k,inct}^{ertps}$, are Reference Incentive flat prices payable by admitted UGS, rtps, ertPs traffic; $P_{inct}^{HPU} =$ Reference Incentive flat Price payable by admitted high priority users; $p_{l,inct}^{nrtps}$, $p_{q,inct}^{BE}$ Incentive Price payable by admitted nrtps, and BE traffic; p_{inct}^{LPU} Incentive price payable by admitted Low Priority Users; $\alpha(t)_{l,inct}^{nrtps}$, $\alpha(t)_{q,inct}^{BE}$, Instantaneous Bandwidth Utilization by nrtPs and BE traffic in an incentive region; $\alpha_{i,w}^{HPU}$ is the Total Bandwidth Utilization by High Priority Users; $\alpha_{i,w}^{LPU}$ is the Total Bandwidth Utilization by Low Priority Users; $\alpha_{i,w}^{ic}$ is the Incentive Cut-off Bandwidth Utilization $\alpha_{i,w}^{th}$ is the Threshold for Bandwidth Utilization; $m_{i,w}^{inct}$ is the Price Leveling Factor (PLF) in the incentive region and this provides additional flexibility to the Network Service Providers (NSPs) to modify their LPU pricing curves in the incentive region; $N_{l,inct}^{LPU} = N_{l,inct}^{nrtps} + N_{q,inct}^{BE}$ is the total Number of admitted nrtPs and BE traffic in the incentive region.

2.2 The Behavior of the Proposed Model

Figure 1 shows the LPU price normalized versus the bandwidth utilization (BU) for the proposed model without HPU utilization having a PLF = 0, 0.1, 1, and 5. The BU curves for PLF = 0 is a straight line at LPU = 0.5, this indicates, the HPU reference price above which the BU price is increased exponentially to discourage the utilization above incentive cut off limit. In the proposed model without HPU utilization, the price increment is above the HPU reference price and it goes to 1 while approaching the BU threshold limit of 0.9. In the incentive region the lower PLF corresponding to the values of 0 and 0.1 generates BU curves with higher revenue than those with PLF = 1 and 5. While in the congestion region, the reverse is the case. The difference with the existing model is that there is an initial HPU bandwith utilization of 0.4 and congestion control can be activated by tuning the values of PLFs according to the introduced concept of the proposed utility and acceptance probability models in [9].

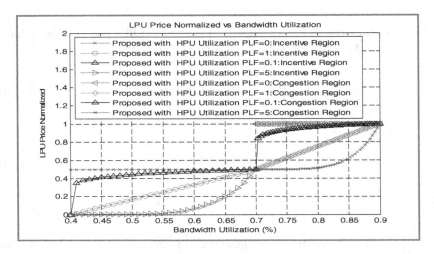

Fig. 1. HPU BW Price Normalized vs. Bandwidth Utilization

3   Resource Efficiency Index

The metric in [7] is used for the comparative and performance analysis of the proposed model and the existing model.

$$E = \frac{R}{B} \tag{7}$$

E = Resource Efficiency Index, R = Total revenue generated from the admitted users and B = Total Allocated Resources to the admitted users.

4   Performance Analysis

The NSPs need to have a mechanism for price flexibility to enable price adjustment for profit maximization and for competing with the prices set by the other NSPs in the region. To aid this purpose, the Price Leveling Factor (PLF) is introduced [5]. This factor allows the adjustment in LPU prices according to NSP requirements, keeping the configuration parameters $\alpha_{i,w}^{ic}$ and $\alpha_{i,w}^{th}$ set by the NSP unchanged. The PLFs for these simulations are 0, 0.1, 1, and 5. These three pricing models inherently handle LPU admission control by dynamically modulating the prices with respect to the fixed reference HPU price and based on the HPU demand. HPU price is the reference price used in these models to reflect the monetary incentives or penalties charged to the LPUs. The BU from 0.4 to 0.7 is called the incentive or non congestion region, while, the interval 0.7 to 0.9 is called the penalty region. The BU curves for PLF = 0 is a straight line at LPU = 0.5, this indicates, the HPU reference price above which the BU price is increased exponentially to discourage the utilization above the incentive cut off limit. Other values of Incentive cut-off and threshold could be chosen by the NSPs for revenue maximization in a competitive environment.

Figure 2 shows the cumulative revenue (CR) of the BS versus the cumulative bandwidth utilization (CBU) of all the three models. The Dixit without HPU utilization and the proposed modified dixit with HPU utilization and proposed with HPU utilization all having a PLF = 5. It is evident that the CR of the proposed model outperformed the CR of both Dixit without HPU utilization and the proposed modified dixit with HPU utilization in the CBU range between 0% and 3700%. It is also evident that the CR of both Dixit without HPU utilization and the proposed modified dixit with HPU utilization outperformed the proposed model in the CBU range between 3700% and 4500% possibly because the BU price overshoots to infinity as BU approaches the threshold limit of 0.9.

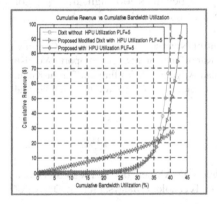

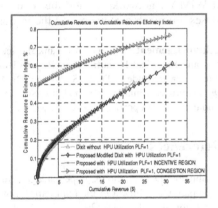

Fig. 2. Cumulative Revenue vs. Cumulative Bandwidth Utilization

Fig. 3. Cumulative Resource Efficiency Index vs. Cumulative Revenue

Figure 3 shows the Cumulative Resource efficiency index (CRI) of the BS versus the cumulative revenue (CR) for the Dixit without HPU utilization, proposed modified Dixit with HPU utilization and the proposed with HPU utilization all of them having a PLF = 1. The proposed model with HPU utilization is a distribution of the BU in the incentive and congestion regions both of them having a PLF = 1. The CRI of the proposed model with HPU utilization in the congestion region increase linearly from 0.5 to 0.75 across the range of CR from $0 to $32, while in the incentive region it has a maximum CRI of 0.28 across the range of CR from $0 to $8. The CRI of Dixit without

HPU utilization and the proposed modified Dixit with HPU utilization increases exponentially from 0 to 0.6 across the range of CR from \$0 to \$23 and \$0 to \$32, respectively. The % improvement of the CRI generated by the proposed modified dixit model with HPU utilization over CR generated by the Dixit model without HPU utilization at PLF = 1 is 50%.

5 Conclusions

In this paper, a mathematical model for an efficient dynamic pricing is developed for optimal network resource utilization using a modified log barrier function in Mobile WiMAX network. The percentage improvement of the Cumulative Resource Efficiency Index (CREI) generated by the proposed model over the existing model ranges between 6% and 7.1% depending on the values of the Price Leveling Factor (PLF). The scheme proved to generate more revenue per Bandwidth Utilization. For further improvement, a model with HPU utilization and a price increment which approaches 1 above the HPU reference price instead of infinity has been developed. Congestion control could be possible by tuning the values of PLFs according to the introduced concept of the proposed utility and acceptance probability models. The proposed scheme is evaluated and compared with existing schemes for similar traffic scenarios. The results show that the scheme can achieve higher bandwidth utilization and lower the blocking probability in WiMAX networks. When the required BW price becomes too high, the operator looses too much customers and the resources are then under-utilized.

Acknowlegement. We wish to thank the management of Nigerian Communications Commission and Electrical Department of Bayero University Kano for their financial support. We also extend our gratitude to Dr. S. S. Adamu, Dr. Muhammad Ajiya, Dr. Sabo Ibrahim Birnin Kudu, Dr. Dahiru S. Shuaibu, Dr. Yakubu Suleiman and Dr. Sulaiman Garba for their intellectual guidance and support.

References

1. Shuaibu, D.S.: Radio resource management for mobile WiMAX network. A Thesis Submitted in partial fulfillment of the requirements of Universiti Technologi Malaysia for the Degree of Doctor of Philosophy (2012)
2. Ramad, K., Jain, R.: WiMAX System evaluation Methodology. WiMAX Forum, version 2.1, July 2008
3. Akyildiz, I., Lee, W., Vuran, M., Mohanty, S.: NeXt generation/dynamic spectrum access/ cognitive radio wireless networks. Surv. Comput. Netw. **50**(13), 2127–2159 (2006)
4. Mowafi, M.Y., Al-Mistarihi, M.F., Marei, M.S.: A Dual Usage of Cognitive Radio in Managing the WiMAX Band width MIPRO/CTI (2012)
5. Dixit, S., Periyalwar, S., Yanikomeroglu, H.: Secondary user access in LTE architecture based on a base-station-centric framework with dynamic pricing. IEEE Trans. Veh. Technol. **62**(1), 284–296 (2013)
6. Badia, L., Lindstrom, J., Zorzi, M.: On utility-based radio resource management with and without service guarantees. In: Proceedings of the 7th ACM International Symposium on Modeling, Analysis and Simulation of Wireless and Mobile Systems, Venice, Italy, pp. 244–251 (2004)

7. Vuong, Q.N.: Mobility management in 4G wireless heterogeneous networks. A Thesis Submitted in partial fulfillment of the requirements of Universite D'evry Val-D'essonne for the Degree of Doctor of Philosophy (2008)
8. Danbatta, K.B., Danbatta, U.G.: Dynamic pricing scheme for effective bandwidth utilization in mobile Wimax. Int. J. Comput. Appl. **104**(15), 7–12 (2014)
9. Danbatta, K.B., Danbatta, U.G.: Efficient price and utility based congestion control in the next generation networks 4G. Int. J. Comput. Appl. **104**(15), 1–6 (2014)

Dynamic Congestion Control Based on Delay, Service Partitioning and Prioritization in Mobile WiMAX IEEE802.16e

Kafilu Barau Danbatta[1(✉)] and Umar Garba Danbatta[2]

[1] Nigerian Communications Commission, Abuja, Nigeria
kdanbatta@ncc.gov.ng
[2] Department of Electrical Engineering, Bayero University Kano, Kano, Nigeria

Abstract. In the next Generation Networks like 4G, it is highly essential to create a market mechanism that would allow the customer to communicate with network and negotiate a contract based on some QoS parameters like blocking probability, delay, arrival rate, spectral efficiency, resource allocation and price. However, the mechanisms, rather than technical-oriented scheme, that involve the use of economic theories may provide better solutions to accommodate the high demand of mobile services. The purpose of this research work is to propose and validate mathematical model that study the effect of pricing incentives as an additional strategy that optimally shapes the users' traffic in terms of delay, service class partitioning, and prioritization for wireless users in Mobile WiMAX network. The percentage improvement of the Cumulative Revenue (CR) generated by the proposed model over Yaipairoj model ranges between 25 % and 100 %. The proposed model is able to reduce congestion by 21 %.

Keywords: Price Leveling Factor (PLF) · Total revenue generated · Total allocated resources · Cumulative Resource Allocated (CRA) · Incentive price · Incentive Cut-off · Threshold for bandwidth utilization

1 Introduction

The IEEE 802.16e standard considers five QoS classes in order to have a heterogeneous WiMAX environment with real-time and non-real-time users: Unsolicited Granted Service (UGS), Real-Time Polling Service (rtPS), Extended Real-Time Polling Service (ertPS), Non-Real Time Polling Service (nrtPS), and Best Effort (BE). [1]. The BE class, designed for non-real-time applications, has no QoS guarantees and then should be identified as LPU and they are evidently be the cheapest one. The other three QoS classes in this thesis shall be identified as HPUs.

The system is composed of three functional blocks: CAC block, dual partitioning block and Pricing block. Here, a guard channel scheme is used at the CAC block. The pricing block works as follows: When the traffic load is such that the bandwidth utilization level is less than the congestion threshold value, a minimum price is charged to each user. The minimum price is the price that is acceptable to every user. When the traffic load increases beyond the congestion threshold value, dynamic peak hour price will be charged to users who want to place their calls at this time. They would be

© Institute for Computer Sciences, Social Informatics and Telecommunications Engineering 2015
S. Mumtaz et al. (Eds.): WICON 2014, LNICST 146, pp. 278–283, 2015.
DOI: 10.1007/978-3-319-18802-7_37

queued on priority queue. This is a range of price between p_{max} and p_{min} depending on the individual users demand. Base stations broadcast the current unit price to the users when they try to make the call. It should be noted here that, according to the proposed scheme, the decision about the peak hour fee is based on the actual network conditions and not only on the time of the day. This means that the price is continuously and dynamically adjusted according to the changes in the system condition as the system evolves [3].

In [2], the dual partitioning commences immediately after the Service Flow (SF) reaches a certain threshold. In the proposed scheme, the two queues are identified as: conventional and priority queues. The traffic is initially partitioned in two; HPU and LPU and charged with normal pricing if congestion threshold is not reached. If the Network enters into a congestion state, then the pricing scheme would be activated and those that are willing to accept a new range of price $p_m \leq p \leq p_{max}$ are placed under priority queue, while those that are just willing to accept $p_{min} \leq p \leq p_m$ are placed under conventional queue. They pay this range of price, but with a little bit longer delays and lower QoS.

2 System Model

In the proposed model as depicted in Fig. 1, the arrival rate of the incoming users is characterized by Poisson arrival. The network would test the congestion level based on the current load and determines whether the system is congested or not [5]. If the system is not congested, then the traffic would not be differentiated and it is directed towards the conventional queuing system as they would be charged with normal price (minimum price).

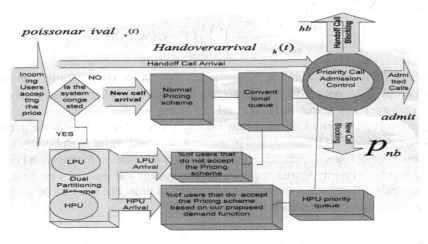

Fig. 1. The schematic representation of the proposed dynamic congestion control model based on price, delay, service partitioning and prioritization.

On the other hand if the system is congested, the traffic would be differentiated and according to the proposed scheme, instead of charging directly congestion price to higher priority users, a price between a minimum and maximum is charged according to the developed demand function in [6], which is entirely different from the one normally used by the existing literatures like the one used by [4].

For the dynamic price-based congestion control, the following demand function is proposed as:

$$
\lambda\left(p_i^{traffic\,class}(t)\right) = \lambda_{max}^{traffic\,class}
$$
$$
* \left(1 - \left(\frac{p_i^{traffic\,class}(t) - p_{min}^{traffic\,class}}{p_{max}^{traffic\,class} - p_{min}^{traffic\,class}}\right)^{\alpha}\right) \tag{1}
$$

$p_i^{traffic\,class}(t)$ is the price paid by a traffic class; $\lambda_{max}^{traffic\,class}$ is the maximum arrival rate of a traffic class; $p_{min}^{traffic\,class}$ Minimum Price quoted to a traffic class acceptable to all users; $p_{max}^{traffic\,class}$ Maximum Price quoted to a traffic class; is the maximum price threshold. If this price is exceeded no any user is willing to pay.

3   Revenue Generated by High Priority Users in a Network Congestion State

This is the revenue generated by HPUs in a network congestion state. The revenue tends to be very high despite the fact that number of users in the network has been reduced as a result of the ability of the model to shape the incoming arrival rates.

$$
R(p)^{HPU} = \sum_{i=1}^{N_{HPU}} p_i^{HPU}(t) * \lambda_{max}^{HPU}
$$
$$
* \left(\left(1 - \left(\frac{p_i^{HPU}(t) - p_{min}^{HPU}}{p_{max}^{HPU} - p_{min}^{HPU}}\right)^{\alpha}\right)\right)\left(1 - C(N_p, a_p)cr * e^{-N_p\mu(1-\rho_p)t_p}\right) \tag{2}
$$

Where $C(N_p, a_p), C(N_c, a_c)$ is the Earlang-C formula for High Priority Users and Low Priority Users respectively, a_p and a_c are the loads from High Priority Users and Low Priority Users respectively, N_p and N_c is the number of channels logically assigned to High Priority Users and Low Priority Users respectively, μ is the average departure rate of users $(1/T_{avg})$, ρ_p and ρ_c are the load per server for High Priority Users and Low Priority Users respectively, t_p and t_c are QoS requirement for the High Priority Queue and Low Priority Queue respectively. The system will guarantee the time that mobile user's call request would not exceed amount of time. The t_p would be a lot less than t_c when the system enters into congestion [5].

4   Performance Analysis

Mat Lab simulation software has been utilized to evaluate the performance of the proposed integrated pricing and call admission control in terms of congestion prevention, achievable total user utility, and obtained revenue. Figure 2 shows the arrival rates of 0.25 calls/minute is the lowest for both the two models when the Bandwidth (BW) price is at its maximum $22 per Kbps. This implies that most of the users are rejecting the quoted maximum BW price and join the conventional queue during congestion. At a BW price of $8 per Kbps, all the two models have the same maximum arrival rates of 4.5 calls/minute. This is the normal range of price acceptable to all the users in the two models during non congestion state. The percentage improvement of the arrival rate generated by the proposed model over Yaipairoj et al. model, at the selected BW price of $14 per Kbps, is 35.7 %.

Figure 3 shows the revenue generated by both the two models are at the lowest when the BW price is at its maximum $22. The proposed model generated a maximum revenue of $51 at a BW price of $14 per Kbps. The least is a maximum revenue of $42 generated by Yaipairoj et al. model at a BW price of $11 per Kbps.

The simulation parameters for the proposedmodel and Yaipairoj et al. model are represented in (Table. 1).

Table 1. The simulation parameters for the proposed model and Yaipairoj et al. model

Parameters	Settings
Blocking Probability model	Earlang B model
Waiting Probability model	Earlang C model
Average Holding Time for priority users	200sec
Average Holding Time for conventional users	200sec
Total Number channels	30
Proposed models parameters	
Minimum acceptable Price	$8
HPU maximum Congestion Price	$22
Demand function Used	Proposed demand function
Yaipairoj et al. model parameters	
Minimum acceptable Price	$8
HPU maximum Congestion Price	Infinity
Demand function Used	Odlyzko, A. (2001).
Priority factor	0.8
Total Number of channels	30

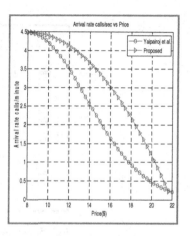

Fig. 2. Arrival rate vs. BW price

Figure 4 shows that the lowest revenue of $5 generated by both the two models is when the BW utilization is at its minimum value of 2 %. The proposed model generated a maximum revenue of $51 at a BW utilization of 51 %. The least is maximum revenue of $42 generated by Yaipairoj et al. model at a BW utilization of 55 %. As the BW utilization increases from 5 % to 62 %, the revenue increases to the maximum values quoted above for each model, then decreases exponentially to $35 at 62 % utilization. The percentage improvement of the maximum revenue generated by the proposed model at the BW utilization of 51 % over Yaipairoj et al. model at the BW utilization of 55 % is 35.7 %.

Figure 5 shows that the highest cumulative revenues generated by both the two models are at the highest BW price of $22. At this BW price the proposed model

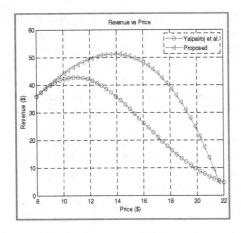
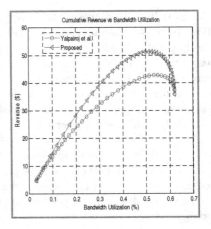

Fig. 3. Revenue vs. BW price   **Fig. 4.** Revenue vs. bandwidth utilization

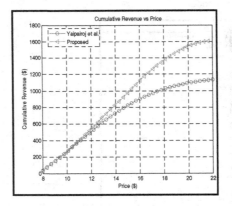

Fig. 5. Cumulative revenue vs. BW price

generated a CR of $1600 and the least is a CR of $1050 generated by Yaipairoj et al. model. The two models achieved the same range of CR from 0 to $500 for the BW price range of $8 to $12. As the BW price increases from $12 to $22, the CR increases exponentially from $500 to the highest values quoted above. The percentage improvement of CR generated by the proposed model over Yaipairoj et al. model at the BW price of $22 is 71.4 %.

5 Conclusions

The analytical results show that the proposed dynamic pricing is capable of preventing network congestion, similar to the conventional dynamic pricing schemes. The mobile network can reduce the level of arrival rate if the users are incentivized. Mobile users are potentially more satisfied with the proposed dynamic pricing since they can choose either to be charged according to the dynamic pricing scheme for superior QoS or the flat-rate pricing scheme for predictable BW prices. The model is able to reduce congestion by 21 % at 0.045 maximum blocking probability.

Acknowledgement. We wish to thank the management of Nigerian Communications Commission and Bayero University Kano for their financial support. We also extend our gratitude to Dr. S. S. Adamu, Dr. Muhammad Ajiya, Dr. Sabo Ibrahim Birnin Kudu, Dr. Dahiru S. Shuaibu, Dr. Yakubu Suleiman Baguda and Dr. Sulaiman Garba for their intellectual guidance and support.

References

1. Mowafi, M.Y., Al-Mistarihi, M.F., Marei, M.S.: A Dual Usage of Cognitive Radio in Managing the WiMAX Band width MIPRO /CTI (2012)
2. Shuaibu, D.S.: Radio Resource Management for Mobile WiMAX Network. A Thesis Submitted in partial fulfillment of the requirements of Universiti Technologi Malaysia for the Degree of Doctor of Philosophy (2012)
3. Hou, J., Yang, J., Papavassiliou, S.: Integration of pricing with call admission control to meet QOS requirements in cellular networks. IEEE Trans. Parallel Distrib. Syst. **13**(19), 898–910 (2002)
4. Fishburn, P.C., Odlyzko, A.M.: Dynamic behavior of differential pricing and quality of service options for the internet. In: ICE 1998, pp. 128–139 (1998)
5. Yaipairoj, S.: Enhancing Performance of Mobile Services through Pricing Mechanisms. A Thesis Submitted in partial fulfillment of the requirements of Stevens Institute of Technology for the Degree of Doctor of Philosophy (2006)
6. Danbatta, K.B., Danbatta, U.G.: Efficient price and utility based congestion control in the next generation networks 4G. Int. J. Comput. Appl. **104**(15), 1–6 (2014)

Experimental Assessment of a Propagation Model for TV White Spaces

Rogério Dionísio[1,2(✉)], Paulo Marques[1], and Jonathan Rodriguez[1]

[1] Instituto de Telecomunicações, Campus de Santiago, 3810-193 Aveiro, Portugal
{rdionisio,pmarques,jonathan}@av.it.pt
[2] Instituto Politécnico de Castelo Branco, Avenida do Empresário,
600-767 Castelo Branco, Portugal

Abstract. This paper describes outdoor field measurements in television white spaces (TVWS) carried out in Munich, Germany. Fixed and mobile measurements in rural, sub-urban and urban scenarios showed that the modified Hata model is appropriate to describe the path loss over distances up to few kilometers, and may be used in the process to populate a geo-location database.

Keywords: Field measurements · TV white space · Geolocation database

1 Introduction

TVWS refer to geographically unused UHF television broadcasting frequency channels. Such radio signals have singular and attractive propagation characteristics, high coverage areas with lower power and good building penetration. However, the availability of TVWS depends on the location and the protection requirements of DVB-T commercial reception.

The FP7 project COGEU aimed to take advantage of the transition to digital TV, to design, implement and demonstrate enabling technologies to allow an efficient use of TVWS for radio communications, while addressing coexistence with the DVB-T European standard [1]. The first opportunity to test the equipment in a real environment, i.e., operate in realistic White Spaces, took place with the Munich trial. As no commercial WSDs are available on the European market for the trials, we used prototype equipment. For WSD transmitter and receiver, we used ETTUS USRP hardware [2]. This prototype cannot be representative for future commercial off-the-shelf WSDs, so our objective for the trials was to investigate if modified Hata propagation model [3] is appropriate for Maximum EIRP calculations to populate the geo-location database. The paper is structured as follows: Section II presents an overview of the geo-location database features and implementation. Section III describes the transmission trials and field measurements realized in Munich. Finally, in Section IV we present the conclusions of the work.

© Institute for Computer Sciences, Social Informatics and Telecommunications Engineering 2015
S. Mumtaz et al. (Eds.): WICON 2014, LNICST 146, pp. 284–290, 2015.
DOI: 10.1007/978-3-319-18802-7_38

2 TVWS Geolocation Database

A geo-location database is a crucial element for a secondary spectrum system to work and avoid interference to DVB-T signals. The methodology to estimate TVWS is aligned to ECC Report 186 [4]. In principle, in a first step for each considered location, the wanted and interfering field strengths (for the broadcast only, i.e. without WSD) need to be calculated. From this the location probability for the case without active WSDs can be determined.

Accepting a degradation of location probability allows higher interfering signal. By applying the approximation (A.7.1-1) given in ECC Report 159 [5], the maximum acceptable WSD signal strength in the considered TV channel at the possible location of DVB-T reception antenna can be calculated. To determine maximum WSD transmit power, further information is required, e.g. on minimum distance to DVB-T reception antenna, channel separation, protection ratios, among other parameters.

For the propagation of DVB-T signals, a terrain-based model is used which also takes (to some extend) the morphology into account. For the propagation of WSD signals which range, due to the possible transmit power, antenna height, antenna gain, etc., is typically below 10 km, simpler non-terrain based models like extended Hata are commonly used. The transmission trials described in the following sections are meant to verify the accuracy of such a propagation model to populate a TVWS geo-location database.

3 TVWS Trial in Munich

The Hata propagation model is widely used for mobile network applications. It is an empirical non-terrain-based model applicable for distances up to 20 km, which is based on measurements made by Okumura in Japan in Tokyo region [6, 7]. Following the Hata propagation model classification, we chose three scenarios in Munich, for outdoor tests using trial licenses: Neuperlach (urban); Freimann (suburban) and Parsdorf (rural).

3.1 Measurement Setup

For the coverage and link measurements, the set-up used for transmission uses a notebook to control the WSD (USRP) transmitter, followed by a power amplifier and a band-pass filter to reduce the interfering power in the adjacent TV channels, as shown in Fig. 1a. The transmitting antenna is vertically polarized and omnidirectional, in a height of 10 m.

For the fixed reception coverage measurement in 10 m height, the transmitting equipment was installed in a limousine and the antenna was on a pump-up mast. The receiving set-up for the fixed reception measurements is shown in Fig. 1b. The signal from the receiving log-periodic antenna is split by a 3 dB power divider and fed to the WSD receiver USRP and to a spectrum analyzer, where the channel power is measured.

For the mobile reception measurements the transmitter was installed in the bus and the receiver in a limousine. The measurement set-up was the same as the one used for fixed measurements. The transmitting antenna used was a vertically polarized omni-directional antenna.

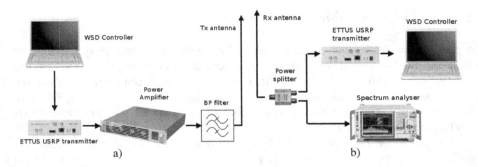

Fig. 1 WSD setup for fixed and mobile measurements: a) Transmitter; b) Receiver.

The receiving equipment was installed in a limousine and the antenna was fixed on the car roof. The limousine is equipped with a path sensor at the wheel. The sensor generates an impulse each 5 cm of vehicle movement. This impulse triggers the measuring receiver, which sends one measured value to the controller PC for each impulse. The PC is also connected to a GPS which records the limousine's location each 2 seconds. The impulses are aligned with the GPS data to determine the exact location of the receiver. With this configuration, it has been possible to measure while the car was driven on the streets around the transmitting antenna. One measurement was generated for each 5 cm driven. For a route of 3 km length we've retrieve 60.000 values. The average (median) was built over 10 m distances (200 values) to eliminate fast fading. For the measurements a 5 MHz LTE signal (OFDM) was used. The duty cycle was 100 % (continuous transmission).

3.2   Experimental Results

For all the measurements, we chose two DVB-T channels:

- Channel 41, where in the Munich region also the adjacent channels are free.
- Channel 55, where in the Munich area the adjacent channels 54 and 56 are in use.

We previously verify that the WSD sensitivity is quite low for both modulations because of the WSD Slave receiver poor radio frequency qualities [8]. For that reason the field transmission measurements were restricted to a short range and a 10 dB attenuator had to be used to avoid overloading the measuring receiver. With the attenuator, the sensitivity of the receiver ends 10 dB above noise level at ~48 dBμV/m. Without the attenuator, lowest measured values are ~38 dBμV/m (which is the noise level for 5 MHz band width and 11 dB noise figure of the measurement receiver). For the fixed transmission trials, the bus was moved to reception points at several distances to the transmitter. At each location the mast was lifted up to 10 m and the log-per antenna directed to the transmitter antenna. Table 1 present the link budget parameters for this measurement campaign.

Table 1. Link budget for fixed measurements.

	Channel		Units
	41	55	
Frequency	634	746	MHz
Power Amplifier Input	4.6	2.1	dBm
Amplification	33	33.6	dB
Power Amplifier output	37.6	35.7	dBm
Cable Attenuation	4.5	4.5	dB
BP filter insertion loss	2.4	2.4	dB
Antenna Input power	30.7	28.8	dBm
Antenna gain	-2.9	-1	dBd
Radiated power dipole ERP	27.8	27.8	dBm
Radiated isotropic EIRP	30	30	dBm
Radiated power isotropic	1	1	W EIRP

Fig. 2 shows the results for the fixed reception measurements, i.e. 10 m transmitter and receiver height. The lines show the predictions of the Hata model for rural (red), suburban (green) and urban (blue) areas. The symbols show the corresponding measurements. For the rural and suburban measurements the results are close to the theoretical curve. The black dotted line, which is identical for up to 2 km with the Hata rural curve describes free space propagation. We found higher signals than for free space propagation since this curve does not take into account reflections from objects in the vicinity like ground, trees or buildings. For the urban measurements our results are clearly below the theoretical curve, which indicates that the locations we chose at Neuperlach area are worse than the average situation for urban areas.

Fig. 3 shows the results of mobile measurements. The lines show the Hata curves. The black dotted line above the curves represents free space propagation. The antennas were of different heights (10 m for the transmitter, 1.5 m for the receiver). For this case the extended Hata model contains corrections, which cause the curves to bend down below free space propagation for short distances (few meters). The black dotted horizontal line below the curves (at 38 dBμV / m) stands for the noise field level. As expected, increasing distance the signal strength drops. Three data groups can be distinguished for rural, suburban and urban locations. The urban data (blue) scatter well around the theoretical curve with more values above the curve than below, indicating that the selected area in Neuperlach is somewhat better than the 'average' urban location from the Hata curve. The suburban data (green) fit well with the corresponding Hata curve for distances above 200 m. For distances below 200 m, many values lie above the green curve. This is caused by the measurements with line of sight conditions in this range, so the values

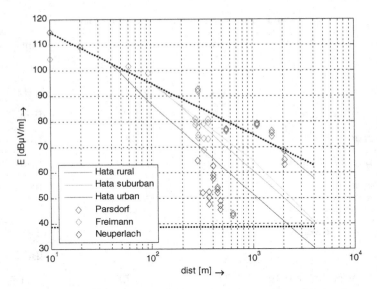

Fig. 2 Comparison of measurements with Hata propagation curves with fixed measurements: Red: rural scenario (Parsdorf); Green: Suburban scenario (Freimann); Blue: Urban scenario (Neuperlach). The horizontal black dotted line is the noise threshold and the slopped black dotted line represented free space propagation model values (Color figure online).

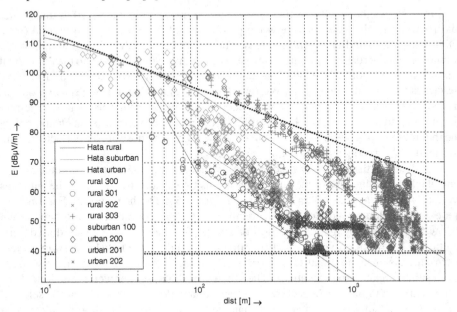

Fig. 3 Comparison of measurements with Hata propagation curves with mobile measurements: Red: rural scenario (Parsdorf); Green: Suburban scenario (Freimann); Blue: Urban scenario (Neuperlach). The horizontal black dotted line is the noise threshold and the slopped black dotted line represented free space propagation model values (Color figure online).

are between suburban Hata curve and free space propagation curve. For the rural measurements for distances at 1 km, a sharp drop can be seen; this is due to shielding of signal by a forest. On the rural measurements between 1.5 and 3 km distance to the transmitter, many locations are line of sight and so the signals are very good, up to free space values (circles). Due to the noise level, signals field strength cannot drop below 38 dBμV / m.

4   Conclusions

From the comparison of theoretical results with propagation measurements, we can conclude that modified Hata model is well appropriate to describe the path loss in TVWS links over distances up to few km. However some care is necessary due to non-terrain-based model's mean error and large standard deviation. Due to the real situation, e.g. shading by buildings, absorption of signals by vegetation, ground reflections etc., the calculated path loss values experience a very large variation. For non-terrain based models to which Hata model belongs to, this can be more than 30 dB for > 99% of measured values. As a consequence, to protect incumbent's reception a propagation margin would be required, reducing WSD transmit power due to possibly better propagation to guarantee non-interfering operation of WSD. The level of protection of incumbents and hence the height of the propagation margin is a matter of regulation and should be fixed by corresponding groups at international level. The safety margin becomes a compromise between the level of reliability for reception and operational range of the White Space Device. This value has to be carefully balanced between both needs.

Acknowledgments. The work presented in this paper was supported by the European Commission, Seventh Framework Programme, under the project 248560, ICT-COGEU and coordination action project 318563, CRS-i. The authors gratefully acknowledge CTVR – The national telecommunications research centre at Trinity College Dublin and IRT - Institut für Rundfunktechnik, at Munich, Germany.

References

1. COGEU – Cognitive radio system for efficient sharing of TV white spaces in European context http://www.ict-cogeu.eu
2. Ettus Research LLC, http://www.ettus.com
3. Joslyn, D., Roberts, R.: Protocol for Communication between White Space Device and White Space Database. Draft PAWS protocol, (2012), http://www.ietf.org
4. Technical and operational requirements for the operation of white space devices under geo-location approach", Technical report 186, ECC (2013), http://www.erodocdb.dk
5. Technical and operational requirements for the possible operation of cognitive radio systems in the 'whitespaces' of the frequency band 470-790 MHz. Technical report 159, ECC (2011), http://www.erodocdb.dk
6. Okumura, Y., Ohmori, E., Kawano, T., Fukuda, K.: Field strength and its variability in VHF and UHF land-mobile service. Rev. Elec. Comm. Lab. **16**(9–10), 825–873 (1968)

7. Hata, M.: Empirical formula for propagation loss in land mobile radio services. IEEE Trans. Veh. Tech. **29**(3), 317–325 (1980)
8. Charalambous, E. et Al.: Demonstrations and validation of COGEU secondary spectrum trading platform. Technical report 7.3, COGEU (2012), http://www.ict-cogeu.eu

Platform for Quality of Experience Evaluation in Real Time Applications over LTE Networks

L. Pereira[1], F. Mateus[2], V. Monteiro[3]([✉]), Jonathan Rodriguez[3], W. Lage[4], A. Gomes[4], and M. Feitosa[4]

[1] Escola Superior de Tecnologia, IPCB, Av. Do Empresário, 6000-767 Castelo Branco, Portugal
`luis_pereira87@ipcbcampus.pt`
[2] MECALBI, Rua J, Lote 14, Zona Industrial, 6000-459 Castelo Branco, Portugal
[3] Instituto de Telecomunicações, Campus de Santiago, 3010-193 Aveiro, Portugal
`vmonteiro@av.it.pt`
[4] Portugal Telecom Inovação e Sistemas, Rua Eng. José Ferreira Pinto Basto,
3810-106 Aveiro, Portugal

Abstract. GREEN-T is a CELTIC-Plus project which lists as one of its goals to develop and implement a 4G emulator, allowing the end-user to evaluate the quality of experience of real-time based services. There are many simulators for various wireless technologies (LTE, UMTS, WI-FI) and almost all of them have as outputs different values, such as bitrate, received power, SNR, depending on the simulation type. In spite of the reliability of these simulators, it is difficult to understand the impact of those values in real communication. This paper describes the implementation of an LTE emulator based on system simulator results where the end user can experience real time and real scenario communication conditions and interactivity with applications. This platform aims to convert the merely numerical values, obtained through the use of simulation tools, to a real-time experience for the simulated scenario. We demonstrate a 2Mbits/s bitrate video application, with a BER value of around 1×10^{-6} or a received power around 1 nW in a simulation scenario. In spite of the fact that the implementation was based on the LTE, protocols of other 4G and 5G networks will be allowed to be used and tested, since they are IP based protocols like LTE.

Keywords: LTE · Real Time Link · QoE · Interactivity

1 Introduction

One of the biggest impediments of future wireless communications systems is the need to limit the energy consumption of the battery-driven devices so as to prolong the operational times and to avoid active cooling.

GREEN-T [1] aims to overcome the energy trap of 4G mobile systems by investigating and demonstrating energy saving technologies for multi-standard wireless mobile devices, exploiting the combination of cognitive radio and cooperative strategies while still enabling the required performance in terms of data rate and QoS to support active applications. This notion is further extended by investigating lightweight security

© Institute for Computer Sciences, Social Informatics and Telecommunications Engineering 2015
S. Mumtaz et al. (Eds.): WICON 2014, LNICST 146, pp. 291–297, 2015.
DOI: 10.1007/978-3-319-18802-7_39

approaches, which is a pivotal requirement of 4G systems that will constitute a multitude of players from network operators to services providers cooperating under a converged service platform. In this scope, this paper describes the implementation of an LTE emulator, which allows users to measure their quality of experience, in this specific case, of multimedia services. Given the need to analyse in real time various parameters such as quality of service (QoS) and quality of experience (QoE), we propose to develop a platform to meet those requirements. The intended platform must support the most commonly used services on the internet like Web Browsing, File Download, IPTV / Online Media and Voice over LTE.

This paper is organized as follows: in Sect. 2 we present the features of the system level simulator used in this work, mainly the interface with physical layer and most important parameters of the LTE system that we are evaluating. In Sect. 3 we describe the real time link implementation, which allows the running of the real time applications. In Sect. 3.2 we describe the integration of the Real-time link with the system simulator, in order to compose the emulator that we are proposing. In Sect. 4 we discuss the results and the conclusions of the presented work.

2 System Level Simulator

In the development and standardization of new wireless access technologies (such as 4G LTE), as well as in the implementation process of equipment manufacturers and optimization by the operators, simulations are necessary to test and optimize algorithms and procedures. These simulations have to be carried out on the physical layer (link level) and on the network layer (system level). In this section we describe the system level simulator that was used in this work.

In particular, the following aspects must be considered with care when developing a system level tool and performing system level simulations: **Network Scenario**, related to the considered environment (urban, rural, vehicular or indoor); **Network Layout**: the number of tiers, number of base stations simulated and the type of cells (omnidirectional, sectored); **Radio Resource Management**, which enables dynamic resource allocation, including the scheduler process; **Physical Layer Modeling** and Abstraction, used to map physical layer performance to higher layers of the protocol stack defining the interfaces (LTE, HSPA, WiMAX); **Channel Propagation modeling**, which includes the path loss, slow fading (shadowing) and the fast fading; **Interference modeling**; **Traffic models for application services** and **Performance metrics**, the metrics for network performance evaluation. More specific details of these aspects can be evaluated with detail in the report provided in the scope of the GREEN-T project [2].

2.1 Interface with LTE Physical Layer

This section summarizes the most recent link level Interface LUTs for the LTE. These LUTs are achieved from physical layer simulations and are used in the system level simulation. The performances of BLER versus SINR are given for a specific environment/channel and a specific MCS. We consider the, Urban (BRAN E channel, 60 km/h).

Table 1 lists the possible Modulation and Coding Scheme (MCS) to be used, and the theoretical throughput for the 20 MHz bandwidth case. Other bandwidth can be selected, as can stated in the Table 2 bellow.

Table 1. Modulation and coding schemes and maximum throughput

Modulation and coding scheme	Theoretical throughput (Mbps)
QPSK 1/2	16.80
QPSK 2/3	22.40
QPSK 3/4	25.20
QPSK 5/6	28.00
16QAM 1/2	33.60
16QAM 2/3	44.80
16QAM 3/4	50.40
16QAM 5/6	56.00
64 QAM 1/2	50.40
64 QAM 2/3	67.20
64 QAM 3/4	75.60
64 QAM 5/6	84.00

2.2 Simulation Scenario and Parameters

The simulations are performed on a dynamic simulation, where the mobiles are created at the beginning of each run, and remain active for the complete run duration. The path loss values are updated on each TTI. Simulations are conducted in an urban environment where each run corresponds normally to 300 seconds of real time (5 minutes), and each TTI is 1ms. The simulation parameters are presented in the table below.

3 The Real-time Link

3.1 Concepts

To emulate an eNodeB independent from the emulation of the User Equipment, we present a solution based on two devices, with two different computers, which allows a better processing performance. Figure 1 shows a simplified schematic of the connection between UE and eNB, with one computer that emulates a UE and another that emulates an eNodeB. In this initial approach the EPC is not considered and the eNodeB provides Internet connection to the UE's instead of the PDN-GW [3].

Table 2. LTE simulation parameters

LTE simulation parameters	
Download transmission technique	OFDMA
Duplex method	FDD
Channel bandwidth[MHz]	1.4, 3, 5, 10, 15, 20
Number of resource Blocks	6, 15, 25, 50, 75, 100
Subcarrier spacing	15Khz
Frame size	10ms with 10 sub-frame
Scheduling speed	Every sub-frame (1ms)
Modulation	QPSK,16QAM,64 QAM
Coding	Turbo code (1/2, 2/3…)
Link adaptation	EESM with 3 HARQ process
Scheduler	Round Robin, Max C/I, Proportional fairness
Traffic	Mix/Full Queue
Channel modelling	Path loss
Cell deployment	Hexagonal

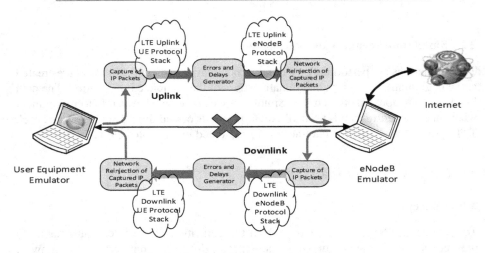

Fig. 1. Emulator implementation scheme.

The purpose of this connection is to demonstrate, in real time, the functionalities of the services and applications in a simulated environment, both for the evaluation of the QoE and the QoS at the UE and eNB (UL/DL). One of the crucial aspects here is the simulation time, which cannot be greater than the time defined for LTE. Another aspect to consider is that the connection between the two emulators, besides having to work in a transparent mode, should not introduce errors or delays (greater than 2ms) to prevent significant interference with the simulation time – though we might want to introduce simulated errors for testing purposes. It is necessary to develop a highly efficient platform, since the operations to perform require processing heavy amounts of information in real time.

Implementation. The RTL can be split in two main blocks: (1) One that captures TCP/IP [4] packets generated by the UE, transfers those packets to the eNodeB and re-injects the packets towards the internet, as depicted in Fig. 1; (2) Implementation of the LTE protocol stack.

In an uplink message, the following steps are applied: (1) Capture of IP packets generated at UE; (2) Apply LTE protocol stack to IP packets; (3) Create errors and delays for each packet; (4) Transfer data to the eNodeB Emulator; (5) Apply LTE protocol stack; (6) Recover IP packet (if it is possible, due to errors); (7) Send IP packet, for example to the Internet.

3.2 Integration with the System Simulator

The LTE emulator is composed by different software modules, the System Level Simulator (SLS) including the Graphical User Interface, the real time link composed by the eNodeB and the User Equipment (UE) as presented in Fig. 2. These software modules have to communicate between them so communication interfaces were developed. In this section we present some of the communication interfaces that connect the main software modules/blocks for proper operation.

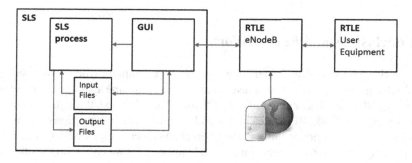

Fig. 2. LTE emulator, main software modules

As described previously the GUI communicates with the SLS process and the RTLE eNodeB, which in turn, RTLE eNodeB communicates with the RTLE User Equipment.

At this stage simulation had been performed previously with the 'offline' results stored in text files and accessed for the real-time emulation process. The emulation process allow both the running of new simulation to collect data or the usage pre-stored results from a previous simulation.

3.3   Testing, Video Service Emulation and Discussion

In order to verify the effects of insert delays in communication the ping utility is used [5]. Two situations were tested: one, where no delays were added during communication; and a second scenario where we add a 25000 microseconds (25 milliseconds). In the first test a delay of 1 ms was verified, but in the second test a 25 ms higher latency was verified in the communication. We've noticed that in a communication where a high number of packets should be transmitted this second delay can be enough to block the connection between the two hosts.

In a second test a video service (video streaming) was used to analyse the effect of errors in communication (with UDP protocol [6]). As performed with the Ping utility test, two situations were observed, in Fig. 3, one with no errors in the communication, and other with a bit error rate of 1×10^{-5} Looking at the images, one can easily see the effect of communication errors in the Quality-of-Experience of the user.

Fig. 3.   Received stream without errors (left) and with $BER = $ 1E-5 (right)

4   Conclusions and Future Work

In this work we presented an implementation of an LTE emulator where with a real Time Link Platform is possible for the end user to experience real time applications in different scenario conditions. The emulator uses off-line data obtained through system level simulator which include BER rates, delay and bitrate control connection options.

In fact it was experienced that when radio channels conditions bellow a threshold, the experienced interactivity between user and applications was poor; on the other hand when channel conditions were above this threshold, user experiences a transparent communication. Since this platform allows changes in IP Packet, new communication protocols for other 4G systems or 5G can also be developed and tested inside this platform.

Acknowledgments. The authors would like to acknowledge the project N. 23205 – GREEN-T, co-financed by the European Funds for Regional Development (FEDER) by COMPETE – Programa Operacional do Centro (PO Centro) of QREN.

References

1. CELTIC GREEN-T project. http://greent.av.it.pt/index.html
2. Project GREEN-T, N° Projeto: 23205, "Relatório técnico-científico intercalar do 5° Semestre (01/01/2014 – 30/06/2014)", AdI. http://www.adi.pt/, July, 2014
3. Dahlman, E., Parkvall, S., Sköld, J.: 4G LTE/LTE-Advanced for Mobile Broadband. Elsevier Ltd, UK (2011)
4. Microsoft: TCP/IP Protocol Architecture (2014). http://technet.microsoft.com/en-us/library/cc958821.aspx. [Accessed 11 02 2014]
5. Microsoft: Ping (2014). http://technet.microsoft.com/en-us/library/bb490968.aspx. [Accessed 12 02 2014]
6. Microsoft: User Datagram Protocol (UDP) (2014). http://msdn.microsoft.com/en-us/library/aa915632.aspx. [Accessed 12 02 2014]

A Miniaturised Monopole Wideband Antenna with Reconfigurable Band Rejection for WLAN/WiMAX

Issa T. E. Elfergani[1(✉)], Abubakar Sadiq Hussaini[1,3,5], C.H. See[3,4],
Jonathan Rodriguez[1,2], Raed Abd-Alhameed[3], and Paulo Marques[6]

[1] Instituto de Telecomunicações, Aveiro, Portugal
{i.t.e.elfergani,ash,jonathan}@av.it.pt
[2] Universidade de Aveiro, Aveiro, Portugal
[3] Radio Frequency, Antennas, Propagation and Computational Electromagnetics Research
Group, School of Electrical Engineering and Computer Sciences, University of Bradford,
Bradford, BD7 1DP, UK
r.a.a.abd@bradford.ac.uk
[4] Engineering, Sport and Science (ESS) Academic Group, University of Bolton,
Bolton, BL5AB, UK
[5] School of Information Technology and Communications,
American University of Nigeria, Yola Nigeria
[6] Escola Superior de Tecnologia - Instituto Politécnico de Castelo Branco,
Castelo Branco, Portugal

Abstract. This paper proposes a tuneable band-rejected miniaturised monopole antenna. The band-notching was achieved by printing an inner chorded crescent shape over the surface of the substrate. By placing a small varactor between the inner and outer arches, the centre frequency of each notch can be individually shifted downwards. The design of the proposed structure has a controllable rejection in the range from 2.38 to 3.87 GHz maintaining a wideband performance from 1.5 to 5 GHz based on VSWR ≤ 2. The antenna prototype was fabricated and tested. Simulated and measured results are performed and analysed. With a compact size, the proposed monopole antenna may well work as an internal antenna in a portable device.

Keywords: Monopole antenna · Tunability · VSWR · WLAN · WiMAX

1   Introduction

Printed wideband monopole technology has been widely adopted in commercial and military domains. Because of its attractive features, such as low cost, small size and easy fabrication, the printed wideband monopole antenna has received more and more attention with developments in communication technology. Similar versions of this antenna have been reported and it can cover a very wide frequency band or several bands [1–5]. However, radiation in some of these frequency bands may generate interference to (or from) the Wireless local area networks (WLAN) of IEEE802.11b/g and IEEE802.11a

© Institute for Computer Sciences, Social Informatics and Telecommunications Engineering 2015
S. Mumtaz et al. (Eds.): WICON 2014, LNICST 146, pp. 298–304, 2015.
DOI: 10.1007/978-3-319-18802-7_40

standard (2.4–2.485 GHz) and World Interoperability for Microwave Access (WIMAX) for IEEE802.16 bands (3.3–3.7 MHz).

On the other hand, some wideband antennas with a notch capability have been early reported in the published literature [6–8]. However, these antennas have fixed rejected frequency bands which cannot be altered after fabrication. Hence adaptive frequency suppression methods have been studied by using tuneable techniques [9–11]. These have the advantage that once the monopole antenna is constructed, the notch centre frequency can be easily changed by a capacitor inserted inside the antenna structure. This has enabled the antenna to adaptively tune the band-reject notch to the correct frequency band whenever interference from other systems significantly impairs the wide band system performance.

By implementing similar design principles as in [12, 13], this paper documents a compact tuneable notch monopole antenna that achieves a size reduction compared to some existing published results. The antenna occupies an envelope size of $57 \times 37.5 \times 0.8$ mm^3, making it a good candidate for portable wide band applications.

2 Antenna Design and Concept

The antenna geometry is given in Fig. 1. The chorded crescent-shaped patch prototypes are printed on an FR4 material of relative permittivity $\varepsilon_r = 4.4$ and of loss tangent of 0.017, with no ground plane directly underneath it. The substrate thickness is 0.8 mm. The radiator is fed by an 17.95×1mm microstrip line, printed on the surface of the substrate that is partially backed by a ground plane.

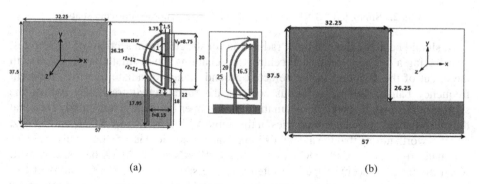

(a)   (b)

Fig. 1. Basic antenna structure, (a) Top view, (b) Bottom view.

The microstrip line is formed by two sections, i.e. upper section (6.75 mm) and lower section (11.25 mm). The lower section has a characteristic impedance of 64 Ω and is required for matching 50 Ω at the input port which is at the lower edge of the ground plane. The ground plane has dimensions of 57 mm × 37.5 mm. This antenna is a modified version of the authors' previous work as in [12, 13], but achieves a wider band compared to published results in [12], and offering the tuneable notched band characteristic in contrast to [13]. Moreover, an inner crescent shape is added to create the notch frequency as well as to accommodate a capacitor or varactor at a fixed location between the two crescent shapes for tuning the rejection band.

3 Results and Discussions

Figure 2 shows the simulated VSWR for the proposed antenna with the inner chorded crescent shape and both inner and outer chorded crescent shapes. As can be seen in Fig. 2, by adding a strip to the outer crescent shape the proposed antenna resonates from 1.5 to 5 GHz, achieving a wider frequency range compared to the authors' previous work [12].

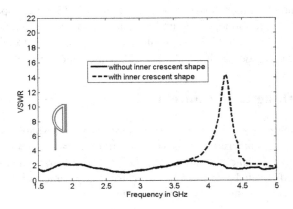

Fig. 2. Simulated VSWR with the inner and outer chorded crescent shapes

It should be noted that the outer radiator is constructed from sections of two circles, each having a different radius and centre, thus enabling the resultant patch, taken with the effect of the coupling to the defected ground plane, to radiate over two different frequency bands. The larger radius controls the fundamental frequency, whilst the shorter radius may be tuned to obtain the desired upper frequency. It is clearly seen that the two adjacent resonant frequencies in the range VSWR ≤ 2, are 1.5 GHz and 5 GHz, and it is worth noting that the antenna's impedance bandwidth is 3.5 GHz. This provides adequate coverage for GPS, DCS, PCS, UMTS, WLAN and WiMAX bands. However, when the inner crescent shape is printed with the same construction (sections of two circles) as the outer one, the notch can be created at 4.25 GHz, while the same frequency with only one crescent shape (1.5–5 GHz) is accomplished as shown in Fig. 2.

To suggest the optimum position for the varactor effectively, the surface currents of the antenna in [12] and proposed antenna without varactor for three selected operating frequencies, i.e. 1.6, 2.7 and 4.25 GHz covering the aggregate bandwidth of the frequency band, are studied in Fig. 3. As can be observed, the surface current for the selected operating frequencies of 1.6, 2.7 and 4.25 GHz for the outer chorded crescent-shaped proposed antenna is induced mainly around the antenna feed port and almost negligible over the ground plane. This observation could validate the findings from the ground plane size analysis, in which increasing the ground plane size does not impair impedance matching [12]. By comparing these two antennas, it was noticeable that the current distributions are almost same at 1.6 and 2.7, which indicates the proposed antenna preserves the same performance as the one in [12] at lower operating frequency band. It was clearly seen the most of the current exist around the antenna feed-line. While at 4.25 GHz, the proposed antenna shows strong electric currents are concentrated in the inner and outer chorded crescent-shape and feed-line areas of the radiator compared with those seen at other operating frequencies. This is due to the added parasitic inner chorded crescent-shape acting as a resonator to trap the current within the radiator and hence to suppress the unwanted 4.25 GHz band. Moreover, it is suggested the varactor should be attached in the area where the current is less induced in order to prevent the performance degradation at desired operation frequency band.

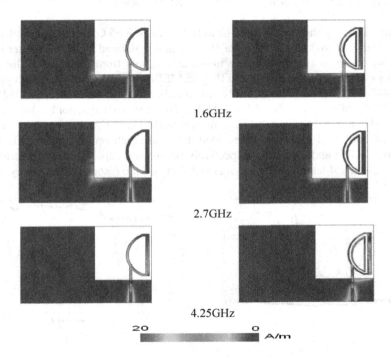

Fig. 3. Current surface for the outer chorded crescent shape and both chorded crescent shapes at, (a) 1.6 GHz, (b) 2.7 GHz and (c) 4.25 GHz.

Figure 4 shows the simulated VSWR for the proposed antenna when the value of the capacitor between the two crescents shapes was varied from 0.25 to 10.5 pF. This causes the notch-band centre frequency to vary from 2.38 to 3.87 GHz. All of the simulations described were performed using Ansoft HFSS [14].

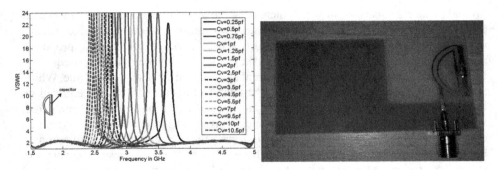

Fig. 4. Simulated VSWR with loaded capacitor (from 0.25 to 10.5 pF).

Fig. 5. The proposed antenna prototype with loaded capacitor.

Figure 4 clearly shows a rejected band from 3.28 to 3.65 GHz for the 0.5 pF loaded antenna and 2.42 to 2.55 GHz for the 10 pF loading, defined at VSWR better than 2. This is sufficient to suppress, where unwanted, signals from the wireless local area networks (WLAN) of the IEEE802.11b/g and IEEE802.11a standards employing the band 2.4–2.485 GHz, and the World Interoperability for Microwave Access (WIMAX) standard IEEE802.16 in the band 3.3–3.7 GHz. The proposed capacitor loaded prototype is depicted in Fig. 5. Its measured VSWR is shown in Fig. 6a. As can be observed, once the 0.5 pF and 10 pF capacitors are added the band-notch centre frequency is shifted down to 3.5 GHz and 2.48 GHz respectively (increasing capacitance will increase the effective electrical length of the antenna and decrease the resonance frequency).

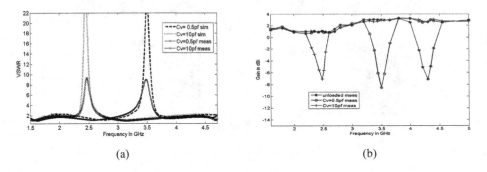

(a)   (b)

Fig. 6. Measured and simulated VSWR at 0.5 and 10.5 pF (a), Measured peak gain for proposed antenna at 0.5 and 10.5 pF

Figure 6b shows the measured gain of the monopole antenna in the case of unloaded and loaded design. It is noted that the presence of the varactor only shifts the notches and the gain does not change substantially. The unloaded antenna has a gain of 2.8 dBi at the notch band centre frequency of 3.5 GHz and 1.9 dBi at 2.48 GHz. The peak antenna gain at 10.5 pF excitation is reduced to −9 dBi and to −7.5 dBi at 0.5 pF. This indicates that there is approximately 11.8 dB and 9.4 dB of gain suppression for the capacitance of 0.5 pF and 10 pF respectively.

4 Conclusions

A small printed on a single-layer commercial substrate has been designed and used to introduce desired frequency notches in a printed UWB monopole antenna. The proposed antenna occupies a compact envelope dimension of $57 \times 37.5 \times 0.8$ mm^3 while covering the required wide band with sufficient tuneable rejection frequency band spectrum ranging from WLAN (2.4–2.485 GHz) to WIMAX (3.3–3.7 MHz). The notch centre frequencies shifts were quite stable and consistent over the selected spectrum without a serious change in notch bandwidth. The antenna is optimized for best results through simulation .The computed results are in good agreement with the measured results; showing that the antenna will easily satisfy current trend of wireless communications guidelines.

Acknowledgments. This work is carried out under the BENEFIC project (CA505), a project labelled within the framework of CATRENE, the EUREKA cluster for Application and Technology Research in Europe on NanoElectronics, co-financed by the European Funds for Regional Development (FEDER) by COMPETE – Programa Operacional do Centro (PO Centro) of QREN [Project number 38887 – BENEFIC. Also, this work is supported by the VALUE project (PEst-OE/EEI/LA0008/2013 and, through its first author, by the grant of the Fundacão para a Ciência e a Tecnologia (FCT - Portugal), with the reference number: SFRH/BPD/95110/2013.

References

1. Yang, F., Zhang, X.-X., Ye, X., Rahmat-Samii, Y.: Wide-band E shaped patch antennas for wireless communications. IEEE Trans. Antennas Propag. **AP-49**(7), 1094–1099 (2001)
2. Koohestani, M., Khaghani, M., Asadi, H.: A compact wideband antenna with CPW-fed monopole for WLAN/WiMAX operation. J. Telecommun. **10**(2), 10–13 (2011)
3. Zhu, R., Wang, R., Yang, G.: A wideband monopole antenna using parasitic elements. In: Mark, Z. (ed.) Applied Mechanics and Materials, vol. 52–54, pp. 1515–1519. Trans Tech Publications, Dürnten (2011)
4. Tseng, C.-F., Huang, C.-L., Hsu, C.-H.: Microstrip-FED monopole antenna with a shorted parasitic element for wideband application. Prog. Electromagn. Res. Lett. **7**, 115–125 (2009)
5. Ruan, Y.-F., Guo, Y.-X., Khoo, K.-W., Sh, X.-Q.: Compact wideband antenna for wireless communications. IET Microw. Antennas Propag. **1**(3), 556–560 (2007)
6. Chen, W-S., Chang, P-Y., Lee, B-Y., Chen, H-T., Kuo, J-S.: A Compact Microstrip-Fed slot antenna with a dual-band notched function for WiMAX operation. In: Antennas and Propagation Society International Symposium (APSURSI), pp. 1–4 (2010)
7. Lee, W.-S., Kim, D.-Z., Kim, K.-J., Yu, J.-W.: Wideband planar monopole antennas with dual band-notched characteristics. IEEE Trans. Microwave Theory Tech. **54**(6), 2800–2806 (2006)
8. Lee, W.-S., Kim, D.-Z., Jong-Won, Yu.: Wideband crossed planar monopole antenna with the band-notched characteristic. Microwave Opt. Technol. Lett. **48**(3), 543–545 (2006)
9. Hamid, M.R., Gardner, P., Hall, P.S., Ghanem, F.: Vivaldi with tunable narrow band rejection. Microw. Opt. Technol. Lett **53**(5), 1225–1228 (2011)
10. Perruisseau-Carrier, J., Pardo-Carrera, P., Miskovsky, P.: Modeling, design and characterization of a very wideband slot antenna with reconfigurable band rejection. IEEE Trans. Antennas Propag. **AP-58**(7), 2218–2225 (2010)

11. Scardelletti, M.C., Ponchak, G.E., Jordan, J.L., Jastram, N., Mahaffey, V.: Tunable reduced size planar folded slot antenna utilizing varactor diodes. In: RWS, .pp. 547–550 (2010)

12. See, C.H., Abd-Alhameed, R.A., Zhou, D., Lee, T.H., Excell, P.S.: A crescent-shaped multiband planar monopole antenna for mobile wireless applications. IEEE Antennas Wirel. Propag. Lett. **9**, 152–155 (2010)

13. See, C.H., Abd-Alhameed, R.A., Elmegri, F., Zhou, D., Noras, J.M., McEwan, N.J., Jones, S.M.R., Excell, P.S.: Planar monopole antennas for new generation mobile and lower band ultra-wide band applications. IET Microwave Antennas Propag. **6**(11), 1207–1214 (2012)

14. Ansoft High Frequency Structure Simulator v10 Uses Guide, CA, USA

A Multi-service Cluster-Based Decentralized Group Key Management Scheme for High Mobility Users

Trust T. Mapoka, Haider M. AlSabbagh, Yousef A.S. Dama,
Simon J. Shepherd, Raed Abd-Alhameed[(✉)],
Mohammad Bin-Melha, and Kelvin O. Anoh

Mobile and Satellite Communications Research Center,
University of Bradford, Engineering and Informatics, Bradford, UK
{ttmapoka, sjshepherd, raaabd, oanoh}@bradford.ac.uk

Abstract. Previous cluster based group key management schemes for wireless mobile multicast communication lack efficiency in rekeying the group key if high mobility users concurrently subscribe to multiple multicast services that co-exist in the same network. This paper proposes an efficient multi-service group key management scheme suitable for high mobility users which perform frequent handoffs while participating seamlessly in multiple multicast services. The users are expected to drop subscriptions after multiple cluster visits hence inducing huge key management overhead due to rekeying the previously visited cluster keys. However we adopt our already proposed SMGKM system with completely decentralised authentication and key management functions to address demands for high mobility environment with same level of security and less overhead. Through comparisons with existing schemes and simulations, SMGKM shows resource economy in terms of rekeying communication overhead in high mobility environment with multi-leaves.

Keywords: Mobile multicast communication · Group key management · Wireless networks · Security

1 Introduction

Multicast is an efficient communication technology for the provision of group-oriented services over the internet. These include services such as VOD (Video on Demand) and video conferencing. The services could be deployed more comfortably in wireless mobile networks than in wired networks because the entire receiving nodes within the transmission range of the broadcast medium can receive the services in a single transmission. Thus, the multicast services are expected to be dominating services by considering the fact that majority of the recent standards committees of wireless networks such as E-MBMS in LTE 1 have standardized them. However in order to provide access control to the broadcasted multicast services, a symmetric group key, known as the Traffic Encryption Key (TEK), has been widely deployed to guarantee secure group communications among the subscribed group members. Thus the broadcasted services encrypted by the TEK at the Service Provider (SP) end are

© Institute for Computer Sciences, Social Informatics and Telecommunications Engineering 2015
S. Mumtaz et al. (Eds.): WICON 2014, LNICST 146, pp. 305–312, 2015.
DOI: 10.1007/978-3-319-18802-7_41

decrypted by the authorised group members holding the same valid TEK at the receivers end assuming multicast routing protocols are in place.

Although symmetric effort provide efficiency in achieving secure group communications than asymmetric effort with heavier computation effort, it causes some challenges in Group Key Management (GKM) because the TEK need to be updated for both *forward* and *backward secrecy* [1] during group membership dynamics caused by joins, leaves and mobility. Convectional GKM schemes for secure wired [1] and wireless [2] multicast networks were specifically designed for a single multicast service subscribed by low mobility users. Instead, wireless GKM schemes [2] may induce huge rekeying communication overhead in rekeying the TEK when the group become flooded with high mobility users which perform frequent handoffs while participating in diverse multicast services. In addition to frequent moves, high mobility users maintain the local cluster keys (KEKs) for the previously visited clusters during frequent handoffs. Eventually when users leave or drop the subscriptions after multiple visits, this triggers repeated rekeying of the entire keys (TEKs and local KEKs) held by the user in all the previously visited clusters for *forward secrecy* hence causing extra rekeying signalling overhead. During frequent handoffs, the schemes also require synchronisation with the trusted Domain Key Distributor (DKD) for requesting the TEK as well as for tracking mobility hence the name key-request schemes [3] which are Decleene et al. [4], GKMF [5] and Kellil et al. [6]. The DKD in key-request schemes controls the entire local cluster managers called the Area Key Distributors in a decentralised environment.

However, this is not practical that a single entity controls the entire network consisting of millions of mobile users and huge AKDs. Additionally frequent handoffs constitute to huge number of notifications to the DKD which cannot be a negligible communication overhead any more especially in vehicle-related services, such as telematics services where high speed vehicles handover frequently hence repeated rekeying. Also, if the entire key management functions of the TEK are concentrated on the DKD which is single point of failure and maybe far from the serving AKD, the multicast services become very vulnerable to service disruptions due to rekeying delivery delays. Therefore key-request schemes characteristics inhibits suitability for high speed wireless networks with multiple services and this has motivated the need to build a multi-service communication-efficient key management scheme suitable for high mobility users in this paper. In addition to our multi-service group key management scheme known as SMGKM [7, 8] dedicated to provide secure multi-group oriented services to mobile users who dynamically perform handoff while seamlessly participating in multiple multicast services we now consider rekeying during dynamic movement of high mobility users in multi-service subscriptions who then leave subscriptions after multiple visits.

The rest of the paper is organized as follows: the scenario for high mobility environment with multi-leaves in SMGKM scheme is described in Sect. 2, the performance analysis of the SMGKM in terms of communication overheads in high mobility environment in comparison to key-request schemes is discussed in Sect. 3 and finally, the conclusions are drawn in Sect. 4.

2 The SMGKM Scheme for High Mobility Situation

Assuming the network model and assumptions of the SMGKM are maintained [7, 8], we further explore the performance of the SMGKM in the presence of high mobility users which perform frequent handoffs across multiple clusters then finally leave the multicast services concurrently from the concerned clusters after visiting multiple clusters. Let us consider a scenario where mobile subscribers belong to the same service group G_K. The service group determines users accessing exactly same set of services $(s_1, s_2, ..., s_j)$ and this simplifies key management with multi-services. Suppose users M_1, M_2, M_5 and M_9 in Fig. 1 access three of the pay-TV services concurrently such as sports (s_1), movie (s_2) and music (s_2) out of 8 services provided by the SP. The assumption is that users can seamlessly access these services in a high mobility environment such as vehicular networks where frequent handoffs may occur hence making multiple visits possible before users leave the multi-services. In the cellular clusters of the SMGKM scheme illustrated in Fig. 1 we define two types of subscribed users:

- Present in the cluster (PIC) users currently being served by the AKD_i. This are considered as low mobility users assuming they stay long in the service.
- Absent in the cluster (AIC) users who have visited multiple clusters served by the target AKD_v after frequent handoffs. These users are considered to have high mobility.

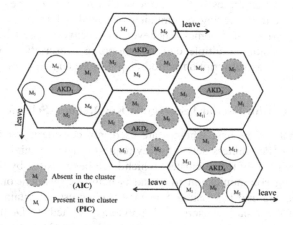

Fig. 1. High mobile users leaving after multiple cluster visits

Clearly from Fig. 1, it can be observed that from the AIC mobile users in SMGKM, M_1 and M_2 in G_K have previously visited AKD_0, AKD_1, AKD_2 and AKD_3 by performing frequent handoffs then finally stay at the target AKD_5 before leaving the multicast services. M_9 have previously visited AKD_5 and AKD_0 before leaving at AKD_2. Similarly, M_5 have previously visited AKD_4, AKD_3 and AKD_0 before leaving at AKD_1. The assumption is that all M_i in G_K follow the same mobility pattern and the

SMGKM has already carried out the multi-service rekeying strategy based on Key Update Slots (KUS) [7, 8] to satisfy *backward secrecy* during frequent handoffs at the visited AKD_v and *forward secrecy* where M_1, M_2, M_5 and M_9 currently leaves. The rekeying strategy detect the affected services during group dynamics so that the AKDs generate and securely deliver new TEK shares for the affected services to the PIC users where a join or leave occur [7]. The assumption is that Authentication phase of users is also performed at the target cluster during handoff using Session Key Distribution List (SKDL) concept which tracks mobility at the AKD level [4].

3   Performance Analysis

This section investigates the performance of the SMGKM scheme with comparisons to legacy key-request schemes. We only focus on the extra rekeying communication overhead as a result of unicast transmissions caused by delivering rekeying messages, under the assumption that this overhead is the most vital factor in wireless networks where radio resources is limited in the presence of high mobility users and multi-services. We also consider the communication overhead induced by the control messages emanating from handoff at the wired network beyond each AKD. In this network let's assume that various multicast services provided by the SP covers a huge area consisting of C clusters, and the number of mobile users M_i existing in each cluster is maintained at N. Let's define a random variable X as the number of clusters that M_i has visited before leaving the multicast services. Thus the expected number of clusters previously visited which represent the degree of user mobility can be denoted as $E(X)$. Now let's contrast the rekeying communication overhead induced in SMGKM in contrast to the key-request schemes whenever multi-leaves caused by high mobility users occur after visiting multiple clusters. Stopping subscriptions may be due to various reasons such as subscription period elapse or battery failures.

3.1   Multi-leaves with Forward Secrecy in Key Request Schemes

First consider that key request schemes are used, not considering multi-services and multi-leaves in mobile wireless network. Key request schemes achieve more efficiency by limiting rekeying only to the clusters which have been visited by the leaving user. Thus, the rekeying communication overhead is mainly dependent on the number of clusters that a leaving user has visited. Since the leaving user maintain the local cluster keys for each of the visited clusters, each previously visited AKD_i should unicast O (N) rekeying messages including the updated local cluster keys to PIC users of the visited clusters. After updating the local cluster keys, each AKD_i distribute the new TEK from the DKD. This induces rekeying communication overhead in the entire wireless network of

$$E(X)O(N) + C. \tag{1}$$

The key-request schemes require notifying the DKD about users' handoff as well as the TEK update. Though the notifications may be negligible in size, they cannot be overlooked in the presence of high mobility users and multi-services requiring TEK update in the network. The notifications should be delivered to and from the DKD as a form of a control messages at the wired network beyond the AKDs.

Therefore the total number of notifications at the wired network on average gives

$$E(X)O(N)C. \tag{2}$$

Let now employ the wireless weight denoted as α in [5] to demonstrate the importance of the wireless cost. Therefore, the total rekeying communication overhead for the key request schemes induced at both parts of network becomes,

$$RO_{KEYREQUEST} = \alpha\{E(X)O(N) + C\} + (1-\alpha)\{E(X)O(N)C\}. \tag{3}$$

where $0 \leq \alpha \leq 1$.

However in the presence of S-multi-services and x services require rekeying at user departure, key-request schemes requires independent rekeying of the affected services whenever multiple leaves occur at the target cluster after visiting $E(X)$ clusters. Thus Eq. (3) gives

$$RO_{KEYREQUEST} = \alpha\frac{x}{S}\{E(X)O(N) + C\} + (1-\alpha)\frac{x}{S}\{E(X)O(N)C\}. \tag{4}$$

3.2   Multi-leaves with Forward Secrecy in SMGKM Scheme

In contrast with the key request scheme, the SMGKM only perform rekeying at the target cluster where multi-leaves occur regardless of the visited number of clusters. The DKD does not need to keep track of mobile subscribers because each AKD$_i$ independently controls its own users due to cryptographically separate keys adopted per cluster in SMGKM. Thus on every handoff, the SMGKM provide access control mechanism which uses the SKDL concept for authentication of mobile users before obtaining the new service group keys used at the target cluster. Whenever mobile user completely handoff, the cluster local keys for the previously visited clusters are automatically revoked under the assumption that mobile users have the capability to store keys only for the target cluster. This is what differentiates the SMGKM to key request schemes hence less storage complexity at the mobile receiver. This additionally lessens the number of rekeying communication overheads significantly.

Now let's consider M_1 and M_2 in G_K which finally stop x services after visiting E (X) clusters, we first compute the number of AIC in the visited clusters at user departure.

The assumption is that handoff that occurs between two non-adjacent clusters can be likely, which is tolerable enough to make the performance comparison. Consider a certain cluster v whose AKD initially consist of N mobile users. Assuming N individual users move from one cluster to another at least $E(X)$ times, i.e., it visits $E(X)$ clusters. Whenever users finally drop the subscriptions at departure, only $E(X)$ of the initial N users remain in cluster v while $E(X) - 1/E(X)$ of N users have left cluster v.

Furthermore, let's also consider other users participating in the same set of services in G_K from other clusters with the exception of cluster v. A user of the other clusters can be considered to pick $E(X) - 1$ visiting clusters amongst $C - 1$ clusters. Therefore the probability that the user does not visit cluster v is $\left(\begin{array}{c} C - 2 \\ E(X) - 1 \end{array} \right) / \left(\begin{array}{c} C - 1 \\ E(X) - 1 \end{array} \right)$. It means now that $1 - \left(\begin{array}{c} C - 2 \\ E(X) - 1 \end{array} \right) / \left(\begin{array}{c} C - 1 \\ E(X) - 1 \end{array} \right) \cdot N$ mobile users from other clusters can visit cluster v. Likewise, only $1/E(X)$ of the N users remain in cluster v while $E(X)-1/E(X)$ of the N users have left. Consequently, this evaluate the number of AIC in the visited clusters denoted by L as:

$$L = E(X) - 1/E(X)[N + 1 - \left(\begin{array}{c} C - 2 \\ E(X) - 1 \end{array} \right) / \left(\begin{array}{c} C - 1 \\ E(X) - 1 \end{array} \right) \cdot N \cdot (C - 1)] \quad (5)$$

In contrast to key-request schemes, since the SMGKM independently manages its own TEK per cluster, the visited AKDs do not undergo rekeying except the target cluster where multi-leaves currently occur under the assumption that leaves occur concurrently while participating in multi-services. It should be noted that it is possible for multi-leaves to occur at various locations visited (i.e. $E(X)$) in SMGKM as shown in Fig. 1. Therefore in order to guarantee forward secrecy at the concerned cluster, SMGKM need to unicast $O(N + L)$ rekeying messages to the PIC user of the concerned clusters in order to deliver the updated TEK shares for the services affected by multi-leaves. Additionally the SMGKM does not need to notify the DKD about the user mobility since the AKD_i automatically revoke the rows for the corresponding departures from the $SKDL_i$; however notification of the updated TEK shares at the concerned AKD_i to the SP is absolutely necessary at the wired part of the SMGKM. The notification/control message uses the KUS notifier which is negligible in size and dependent on the number of affected services S assuming that the SP also has prior knowledge of the KUS operation to update the service keys. This on average gives total number of notifications beyond the concerned clusters as

$$E(X)O(\frac{x}{S}). \quad (6)$$

Therefore in the presence of S-multi-services and x services requires rekeying if L-users departure, SMGKM scheme induces total rekeying communication overhead of

$$RO_{SMGKM} = \alpha\{E(X)O(N + L)\} + (1-\alpha)\{ E(X)O(\frac{x}{S})\}. \quad (7)$$

3.3   Simulation Results and Discussion

In order to contrast the performances of the above scheme, we consider S-multicast services covering a huge cellular cluster areas consisting of 1000 cells under the assumption that each cluster has a total of 400 mobile users subscribed to these services from various locations. The expectation is that each user is likely to visit $E(X)$ clusters on average before leaving the subscribed multicast services simultaneously, where E (X) varies from 10 to 60. The higher $E(X)$ means the user has the higher mobility. Also the assumption is that wireless cost of the network is much greater than wireline cost hence we set the wireless weight to be 0.999 in order to weight wireless links much more than wired links. To summarize, we set $x = 3$ to be the number of affected services requiring rekeying out of $S = 8$ services provided by the SP, $C = 1000$, $N = 400$, $\alpha = 0.999$, respectively.

From the simulation results in Fig. 2(a), we compare the communication overheads emanating from rekeying and handover control messages at the wireless and wireline parts of the network. It can be seen that the performances of both schemes worsens with high user mobility and multi-leaves participating in multi-services. However SMGKM overhead outperforms that of key-request schemes because high mobility in users in key-request schemes maintains key management keys for the local $E(X)$ clusters. This requires rekeying that incurs substantial rekeying communication overhead. In contrast, SMGKM only rekeys the concerned clusters where user departure occurs hence reducing communication overheads significantly.

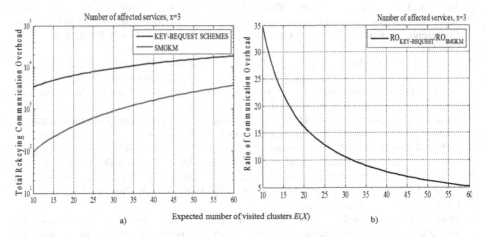

Fig. 2. Rekeying communication overheads induced by multi-leaves at multiple clusters

Additionally, in Fig. 2(b) we compare the ratio of the communication overheads for the concerned schemes. When $E(X) = 30$, key-request schemes incur 10.6 times communication overheads as much as that of the SMGKM. Therefore SMGKM obtains quantitative advantage of less communication overheads and qualitative advantage of distributing some parts of the DKD functions to the AKDs.

4 Conclusion

This paper has addressed inefficiency of existing key-request GKM schemes for secure multicast in high mobility wireless networks by proposing an efficient and practical solution. The core of the proposed scheme is to decentralize the DKD key management and authentication functions. While the DKD only does the initial setup phase of the entire group membership, each AKD keeps track of users during handoff and manages the group TEK shares for multiple services independently per cluster to ensure *backward* and *forward secrecies* when frequent handoffs and multi-leaves participating in multi-services occur respectively. The proposed scheme also achieves high efficiency of rekeying and reduces the overburden of the DKD by distributing it to each AKD in high mobility environments. Therefore, it is expected that the proposed protocol can be a practical solution for securing group communication with multi-services in high mobility wireless environment.

References

1. Challal, Y., Seba, H.: Group key management protocols: a novel taxonomy. Enformatika Int. J. Inf. Technol. **2**, 105–118 (2005)
2. Mapoka, T.T.: Group key management protocols for secure mobile multicast communication: a comprehensive survey. Int. J. Comput. Appl. **84**(12), 28–38 (2013)
3. Mapoka, T.T., Shepherd, S., Abd-Alhameed, R., Anoh, K.: Efficient authenticated multi-service group key management for secure wireless mobile multicast. In: 3rd International Conference on Future Generation Communication Technologies (FGCT 2014), Luton, UK, (2014)
4. DeCleene, B., Dondeti, L., Griffin, S., Hardjono, T., Kiwior, D., Kurose, J., et al.: Secure group communications for wireless networks. In: Military Communications Conference, MILCOM 2001, Communications for Network-Centric Operations: Creating the Information Force, vol.1, pp. 113–117. IEEE (2001)
5. Kiah, M.L.M., Martin, K.M.: Host mobility protocol for secure group communication in wireless mobile environments. Int. J. Secur. Appl. **2**, 39–52 (2008)
6. Kellil, M., Olivereau, J.C.A., Janneteau, P.: Rekeying in secure mobile multicast communications, United States Patent Application Publications, US 2007/ 0143600 A1 (2007)
7. Mapoka, T.T., Shepherd, S., Abd-Alhameed, R.: A new multiple service key management scheme for secure wireless mobile multicast. IEEE Trans. Mobile Comput. 1–15 (2014, in press). doi:10.1109/TMC.2014.2362760
8. Mapoka, T.T., Shepherd, S., Abd-Alhameed, R., Anoh, K.O.O.: Novel rekeying approach for secure multiple multicast groups over wireless mobile networks. In: IEEE 10th International Conference on Wireless Communications and Mobile Computing (IWCMC), pp. 839–844, Nicosia, Cyprus (2014)

An Evaluation of Spatial Modulation
for MIMO Systems with QO-STBC

Kelvin O. Anoh[1], Y.A.S. Dama[2], H.M. AlSabbagh[3], E. Ibrahim[4],
R.A. Abd-Alhameed[1(✉)], Fauzi Elmegri[1], Trust T. Mapoka[1],
Mohammad Ngala[1], and S.M.R. Jones[1]

[1] Mobile and Satellite Communications Centre,
University of Bradford, Bradford, UK
r.a.a.abd@bradford.ac.uk
[2] Department of Telecommunications Engineering,
An Najah National University, Nablus, Palestine
[3] College of Engineering, Basrah University, Basrah, Iraq
[4] College of Electronic Technology, Bani Walid, Libya

Abstract. Simplified designs of multi-antenna systems with optimum efficiency
are receiving attentions. Such simplicities also involve low cost architectures. In
this study, we report an evaluation of a new multi-antenna scheme, namely,
spatial modulation (SM) that is compared with quasi-orthogonal space time
block codes (QOSTBC) scheme over Rayleigh fading channel. The SM scheme
has been, earlier, compared with space time block codes (STBC) – a two
antenna transmit diversity scheme that achieves full diversity when only two
antennas are used. This is extended to QOSTBC scheme that absolves
some decoding limitations to attain full diversity. It will be shown that, using the
QOSTBC of similar architecture with the SM, even better performance can be
achieved in favour of QOSTBC.

Keywords: Spatial modulation · Space time block codes · Quasi-orthogonal
space time block codes · MIMO

1 Introduction

Modern telecommunications expect to deliver the most dependable seamless quality of
service to support infotainment, data and video transmissions. Data delivery is however
by wireless communication and different data, infotainment and video delivery techniques are still evolving to offer the best service. Multiple input multiple output
(MIMO) scheme exploits the fact that no two channel paths can be equally likely badly
impaired. Thus increasing the number of transmitting and/or receiver elements can help
a great deal in mitigating the hostile multipath channel fading problems. Because the
receiver equipment exists in small sizes (miniature), then diversity techniques are
best explored in the transmitter. Different and varied transmitter diversity techniques
have been considered over time. Most recently is the spatial modulation (SM) technique [1, 2]. In SM diversity technique, multi-antenna systems can be designed that

© Institute for Computer Sciences, Social Informatics and Telecommunications Engineering 2015
S. Mumtaz et al. (Eds.): WICON 2014, LNICST 146, pp. 313–321, 2015.
DOI: 10.1007/978-3-319-18802-7_42

involves only one RF-chain in the transmitter. This technique is explored in this study and will be compared with QOSTBC alongside STBC.

Spatial modulation (SM) is a tractive multi-antenna transceiver technique for MIMO systems deployment. It promises spectral efficiency and no-inter channel interference (ICI) at the receiver (provided the pulse shaping period does not overlap amongst antennas) [3]. SM reduces transmitter complexity and cost since only one transmitting antenna is enabled during a transmission period thus reducing the number of radio frequency (RF)-chain to one. When SM was introduced, it was compared with space time block codes (STBC) with up to 4-receive antennas [4]. STBC improves power efficiency by maximizing spatial diversity. It improves capacity from diversity gain which reduces error probability over the same spectral efficiency [2, 4].

In this study, the SM, STBC and QOSTBC will be compared in terms of bit error ratio (BER). Each of these will be discussed in Sect. 2 and the results will be shown in Sect. 3 with the Conclusion in Sect. 4.

2   System Models

We discuss the different system models to be considered in this paper here. They involve the STBC, QOSTBC and SM. QOSTBC is a class of STBC used to enable more than two transmit antenna diversity with full rate transmission. SM on the other hand is a three-dimensional signal modulation scheme that enables multi-antenna transmitter design with only one RF-chain.

2.1   Spatial Modulation

Signal modulation involves mapping fixed number of information into one symbol. Each symbol represents a constellation point in the complex two dimensional signal plane [2]. Extending this plane to three dimension yields what has been referred to as spatial modulation [2, 4]. Thus, spatial modulation is a three-dimensional signal mapping (modulation) scheme that simplifies (reduces) RF-chain of a communication system although only one transmit antenna is made active in each time slot.

In signal modulation, for instance using M-QAM (or PSK as explored in this study), the number of bits that can be transmitted is given by:

$$m = \log_2(M) \tag{1}$$

for any M-PSK scheme. On the other hand, the spatial modulation permits the mapping/transmission of n bits according to:

$$n = \log_2(N_t) + m \tag{2}$$

where N_t is the number of transmitting elements. This is done by mapping the information in q-vector of n bits into a new x-vector of N_t bits at each time slot such that only one element in the resulting vector is non-zero. The position of the element in the x-vector chooses the transmit antenna element over which the symbol will be transmitted (or that can be made active) at such transmission time slot. Let the active antenna be designated as x_l; notice that,

$$x_l \in [1, \cdots, N_t] \tag{3}$$

Because data are encoded in information symbol and antenna number (as in Eq. 3), then the estimation of antenna number is highly required. For a noiseless system of the form $y = hx$, where h is channel matrix, then the estimate of the transmit symbol can be expressed as [4]:

$$g = h^H y \tag{4}$$

where $(.)^H$ is a Hermitian operator. The antenna number can then be estimated as [2]:

$$\hat{l} = \arg \max_{\forall i}(|g_i|) \qquad i = 1, \cdots, N_t \tag{5}$$

Then, based on the estimated antenna index, the estimate of the transmitted symbol can be discussed as:

$$\hat{x} = D(g_{i=\hat{l}}) \tag{6}$$

where D is the constellation demodulator function [3].

2.2   Orthogonal Space Time Block Codes

The space time block code or STBC is proposed to improve multi-antenna design over constrained bandwidth. It achieves full diversity and full rate transmissions over two antenna transmission, for example [5];

$$s = \begin{bmatrix} s_1 & s_2 \\ -s_2^* & s_1^* \end{bmatrix} \tag{7}$$

where s is the symbol. Its equivalent channel matrix is defined as [5];

$$h = \begin{bmatrix} h_1 & h_2 \\ h_2^* & -h_1^* \end{bmatrix} \tag{8}$$

Using the channel matrix simplifies the implementation of STBC scheme. A major limitation in the use of STBC is that, more than two transmit diversity is not supported.

2.3   Quasi-Orthogonal Space Time Block Codes

QOSTBC is a class of STBC that absolves the two-transmit antenna limitation. Traditional QOSTBC achieves full transmission rate but not full diversity [6]. The QOSTBC sacrifices both BER measure with increasing signal-to-noise ratio (SNR) and full transmission diversity although it offers full rate transmission. Some coupling (interference) terms in the decoding matrix exist that degrade the BER statistics. Assuming that the channel matrix of a QOSTBC system is given as [7]:

$$
h_v = \begin{bmatrix} h_1 & h_2 & h_3 & h_4 \\ h_2^* & -h_1^* & h_4^* & -h_3^* \\ h_3 & h_4 & h_1 & h_2 \\ h_4^* & -h_3^* & h_2^* & -h_1^* \end{bmatrix}
\tag{9}
$$

Suppose that the rank of the channel temporal correlation matrix is κ, then the maximum achievable diversity level has been obtained as $\kappa N_T N_R$ [8], where N_T is the number of transmit elements and N_R is the number of receiver elements. The decoding matrix following from Eq. 9 does not permit linear decoding [9]. Thus, the scheme does not attain full diversity. Some handy examples of interference free QOSTBC techniques include Givens rotation [10], eigen-value [9] and Hadamard matrices [7] approaches. Givens rotation and eigen-value approaches yield similar results and will be explored in this study. Since both give similar results, the eigen-value approach will be followed due to its simplicity. QOSTBC by eigen-values shall henceforth be used as eQOSTBC. The eigen-value of the detection matrix of channel matrix can be defined as [9];

$$
V = \begin{bmatrix} 1 & 0 & -1 & 0 \\ 0 & 1 & 0 & -1 \\ 1 & 0 & 1 & 0 \\ 0 & 1 & 0 & 1 \end{bmatrix}
\tag{10}
$$

The new channel matrix can be formed as:

$$
\begin{aligned}
h_{new} &= h_v \times V \\
&= \begin{bmatrix} h_1 + h_3 & h_2 + h_4 & h_3 - h_1 & h_4 - h_2 \\ h_2^* + h_4^* & -h_1^* - h_3^* & h_4^* - h_2^* & h_1^* - h_3^* \\ h_1 + h_3 & h_2 + h_4 & h_1 - h_3 & h_2 - h_4 \\ h_2^* + h_4^* & -h_1^* - h_3^* & h_2^* - h_4^* & h_3^* - h_1^* \end{bmatrix}
\end{aligned}
\tag{11}
$$

From Eq. 11, one can define the channel matrix of an interference free QOSTBC matrix as follows:

$$
h_{new} = \begin{bmatrix} \vec{h}_1 & \vec{h}_2 & \vec{h}_3 & \vec{h}_4 \\ \vec{h}_2^* & -\vec{h}_1^* & \vec{h}_4^* & -\vec{h}_3^* \\ \vec{h}_1 & \vec{h}_2 & -\vec{h}_3 & -\vec{h}_4 \\ \vec{h}_2^* & \vec{h}_1^* & -\vec{h}_4^* & \vec{h}_3^* \end{bmatrix}
\tag{12}
$$

where $\vec{h}_1 = h_1 + h_2$, $\vec{h}_2 = h_2 + h_4$, $\vec{h}_3 = h_3 - h_1$ and $\vec{h}_4 = h_4 - h_2$. Hence, as a linear system with linear decoding, the system that implements an interference-free QOSTBC can be represented as:

$$y = h_{new}s + \eta$$

where s is a vector of transmit symbols having the form $s = [s_1 \cdots s_4]^T$. The detection (ignoring η) can be expressed as: $\hat{s} = h_{new}^H h_{new}s = \alpha(I_4s)$, where α is the channel gain and I_4 is an identity matrix. η is the noise term, notably, an additive white Gaussian noise (AWGN). In the receiver, the maximal ratio combining (MRC) is applied.

3 Simulation Results and Discussion

In this section, the simulation results are discussed. The results involve comparisons of the spatial modulation scheme as a method for MIMO transmission with STBC and QOSTBC schemes. Assuming a Raleigh fading channel, the receiver is equipped with the full knowledge of the channel and the antennas are reasonably separated to avoid correlation.

3.1 Comparison of Analytical and Simulation Results

To validate our results, we first show comparisons of analytical results with the simulation results in Fig. 1.

The simulation results shown in Fig. 1 are for QOSTBC diversity scheme using 4 × 1-QPSK. It can be found that simulation result of eQOSTBC and analytical eQOSTBC perfectly agree. Meanwhile, the interference terms in the detection matrix of the traditional QOSTBC degrade its performance, hence the eQOSTBC outperformed the traditional QOSTBC both analytically and in simulations.

3.2 Two Bits Transmission

At first, we transmit two bits for SM, STBC and QOSTBC. The two bits from the SM scheme are provided by two transmit antennas and BPSK scheme sequel to Eq. 2 with four receiving elements. The results are shown in Fig. 2.

From Fig. 2, it is found that transmitting with two antennas and receiving with four antennas for STBC scheme is better by circa 2 dB than transmitting with four antennas and receiving by two antennas using QOSTBC scheme. However, comparing the results of QOSTBC and SM schemes, it is found that QOSTBC scheme outperforms SM about 10 dB.

3.3 Three Bits Transmission

In Fig. 3, we compare the results of the SM, STBC and QOSTBC schemes for three bits transmission. The three bits transmission investigation is typical of the ones reported in Fig. 3 of [2].

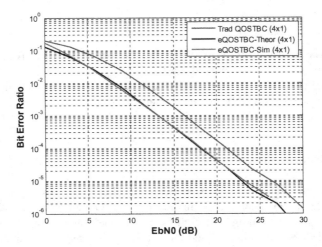

Fig. 1. Performance comparison of analytical and simulation results

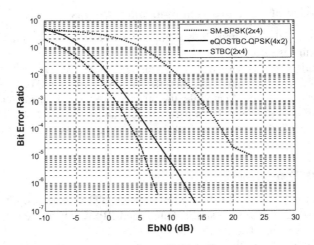

Fig. 2. Comparison of two bits transmissions using SM, STBC and QOSTBC

Like in [2], it can be seen that transmitting on two antennas and receiving on four antennas using SM scheme is better than transmitting on four antennas and receiving on four antennas by about 1 dB. However, comparing the STBC and QOSTBC schemes, both performed nearly equally likely. Then comparing them with the SM scheme, it is found that both STBC and QOSTBC outperformed SM scheme (2 × 4-QPSK) by about 9 dB and SM scheme (4 × 4-BPSK) by about 9 dB respectively. The benefit of the discussed QOSTBC scheme is in its ability to attain full diversity and full rate consequent on the elimination of the coupling terms.

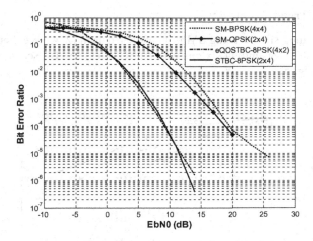

Fig. 3. Comparison of three bits transmissions using SM, STBC and QOSTBC

3.4   Four Bits Transmission

Again, we investigate the performance of STBC and QOSTBC with SM scheme when four bits are transmitted. The results are shown in Fig. 4. Both 4×4-QPSK and 2×4-8PSK SM schemes performed alike up to 10^{-2} BER. On the other hand, QOSTBC outperformed STBC at 10^{-4} BER by about 3 dB. Then comparing SM and QOSTBC, it is better (by about 6 dB) to transmit over two antennas and receiving over two antennas using 16-PSK for QOSTBC than transmitting by two transmit antennas and receiving with four antennas using 8-PSK for SM scheme. Also, it is better to transmit and receive using 4×4 QPSK for QOSTBC than using 4×4-QPSK SM scheme by about 8 dB.

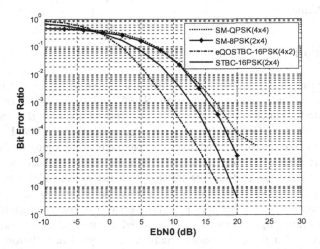

Fig. 4. Comparison of four bits transmissions using SM, STBC and QOSTBC

3.5 Six Bits Transmission

Finally, transmitting six bits using SM is investigated as in [2, 4]. We then compare the results with that of transmitting six bits with STBC and QOSTBC schemes. The results are shown in Fig. 5.

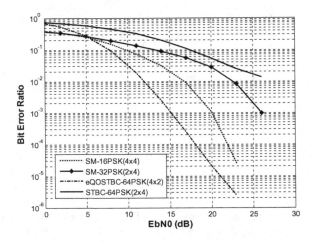

Fig. 5. Comparison of five bits transmissions using SM, STBC and QOSTBC

Like in [2, 4], Fig. 5 shows that SM schemes for six bits transmission outperformed STBC scheme. However, SM showed increased performance as the signal modulation order increased. The SM scheme transmission of six bits with 4 × 4-16PSK outperformed 2 × 4-32PSK increasingly. On the other hand, comparing the QOSTBC and SM schemes, 4 × 2-64PSK of the QOSTBC scheme outperformed all other SM schemes and STBC scheme.

4 Conclusion

In this study three different diversity schemes that enable MIMO systems are studied. These schemes include spatial modulation, STBC and QOSTBC. The investigation explored the performance of the schemes at low and relatively high spectral efficiencies. In all, the MIMO QOSTBC (4 × 2) performed better than the SM. From the study, it can be said that the strength of SM diversity scheme is in the signal modulation order, that is, the performance of the SM diversity scheme recuperates as the signal modulation order increases up to four bits transmission (as investigated above). Notwithstanding, using the QOSTBC with only two receive antennas, the performance of SM diversity scheme is less comparable. For all diversity schemes, transmitting on lower number of transmitter antenna elements is favoured when using lower number of signal modulation order. On the other hand, where higher signal modulation order is preferred, then higher number of transmitting elements will be preferred.

References

1. Di Renzo, M., Haas, H., Grant, P.M.: Spatial modulation for multiple-antenna wireless systems: a survey. IEEE Commun. Mag. **49**, 182–191 (2011)
2. Mesleh, R., Haas, H., Ahn, C. W., Yun, S.: "Spatial modulation-a new low complexity spectral efficiency enhancing technique," In: First International Conference on Communications and Networking in China, ChinaCom *2006*, pp. 1–5 (2006)
3. Jeganathan, J., Ghrayeb, A., Szczecinski, L., Ceron, A.: Space shift keying modulation for MIMO channels. IEEE Trans. Wireless Commun. **8**, 3692–3703 (2009)
4. Mesleh, R.Y., Haas, H., Sinanovic, S., Ahn, C.W., Yun, S.: Spatial modulation. IEEE Trans. Veh. Technol. **57**, 2228–2241 (2008)
5. Anoh, K., Ochonogor, O., Abd-Alhameed, R., Jones, S., Mapuka, T.: Improved Alamouti STBC Multi-Antenna System Using Hadamard Matrices. Int. J. Commun. Netw. Syst. Sci. **7** (3), 83–89 (2014)
6. Su, W., Xia, X.-G.: Signal constellations for quasi-orthogonal space-time block codes with full diversity. IEEE Trans. Inf. Theory **50**, 2331–2347 (2004)
7. Anoh, K., Dama, Y., Abd-Alhameed, R., Jones, S.: A simplified improvement on the design of QO-STBC based on hadamard matrices. Int. J. Commun. Netw. Syst. Sci. **7**, 37 (2014)
8. Su, W., Safar, Z., Liu, K.R.: Towards maximum achievable diversity in space, time, and frequency: performance analysis and code design. IEEE Trans. Wireless Commun. **4**, 1847–1857 (2005)
9. Dama, Y.A.S., Abd-Alhameed, R.A., Jones, S.M.R., Migdadi, H.S.O., Excell, P.S.: "A new approach to quasi-orthogonal space-time block coding applied to quadruple mimo transmit antennas," In: Fourth International Conference on Internet Technologies and Applications, September 2011
10. Park, U., Kim, S., Lim, K., Li, J.: A novel QO-STBC scheme with linear decoding for three and four transmit antennas. IEEE Commun. Lett. **12**, 868–870 (2008)

Nigeria: Cyber Space Security Vis a Vis Computerisation, Miniaturisation and Location-Based Authentication

Muhammad Adeka[1(✉)], Mohammad Ngala[1], Mohammad Bin-Melha[1],
E. Ibrahim[2], Simon J. Shepherd[1], Issa T.E. Elfergani[3], Ash S. Hussaini[3],
Fauzi Elmegri[1], and Raed Abd-Alhameed[1]

[1] Mobile and Satellite Communications Centre, University of Bradford,
Bradford, UK
M.I.Adeka@student.Bradford.ac.uk,
{S.J.Shepherd,R.A.A.Abd}@Bradford.ac.uk
[2] College of Electronic Technology, Bani Walid, Libya
[3] Instituto de Telecomunicacoes, Aveiro, Portugal

Abstract. The degree of insecurity occasioned by fraudulent practices in Nigeria has been of great concern economically, especially as it relates to overseas transactions. This paper was designed to mitigate this problem for Nigeria and countries with similar dispositions. Based on a survey involving field trip to Nigeria, the paper examines the general security situation in Nigeria and its mutual impacts with computerisation, miniaturisation and Location-Based Authentication (LBA). It was discovered that both computerisation and miniaturisation had some negative effects on cyber-security, as these were being exploited by fraudsters, especially using 'advance fee fraud;' popularly called *419*. As a countermeasure, the research examined the possibility of using LBA and further digitisation of the GSM Mobile country codes down to City/Area codes along with GSM Mobile/ Global Positioning System (GPS) authentications. Where necessary, these could be combined with the use of a web-based Secret Sharing Scheme for services with very high security demands. The anticipated challenges were also examined and considered to be of negligible impacts; especially roaming.

Keywords: Cyber space · Computerisation · Miniaturisation · Authentication · Advance fee fraud (419) · Digitisation and tele-density

1 Introduction

The degree of cyber-related insecurity occasioned by fraudulent practices in Nigeria has been an issue of great concern economically, especially as it relates to foreign direct investments and dealings with other international partners. Apart from the economic costs to the nation, corporate organisations and individuals, it has also been an image problem for Nigeria in various international fora. It was in an effort to find ways of using technology to mitigate the negative effects of this state of insecurity that this research was designed. Although it was tailored, specifically, for the Nigerian environment, the results are applicable to all countries with similar situations.

© Institute for Computer Sciences, Social Informatics and Telecommunications Engineering 2015
S. Mumtaz et al. (Eds.): WICON 2014, LNICST 146, pp. 322–334, 2015.
DOI: 10.1007/978-3-319-18802-7_43

Based on a survey involving a field trip to Nigeria in November 2013, among other resources, this paper begins by examining the general security situation in Nigerian environment, with a focus on cyber-security, especially as it relates to the use of Global System for Mobile Communications (GSM). This would be after undertaking some basic clarifications of some relevant concepts, including cyber space, computerisation, miniaturisation, Location Based Authentication (LBA), advance fee fraud (419), digitisation and tele-density, as they affect Nigeria. Next, both the forward and backward effects of these technological developments are then assessed vis a vis the national security posture with a focus on the security of cyber space. This would be followed by discussions on identifiable measures aimed at countering or mitigating possible security threats in the system. These would include the possibility of using LBA and further digitisation of the GSM Mobile country codes down to City/Area codes along with GSM Mobile/Global Positioning System (GPS) authentications. Where necessary, these could be combined with the use of a web-based Secret Sharing Scheme for services with very high security demands. Possible challenges to the suggested mitigating measures would also be considered.

2   Basic Conceptual Clarifications

The term cyberspace does not have a standard and objective definition [1]. Generally, it is used to describe the virtual world of computers. In other words, while the term *'cyber'* denotes the computer and anything that relates to it, *cyberspace* refers to the notional environment in which communications over computer networks occur [2]. It is "the domain characterized by the use of electronics and the electromagnetic spectrum to store, modify and exchange data via networked systems and associated physical infrastructures" [3]. On the other hand, computerisation is to cause certain operations or processes to be performed by a computer, particularly, as a replacement for human labour. Digitisation is the process of converting real-world analogue quantities (texts, images, audio, video, etc.) into a digital format [4]. In this format, information is organised into discrete small units of data (bits) which are grouped into bytes. This is the binary data that computers and several devices with computing capacity can process. Thus, digitisation involves a process that results in the breaking down of a given whole into its smaller parts.

Miniaturisation is the continuous reduction in the sizes of manufactured items, regardless of whether they are mechanical, optical and electronic products and devices; e.g., mobile phones, computers, vehicle engine downsizing, etcetera [5]. This trend is made possible by the emergence of *micro* and *nano* technologies. Authentication is the process of establishing the true identity of a user or an entity [6]. Thus, LBA is a form of authentication where the identification factor is related to the physical location of the user/entity. Tele-density used to be computed as the number of fixed telephone lines per hundred inhabitants. With the advent of GSM, where mobile cellular subscribers outnumber the fixed line connections in some countries, the term Mobidensity is preferred in such countries; i.e., mobile cellular subscribers per hundred inhabitants. Since the two terms may lead to mutual disadvantages for countries with well-established fixed lines and those whose GSM network is still at the initial stage of development, ITU has proposed the use of Effective Tele-density; defined as either fixed line connections or mobile subscribers per hundred inhabitants – whichever of the two is higher [7, 8].

Advance fee fraud (alias 419), which is also known as the *Nigerian Scam*, has grown into an epidemic [9]. The term *'419'* was coined from Sect. 419 of the Nigerian Criminal Code (part of Chapter 38: Obtaining Property by False Pretences; Cheating) [10]. Basically, 419 is a form of confidence trick which the confidence *artists* use to defraud unassuming innocent business partners, both locally and abroad.

3 The State of Cyber Insecurity in Nigeria

Every society has its bad eggs; research estimates show that only about 4 % of Nigerians engage in cybercrimes [11]. Regardless of the smallness of this percentage, Nigerian 419 Scam is a major concern, not only for the Nigerian Government and its citizens, but the entire global community [10].

Cybercrime refers to any unlawful act perpetrated using the computer, electronics and ancillary devices as tools within the cyberspace [12]. It involves disruption of network traffic along with virtually an endless list of major and sundry crimes including terrorism and outright warfare [3]. It targets individuals, individual properties, corporate organisations, governments, the entire nation and the global community at large [3, 12]. Discussions with and statistics from the Economic and Financial Crimes Commission (EFCC), Abuja, and the Special Fraud Unit (SFU) of the Nigeria Police, Lagos, Nigeria, indicate that cybercrimes that are prevalent in Nigeria include [13, 14]: fishing and spoofing activities targeting bank customers; skimming of standard issue magnetic-stripe ATM (Automated Teller Machine) cards; cloning and/or defacing of government and business websites; spamming activities involving 419 Scam solicitations (for lottery, inheritance, charity, romance, crude oil, fund transfer, employment, contracts, etcetera); fraudulent online purchases from e-commerce sites made with fake foreign financial instruments and stolen credit card information; online investment scams targeting local victims; deployment of malicious programmes – mostly off-the-shelve spyware, key stroke loggers, Trojans and extractors on target systems; targeting of emotionally vulnerable persons on free social networking sites; and the use of free email services (especially g-mail, yahoo-mail and hotmail) in cybercrime related communications.

Cybercrimes are very common in Nigeria. Statistics reveal that these crimes are mostly committed by males between the ages of 20–35, and mostly based in University towns [13]. Nigeria currently ranks first in Africa, and third in the world, after the US and UK, with 5.7 % cybercrime perpetrators (down by 0.2 % from 2006), as illustrated in Table 1 [12]. From Table 2, all the indices for the incidence of cybercrime in Nigeria are on the increase for the three years; some astronomically, bearing in mind that the indicators for 2014 are incomplete. Virtually all researchers agree that globalization occasioned by the revolution in Information and Communication Technology (ICT) has greatly contributed to the rise in cybercrimes in Nigeria. However, this does not explain why Nigeria should be far ahead of South Africa, for instance, with 5.7 % against 0.9 %, given that the Internet users in South Africa are more than 50 % of their Nigerian counterparts: about 26.5 % of Nigerians use the Internet, giving about 45million Internet users; South Africa has about 48.9 % of its population on the net, yielding about 23.6 million users [15]. Many researchers agree that it is the Nigerian 419 Scam that has sharply differentiated her from South Africa, and this was enhanced by miniaturization of communication devices among other factors, especially the mobile phone which is very portable and more amenable to deception in respect of callers' location information [10–13].

Table 1. Top ten countries by count (Cybercrime perpetrators)

Country	Percentage
1. United States	63.2%
2. United Kingdom	15.3%
3. Nigeria	5.7%
4. Canada	5.6%
5. Romania	1.5%
6. Italy	1.3%
7. Spain	0.9%
8. South Africa	0.9%
9. Russia	0.8%
10. Ghana	0.7%

Source: Internet Crime Report 2007

The implication of this finding would be fully appreciated only if it is realized that, the annual statistics for mobile phone subscribers in Nigeria indicates a leap from 266,461 to 135,253,599 between 2001 and 2012, respectively. The tele-density for the corresponding periods also witnessed a quantum leap from 0.73 to 80.85 respectively [16]. Nigerian Governments have been fighting fraudulent crimes for long without much result. This led to the establishment of various outfits, in addition to the Nigerian Criminal Code Act. Thus, it could be said that while globalization has enhanced the socio-economic life of the people, it has also come along with insecurity problems that have so far defied solutions.

Table 2. Cyber fraudulent crime statistics in Nigeria (EFCC/NFIU) - 2012–2014

Year	Description	Quantity
2012	No of Cases Reported	89
	No of Suspects Arrested	100
	Financial Recoveries (Naira)	2.4 Billion
2013	No of Cases Reported	99
	No of Suspects Arrested	188
	Financial Recoveries (Naira)	8.4 Billion
2014*	No of Cases Reported	93
	No of Suspects Arrested	–
	Financial Recoveries (Naira)	630 Billion

Source: Nigeria Police (SFU) and EFCC Crime Statistics

2014* For the First Quarter Only

4   Countering Feigned-Location Fraud Related Crimes in Nigeria

It is noteworthy that most of the measures so far employed in Nigeria to counter the cyber and other fraud-related crimes are mostly based on legal instruments; in terms of enactments and enforcements. Since the most valuable tool for the 419 fraudsters is the mobile phone, it seems reasonable to approach the problem from a technological angle as one of the most optimistic ways forward. It is hereby proposed that location-based authentication be employed in two versions in Nigeria. While one version is to actually detect the exact physical location of the fraudster, the other is to deter him/her from committing the crime. For actual detection, there would be need to make all transceivers GPS-compliant, with inherent capabilities for location-based mutual authentication as advocated in [6]. This would be able to detect the locations of both static and mobile cyber criminals; please note that a mobile phone is being treated here as a computer – smart phones are computers with phone capabilities. The deterrence approach would be realised by a further digitisation of the country codes for the GSM cellular phone systems, as explained in the next segment. This could be very effective against 419 fraudsters who use the mobile phone as their main tool. Where necessary, the two approaches could be combined with the use of a modified web-based secret sharing scheme for services with very high security demands.

4.1   Background to the Deterrence Approach

In the evolution of cellular phones, one major reason for dropping certain standards stemmed from security limitations and incompatibility of diverse standards. Researches were heated up to solve this challenge. Breakthroughs yielded the Long Term Evolution (LTE) today [17, 18]. Since then, subsequent cellular standards have become more mobile, secure and compatible with earlier standards across different national boundaries. Aside these improvements, security challenges still abound such as location identification of a mobile user. Recently, the 3GPP working group proposed the inclusion of the Time Difference of Arrival (TDOA) algorithm [19] in the LTE-Advanced (LTE-A) Release 10 and beyond (which has been revised to inherit Rel-8/9 features) to identify the location of a mobile caller [20, 21]. .In cellular phone networks, although the term Enhanced Observed Time Difference (E-OTD) is often used instead of TDOA, the principle is the same [6], except that the former involves the broadcast of cell-ID [21].

In contrast to mobile phones, fixed telephones are more secure and mostly preferred in official involvements, since it is tractable more accurately. Its address can be easily traced since the address (including the city codes) assigned to a user is known. This feature makes it more dependable to transact businesses using fixed telephones than mobile phones. This proposal considers mapping the security advantage of the fixed telephones on to the mobiles (with variety of modifications) such that it can be more dependable than it has been. Of course, most business organizations would benefit should the mobile lines provide security trust-head that can be dependable.

In the meantime, area codes are known to be common and are defined differently for different countries [22, 23]; e.g., three digits for USA, Canada and Nigeria, two digits for Brazil and one digit for Australia and New Zeeland. We also have variable lengths for United Kingdom, Germany, Austria, etcetera. Sometimes, and in some countries also, these area codes are part of caller's mobile number. It is hoped that another variety can be exploited as the proposed would travel with the permanent caller mobile number. First of its kind, it is possible that this research may revolutionize area/city coding for mobile nodes and that the security breaches volunteered by the cellular telecommunication security orifice will be solved permanently, within the context of current technology.

This proposal does not suggest any change in the numbering plan or hardware of any telecommunication network operator, but integration into the software configuration of the radio routing elements of the network operator's systems – base station (Node-B, evolved-Node B or Home-eNB). It does not affect the traditional design of the mobile handsets nor would the handsets be reconfigured for the purpose.

4.2 The Proposed Technology

In the meantime, a mobile phone caller can be traced to the country of origin using the country calling code. It makes it very possible that fraudulent activities can thrive since the exact location of the mobile caller cannot be estimated by the ordinary users. In LTE-A Release 10 and beyond, mobile phones are proposed to incorporate the TDOA in determining the location of the mobile caller [21, 22]. This tracking functionality permits that only the network operators and/or the security agencies such as the police would be able to trace the origin of a mobile caller, depending on the TDOA parameters [19] extracted from the caller. It can be reasoned that this still makes the acquisition of the space-time information of a mobile caller vague, perilous, tedious, and expensive. The proximity of a caller's location characteristics to the parameters extracted from the

TDOA algorithm cannot define the position of a caller closer than 10 meters. In addition, the time it takes to compute and then trace the origin of the caller can as well leverage fraud. The proposed initiative can be combined with the TDOA to improve the identification of a mobile user's geographical location faster. In fact, at least four cells are required to perform Observed Time Difference of Arrival (OTDOA) [19, 24], and the disadvantages cannot be overstressed.

Just like the landlines wherein a caller location can be easily identified, a similar situation is being advocated for a mobile user. This could be achieved by a further digitisation of the GSM country code into city/area codes. Thus, the caller ID travels with the city/area codes as well, instead of country code alone. With proper public awareness education, it would become clear to all users that such phones would no longer be safely used in defrauding people by falsifying the city location of the caller. The exact city location can be extended to a mobile phone user to reduce and also discourage fraudulent activities among mobile phone users. The city/area codes will be incorporated in the base stations within an area. Each base station will bear a code of the area within which it is domiciled; i.e., its *cell*, as illustrated in Fig. 1 below. The radio signal originating from such base stations will be routed with city/area code parameters to disclose the origin of a call via the Cell of Origin (COO). Further binning of the available area codes, as defined by the Nigerian Communications Commission (NCC) [22], like in the case of USA [25], can be made to ensure discrete proximity to the COO of a mobile phone radio information. Thus, for each call placed by a user, the trunk prefix in the trunk code [22] (i.e. the '0' in '043' of 043-805123456, for example) will remain, but the trunk code will be modified to characterise the discrete area in the city from where a call originated.

The hierarchical structure of a cellular network is illustrated in Fig. 1 [45]. The structure is formed by connecting the major components like mobile phones, Base stations (BS) and Mobile Switching Centres (MSC). The BS serves a cell which could be a few kilometres in diameter as shown in Fig. 1 (a); instead of using a circle to depict an ideal situation, the hexagon is used for convenience. When the cells are grouped together, they form a Cluster as shown in Fig. 1 (b). Usually, the number of cells in a cluster is limited by the requirement that the clusters must fit together like jig-saw pieces. The possible cell clusters are the 4-,7-,12- and 21-cell clusters [45]. The size of a cell can be changed or reduced by splitting the original cell. Figure 1 (c) illustrates how a cell can be split into four; this involves reducing the radius of the original cell by half [45]. As illustrated in Fig. 1 (d), all BSs in a cluster are connected to the MSC using land lines. Each MSC of a cluster is then connected to the MSC of other clusters and a Public Switched Telephone Network (PSTN) main switching centre. The MSC stores information about the subscribers located within the cluster and is responsible for directing calls to them [45].

The advantage of these codes is that it will be relative to the specific geographical location of a mobile phone; for instance, if a user leaves *Gwarimpa* for *Nyanya* (two different areas in Abuja, Nigeria), the area code would change and would identify where the caller resides at the time of call. This is also the case for inter-states. Genuine privacy issues may not be relevant since, as in the current situation, users would be at liberty to either activate or de-activate the Caller ID facility [6].

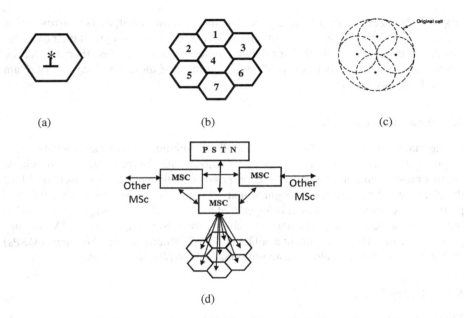

Fig. 1. Hierarchical structure of cellular network: (a) Base station (BS) for a Cell; (b) A 7-Cell Cluster; (c) Cell splitting; and (d) Cellular network structure.

In security related terminologies, this proposal is inherently a location-based authentication initiative; though it does not comprise all the ingredients of AAA (Authentication, Authorisation and Accounting) [26–28]. However, all the processes of AAA [6] would be a security requirement for the operations of special security agencies. These security agents and some designated top government functionaries could be permitted by the NCC and the network operators at the instance of necessary legislations to operate special mobile numbers and phones that would not reveal these city/area codes.

5 Anticipated Challenges

Every technology evolves with its challenges; this is no exception. In this section, the possible challenges that may evolve with this proposal are enumerated, with possible countermeasures spelt out.

5.1 Roaming

Most times, the mobile phone user travels abroad for conferences, trainings, workshops, businesses, health, etcetera. Most of these users prefer to roam their calling IDs. This technology (if operated in Nigeria only) cannot provide the city codes of the foreign countries (unless it is adopted there or globally). However, except for the case of roaming, the proposed city codes provide well-binned space-time information of a mobile phone user based on city/area codes. The possible effect of roaming on the reliability of the proposed system will be quantified in the course of implementing this proposal; this is expected to be negligible. The survey showed that, users who roam their mobile audio communications and use the service effectively throughout their overseas travels are in the region of 10 % for the upper class citizens, and less than 2 % for the lower class citizens. Statistics also showed that most of those involved in 419 Scam belong to the lower class.

5.2 Awareness Education

In Nigeria, most users tend to believe that all telecommunications caller numbers not starting with the trunk prefix (zero) is an international call. This has been used to swindle victims most often than not. When this proposal is implemented, most users will face the challenge of adjusting to recognize that all numbers not beginning with the zero prefix are not foreign numbers. It is hoped that a sensitization campaign will be carried out to educate the general public about the change using Newspapers, radio, TV stations, posters, etcetera. The Government at all levels, NCC, Mobile Service Providers (MSPs) and security agencies would have an important role to play in this regard.

5.3 Cloning Fraud

This is a high-tech problem that can be perpetrated only by some experts who are capable of knowingly, wittingly or fraudulently obtaining the factory details of a mobile-phone or by monitoring the radio characteristics of a particular mobile phone for a long time. Cloning fraud occurs when the factory-set Electronic Serial Number (ESN) and telephone Mobile Identification Number (MIN) has been dubbed and used to programme a different phone so that when the legal, as well as illegal (cloned), user places a call, the ESN/MIN of the legitimate mobile will be transmitted [25, 29]. The transmission of similar ESN/MIN from different mobile nodes is already known [29] and described as Sybil attack in, for example, wireless sensor networks [31–35], and several solutions have been suggested [36–40]. It will be easy to identify the location from which the fraudulent user calls when the proposed method is adopted, since the city/area codes would be different. This can easily isolate the legitimate user from the illegal user. Meanwhile, for cell phone cloning fraud, the cellular equipment manufacturing industry has deployed authentication systems that have proven to be a very effective countermeasure [30].

5.4 Immunity/Security of Special Security Agencies and Authorised Government Functionaries

It may be delicate to always reveal the space-time information of a security professional, such as the State Security Service (SSS). These security agents and some designated top government functionaries could be permitted by the NCC and the MSPs, at the instance of necessary legislations, to operate special mobile numbers and phones that would not reveal these city/area codes.

5.5 Man-in-the-Middle and Rogue Base-Station Attacks

The man-in-the-middle (MitM) attack involves intercepting a call and re-routing it through a third party to the receiver at the other end, such that both the original source and the sink do not know that the link is mutilated. This can be tackled by authenticating the (MU) and a Home e-Node B (HeNB or LTE Femtocell) from a contractual proxy-signature already established between the HeNB and OAM (Operation, Admission and Maintenance) [41]. A rogue base station may lead to a Denial of Service (DoS). Meanwhile, DoS due to a rogue base station has been discovered and solution proffered in [42] including impersonation [43].

5.6 Compatibility with Future Evolutions

LTE-A Rel-10 and beyond, is not a new radio-access technology but the *evolution* of LTE to further improve the performance [43]. This evolution inherited all the Rel-8/9 functionalities with additions such as carrier aggregation, enhanced multi-antenna support, improved support for heterogeneous deployments, and relaying [43]. The Rel-9 uses OTDOA for uplink and E-CID (Enhanced-Cell ID) for both uplink and downlink [24]. The E-CID positioning algorithm, in addition to the serving eNB (in other words the radio cell) and the broadcast cell ID which was defined in LTE Rel.8, the information such as propagation delay calculated from the difference in timing of signal transmission and reception and the Angle of Arrival (AoA), are utilised to estimate the MU position [21]. For other lower standards, the proposed technology would comfortably fit in.

5.7 Replacement for Other Positioning Algorithms

This algorithm may rather be seen as the primary algorithm to which any other possible geographical positioning algorithm can be appended. For instance, the use of GPS can be added to the city code algorithm. After all, the Rel-9 was defined to involve assisted-GPS (A-GPS), OTDOA and E-CID [24].

6 Conclusion

The degree of insecurity occasioned by fraudulent practices in Nigeria has been an issue of great concern economically, especially as it relates to foreign direct investments and dealings with other international partners. Apart from the economic costs to the nation and individuals, it has also been an image problem for Nigeria in various international fora. This paper examined possible technological means of addressing this problem. The suggested solutions, though tailored specifically for the Nigerian environment, are applicable to all countries with similar situations.

The paper used the results of survey involving a field trip to Nigeria in November 2013, among other resources, to look at the cyber security problems in Nigeria and arrived at some promising solutions. It was realised that most previous efforts at countering cyber and other fraud-related crimes in Nigeria depended mainly on the use of legal instruments.

It was also realised that the 419 Scam is a major contributor to Nigeria's third position in the world, with 5.7 % of cybercrime perpetrators.

The main technological proposal to tackle this problem is to further digitise the GSM country code into city/area codes which will be transmitted along with caller IDs to give away the position of the caller as being done with the fixed telephones. Anticipated challenges, which include the possible impact of mobile communication roaming on the efficacy of the proposed system, were also highlighted, and found to be minimal.

Acknowledgments. The role of the Petroleum Technology Development Fund (PTDF, Nigeria) for sponsoring the main PhD Programme, which produced this paper, is hereby acknowledged. The same is true of the Nigerian Army which approved the programme. The authors also appreciate the contributions of the various staffs and departments of the School of Engineering and Informatics, University of Bradford, UK.

References

1. The Tech Terms Computer Dictionary. http://www.techterms.com/definition/cyberspace. Accessed 28 September 2014
2. Oxford Dictionaries. http://www.oxforddictionaries.com/definition/english/cyberspace. Accessed 28 September 2014
3. Adeka, M.I.U., Shepherd, S.J Abd-Alhameed, R.A.: Cryptography and Computer Communications Security: Extending the Security Perimeter through a Web of Trus MPhil-PhD Transfer Report, School of Engineering and Informatics, University of Bradford, Bradford (UK), (Ongoing: 2011-)
4. Rouse, M.: Peripherals Glossary (2007). http://whatis.techtarget.com/definition/digitization. Accessed 28 September 2014
5. Moore, G.E.: Cramming More Components onto Integrated Circuits, ed. McGraw-Hill, New York (1965)
6. Adeka, M., Shepherd, S., Abd-Alhameed, R.: Extending the security perimeter through a web of trust: the impact of GPS technology on location-based authentication techniques. In: Proceedings of the Fifth International Conference on Internet Technologies and Applications (ITA 2013), pp. 465–473 (2013)
7. Aslam, H.D., Azhar, M.S., Yasmeen, K., Farhan, H.M., Badar, M., Habib, A.T.: Effects of globalization on developing countries. J. Am. Sci **8**(8), 222–227 (2012)
8. Core ICT Indicators-ITU ed, 2005. http://www.itu.int/pub/D-IND-ICT_CORE-2010/en. Accessed 28. September 2014
9. Hadnagy, C.: Social engineering: The art of human hacking: John Wiley & Sons, 2010
10. Chawki, M.: Nigeria tackles advance free fraud. J. Inf. Law Technol. **1**(1), 1–20 (2009)
11. Ehimen, O., Bola, A.: Cybercrime in Nigeria. Bus Intell. J. **3**, 93–98 (2010)
12. Ashaolu, D.: Combating Cybercrimes in Nigeria Upcoming cyberlaw textbook. Prentice Hall Publishers, Upper Saddle River (2011)
13. EFCC, EFCC Annual Report September 2013
14. N.P. (SFU), Fraudulent Crime Statistics (EFCC/NFIU)–2012–2014 (2014)
15. Internet World Statistics. http://www.internetworldstats.com/af/ng.htm. Accessed 28 September 2014

16. Nigerian Communications Commission. http://ncc.gov.ng/index.php?option=com_content&view=article&id=125:subscriber-statistics&catid=65:industry-information&Itemid=73. Accessed 28.September 2014

17. Rinne, M., Tirkkonen, O.: LTE, the radio technology path towards 4G. Comput. Commun. **33**, 1894–1906 (2010)

18. Akyildiz, I.F., Gutierrez-Estevez, D.M., Reyes, E.C.: The evolution to 4G cellular systems: LTE-Advanced. Phys.Commun. **3**, 217–244 (2010)

19. Sayed, A.H., Tarighat, A., Khajehnouri, N.: Network-based wireless location: challenges faced in developing techniques for accurate wireless location information. Sig. Process. Mag. IEEE **22**, 24–40 (2005)

20. Ghosh, A., Ratasuk, R., Mondal, B., Mangalvedhe, N., Thomas, T.: LTE-advanced: next-generation wireless broadband technology [Invited Paper]. Wireless Communications, IEEE **17**, 10–22 (2010)

21. Abeta, S.: Toward LTE commercial launch and future plan for LTE enhancements (LTE-Advanced). IEEE Int. Conf Commun. Syst. (ICCS) **2010**, 146–150 (2010)

22. Technical Standards: National Numbering Plan. http://www.ncc.gov.ng/index.php?option=com_content&view=category&id=75&Itemid=102. Accessed 2 October 2013

23. Country Codes, Phone Codes, Dialing Codes, Telephone Codes, ISO Country Codes. http://countrycode.org/. Accessed 2 October 2013

24. John, M.: Location Services Part 2: LTE Release 9 Features, LTE University, 2011

25. Area Code History. http://www.area-codes.com/area-code-history.asp. Accessed 2 October 2013

26. Jaros, D., Kuchta, R.: New location-based authentication techniques in the access management. In: 2010 6th International Conference on Wireless and Mobile Communications (ICWMC), pp. 426–430 (2010)

27. Song, Z., Li, Z., Dou, W.: Different approaches for the formal definition of authentication property. In: The 9th Asia-Pacific Conference on Communications, APCC 2003, pp. 854–858 (2003)

28. He, R., Yuan, M., Hu, J., Zhang, H., Kan, Z Ma, J.: A novel service-oriented AAA architecture. In: 14th IEEE Proceedings on Personal, Indoor and Mobile Radio Communications PIMRC 2003, pp. 2833–2837 (2003)

29. Kou, Y., Detecting the sybil attack cooperativelyLu, C.-T., Sirwongwattana, S., Huang, Y.-P.: Survey of fraud detection techniques. In: 2004 IEEE International Conference on Networking, Sensing and Control, pp. 749–754 (2004)

30. Cell Phone Fraud. Available: http://www.fcc.gov/guides/cell-phone-fraud. Accessed 2 October 2013

31. Demirbas, M., Song, Y.: An RSSI-based scheme for sybil attack detection in wireless sensor networks. Proceedings of the 2006 International Symposium on World of Wireless. Mobile and Multimedia Networks, pp. 564–570. IEEE Computer Society, Washington DC (2006)

32. Douceur, J.R.: The sybil attack. In: Druschel, P., Kaashoek, M.F., Rowstron, A. (eds.) IPTPS 2002. LNCS, vol. 2429, pp. 251–260. Springer, Heidelberg (2002)

33. Ssu, K.-F., Wang, W.-T., Chang, W.-C.: Detecting Sybil attacks in Wireless Sensor Networks using neighboring information. Comput. Netw. **53**, 3042–3056 (2009)

34. Yin, J., Madria, S. K.: Sybil attack detection in a hierarchical sensor network In: Third International Conference on Security and Privacy in Communications Networks and the Workshops (SecureComm 2007), pp. 494–503 (2007)

35. Zhang, Q., Wang, P., Reeves, D. S., Ning, P.: Defending against sybil attacks in sensor networks. In: 25th IEEE International Conference on Distributed Computing Systems Workshops 2005, pp. 185–191. IEEE Computer Society, Washington DC (2005)

36. Yu, H., Kaminsky, M., Gibbons, P.B., Flaxman, A.: Sybilguard: Defending against sybil attacks via social networks. ACM SIGCOMM Comput. Commun. Rev. **36**(4), 267–278 (2006)
37. Khalil, I., Bagchi, S., Rotaru, C.N., Shroff, N.B.: Unmask: utilizing neighbor monitoring for attack mitigation in multihop wireless sensor networks. Ad Hoc Netw. **8**, 148–164 (2010)
38. Levine, B.N., Shields, C., Margolin, N.B.: A Survey of Solutions to the Sybil Attack. University of Massachusetts Amherst, Amherst, MA (2006)
39. Lv, S., Wang, X., Zhao, X., Zhou, X.: Detecting the sybil attack cooperatively in wireless sensor networks. In: International Conference on Computational Intelligence and Security, CIS 2008, pp. 442–446 (2008)
40. Danezis, G., Mittal, P.: SybilInfer: Detecting sybil nodes using social networks. In: NDSS (2009)
41. Cao, J., Ma, M., Li, H., Zhang, Y.: A survey on security aspects for lte and lte-a networks. IEEE Commun. Surv. Tutorials **16**(1), 283–302 (2014)
42. Barbeau, M., Robert, J.-M.: Rogue-base station detection in WiMax/802.16 wireless access networks. Ann. Des. Telecommun. **61**(11–12), 1300–1313 (2006)
43. Barbeau, M., Hall, J., An, H.-C.: Detecting impersonation attacks in future wireless and mobile networks. In: Burmester, M., Yasinsac, A. (eds.) MADNES 2005. LNCS, vol. 4074, pp. 80–95. Springer, Heidelberg (2006)
44. Parkvall, S., Furuskär, A., Dahlman, E.: Evolution of lte towards imt-advanced. http://www.ericsson.com/res/docs/2013/evolution-of-lte-towards-imt-advanced.pdf. Accessed 2 October 2013
45. Lee, W.C.: Mobile Cellular Telecommunications: Analog and Digital Systems. McGraw-Hill Professional, New York (1995)

Tunable RF MEMS Bandpass Filter with Coupled Transmission Lines

Issa T.E. Elfergani[1(✉)], Abubakar Sadiq Hussaini[1,3,4],
Jonathan Rodriguez[1,2], Paulo Marques[5], and Raed Abd-Alhameed[3]

[1] Instituto de Telecomunicações, Aveiro, Portugal
{i.t.e.elfergani,ash,jonathan}@av.it.pt
[2] Universidade de Aveiro, Aveiro, Portugal
[3] Radio Frequency, Antennas Propagation and Computational Electromagnetics
Research Group, School of Electrical Engineering and Computer Sciences,
University of Bradford, Bradford BD7 1DP, UK
r.a.a.abd@bradford.ac.uk
[4] School of Information Technology and Communications,
American University of Nigeria, Yola, Nigeria
[5] Escola Superior de Tecnologia, Instituto Politécnico de Castelo Branco,
Castelo Branco, Portugal

Abstract. Passive and active devices are essential devices in mobile and base stations' transceiver. Consequently, these devices dominated the large part of the PCB of the today's transceiver. However, the tomorrow's mobile terminals without circuit tunability would be extremely large in size to accommodate present and future radio access technologies (RATs). The stand-alone transceiver for one single RAT is comprised of single passive and active devices and adding two or more RATs for the same transceiver would require adding two or more devices, since all of these RATs standards work on different frequency bands. Apparently, without tunability approach, this will increase the complexity of the system design and will cover a large part of the circuit space leading to power consumptions, loss which results to the poor efficiency of the transceiver. In this work, a miniaturized RF MEMS tunable bandpass is developed to operate in the frequency range from 1.8 to 2.6 GHz.

Keywords: Coupled lines filter · RF MEMS capacitor · Radio access technologies (RATs)

1 Introduction

The tomorrow mobile terminals and base station transceiver will have to deal with several radio access technologies (RATs) right from GSM up to LTA. This will require two or more RF passive and active devices since all of these standards work on different frequency bands. RF band pass filter, is a passive device that work with one specific frequency band. If we were to upgrade these mobile devices to support future standards, this indeed would entail adding another set of customized RF front end devices leading to extra complexity and power consumption. As a result, future design requirements utter the need for tunable mobile terminals so as to reduce the number of

© Institute for Computer Sciences, Social Informatics and Telecommunications Engineering 2015
S. Mumtaz et al. (Eds.): WICON 2014, LNICST 146, pp. 335–340, 2015.
DOI: 10.1007/978-3-319-18802-7_44

duplicated circuits, and hence the energy consumption, and from a business perspective, to introduce the mobile terminals to the market at a very low cost. Therefore, the design course of action requires a tunable RF filter with high tuning speed, and excellent linearity that have to deal with the wide frequency range, low loss/or high-Q circuits. RF MEMS is a good candidate with good linearity, low power consumption, size reduction; they also offer a high level of integration. MEMS or micro-electro-mechanical systems (a.ka. microsystems technology or micromachines), are electrical-mechanical devices, which are made from micro fabrication and was first developed in the 1970s. Many RF MEMS filter work has been already appeared in the literature [1–7]. Also MEMS technology has been involved in several applications; they include biotechnology, medicine, communication and inertial sensing. RF MEMS filters have good linearity, low power consumption, size reduction, and also have high level of integration. The future mobile handsets will become more sophisticated, providing user centric broadband applications and full mobility within a plethora of wireless access systems. This will lead to power hungry devices and a reduction towards battery lifetime, which eventually will have an impact on the global CO_2 footprint. Therefore, designing a compact tunable RF MEMS filter which is capable of covering the bands of mobile applications, with targeted and desired frequencies range, couple with low power consumption and high Q factor, would be the best candidate for tomorrow's mobile terminals.

By examining the RF MEMS filters in [1–7], it was undoubtedly found that these filters emphasis only on UWB applications [1, 2], Millimetre wave bands [3, 4], C/X bands [5] and Ku bands [6, 7]. Since all these tunable RF MEMS filters in [1–7] have not met the tomorrow's mobile terminals criteria, and in order to meet the required goals, in this paper, we proposed a reconfigurable bandpass filter using RF MEMS technology with design course of action such as: miniaturization, high Q, low power consumption and to cover the bands of frequency from GSM to LTE.

Section 2 explains the filter design and concept, the results of an unloaded filter have shown and discussed in Sect. 3. RF MEMS capacitor position was studied in Sect. 4. Section 5, goes with RF MEMS capacitor loaded results and the conclusion in Sect. 6.

2 Filter Design and Concept

As the aim is to devise a tuneable-frequency bandpass filter having wide tuning range, the underlying passive filter design is vital. The design must ensure good matching below −10 dB (i.e., return losses better than 10 dB) and around 0.2 dB insertion loss, even when the frequencies are shifted to a great extent by changing the capacitance of loaded RF MEMS capacitor. Size of 37.5 × 16 mm RT/duroid 6006/6010LM is used as the substrate throughout the module, with a thickness of 1.27 mm, and the dielectric constant is assumed to be uniformly 10.2 as depicted in Fig. 1a. The substrate is located over ground plane size of 37.5 × 16 mm. The I/O feed lines that set at the edge are parallel microstrip lines with characteristic impedance of 50 Ω and dimensions of 7.5 mm × 1.5 mm as shown in Fig. 1. The design and simulation process are implemented in both 3D electromagnetic simulator HFSS and CST for comparison purposes [8, 9]. The total dimensions of the proposed filter is 37.5 mm × 16 mm which is ideal for application in a mobile device. Table 1 summaries the detailed dimensions of the resonators.

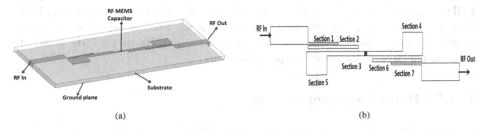

(a)   (b)

Fig. 1. The proposed bandpass filter with RF MEMS capacitor, (a) 3D view, (b) Schematic view

Table 1. Detailed dimensions of resonators

Parameters	Section 1	Section 2	Section 3	Section 4	Section 5	Section 6	Section 7
Trace width (mm)	0.15	0.25	0.375	2	2	0.25	0.15
Trace length (mm)	6	10	15	4	4	10	6
Trace height (mm)	0.02	0.02	0.02	0.02	0.02	0.02	0.02
Trace spacing (mm)	0.25	0.25	0.25	0.25	0.25	0.25	0.25

3 Unloaded Proposed Filter Results

To explain the design concept of the proposed bandpass filter, Fig. 2 shows the S11 and S21 of a reference filter, i.e. the proposed design but without the inclusion of MEMS capacitor.

The design procedure of this filter is elaborated here in order to establish an insight explanation on how this filter operates and why the geometry is proposed. The design

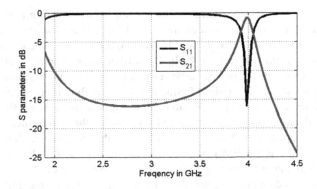

Fig. 2. Simulated S11 and S21 results of unloaded proposed filter

process starts by performing several simulations and modifying the geometry of the proposed bandpass filter for enabling the structure to operate around the 2.6 GHz, i.e. the higher targeted operating frequency and then to be tuned in order to meet the present work target. It was interesting to find that, the unloaded filter resonates at 4 GHz with |S11| better than −10 dB and 0.15 dB insertion loss. However, this band does not meet the design objective. Therefore, a RF MEMS capacitor would be required to down-shift the resonant frequency from 2.6 GHz to 1.8 GHz in which covering the targeted frequency range of this work.

4   RF MEMS Capacitor Position

To suggest the optimum position for the RF MEMS effectively, a parametric study of the RF MEMS capacitor position over the proposed structure was carried out for three selected capacitor values, i.e. 0.7, 1.1 and 4 pF for the operating frequencies of 2.6, 2.4 and 4.25 GHz respectively, covering the aggregate bandwidth of the frequency band as shown Fig. 3. The effect of the capacitor location was examined by considering the variations in the S_{11} and S_{21} against the position of the RF MEMS for the afore-mentioned capacitance values. Figure 3 shows the effect of RF MEMS location with three selected desired frequencies.

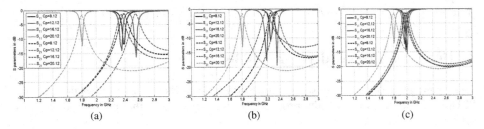

Fig. 3. Capacitor position variation against S11 and S21, loaded with C = (a) 0.7 pF, (b) 1.1 pF, (c) 4 pF

The capacitor position is investigated by starting from 8.12 mm and increasing to 20.12 mm with increments of 4 mm as shown in Fig. 3. It is clear that when it is 8.12 and 16.2 mm, the targeted frequency bands would not be accomplished as the capacitance varies from 0.7, 1.1 to 4 pF. By further increasing it to 20.12 mm, the proposed filter exhibits more or less same resonant modes for all capacitance values in which does not satisfying the desired frequency bands as shown in Fig. 3. However, as it is set at 12.12 mm, a good impedance matching can be achieved over the entire bands at S_{11} < −10 dB and around 0.15 dB insertion loss for three aforementioned capacitance values as depicted in Fig. 3. This leads to the conclusion that for the best impedance match the RF MEMS position should be kept at 12.12 mm in which the filter shows an extensive frequency shift, completely covering the DCS, PCS, UMTS, WLAN and LTE bands and hence suitable in this case for mobile handset applications.

5 RF MEMS Loaded Capacitor Filter Results

The next phase of this work is the filter tuning mechanism, which relies on the introduction of RF MEMS capacitor over the long middle resonator as shown in Fig. 1, which was first derived from the HFSS model.

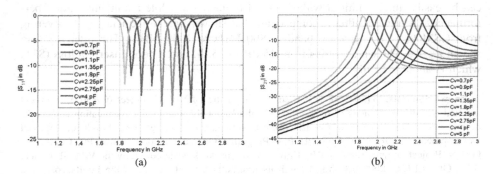

Fig. 4. HFSS results of RF MEMS capacitor filter, (a) S11, (b) S21

For proper realization, this tuning requires the addition of loaded capacitor at fixed location. The target tuning range is obtained by setting the capacitance values from 0.7 pF to 5 pF over the structure of the filter. Figure 4 shows the HFSS simulated scattering parameters (S_{11}, S_{21}) for the loaded proposed bandpass filter. It should be noted that the effect of this capacitive loading cause the structure to resonate over a wide frequency range from 1.8 GHz to 2.6 GHz covering the GSM and LTE systems.

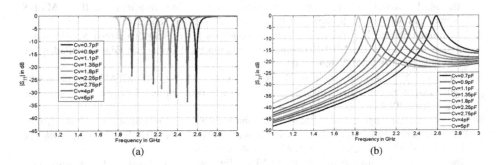

Fig. 5. CST results of RF MEMS capacitor filter, (a) S11, (b) S21

For more validation, the proposed filter was modelled in CST software packages along with tuning capacitor. As can be seen from Fig. 5, the same frequency range from 1.8 GHz to 2.6 GHz was accomplished. Furthermore, S_{11} and S_{21} in HFSS exhibit reasonable agreement with the simulated results computed by CST.

6 Conclusions

By carefully selecting different sets of optimal geometry parameters, a new compact bandpass filter coupled lines with tuneable behaviour has been presented. The tuning method is implemented by loading the filter structure with a RF MEMS capacitor. By means of varying the capacitance values from 0.7 pF to 5 pF, the resonant frequency can be easily tuned within a wide range of frequencies, while maintaining good performance. The tunable filter is compact and has shown a great frequency shift covering from GSM to LTE frequency bands (1800 MHz to 2600 MHz). The filter has also shown a good S11 which varies from 15 dB to 35 dB and a good insertion loss (S21) which is about 0.15 dB.

Acknowledgments. This work is carried out under the BENEFIC project (CA505), a project labelled within the framework of CATRENE, the EUREKA cluster for Application and Technology Research in Europe on NanoElectronics, co-financed by the European Funds for Regional Development (FEDER) by COMPETE – Programa Operacional do Centro (PO Centro) of QREN [Project number 38887 – BENEFIC]. Also, this work is supported by the VALUE project (PEst-OE/EEI/LA0008/2013 and, through its first author, by the grant of the Fundacão para a Ciência e a Tecnologia (FCT - Portugal), with the reference number: SFRH/BPD/95110/2013.

References

1. Entesari, K., Rebeiz, G.M.: A differential 4-bit 6.5-10 GHz RF MEMS tunable filter. IEEE Trans. Microw. Theory Tech. **53**(3), 1103–1110 (2005)
2. Pillans, B., Malczewski, A., Allison, R., Brank, J.: 6-15 GHz RF MEMS tunable filters. In: IEEE MTT-S International Microwave Symposium Digest, Long Beach, CA, USA, pp. 919–922, June 2005
3. Dussopt, L., Rebeiz, G.M.: High-Q millimeter-wave MEMS varactors. In: IEEE MTT-S International Microwave Symposium Digest, pp. 1205–1208, June 2000
4. Lakshminarayanan, B., Weller, T.: Tunable bandpass filter using distributed MEMS transmission lines. In: IEEE MTT-S International Microwave Symposium Digest, Philadelphia, PA, USA, pp. 1789–1792, June 2003
5. Grichener, A., Lakshminarayanan, B., Rebeiz, G.M.: High-Q RF MEMS capacitor with digital/analog tuning capabilities. In: IEEE MTT-S International Microwave Symposium Digest, June 2008
6. Pothier, A., Orlianges, J.-C., Zheng, G., Champeaux, C., Catherinot, A., Cros, P.B.D., Papapolymerou, J.: Low-loss 2-bit tunable bandpass filters using MEMS DC contact switches. IEEE Trans. Microw. Theory Tech. **53**(1), 354–360 (2005)
7. Nordquist, C.D., Muyshondt, A., Pack, M.V., Finnegan, P.S., Dyck, C.W., Reines, I.C., Kraus, G.M., Plut, T.A., Sloan, G.R., Goldsmith, C.L., Sullivan, C.T.: An x- band to Ku-band RF MEMS switched coplanar strip filter. IEEE Microwave Wirel. Compon. Lett. **14**(9), 425–427 (2004)
8. Ansoft High Frequency Structure Simulator v10 Uses Guide, CA, USA
9. CST v.5.0, Microwave Studio. http://www.cst.com

3D Media Distribution over the Internet with Hybrid Client-Server and P2P Approach

Hélio Silva$^{(\boxtimes)}$, Hugo Marques, and Jonathan Rodriguez

Instituto de Telecomunicações, Aveiro, Portugal
{heliosilva,hugo.marques,jonathan}@av.it.pt

Abstract. With the massive deployment of broadband access to the end-users and the improved hardware capabilities of end devices, peer-to-peer (P2P) networking paradigm is consistently gaining terrain over the typical client-server approach. In most of the modern countries, today's Internet connectivity has sufficient conditions to unleash P2P applications such as video-on-demand or real-time television. It is known that the use of P2P based systems to distribute delay sensitive applications raises technical problems mainly associated with the system's instability caused by the peer churn effect. In this article, we propose a framework to distribute delay sensitive 3D video content using a hybrid client-server and P2P approach. The proposed platform uses P2P application-level multicast trees at the access networks, delegating typical server operations at super-peers who are domain and geographically distributed. Results are based on real testbed implementation show quick reaction at peer level.

Keywords: Peer-to-peer · Application-level multicast · Content distribution · Video streaming · 3D media

1 Introduction

In recent years, speed for Internet access has experienced enormous upgrades both in wired and wireless links. This is especially true in the majority of the cities of modern countries, where fibre-to-the-home and Long Term Evolution (LTE) access is becoming a reality. In addition, computers and mobile devices have also become faster and lighter. Facebook and Youtube [1] are the two top contributors for this kind of content distribution. In fact, Internet video from sites such as YouTube, Hulu, Netflix (video-to-TV), online video purchases and rentals, webcam viewing, and web-based video monitoring (excluding P2P video file downloads) are expected to have a compound annual growth rate (CAGR) of 34 % until 2016 [2]. Video mobile data is predicted to have a CAGR of 75 % in the period 2012–2017 [3]. Current developments in 3D technology has raised significant technical challenges mainly due to bandwidth and delay restrictions associated with the multiple views of content. With this in mind, this article proposes a multiple multicast tree distribution mechanism that merges the advantages of both client-server and P2P approaches: centralized decision, administration and content – typical in a client-server paradigm - with the split/balancing of network resources – found on P2P networks.

© Institute for Computer Sciences, Social Informatics and Telecommunications Engineering 2015
S. Mumtaz et al. (Eds.): WICON 2014, LNICST 146, pp. 341–346, 2015.
DOI: 10.1007/978-3-319-18802-7_45

2 Architecture

For the 3D video content, we assume multiple cameras arrangement and multiple description coding (MDC) [4–6] of the resulting streaming media. Considering that each stream [7, 8], needs an average 4 Mbps bandwidth, we would need at least 35 Mbps connection to be able to receive stereoscopic view with depth adjustment and fast viewpoint navigation capability. Given Internet bandwidth constrains and for scalability reasons, the combined video information from the cameras is encoded in multiple IP video streams so that the video can be reconstituted from a subset of these streams, being the video quality proportional to the number of streams received. Each description is sent to the peer as a different IP stream, such that if packets of the corresponding description are lost, then the associated packet in the other description is used to reconstruct the video frame with a slightly downgraded quality.

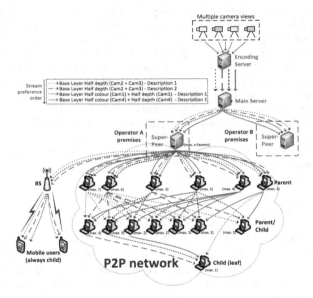

Fig. 1. Distribution of 3D content using P2P concept and application-level multicast trees. Peers with better resources will occupy a higher position on the tree.

The proposed system uses the concept of main server, super-peers, peers and ISP core network. The super-peers are property of the service owner, act as proxies/replicas of the main server and are placed in the premises of every ISP that has an agreement with the service owner, they are responsible to serve peers from a specific geographical area or ISP. The modules which are responsible for overlay management functionality deal with the construction and maintenance of the multiple multicast tree structure for the P2P network and take into account the geographical optimization methods to improve the overall system performance.

Peers are located at the access network and will receive content directly from their nearest super-peer. For each new peer requesting content the super-peer will use the peer's IP address and capabilities to compute the peer's position in an application-level multicast tree, effectively distributing the content via a P2P network. Peers can either assume the role of a parent, a child/parent or a child. Parents receive the content directly from the super-peer and occupy the highest level on the P2P multicast tree. Child/parents are the peers that receive the content from another peer and also feed other peers – they occupy intermediate levels on the multicast tree. At the roof of all trees there is a server that has the role of Super-Peer. It is responsible for constructing of the application-level multicast trees and to trigger the data flow towards the peers. In each tree, a number of peers are directly connected to the Super-Peer. After grouping and sorting operations the multiple P2P multicast trees are computed, one per each requested content and edge router (ER), as depicted in Fig. 1. It will be the ER's responsibility to map each requested content multicast address to specific parent(s) IP addresses(s) – the ER will effectively act as a replicator. To optimize the ER resources, the super-peer predetermines how many top-level peers (parents) can be directly fed by one Edge Router. This means that, when constructing each P2P tree, the super-peer positions a predetermined number of highest ranking peers at the top of the tree and delegates in these the distribution of content to other peers in the same access network. Every time a peer is selected to forward content, its resources are diminished, and if its evaluation becomes lower than other peers, the new highest ranking peer will take the role of parent for additional content streaming. If a peer has insufficient network resources, it will not receive some of the streams.

When a new peer wants to join the P2P network, it will first connect to the main server, the server will then direct it to the nearest Super-Peer and the Super-Peer will insert this new peer to the available multicast trees. To maximize the P2P tree efficiency, the algorithm periodically re-constructs each tree using each peer stored record. The peer can be a fixed computer, a laptop or a smaller mobile device that consumes 3D content. In order to comply with this framework, two modules need to be installed at the peer: a *Topology Controller* (TC) and a *Network Monitoring Subsystem* (NMS). The TC is the module responsible for all tree operations at the peer side. The NMS is responsible for collecting peer hardware and software information, network traffic statistics (such as packet loss, average delay, jitter, available bandwidth) for each received stream and also to compute the *Peer Evaluation* - a value that takes in consideration the peer's hardware (memory and CPU), the peer's network capabilities (upload and download throughput) and the peer's stability. The NMS periodically sends reports with the collected information to the Super-Peer, for tree maintenance operations.

3   System Evaluation

The server and client modules were developed in C++ and implemented in Ubuntu Server 12.10 AMD64 with a Kernel version *3.8.0-19-generic #30-Ubuntu SMP*, powered by an Intel core i7 720QM with 8 GB of RAM.

The evaluation of P2P tree computation time is crucial to understand how the system would perform to the constant changes in the access network. As Fig. 2 shows, the evolution of this performance indicator when computing a single tree versus the number of peers in the system. If we assume we would have 100.000 peers, the system would have taken approximately 500 ms to compute the application-level multicast trees.

At the peer side, the networking operations performed by the TC have a negligible impact (<0,1 %), being the network monitoring and reporting performed by the NMS the most relevant part of the CPU consumption at the peer. As depicted in Fig. 3, when the peer receives the full range of the video streams, the NMS will consume a maximum of 10 % of its CPU resources. For the general cases, the computation of the full P2P multicast trees would be less than 1 s.

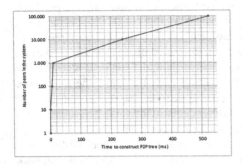
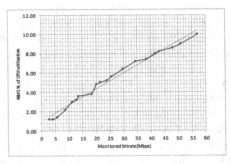

Fig. 2. Time to compute the P2P multicast tree versus number of peers in the system.

Fig. 3. Percentage of CPU utilization at the peer for multiple bitrates received

Figure 4 depicts the memory footprint for the super-peer in light and heavy conditions. The results were computed for P2P tree construction and maintenance operations only. The experiment consisted on the super-peer receiving requests from virtual peers up to a maximum of 100.000 requests. At its maximum, the total memory consumed at the super-peer was approximately 48 Mbytes, which indicate a highly scalable algorithm.

For tree maintenance purposes, each peer periodically sends reports towards the Super-Peer. In our test environment a single report has a size of 387 Bytes, 58 come from Ethernet, IP and TCP related overheads and the remaining from the JavaScript Object Notation (JSON) and report structure, Fig. 5 depicts the worst case scenario in which one single parent will have to support 75 children (this leaves 10 % available bandwidth for other networking operations).

The results measured for the TC are less than 0.1 %, the minimum unit that our tool could capture. The collected values represent a negligible load on the CPU.

4   Related Work

DONet (also known as CoolStreaming) [9], proposes a P2P based data-driven overlay network for efficient live media streaming; video is divided to segments of uniform length and a buffer map is used to identify each video segment and to indicate if it is

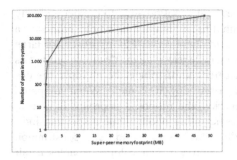
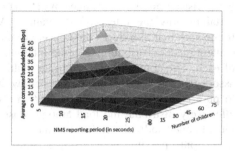

Fig. 4. Memory footprint for the P2P tree construction and maintenance operations versus number of peers in the system

Fig. 5. Average consumed bandwidth by a parent when sending the aggregated NMS reports towards the super-peer

available. DONet proposes a scheduling algorithm that calculates the number of potential suppliers for each video segment; basically the algorithm starts from those with only one supplier and so forth. If there are multiple suppliers, then the algorithm starts by selecting the one with highest bandwidth and enough available time.

iGridMedia [10] aims to provide delay-guaranteed P2P live streaming service over the Internet - safeguarding the ISPs have dedicated servers to support the delay guaranteed interactive applications. For overlay construction, joining nodes must first contact a rendezvous point which is a server maintaining a partial list of current online nodes - then each node randomly finds other 15 nodes to establish a partnership.

CoopNet [11] is a mechanism for distributing streaming media content using P2P cooperative networking; it uses a centralized approach where a central server is responsible to determine the path of distribution, indicating joining peers to which parent they should connect - the peer hierarchy is decided based on each peer available bandwidth (reported upon connection to the server – periodically afterwards) and their proximity (based on IP/BGPP prefix). CoopNet also employs Multiple Description Coding (MDC) to address the interruptions caused by the frequent joining and leaving of individual peers.

SplitStream [12] is also a multicast mechanism for distributing content in P2P cooperative environments, but contrary to CoopNet, it uses a distributed approach; there is no central server and all nodes have the same responsibility - new nodes try to find a parent and join directly to the tree; trees are constructed in a distributed fashion using each peer's upload and download bandwidth.

Our framework enables a fair share of resources among the participating peers, even the peers with scarce resources can have a place in the tree and still receive 3D video.

5 Conclusion

Major challenges for service providers lie ahead, IP multicast technology may have its opportunity to finally be deployed in large scale. Meanwhile, the top sites on the Internet continue to use unicast client-server approach, which is known to be inefficient when distributing large volumes of data. However, it is not possible to predict with any certainty how the Internet will mature. With this in mind this article proposes a framework that introduces the concept of a hybrid client-server/P2P approach for large content media distribution over the Internet, hopefully retaining the desirable properties of each. The approach uses multiple multicast trees to distribute the multiple streams associated with the visualization of bandwidth consuming 3D content. When compared to pure client-server or P2P distribution scenarios, the proposed approach is able to effectively distribute the load among most participating nodes while respecting individual node bandwidth constraints and achieving a fast insertion and tree reconstruction time - only possible when using a centralized approach. Our solution enables a fair share among participating peers – proportional to their rank - being the only exception the leaf peers. Leaf (child) peers are the lowest rank peers and in most situations their participation on the distribution of content should be avoided – mobile terminals are provided as a good example of leaf peers since they have considerable restrictions.

References

1. Alexa - The Web Information Company, The top 500 sites on the web. http://www.alexa.com/topsites
2. Cisco Visual Networking Index: Forecast and Methodology, 2011–2016
3. Cisco Visual Networking Index: Global Mobile Data Traffic Forecast Update, 2012–2017
4. Mohr, A., Riskin, E., Ladner, R.: Unequal loss protection: graceful degredation of image quality over packet erasure channels through forward error correction. IEEE JSAC **18**(6), 819–828 (2000)
5. Apostolopoulos, J.G.: Reliable video communication over lossy packet networks using multiple state encoding and path diversity. In: Visual Communications and Image Processing, January 2001
6. Apostolopoulos, J.G., Wee, S.J.: Unbalanced multiple description video communication using path diversity. In: IEEE International Conference on Image Processing, October 2001
7. MUSCADE project, MUltimedia SCAlable 3D for Europe, large scale integrated project funded by the Europian Union Framework Program 7. http://www.muscade.eu
8. ROMEO project, Remote Collaborative Real-Time Multimedia Experience over the Future Internet, large scale integrated project funded by the European Union Framework Program 7. http://www.ict-romeo.eu/
9. Zhang, X., Liu, J., Li, B., Yum, P.: DONet: a data-driven overlay network for client live media streaming. In: Proceedings of IEEE INFOCOM (2005)
10. Zhang, M., Sun, L., Yang, S.: iGridMedia: providing delay-guaranteed peer-to-peer streaming service on internet. In: Proceedings of IEEE GLOBECOM (2008)
11. Padmanabhan, V., Sripanidkulchai, K.: The case for cooperative networking. In: Druschel, P., Kaashoek, M., Rowstron, A. (eds.) IPTPS 2002. LNCS, vol. 2429, pp. 178–190. Springer, Heidelberg (2002)
12. Castro, M., Druschel, P., Kermarrec, A.-M., Nandi, A., Rowstron, A., Singh, A.: SplitStream: high-bandwidth content distribution in a cooperative environment. Presented at the IPTPS, Berkeley, CA, February 2003

Author Index

Printed in the United States
By Bookmasters